The Study Book for the
NEBOSH National Diploma

in Occupational Health and Safety Practice

Hazardous agents in the workplace

RMS Publishing
Victoria House
Lower High Street
Stourbridge
DY8 1TA

Cover design by Graham Scriven.
Printed and bound in Great Britain by CPI Antony Rowe.

ISBN-13: 978-1-900420-98-3

Editor's Notes

Diagrams and photographs

A number of the diagrams included in the Study Book for the NEBOSH National Diploma in Occupational Health and Safety Practice have been produced in hand-drawn format. In particular these are diagrams that students studying for NEBOSH examinations may be required, or find it helpful, to produce by hand at the time of examination. They are provided to help the student to get an impression of how to do similar drawings of their own. I hope that these diagrams show that such drawings are achievable by hand and also assist in illustrating a standard that might be expected in examination.

We have taken particular care to support the text with a significant number of photographs. They are illustrative of both good and bad working practices and should always be considered in context with supporting text. I am sure that students will find this a useful aid when trying to relate their background and experience to the broad based NEBOSH National Diploma syllabus. They will give an insight into some of the technical areas of the syllabus that people have difficulty relating to when they do not have a strong technical background.

Where diagrams/text extracts are known to be drawn from other publications, a clear source reference is shown and ACT wish to emphasise that reproduction of such diagrams/text extracts within the Study Book is for educational purposes only and the original copyright has not been infringed.

Legal requirements

Legislation is referred to in context in the various elements that comprise the study book. This reflects the interest of the NEBOSH National Diploma syllabus and requirements to study new/amended legislation under the rule from NEBOSH that it has to have been in force for six months before it becomes examinable. In addition, the essential points of legislation relevant to this Unit of the Diploma syllabus are contained in the section of the study book under Relevant Statutory Provisions.

Case law, as specified by the NEBOSH National Diploma syllabus, is referred to in the Hazardous Agents in the Workplace Study Book. It is important to note that these cases are examined in the NEBOSH National Diploma. Additional cases may be referred to in the same element. Though they are not referred to specifically in the syllabus it is useful to be aware of them as they have an influence on the workplace and showing knowledge of them at time of examination may emphasise a greater depth of understanding of the topic. Further information on other significant cases can be found in the other two RMS Publishing Study Books in the series for the NEBOSH National Diploma.

The NEBOSH National Diploma examinations do not assess the students' knowledge of section numbers of the Health and Safety at Work Act or knowledge of regulation numbers in an unhelpful way. Instead questions ask the student to explain something about a section number, or significant regulation, by giving the number and the purpose of that section or regulation. In addition, it should be remembered that the student might choose to refer to a section number when answering a question that requires a broad knowledge of law. Knowledge of significant section and regulation numbers is important when answering the questions for the Diploma examinations. Section and regulation numbers are referred to in the Study Books in order to differentiate different components of the law and to aid the student in referencing legislation in the workplace, if required by their work or Unit D assignment.

Syllabus

Each element of the Study Book has an element overview that sets out the learning outcomes, the contents, the relevant statutory provisions and any connected sources of reference. The Study Book reflects the order and content of the NEBOSH National Diploma syllabus and in this way the student can be confident that the Study Book reflects the themes of the syllabus. In addition, the syllabus, and therefore this study book, is structured in a very useful way; focusing on hazards, their control and core management of health and safety principles which would be useful as reference for any health and safety practitioner..

Higher Level Qualifications

The structure, level and content of this study book is appropriate for those involved in study of health and safety at university level, particularly if the course is one that is accredited by the Institution of Occupational Health and Safety (IOSH).

National Vocational Qualification

We are confident that those working to national vocational qualifications in occupational health and safety will find this Study Book a useful companion. For students working towards the S/NVQ Level 4 in Occupational Health and Safety Practice they will find a good correlation between the scope of the Study Book series for NEBOSH National Diploma and the domain knowledge needs at that level.

Relationship to other RMS Study Books

This study book content is built on the foundation knowledge contained in the RMS Publishing Study Books for Certificate level and should be read in conjunction with them, in particular the study book for the NEBOSH National General Certificate in Occupational Health and Safety.

Acknowledgements

Managing Editor: Ian Coombes CMIOSH – Managing Director, ACT; member of NEBOSH Council, past NEBOSH Board member and NEBOSH examiner; Chairman of IOSH Initial Professional Development Sub-Committee.

RMS Publishing and ACT Associates Ltd wish to acknowledge the following contributors and thank them for their assistance in the preparation of the Unit B Study Book for the NEBOSH National Diploma: Nick Attwood, Dean Johnson, Geoff Littley, Janice McTiernan, Barrie Newell, and Julie Skett.

NEBOSH Study Books also available from RMS:

Publication	Edition	10-digit ISBN	13-digit ISBN	EAN
The Study Book for the NEBOSH General Certificate	Fifth	1 900420 97 X	978-1-900420-97-6	9781900420976
The Study Book for the NEBOSH International General Certificate	First	1 900420 90 2	978-1-900420-90-7	9781900420907
A Study Book for the NEBOSH Certificate in Fire Safety and Risk Management	Second	1 900420 88 0	978-1-900420-88-4	9781900420884
The Study Book for the NEBOSH National Certificate in Construction Safety and Health	Second	1 900420 89 9	978-1-900420-89-1	9781900420891
The Study Books for the NEBOSH National Diploma in Occupational Safety and Health:	A series of three study books, including this study book.			
■ (Unit A) Managing Health and Safety	Third	1 906674 02 7	978-1-906674-02-1	9781906674021
■ (Unit C) Workplace and Work Equipment	Third	1 906674 01 9	978-1-906674-01-4	9781906674014

Contents

Figure List (including tables and quotes)

Element B9

Element B10

Element B11

List of abbreviations

LEGISLATION

CAR	Control of Asbestos Regulations 2006
CDGUTPER	Carriage of Dangerous Goods and Use of Transportable Pressure Group Regulations 2004
CHIP	Chemicals (Hazard Information and Packaging for Supply) Regulations 2002
CHPR	Construction (Head Protection) Regulations 1989
CLAW	Control of Lead at Work Regulations 2002
CNWR	Control of Noise at Work Regulations 2005
COMAH	Control of Major Accident Hazards Regulations 1999
COSHH	Control of Substances Hazardous to Health Regulations 2002
CVWR	Control of Vibration at Work Regulations 2005
DDA	Disability Discrimination Act 1995
DSE	Health and Safety (Display Screen Equipment) Regulations 1992
FAR	Health and Safety (First-Aid) Regulations 1981
HASAWA	Health and Safety at Work etc Act 1974
HSCER	Health and Safety (Consultation with Employees) Regulations 1996
IRMER	Ionising Radiation (Medical Exposure) Regulations 2000
IRR	Ionising Radiations Regulations 1999
LA	Limitations Act 1980
LOLER	Lifting Operations and Lifting Equipment Regulations 1998
MAR	Health and Safety (Miscellaneous Amendments) Regulations 2002
MDA	Misuse of Drugs Act 1971
MHOR	Manual Handling Operations Regulations 1992
MHSWR	Management of Health and Safety at Work Regulations 1999
NNSR	Notification of New Substances Regulations 1993
NONS	Notification of New Substances at Work Regulations 1993
POA	Public Order Act 1986
PPER	Personal Protective Equipment at Work Regulations 1992
PUWER	Provision and Use of Work Equipment Regulations 1998
REPPIR	Radiation (Emergency Preparedness and Public Information) Regulations 2001
RIDDOR	Reporting of Injuries, Diseases and Dangerous Occurrences Regulations 1995
RM(RT)	Radioactive Material (Road Transport) Regulations 2002
RSA	Radioactive Substances Act 1993
SD Act	Sex Discrimination Act 1974
SRSC	Safety Representatives and Safety Committees Regulations 1977
WHSWR	Workplace (Health, Safety and Welfare) Regulations 1992
WTR	Working Time Regulations 1998

GENERAL

AC	Alternating Current
ACGIH	American Conference of Governmental Industrial Hygienists
ACOP	Approved Code of Practice
ACTS	Advisory Committee on Toxic Substances
ADI	Acceptable Daily Intake
AGIR	Advisory Group on Ionising Radiation
AGNIR	Advisory Group on Non-Ionising Radiation
AIDS	Acquired Immune Deficiency Syndrome
ALARP	As Low As is Reasonably Practicable
ANR	Active Noise Reduction
APF	Assigned Protection Factor
ASL	Approved Supply List
BBV	Bloodborne Virus
BCS	British Crime Survey
BMGV	Biological Monitoring Guidance Values
BS	British Standards
BSC	British Safety Council
BSI	British Standards Institution
CA	Competent Authority
CAS	Co-operating with other member state
CEC	Co-operating with the European Commission
CET	Corrected Effective Temperature
CFM	Cubic Feet Per Minute
CGI	Convertible Gas Indicator
CGRO	The Compton Gamma Ray Observatory
CL	Control Limit
CRE	Commission for Racial Equality
dB	Decibel
DLBA	Direct Line Breathing Apparatus
DNA	Deoxyribonucleic Acid

DoE	Department of the Environment
DSE	Display Screen Equipment
EAV	Exposure Action Values
EC	European Community
ECD	Electron Capture
ED	Effective Dose
EDS	Energy Dispersive X-Ray Spectrometry
EEA	European Economic Area
EFTA	European Free Trade Association
EH	Environmental Health
EHO	Environmental Health Office
EINECS	European Inventory of Existing Commercial Chemical Substances
ELV	Exposure Limit Values
EMAS	Employment Medical Advisory Service
EOC	Equal Opportunities Commission
ET	Effective Temperature
EU	European Union
FID	Flame Ionisation Detector
GIT	Gastro-intestinal Tract
GLC	Gas Liquid Chromatography
GM	Geiger Mueller
GP	General Practitioner
HAEO-1	The first High Energy Astrophysical Observatory
HAVS	Hand-arm Vibration Syndrome
HBV	Hepatitus B Virus
HEPA	High Efficiency Particulate Air
HGV	Health Guidance Value
HIV	Human Immunodeficiency Virus
HML	High, Medium and Low
HPA	Health Protection Agency
HPLC	High Performance Liquid Chromatography
HRA	Human Reliability Analysis
HRT	Hormone Replacement Therapy
HSC	Health and Safety Commission
HSE	Health and Safety Executive
HSG	Health and Safety Guidance
HIS	Heat Street Index
IBS	Irritable bowel syndrome
ICD	International Classification of Diseases Injuries and causes of death coding system
ICNIRP	International Commission on Non-Ionising Radiation Protection
ICRP	International Commission on Radiological Protection
IOM	Institute of Occupational Medicine
IR	Infra Red
ISO	International Organisation for Standardization
LD	Lethal Dose
LEV	Local Exhaust Ventilation
LTEL	Long Term Exposure Limit
MCE	Mixed Cellulose Ester
MDHS	Methods for Determinations of Hazardous Substances
MDI	Methylene Bisphenyl di-isocyanate
MELS	Maximum Exposure Limits
MF	Medium Frequency
MMMF	Man Made Mineral Fibres
NC	Noise Criteria
NDT	Non-Destructive Testing
NIHL	Noise induced Hearing Loss
NOAEL	No observed adverse effect level
NR	Noise Rating
NRPB	National Radiological Protection Board
NVQ	National Vocational Qualification
OEL	Occupational Exposure Limit
OES	Occupational Exposure Standard
OHS	Occupational Health Service
OPCS	Office of Population Census and Surveys
OSHA	Occupational Safety and Health Administration
P4SR	Predicted 4-hour Sweat Rate
PCLM	Phase Contrast Light Microscopy
PID	Photo-ionisation Detector
PLM	Polarised Light Microscopy
PMT	Photo Multiplier Tubes
PNS	Peripheral Nervous System
PPE	Personal Protective Equipment

PTSD	Post Traumatic Stress Disorder
PVC	Polyvinyl Chloride
RF	Radio Frequency
RH	Relative Humidity
RL	Recommended Limits
RMS	Root Mean Square
ROSPA	Royal Society for Prevention of Accidents
RPA	Radiation Protected Advisors
RPE	Respiratory Protective Equipment
RRSAG	Radiation, Risk and Society Advisory Group
RSI	Repetitive Strain Injury
RXTE	Rossl X-Ray Timing Explorer
SAR	Specific Absorption Rate
SNR	Single Number Rating
SPHA	Special Health Authority
SPL	Sound Pressure Level
STEL	Short Term Exposure Limit
SWORD	Surveillance of Work related and Occupational Respiratory Disease
TC	Thermal Conductivity
TDI	Toluene di-isocyanate
TLD	Thermoluminescent Dosimeters
TLV	Threshold Limit Value
TTS	Temporary Threshold Shift
TWA	Time Weighted Average
UK	United Kingdom
UV	Ultra Violet
VCM	Vinyl Chloride Monomer
VDU	Visual Display Unit
VHF	Very High Frequency
WATCH	Working on Action to Control Chemicals
WBGT	Wet Bulb Globe Temperature
WBV	Whole Body Vibration
WCI	Wind Chill Index
WEL	Workplace Exposure Limits
WRULD	Work Related Upper Limb Disorder
WRV	Work Related Violence
XRD	X-Ray Diffraction

This page is intentionally blank

General aspects of occupational health and hygiene

Learning outcomes

On completion of this element, candidates should be able to:

B1.1   Outline the purpose and nature of the occupational health and hygiene discipline and practice.

B1.2   Describe the role, organisation, function and composition of occupational health and hygiene staff.

B1.3   Describe human anatomical systems and sensory organs.

Contents

This page is intentionally blank

B1.1 - Nature and history of occupational health and hygiene

The relationship between occupational exposure to an agent and its associated diseases has been long established. In the 19th century, for example, felt hat makers showed symptoms of the effects on the central nervous system of the mercury salts used in the production process (hence the term 'as mad as a hatter'). Coal miners have become respiratorally disabled due to the effects of coal dust on the lungs and painters have become unable to work in their chosen field due to occupational asthma. Despite this, occupational health medicine is a relatively junior science. The Royal College of Physicians did not create a faculty of equal status to surgeons and physicians until 1978. However, observations relating to the relationship between the disease and occupation have been made since ancient times.

Hippocrates was among the first to observe this relationship when he commented on the illness associated with mercury sulphide workers.

In the Middle Ages, Agricola wrote, "In the mines of the Carpathian mountains, women are found who have married seven husbands, all of whom this terrible consumption has carried off to a premature death". Paracelsus also described the effects of mercury poisoning in Austria.

The first definitive work was done in 1700 by Ramazzini, Professor of Medicine in Padua, 'De Morbis Artificum Diatriba'. This is now recognised as the first formal study of industrial disease. Ramazzini was the first to ask: "What is your occupation?" - a question not always asked by doctors today.

Charles Thackrah, a Leeds physician, published the first British work on occupational diseases in 1832 entitled 'The Effects of the Principal Arts, Trades and Professions and of Civic States and Habits of Living on Health and Longevity'. Following this work the General Register Office recorded deaths related to occupation. From this work the science of epidemiology has grown.

Epidemiology is the study of categories of persons (populations) and the patterns of diseases from which they suffer so as to determine the events or circumstances causing these diseases. Thus the epidemiologist applies statistical techniques in the investigation of medical problems.

In 1833 the first Factory Inspectors were appointed, together with Certifying Surgeons (in 1855), who were required to certify that young persons were not incapacitated for work by disease or bodily infirmity. Over the following years a variety of specific work related industrial diseases were identified.

- Mule spinners in Lancashire developed skin cancer of the abdominal wall and scrotum from contact with shale oil lubricants.
- Female workers developed bone marrow disorders using radium based luminescent paints in the manufacture of watch dials; the paint was applied by brush, the tip of which was maintained by moistening with saliva from the mouth.
- Knife grinders developed silicosis of the lung from grinding wheel dust.

Thomas Legge was appointed as the first Medical Inspector of Factories in 1898, following his studies concerning working with lead. Lead poisoning was made a notifiable disease in 1899. Following his work as a Factory Inspector he published the results of his experiences in 1934 as 'Industrial Maladies'.

Donald Hunter is regarded as the last great general physician and his book 'Diseases of Occupations' is still regarded as the current classic. Hunter, as with Ramazzini, added another question to the list started by Hippocrates: "Ask whether any similar disease has occurred in a fellow worker". Hunter observed that: "Many workers are intelligent, co-operative and good witnesses. Although some may be deaf, disconsolate, forgetful, obtuse, garrulous, monosyllabic, the worker is still the best witness to what happened".

The stages in occupational health and hygiene practice

The four main stages of occupational health and hygiene practice have been established for many years. They reflect the four stages from determining that a health issue exists to the control of the health issue.

RECOGNITION/IDENTIFICATION

Recognising and identifying health hazards can be done in a number of ways. They may be well known in the industry, for example processes involving solvents, or noise from a bottling plant. The information may come from the manufacturer's safety data sheet for the substance or the labels on containers. They could also be highlighted because of complaints from the operatives of headaches or generally feeling unwell, or from absenteeism and sickness records.

MEASUREMENT

In order to know if the hazard is in sufficient quantities to cause a risk to health, it will need to be measured. For example, to a certain extent, noise is subjective. Sound may be classed as noise if it is something you do not enjoy, maybe rock music, but it is good music, not noise, if that is what you want to listen to. Noise levels need to be measured to ascertain if they are exceeding the personal action levels laid down by law. The lower they are below the action levels, the less likely they are to do any damage to hearing. Subjectively, sound may be considered a noise, but until the levels are measured it will not be known if it is a risk to hearing.

Measuring the amount of a substance in the air is important to ascertain whether at that level it is a risk to health or not. The amount measured can be compared to the workplace exposure limits (WELs) in EH40.

EVALUATION

Once it is decided that there is a hazard present then the extent of which it is a risk needs to be evaluated. This is done by looking at the nature of the hazard, who may be affected, how the agent does its damage, how it gets into or onto the body and the resulting ill-health. The risk to health is then evaluated taking into account the existing control measures.

CONTROL

Further controls may be necessary if it is decided that the existing controls do not reduce the risk to health to an acceptable or tolerable level. The controls depend on the type of agent that is causing the risk to health. For example, where the risk to health is high or the resulting harm is severe, a process may have to be totally enclosed. Hearing loss from noise may be prevented by engineering the problem out, reducing exposure time and/or wearing hearing protection.

Whatever controls are chosen, they should be workable and not introduce a further hazard.

RISK ASSESSMENTS

Commonly today the stages of occupational health and hygiene practice have been blended into an overarching approach called risk assessments. The original approach of four stages was driven by good practice and experience; the risk assessment approach has been led by what is seen as legal requirements. Both approaches have common elements, stressing the need for risk evaluation.

It should be noted that in addition to the general risk assessment required under Regulation 3 of the Management of Health and Safety at Work Regulations, there are many pieces of legislation which require the assessment of risks to health from hazardous substances and agents. These include:

- The Control of Substances Hazardous to Health Regulations (COSHH) 2002.
- The Control of Lead at Work Regulations (CLAW) 2002.
- The Control of Asbestos Regulations (CAR) 2006.
- The Control of Noise at Work Regulations (CNWR) 2005.

Although these Regulations require risk assessments to be made of substances and agents hazardous to health, they do not specify the form they should take. In the most simple and obvious cases a risk assessment may not need recording as it can be readily explained. However, in most situations a record will be required in order to ensure compliance, accuracy and continuity.

Making an assessment

There are six major steps involved in making any assessment of hazardous substances:

1. The gathering of information about the substances, the work and the working practices, including how substances are used.
2. The evaluation of risks to health.
3. Deciding if any further precautions are required and what these will be.
4. Recording the assessment.
5. Providing information to those who are, or may be, at risk.
6. Deciding when the assessment needs to be reviewed.

Categories of occupational health hazard

CHEMICAL

Chemical hazards - examples include:

- *Acids and alkalis* - dermatitis.
- *Metals* - lead and mercury poisoning.
- *Non metals* - arsenic and phosphorus poisoning.
- *Gases* - carbon monoxide poisoning, arsine poisoning.
- *Organic compounds* - occupational cancers, e.g. bladder cancer.
- *Dust* - silicosis, coal worker's pneumoconiosis.
- *Fibres* - asbestosis.

PHYSICAL

Physical hazards - examples include:

- *Heat* - heat cataract, heat stroke.
- *Lighting* - miner's nystagmus.
- *Noise* - noise induced hearing loss (occupational deafness).
- *Vibration* - vibration induced white finger.
- *Radiation* - radiation sickness (at ionising wavelengths), burns, arc eye.
- *Pressure* - decompression sickness.

BIOLOGICAL

Biological hazards - examples include:

- *Animal-borne bacteria* - anthrax, brucellosis.
- *Human-borne viruses* - viral hepatitis.
- *Vegetable-borne fungi, moulds, yeasts* - aspergillosis (farmer's lung).
- *Environmental bacteria* - legionnaires' disease.

PSYCHO-SOCIAL

Psycho-social hazards - examples include:

- Stress.
- Violence.
- Drugs.
- Alcohol.

ERGONOMIC

Ergonomic hazards - examples include:

- **Job movements** - cramps (in relation to handwriting or typewriting).
- **Friction & pressure** - bursitis, cellulitis, i.e. beat hand, traumatic inflammation of the tendons or associated tendon sheaths of the hand or forearm, i.e. tenosynovitis.

INTERNAL AND EXTERNAL SOURCES OF INFORMATION

Information that can assist in identifying health hazards can be sourced from internal data and external bodies.

Internal data

The information gathered during accident investigation, health surveillance and survey of absence records can provide useful data on the types of hazards within a workplace. Several cases of dermatitis can show a problem with a particular cleaning fluid, whereas one case, when analysed, may show the problem could have been caused by the person's own individual sensitivity or possibly pursuit of a leisure time hobby. Health professionals such as an individual's GP or occupational physician can provide information on health conditions related to workplace exposure.

External data

Health and Safety Commission (HSC) / Health and Safety Executive (HSE)

A major source of information is regulations produced in response to health hazards such as the Control of Noise at Work Regulations or Control of Asbestos Regulations. These regulations and their associated guidance, typically approved codes of practice aid the identification of conditions hazardous to health. In addition, the HSE produce documents including the legal series, guidance notes, information sheets and leaflets providing greater detail on certain topics. Specifically, the HSE guidance note EH40 provides information on chemical and biological hazards, including the lists of Workplace Exposure Limits (WEL) for use with the Control of Substances Hazardous to Health Regulations.

Other relevant bodies

Information can be sourced from agencies from such as Health Protection Agency, whose role is to provide an integrated approach to protecting UK public health through the provision of support and advice to the NHS, local authorities, emergency services and others, on infectious diseases and radiation protection. Other bodies include:

- European Safety Agency.
- Environment Agency.
- Fire Authority.
- Health and Safety Laboratory.
- World Health Organisation.
- Professional and trade bodies.

B1.2 - Occupational health and hygiene specialists

The role and function of specialists

THE OCCUPATIONAL HYGIENIST

Role: to identify risks to health in the workplace. Occupational hygienists take airborne samples and measurements. Identify when exposure is likely to be high and make suggestions in relation to control strategies to meet legal standards, in particular, regarding short-term exposure limits (STELs).

THE OCCUPATIONAL HEALTH PHYSICIAN

They act in the role of consultant and advise organisations of likely health risks associated with their current practices. They make recommendations with respect to employee selection, i.e. to meet statutory requirements, e.g. atopic screening - hayfever sufferers may not be ideal employees to work with known respiratory sensitisers such as flour or paints containing isocyanates.

The physician will be also carry out medicals on behalf of the Company and establish systems of employee examination and monitor the work of the Occupational Health Nurse.

THE OCCUPATIONAL HEALTH NURSE

The Occupational Health Nurse will be trained to identify symptoms resulting from exposure to specific workplace hazards and will carry out specific health monitoring, e.g. those working with lead - blood tests; those working with compounds - nasal examination for "chrome ulcer".

THE EMPLOYMENT MEDICAL ADVISORY SERVICE (EMAS)

EMAS is the occupational health unit of the HSE. The unit monitors workplace illness trends and makes recommendations to industry, establishes limits and makes recommendations, which usually become statutory requirements, e.g. COSHH. EMAS also provides a confidential helpline to employees who may be concerned regarding workplace exposure.

The role, function and composition of an occupational health service

Growth in the Occupational Health Service in private industry has been a slow affair. Companies seeking medical advice were originally protecting against employees' claims for compensation.

There was a growth in the occupational health service in World War II, when doctors were required for larger factories. Some industries developed their own medical services offering X-rays and other facilities. The Nuffield Foundation set up schemes whereby smaller factories shared medical services.

In 1978, the Royal College of Physicians of London set up a Faculty of Occupational Medicine, to train specialists. Recently, a Society of Occupational Health Nursing has been set up by the Royal College of Nursing to provide training courses.

An Occupational Health Service may provide the following services:

HEALTH PROMOTION

Health promotions may reflect topical national issues, e.g. smoking and weight, or issues that are specifically relevant to the organisation carrying out the promotion, e.g. skin care promotion in a company where dermatitis is a problem.

PRE-EMPLOYMENT MEDICAL SCREENING

This can identify certain health problems in workers before employment commences, which can help avoid placing workers in a work situation that could exacerbate a current health condition. For example, an asthma sufferer would not be employed to work with or near respiratory sensitisers or assessment of hearing loss in someone, who has previously worked in a noisy environment. This is important for safety reasons and to avoid any claims for compensation against the innocent company.

MEDICAL/HEALTH SURVEILLANCE (INCLUDING AUDIOMETRY)

The Management of Health and Safety at Work Regulations 1999, Regulation 6 deals with Health Surveillance and gives employers a duty to provide it where it is appropriate and links it in to the outcome of risk assessments.

Further details on medical/health surveillance are also contained in other Regulations e.g. The CLAW Regulations 2002; also The COSHH Regulations 2002, Approved Code of Practice schedule 5 states:

Substances for which medical surveillance is appropriate	Processes
Vinyl Chloride Monomer (VCM)	In manufacturing, production, reclamation, storage, discharge, transport, use or polymerization.
Nitro or Amino derivatives of Phenol and of Benzene or its Homologues	In the manufacture of Nitro or Amino derivatives of Phenol and of Benzene or its Homologues and the making of explosives with the use of any of these substances.
1-Napthylamine and its salts Orthotolidine and its salts Dianisidine and its salts Dichlorbenzidene and its salts	In manufacture, formation or use of these substances.
Auramine Magenta	In manufacture.
Carbon Disulphide Disulphur Dichloride Benzene, including Benzol Carbon Tetrachloride Trichloroethylene	Processes in which these substances are used, or given off as a vapour, in the manufacture of indiarubber or of articles or goods made wholly or partially of indiarubber.
Pitch	In manufacture of blocks of fuel consisting of coal, coal dust, coke or slurry with pitch as a binding substance.

Figure B1-1: Medical / health surveillance.   *Source: ACT.*

Other than the cases stated in the COSHH schedule, surveillance might be appropriate where exposure to hazardous substances is such that an identifiable disease or adverse health effect may be linked to the exposure. There must be a reasonable likelihood that the disease or effect may occur under the particular conditions of work prevailing and that valid techniques exist to detect such conditions and effects.

The employer must keep records of surveillance in respect of each employee for at least 40 years. This requirement still applies where companies cease to trade, in which case the records must be offered to the HSE.

The majority of ventilation systems, although effective in protecting workers health from airborne contaminants, can create other hazards. One of the main hazards that needs to be considered when designing LEV systems is that of noise.

Even if it has been made a design feature that the LEV is noise efficient, when monitoring for engineering control efficiency and effectiveness noise should be considered at the same time and measured.

As part of health surveillance, noise levels and its effects should be considered. Audiometry testing should be carried out on individuals to monitor hearing levels and to scrutinise results for any signs of hearing deficiency. This means preventative action can be taken early on to protect the individual and can also highlight problems with equipment that can be corrected before any other workers are affected.

ASSESSMENT OF FITNESS FOR WORK AND COUNSELLING

The occupational health service (OHS) can carry out an assessment of the fitness of a person returning to work. This may follow ill-health or an accident. The level of fitness would depend on the industry and the type of work a person does. For example, a person in the food industry would have to be free of the strain of bacterium that caused gastro-enteritis before being allowed back to work. A person working in an office environment may be deemed fit to return to work following a hernia operation much sooner than someone working in heavy engineering.

The OHS can devise a programme of gradual return to work after serious illness and monitor the person's progress.

Counselling is offered by some occupational health services for employees who may be suffering bereavement, personal problems, alcohol problems or anything else which may affect their performance at work.

B1.3 - Physiology

Human anatomical systems

RESPIRATORY

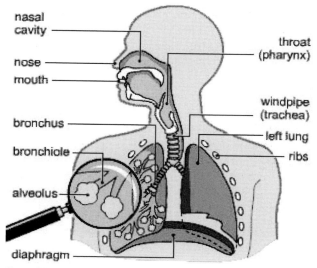

Figure B1-2: Respiratory system.   *Source: BBC.*

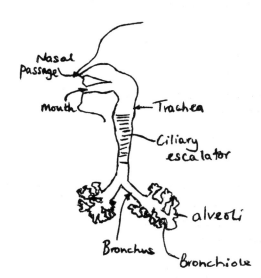

Figure B1-3: Hand drawn respiratory system.   *Source: ACT.*

Main structures

Epiglottis: Cartilage 'lid' closes over trachea when swallowing.

Trachea: Commonly called the windpipe. It is held open by rings of cartilage, to allow free flow of air.

Bronchus: Branch of trachea that leads into the lung, again held open with cartilage rings.

Bronchioles: Branches of the bronchus.

Alveoli: Small sacs arising at the ends of bronchioles. They lie on the lung's outer surface surrounded by blood vessels. It is here that gas exchange occurs.

Pleura: The lungs are surrounded by a double membrane known as the pleura. These 'lubricate' the lungs by allowing them to expand and contract freely within the chest cavity as breathing takes place.

Important terms

Gas exchange: The exchange of oxygen for carbon dioxide. It occurs at the lung surface in the alveoli.

Ciliary Escalator: The respiratory system, excluding the alveoli, is lined with fine hairs called cilia and mucous secreting cells. When dust particles enter the lung, they will adhere to the mucus-coated surface. The cilia gently beat upwards gradually pushing the mucus and dust particles into the throat, enabling their removal as a result of the cough reflex.

Particle size: The size of dust particles is measured in microns. The smaller the particle, the further down the respiratory tract it can go. The nose will filter out the larger particles.

Macrophages: These are scavenger cells that engulf particles that have entered the alveoli.

DIGESTIVE

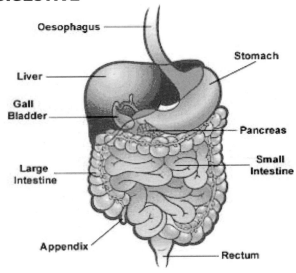

Figure B1-4: Digestive system.   *Source: STEM.*

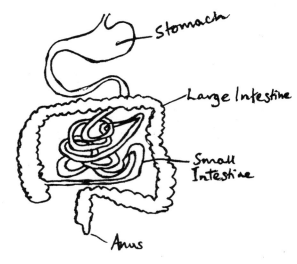

Figure B1-5: Hand drawn digestive system.   *Source: ACT.*

Main structures

Upper digestive tract:

This consists of the buccal cavity, pharynx, oesophagus and stomach. Food enters the buccal cavity (mouth), it is masticated with saliva then passed to the stomach. Here partial digestion of food takes place in low ph (acidic) conditions.

Small intestine:

Partially digested food enters the small intestine where digestion, using enzymes, is completed. Proteins are broken down into poly-peptides, carbohydrates in simple sugars. The majority of food is absorbed into the bloodstream in the small intestine.

Large intestine and anus (colon and rectum):

Fibre and other indigestible materials pass into the colon. Water is absorbed from this material and then the remainder passes into the rectum for excretion.

Liver:

The liver is the body's chemical processing organ. For example, it stores excess sugars and carbohydrates. It also acts as the body's waste treatment plant. It absorbs and destroys poisons that have been ingested. For example, the liver breaks down the poison alcohol, into harmless components which are then excreted. Excessive exposure can damage the liver and in the case of alcohol this results in cirrhosis.

Important terms

Defences:

The digestive system has a number of defences against ingesting harmful substances. Taste may warn of potential contamination. Vomiting enables contaminated food to be regurgitated though the stimulation of vomiting by some chemicals can in itself be very dangerous. Detoxificated, the liver has the capacity to break down harmful chemicals. Finally excretion of digested or semi-digested food assists in the removal of poisons, or micro-organisms from the body.

Cross contamination:

Food or drink that come into contact with chemicals or micro-organisms can become contaminated. For example, foundry workers can contaminate their meals with lead dusts, unless they follow strict hygiene controls before eating.

Accidental contamination:

Food or drink can also be contaminated and consumed accidentally.

CIRCULATORY

The circulatory system comprises the heart and blood vessels which maintain a constant flow of blood to all parts of the body. The blood provides a regular supply of oxygen to the tissues and carries away carbon dioxide and other waste products.

The system comprises two parts: the **systemic circulation** which comprises the blood supply to all parts of the body except the lungs and the **pulmonary circulation** which is responsible for reoxygenating the blood via the lungs.

NERVOUS

The nervous system can be defined as the body's information gathering, control and storage system. It comprises the central nervous system (CNS: brain and spinal cord) which consists of billions of interconnected nerve cells called neurons. Input to the CNS is via the special sense organs (e.g. eyes). Output, or motor instructions, go to muscles, internal organs and glands - including the sweat glands of the skin for temperature regulation; this is known as the **peripheral nervous system (PNS)**. Some of these systems are **automatic** or unconscious whereas others are voluntary, requiring a conscious effort of will.

THE SPECIAL SENSORY ORGANS

Skin

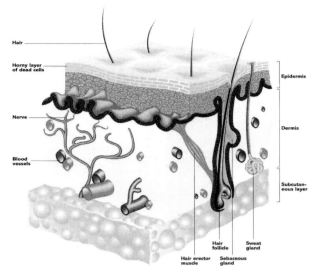

Figure B1-6: Skin layers.   *Source: SHP.*   Figure B1-7: Hand drawn skin layers.   *Source: ACT.*

Main structures

Epidermis:

The outer horny layer consisting of dead skin cells, held together with natural oils secreted by the skin. It acts as an impermeable barrier, though organic based compounds can be absorbed through this layer. This layer also protects against mechanical damage, being able to repair itself from major damage.

Dermis:

This layer contains the sweat glands, capillaries and fat cells. If a chemical is absorbed through the epidermis, it can then be transported around the body via the capillaries.

Important terms

Absorption
(skin contact):

Substances can enter through the intact skin, cuts or abrasions, and through the eye. Solvents such as toluene and trichloroethylene can enter either accidentally or if used for washing the hands. These substances may have a local effect, such as de-fatting of the skin, or pass through into the blood system.

Percutaneous absorption:

The absorption of organic based compounds directly through the epidermis, for example, chemicals like benzene, trichloroethylene and organic lead (e.g. tetraethyl lead used as a fuel additive) can be absorbed in this way. The danger is that these chemicals pass into the blood stream and cause a systemic effect.

Eyes

Main structures

The eye consists of structures (the cornea and lens) which focus an image onto the retina which is then converted into a pattern of nerve impulses and transmitted to the brain via the optic nerve. The pupil controls the amount of light entering the eye; the ciliary body alters the shape of the lens to adjust focus.

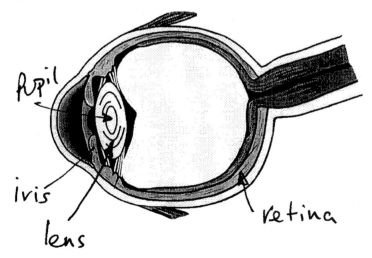

Figure B1-8: Hand drawn diagram of the eye.   *Source: ACT.*

Important terms

Defences   Blinking is a mechanism to clear dust and other contaminants from the surface of the eye.

Lacrimation is the secretion of tears. When the eyes are irritated, tears are produced to wash away the irritant

Ears

The ear senses *sound*, which is transmitted in the form of pressure waves travelling through a substance, e.g., air, water or metals.

Main structures

The ear has three basic regions:

1.   The *outer* ear channels the sound pressure waves through to the eardrum.

2.   In the *middle* ear, the vibrations of the eardrum are transmitted through three small bones (hammer, anvil and stirrup) to the inner ear.

3.   The cochlea in the *inner* ear is filled with fluid and contains tiny hairs (nerves), which respond to the sound. Signals are then sent to the brain via the acoustic nerve.

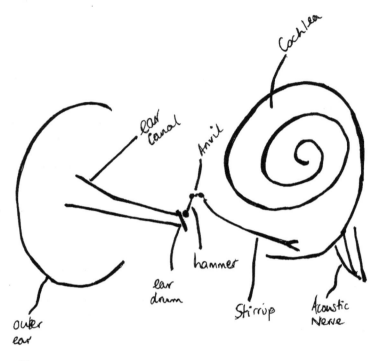

Figure B1-9: Hand drawn diagram of the ear.   *Source: ACT.*

Important terms

Defences   Although the ear doesn't have much by the way of defences against sound pressure, there is the stapedial reflex, which reduces the transmission of intense sound. Stapedial refers to the stapes, which is the stirrup-shaped bone in the middle ear. The reflex causes the stirrup to stiffen and therefore not transfer as much sound pressure through the oval window to the cochlea in the inner ear.

Nose

The nose is the upper part of the respiratory system and the organ of smell.

Main structures

It consists of an air passage from the *nostrils* at the front to the *nasopharynx* at the rear. The *nasal septum*, which is made of cartilage and bone, divides the passage into two chambers. One of the main functions of the nose is to filter, warm and moisten air before it enters the rest of the respiratory tract *(see previous section on the Respiratory System).* The sense of smell is provided by *olfactory nerve* endings, which transmits information to the *olfactory bulb* in the brain when stimulated by inhaled vapours. Finally the nose acts as a resonator that helps to give the voice its individual characteristic tone.

Important terms

Defences   The nasal hair will trap dust up to a certain size, approximately up to 15 microns and prevent it getting into the rest of the respiratory tract.

Mucus produced by the lining of the nostrils will also trap dust.

Principles of toxicology and epidemiology

Learning outcomes

On completion of this element, candidates should be able to:

B2.1   Describe the classification of hazardous substances with reference to appropriate legislation.

B2.2   Describe the main effects and route of attack of hazardous substances on the human body.

B2.3   Explain the relevance of toxicological data to the identification of work related ill-health.

B2.4   Explain the principles of epidemiology and its application in health surveillance of a workforce.

Content

Relevant statutory provisions

Control of Substances Hazardous to Health Regulations (COSHH) 2002 (and as amended 2004)

Chemicals (Hazard Information and Packaging for Supply) Regulations (CHIP) 2002 (and as amended 2004)

Notification of New Substances Regulations (NONS) 1993

This page is intentionally blank

ELEMENT B2 - PRINCIPLES OF TOXICOLOGY AND EPIDEMIOLOGY

B2.1 - Classifying hazardous substances

Physical forms

The form taken by a hazardous substance is a contributory factor to its potential for harm. Principally the form affects how easily a substance gains entry to the body, is absorbed into the body and reaches a susceptible site.

Hazardous substances take many forms and these forms can be changed into more or less harmful forms. For example, a liquid can be heated till it becomes a vapour, a gas can be compressed till it becomes a liquid and a solid can be abraded till it becomes a dust. A substance's natural form, at ambient temperature, may change several times during a process.

The most common physical forms are as follows:

SOLIDS

The ability of a solid to cause ill-health depends on its ability to get onto or into the body, that is, its routes of entry and process of entry into the body. Generally, a solid is more harmful to health when it is finely divided, can become airborne and then inhaled, e.g. hardwood dust. A solid may give off particles which are part of the gas given off when heated; this forms a fume e.g. welding fumes, which may be inhaled.

A solid may be ingested if it is in small enough pieces, e.g. flakes of lead paint.

LIQUIDS

The routes of entry for liquids could be ingestion and skin contact. If finely dispersed, they become a mist and therefore inhalable.

Some liquids are toxic to the human body and ingesting in large amounts can destroy it to the point of death, e.g. alcohol. Some liquids make skin contact and are irritants or corrosives thereby destroying the tissue e.g. acids and alkalis. There are also liquids that pass through cuts and grazes or pass through intact skin, e.g. trichloroethylene.

DUSTS

These are solid airborne particles, often created by operations such as grinding, crushing, milling, sanding or demolition, e.g. silica or hardwood dust. The size of the dust particles is important, whether it is inhalable or respirable.

FIBRES

Dust may be created that is made up of tiny fibres e.g. mineral wool and asbestos. The fibres may become airborne during use , when surfaces are damaged or when a building is being demolished. The fibres may be so small that they fall into the respirable range and as such may be inhaled deep into the alveoli region of the lungs.

MISTS

A mist is a finely dispersed liquid suspended in air. They are created mainly by spraying, foaming, pickling and electro-plating.

GASES

Formless fluids usually produced by chemical processes involving combustion or by the interaction of chemical substance. A gas will normally seek to fill the space completely into which it is liberated, e.g. nitrogen gas widely used in vessels due to its chemically inert properties.

FUMES

Solid particles formed by condensation from the gaseous state, e.g. lead fume. Welding 'fume' may be made up of a number of gases with a variety of solid particles suspended in it, dependent on the type of welding and the metals involved.

VAPOURS

The gaseous form of a material normally encountered in a liquid or solid state at normal room temperature and pressure. Typical examples are solvents, e.g. trichloroethylene that releases vapours when the container is opened.

Risk and safety phrases

The Chemicals (Hazard Information and Packaging for Supply) Regulations (CHIP) 2002 are regularly updated usually by amendment regulations. The aim of the CHIP Regulations is to provide a harmonised basis for the classification, information and labelling of dangerous substances and preparations in accordance with EU Directives. The Regulations are designed to protect people's health and the environment by:

■ Identification of the hazardous properties of materials (classification).
■ Provision of health and safety information to users (safety data sheet and label).
■ Packaging of materials safely.

CHIP requires suppliers to classify substances in accordance with their effects and provide information to users based on a specified classification scheme. The scheme is designed to be used to classify products (including mixtures) based on a calculation method. *See also - Relevant Statutory Provisions - Element B11 - Classification, Data Sheets and Labelling under the Chemical (Hazard Information and Packaging for Supply) Regulations 2002 (CHIP 3) and Chemicals (Hazard Information and Packaging for Supply) (Amendment) Regulations 2005.*

In order to clearly identify the properties of substances and preparations that may present a hazard during normal handling, the following information should be included on the label under Regulation 9 of CHIP Regulations 2002:

1.   Symbols and general indications of danger which highlight the most severe hazards.
2.   Standard risk phrases (r), which specify the hazards arising from (1) above.
3.   Standard safety phrases (s), which give the advice on the necessary precautions.

The criteria for classification, choice of symbols, indication of danger and choice of risk phrases are outlined in the Guidance on Regulations. The classification of carcinogens and mutagens above give an indication of the approach. Other examples include:

No.	Phrase	Criteria
R7	May cause fire	Organic peroxides which have flammable properties even when not in contact with other combustible material.
R28	Very toxic	Acute toxicity results: LD_{50} oral, rat: $\leq$ 25 mg/kg. Less than 100% survival at 5 mg/kg oral, rat, by the fixed dose procedure.
R35	Causes severe burns	If, when applied to healthy intact animal skin, full thickness destruction of skin tissue occurs as a result of 3 minutes exposure, or if this result can be predicted.
R42	May cause sensitisation by inhalation	If there is evidence that the substance or preparation can induce specific respiratory hypersensitivity. Where there are positive tests from appropriate animal tests. If the substance is an isocyanate, unless there is evidence that the substance does not cause respiratory hypersensitivity.

Figure B2-1: Risk phrases.

Source: ACT.

Safety phrases are assigned to dangerous substances and preparations in accordance with general criteria set out by the Guidance on Regulations. Some examples of safety phrases are:

No.	Phrase	Applicability	Criteria for use	
S1	Keep locked up	Very toxic and toxic and corrosive substances and preparations.	Obligatory for certain substances and preparations mentioned if sold to the general public.	
S2	Keep out of reach of children	All dangerous substances and preparations.	Obligatory for all dangerous substances and preparations sold to the general public, except for those only classified as dangerous for the environment.	
S8	Keep container dry	Substances and preparations which may react violently with water. Substances and preparations which on contact with water liberate extremely flammable gases. Substances and preparations which on contact with water liberate very toxic or toxic gases.	When necessary to reinforce warnings R14 Reacts violently with water. R15 Contact with water liberates highly flammable gases. *In particular* R29 Contact with water liberates toxic gas.	

Figure B2-2: Safety phrases.

Source: ACT.

The full text of the R-phrases and S-phrases can be found in Part V of the Approved Supply List (ASL): Information Approved for the Classification and Labelling of Substances and Preparations Dangerous for Supply. Risk phrases are also found in EH40.

For more information on the CHIP Regulations 2002, see also - Relevant Statutory Provisions - Element B11.

Content of safety data sheets and other sources of information

SAFETY DATA SHEETS

Safety data sheets must be provided for classified substances or preparations and will include:

1. Identification of the substance/preparation and the company
   Name of the substance.
   Name, address and telephone number (including emergency number) of supplier.
2. Composition/information on ingredients
   Sufficient information to allow the recipient to identify readily the associated risks.
3. Hazards identification
   Important hazards to man and the environment.
   Adverse health effects and symptoms.
4. First-aid measures
   Whether immediate attention is required.
   Symptoms and effects including delayed effects.
   Specific information according to routes of entry.
   Whether professional advice is advisable.
5. Fire fighting measures
   Suitable extinguishing media.
   Extinguishing media that must not be used.
   Hazards that may arise from combustion e.g., gases, fumes etc.
   Special protective equipment for fire fighters.

6. Accidental release measures

   Personal precautions such as removal of ignition sources, provision of ventilation, avoid eye/skin contact etc.

   Environmental precautions such as keep away from drains, need to alert neighbours etc.

   Methods for cleaning up e.g. absorbent materials. Also, "Never use…."

7. Handling and storage

   Advice on technical measures such as local and general ventilation.

   Measures to prevent aerosol, dust, fire etc.

   Design requirements for specialised storage rooms.

   Incompatible materials.

   Special requirements for packaging/containers.

8. Exposure controls/personal protection

   Engineering measures taken in preference to PPE.

   Where PPE is required, type of equipment necessary e.g. Type of gloves, goggles, barrier cream etc.

9. Physical and chemical properties

   Appearance, e.g. solid, liquid, powder, etc.

   Odour (if perceptible).

   Boiling point, flash point, explosive properties, solubility etc.

10. Stability and reactivity

    Conditions to avoid such as temperature, pressure, light, etc.

    Materials to avoid such as water, acids, alkalis, etc.

    Hazardous by-products given off on decomposition.

11. Toxicological information

    Toxicological effects if the substance comes into contact with a person.

    Carcinogenic, mutagenic, toxic for reproduction etc.

    Acute and chronic effects.

12. Ecological information

    Effects, behaviour and environmental fate that can reasonably be foreseen.

    Short and long term effects on the environment.

13. Disposal considerations

    Appropriate methods of disposal e.g. land-fill, incineration etc.

14. Transport information

    Special precautions in connection with transport or carriage.

    Additional information as detailed in the Carriage of Dangerous Goods by Road (CPL) Regs 1994 may also be given.

15. Regulatory information

    Health and safety information on the label as required by CHIP 3. Reference might also be made to HASAWA and COSHH.

16. Other Information

    Training advice, recommended uses and restrictions, sources of important data used to compile the data sheet.

SUPPLY LABELS

Where a dangerous chemical is supplied in a package, the package must be labelled. Packaging must be safe and able to withstand the conditions. The supply label must state the following information:

- Name, address and telephone number of supplier in the European Economic Area (EEA) - the EU plus Norway, Iceland and Liechtenstein.

- Name of the substance - chemical name, a trade name would not be adequate.

- Indications of danger and corresponding symbol - per schedule 2 of CHIP.

- Risk phrases.

- Safety phrases.

- EC number - usually found in the Approved Supply List (ASL).

- If the substance is listed in the ASL, the label should bear the words 'EC label'.

Figure B2-3: Product labels.

Source: Stocksigns.

Indication of danger	Symbol (orange background)	Category of danger	Characteristic properties and body responses
Irritant		Irritant	A non-corrosive substance which, through immediate, prolonged or repeated contact with the skin or mucous membrane, can cause inflammation e.g. butyl ester, a severe irritant which can cause abdominal pain, vomiting and burning of the skin and eyes.
		Sensitising (by contact)	May cause an allergic skin reaction which will worsen on further exposures (allergic dermatitis), e.g. nickel or epoxy resin.
Corrosive		Corrosive	May destroy living tissues on contact e.g. sulphuric (battery) acid or sodium hydroxide (caustic soda).
Harmful		Harmful	If inhaled or ingested or it penetrates the skin, has an adverse effect on health e.g. some solvents causing narcosis or central nervous system failure.
		Sensitising (by inhalation)	May cause an allergic respiratory reaction, which will progressively worsen on further exposures (asthma), e.g. flour dust, isocyanates
		Carcinogenic (category 3)	Only evidence is from animals, which is of doubtful relevance to humans, e.g. benzyl chloride.
		Mutagenic (category 3)	Evidence of mutation in Ames Test and possible somatic cell mutation.
		Toxic to reproduction (category 3)	Animal data, not necessarily relevant.
Toxic		Toxic	If inhaled or ingested or it penetrates the skin, may involve serious acute or chronic health risks and even death e.g. arsenic, a systemic poison.
		Carcinogenic (categories 1 & 2)	May, if inhaled or it penetrates the skin, induce uncontrolled cell division (cancer) or increase its incidence e.g. benzene affects the bone marrow causing leukaemia.
		Mutagenic (categories 1 & 2)	May cause genetic defects, e.g. 2-Ethoxyethanol may impair fertility.
		Toxic to reproduction (categories 1 & 2)	May cause harm to the unborn child, e.g. lead suspected of causing restricted development of the brain of the foetus.
Very Toxic		Very toxic	If inhaled or ingested or it penetrates the skin, may involve extremely serious acute or chronic health risks and even death e.g. cyanide, a severe irritant and systemic poison.

Figure B2-4: Harmful, toxic.   *Source: ACT.*

Figure B2-5: Toxic.   *Source: ACT.*

Figure B2-6: Table of toxic levels.   *Source: The Chemicals (Hazard Information & Packaging for Supply) Regulations 2002 (CHIP 3).*

OTHER INFORMATION

For example - training advice, recommended uses and restrictions, and sources of important data used to compile the data sheet.

For substances dangerous to the environment, information is required on:

- Acute toxicity to fish, daphnia and algae.
- Biodegradability.
- Bioaccumulation potential.

For supply to the general public, for example from a retail outlet, sufficient information must be available if a person requests a safety data sheet.

- If packaged - information should be available on the product packaging.
- No packaging - e.g. petrol, displayed on a conspicuous notice.

MS SERIES

Available from HSE Books (Health and Safety Executive), the MS Series are a general series of books to provide guidance on specific work-related health risks. Included within the series are publications such as:

MS12	Mercury, medical guidance notes.	MS24	Medical aspects of occupational skin disease.
MS13	Asbestos, medical guidance note.	MS25	Medical aspects of occupational asthma.
MS17	Medical aspects of work-related exposures to organophosphates.	MS26	A guide to audiometric testing programmes.

Available at www.hsebooks.co.uk.

CAS

CAS numbers identify the chemical, but not its concentration or specific mixture. For example, hydrogen chloride (HCL) has the CAS number 7647-01-0; this specific CAS number will appear on containers of anhydrous hydrogen chloride, a 20% solution of HCL in water, and a 2.0 molar solution of HCL in diethyl ether.

It is a good idea to file chemicals, not only by chemical name, but by CAS number. It is one way to avoid the problem of finding a substance name filed on a Material Safety Data Sheet (MSDS) when the name of the substance might not be correctly catalogued or spelt. It is also a good idea to include a CAS number field if data is stored on a computer, especially if the electronic copy is used by a non-chemist to obtain data.

MEDICAL DATABASES

A variety of organisations maintain current information on work-related health effects, such as the HSE; British Medical Association (www.bma.org.uk); Medic8 UK Medical Research Engine and Health Guide, (www.medic8.com).

Toxic

DEFINITION OF TOXICITY

A toxic substance is one which if inhaled or ingested or it penetrates the skin, may involve serious acute or chronic health risks and even death e.g. arsenic, a systemic poison.

All substances can be considered as toxic, given a sufficient amount. Even water ingested in sufficient quantities will cause harm. The toxicity of a substance is defined as its ability to cause death/serious health effects in a population. Thus toxicity is the property of being poisonous and is used to refer to the severity of adverse effects or illness produced by a toxin (e.g. bacteria), a poison or a drug. Highly toxic substances are classified as those which can cause death at relatively low concentrations. There are many measures of toxicity, for example, LD_{50} (lethal dose fifty) is the amount of a substance that will cause 50% of a standardised population of rats to die.

EXAMPLES OF COMMONLY OCCURRING TOXIC SUBSTANCES AND THEIR TOXIC EFFECTS

Trichloroethylene

Its common name is 'trike', a chlorinated hydrocarbon. Trichloroethylene is used commercially for degreasing metal components such as steel vehicle wheels prior to rust proofing or other surface treatments. Workers may develop, through prolonged exposure to solvent vapour, an addiction to trichloroethylene. It is a narcotic (induces unconsciousness) and therefore over exposure can produce drowsiness leading to unconsciousness and death. Although non-flammable, heating causes the formation of phosgene gas (this may occur when contaminated air is drawn through a cigarette so operators must be prohibited from smoking when using this substance) and corrosive hydrochloric acid as a result of its decomposition (exposure to ultra-violet light can have similar effects).

Inhalation of a large amount of trichloroethylene vapour can lead to death, i.e. the acute effect.

In smaller doses over time, the liver will break down the toxin and eventually become damaged. As the liver heals itself, scar tissue will be formed, which does not function as well as the healthy tissue. An increase of this scar tissue will stop the liver functioning correctly and cause deterioration in health. This damage is known as cirrhosis.

Asbestos

Asbestos is a general term used to describe a range of mineral fibres (commonly referred to by colour i.e. white, brown and blue). Asbestos was mainly used as an insulating and fire resisting material. Asbestos fibres readily become airborne when disturbed and may enter the lungs, where they cause fibrosis (scarring and thickening) of the lung tissue, asbestosis (a diffuse form of interstitial pulmonary fibrosis) or mesothelioma (a form of cancer involving thickening of the pleural lining). Asbestosis typically takes more than 10 years to develop. Research suggests that 50 per cent of asbestos sufferers will also develop cancer of the lung or bronchus.

Carbon monoxide

Carbon monoxide has a great affinity (200 times that of oxygen) for the haemoglobin red blood cells. Carbon monoxide will inhibit oxygen uptake by red blood cells resulting in *chemical asphyxiation.*

Isocyanates

Isocyanates are used in the manufacture of resins and urethane foams. Common compounds are toluene di-isocyanate (TDI) and methylene bisphenyl di-isocyanate (MDI). TDI, an extremely volatile vapour, is evolved during the manufacture of foams. TDI and MDI are highly toxic in very small amounts (parts per billion) and inhalation will result In a severe respiratory reaction. Isocyanates are sensitising agents.

Figure B2-7: Asbestos label.
Source: Ambiguous.

Siliceous dusts

Silica exists naturally as crystalline minerals (tridymite, cristobalite) - a common variety is quartz. Industrially silica is used in the morphous (after heating) form e.g. fumed silica, silica gel. Inhalation of silica can result in silicosis, a fibrosis of the lung. Nodular lesions are formed which ultimately destroy lung structure.

Lead

Lead poisoning results from the inhalation of fumes produced from the heating of the metal or certain solders containing lead at temperatures above 500°C or from finely-divided lead dust. Lead poisoning may result from the inhalation of organic lead compounds e.g. tetraethyl lead. Chronic (cumulative) lead poisoning may result in anaemia, mental dullness and is often accompanied by the presence of a blue line around the gums. Acute lead poisoning is often fatal; symptoms include muscular twitch, hallucinations and violent behaviour. Lead can also inhibit the proper development of an unborn foetus and is referred to as having a teratagenic effect.

Carbon dioxide

A *simple asphyxiant* produced as a by-product of the brewing processes. As a simple asphyxiant it displaces oxygen in the air that we breathe and means insufficient oxygen goes to the brain, leading to collapse and death. Available commercially as a frozen solid 'dry ice' used as a refrigerant or to generate 'smoke' in theatre productions. Provides the constituent part of a carbon dioxide fire extinguisher and may be encountered in fixed fire fighting installations in buildings. It may be encountered in confined spaces, such as trenches, in areas with chalky soil as carbon dioxide is evolved naturally; it is heavier than air and tends to gather in low areas.

Corrosive

DEFINITION OF CORROSIVE

Corrosive substances will destroy living tissue on contact by chemical attack. The level of harm will depend on the concentration and polarity of the substance (the ph level). Acids and alkalis are classified as corrosive.

EXAMPLES OF COMMONLY OCCURRING CORROSIVE SUBSTANCES AND THEIR EFFECTS

Acids

Common workplace acids include hydrochloric acid, which is a common bi-product of organic chemical processes used extensively in 'pickling' processes (rust descaling of steel, such as used in the process of steel tube manufacture). Vehicle 'battery acid' (which contains approximately 28 %sulphuric acid) is another common workplace acid. If contact is to the skin, e.g. hands, a burning sensation and reddening of the skin is usually the first indication of contact. Skin damage may result in dermatitis with the potential for bacterial infection.

Ammonia

Ammonia is a gas used extensively as a refrigerant or as an aqueous solution used in cleaning materials. It is a gas usually stored under pressure.

Contact with liquid - it has a corrosive action that will burn the skin on contact and it will severely irritate or burn the cornea.

Gas - it is lighter than air and has a local effect on the lungs. In small concentrations it is an acute irritant but is recoverable, though in larger concentrations it can result in pneumonia and pulmonary failure.

Aqueous - (alkaline liquor) can cause skin damage on contact and the vapours from the liquor are an acute respiratory irritant.

Sodium hydroxide

Common name caustic (burns) soda is available as a solid usually in pellet form or various concentrations in water. The solid is hydroscopic and will rapidly absorb water from the air if in contact with the skin (or lungs if inhaled) and forms a corrosive solution. On contact with the skin the material will feel soap like. This occurs because sodium hydroxide will turn the fat cells of the skin into soap (sodium hydroxide was used to make the original bars of soap from animal waste products). Sodium hydroxide is used extensively in the extraction of aluminium from bauxite and is mainly encountered in the work place as a cleaning agent (for unblocking of drains, degreasing of cooking ovens etc.). Sodium hydroxide is the major cause of industrial chemical sight loss as the cornea and iris of the eye are instantly damaged or destroyed on contact with relatively low concentrations.

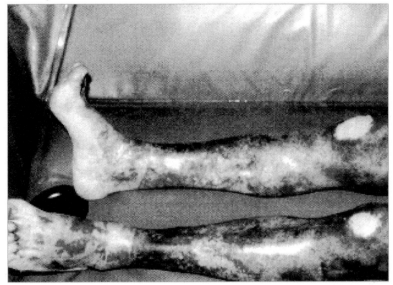

Figure B2-8: Skin burns from wet cement.   *Source: SHP.*

Irritant

DEFINITION OF IRRITANT

An irritant substance is a non-corrosive substance which, through immediate, prolonged or repeated contact with the skin or mucous membrane, can cause inflammation. For example butyl ester - a severe irritant which can cause abdominal pain, vomiting and burning of the skin and eyes.

EXAMPLES OF COMMONLY OCCURRING IRRITANT SUBSTANCES AND THEIR EFFECTS

Cleaning agents

Organic solvents

Include highly volatile / flammable cleaning agents such as acetone, organo-chlorides such as trichloroethylene (used for commercial degreasing) or carbon tetrachloride used in dry cleaning processes. These substances remove the protective oils that cover the skin, penetrate the skin readily and destroy the fats in the subcutaneous layers. In the construction industry they may be encountered as residual contents of storage tanks or may be used as convenient cleaning substances to remove adhesives.

Silicates

Cement is a silicate and prolonged exposure to the skin may result in irritation of the skin, leading to reddening, dryness and dermatitis. Inhalation of cement will result in a progressive chronic irritant effect on the lungs.

Chlorine

It is usually stored under pressure in its liquid state. If a leak occurs a small amount of liquid will give rise to a large amount of gas. It is an acute respiratory irritant; small quantities may lead to chronic lung disease, large quantities result in pneumonia and pulmonary failure. It is a highly reactive chemical gas which supports violent combustion. It is used extensively in water treatment processes, for example, where water is required for human consumption. Compounds of chlorine include sodium hypochlorite e.g. domestic bleach. These compounds liberate chlorine gas readily when mixed with acids, therefore creating a risk to workers who use mixtures of bleaches and acid cleaners.

Harmful

DEFINITION OF HARMFUL

A substance which, if inhaled or ingested or it penetrates the skin in large amounts, has an adverse effect on health.

EXAMPLES OF COMMONLY OCCURRING HARMFUL SUBSTANCES AND THEIR EFFECTS

Certain substances classified under the CHIP Regulations 2002, labelled with a cross (X) on an orange background are harmful. Carbon tetrachloride and trichloroethylene are capable of absorption through the skin and have a harmful narcotic effect. If the vapours are inhaled, it can cause drowsiness very quickly, depress the central nervous system and may lead to liver failure and death if exposure is for prolonged periods. Harmful substances include aqueous solutions of ammonia (ammonium hydroxide) and bleach (sodium hyperchlorite solutions). They will often have an acute effect on the body, including inflammation of the skin, mucous membranes of the eyes or nose, irritation of the lungs.

Dermatitic

DEFINITION OF DERMATITIS

Dermatitis is an inflammatory reaction in the skin and relates to a spectrum of clinical and histopathological characteristics. There are two types of dermatitis, primary (contact) dermatitis and secondary (allergic) dermatitis.

Primary/contact forms of dermatitis

This form of dermatitis is caused by repeated or long contact with substances which interfere with normal skin physiology leading to the acute form of this dermatitis in which inflammation of skin (usually on the hands, wrists and forearms) occurs. It may take the form of dry and cracked skin. Removal from exposure allows normal cell repair, over time. A similar level of repeat exposure usually results in the same response. This class of dermatitis is called primary or contact dermatitis.

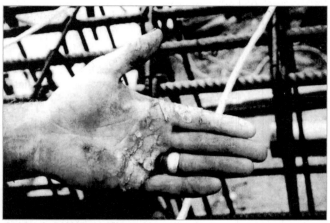

Figure B2-9: Contact dermatitis.   Source: SHP.

Repeat exposures can lead to the chronic form of this dermatitis where cumulative damage leads to failure in the repair mechanism and the symptoms persist even after exposure has ceased. Sufferers of the chronic form of irritant contact dermatitis can develop a rapid flare-up of symptoms even when exposure is relatively minor.

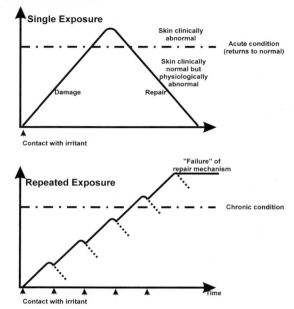

Figure B2-10: Skin - contact with irritant.

Source: ABC of Work Related Disorders, BMJ Publishing Group.

Secondary/allergic or sensitised forms of dermatitis

In this form of dermatitis a person exposed to the substance develops dermatitis in the usual way described above. When exposure ceases, the dermatitis heals but the person develops antibodies as a defence mechanisms in anticipation of further exposure. When a new exposure occurs the anti-bodies react to the exposure leading to inflammation of the skin. Because the anti-bodies are dispersed throughout the body the (allergic) response will usually mean the skin becomes inflamed where the substance has not been in contact as well as in the area of contact. A small exposure, even a few molecules, is enough to cause a major response.

CIRCUMSTANCES LIKELY TO LEAD TO DERMATITIS

Regular contact with causative agents such as cement, acids or alkalis, as discussed above, may result in cell damage and the development of dermatitis. Care needs to be given to personal hygiene (although excessive washing of hands, particularly with pumice based cleaners, must be kept to a minimum to avoid removing the natural oils from the hands), the use of barrier creams and appropriate hand protection. Light or fair-skinned individuals are often found to be particularly prone to dermatitis.

TYPICAL WORKPLACE EXAMPLES OF DERMATITIC SUBSTANCES

Primary/contact dermatitis: greases, mineral oils, detergents and cement.

Secondary, allergic or sensitisation dermatitis: nickel, resins, rubber additives and hair dyes (phenols).

Dermatitis can be prevented by:

- Clean working conditions and properly planned work systems.
- Careful attention to skin hygiene principles.
- Prompt attention to cuts, abrasions and spillages onto the skin.
- Use of protective equipment.
- Barrier cream can help.
- Pre-employment screening for sensitive individuals.

Sensitisation

DEFINITION OF SENSITISATION

A sensitising substance may cause an allergic reaction with the skin or respiratory system. Where the skin or respiratory system is regularly exposed to contact with many workplace substances, there is the potential to develop an allergic reaction on subsequent exposure to the same material at a later date.

The body may produce large amounts of defensive substances such as histamine, causing the eyes, the lung or even the skin to develop adverse effects such as wheezing, shortness of breath, excessive mucous flow from the nose or mouth or reddening or cracking of the skin.

SKIN

Sensitising (by contact) may cause an allergic skin reaction, which will worsen on further exposures (e.g. allergic dermatitis).

RESPIRATORY SYSTEM

Sensitising (by inhalation) may cause an allergic respiratory reaction, which will progressively worsen on further exposures (asthma). In this situation there are no symptoms when a person first becomes sensitised, but the immune system will have "identified a pathogen" i.e. the allergen, which could be flour dust or isocyanates. This "pathogen" will be recognised at the time of next exposure, and at each subsequent exposure the immune system will produce progressively more antibodies to respond to the "pathogen". The large production of antibodies causes the tissue in the respiratory tract to swell, narrowing the airways. Histamine is also produced, which makes the muscles and cartilage stiffen. The tighter and narrower the airways, the more difficult it is to breathe. This respiratory system response is an asthma attack.

HEALTH EFFECTS

Dermatitis (skin) is the most common industrial disease. More than 20,000 individuals are diagnosed with work-related industrial asthma (respiratory system) each year.

TYPICAL WORKPLACE EXAMPLES OF SENSITISING AGENTS

Skin sensitising agents include nickel, chromium salts, cement, epoxy resins, isocyanates. Respiratory system, sensitising agents include flour dust, maize, starch, isocyanates, formaldehyde, coal (anthracitic - very pure carbon form), sulphur dioxide (product of aluminium manufacture).

Carcinogenic

DEFINITION OF CARCINOGEN

A substance if inhaled or absorbed will have the potential to cause uncontrolled cell division at a susceptible site on (skin) or within the body (e.g. liver).

Cancer cells will cause dysfunction of the normal cell activity. Cell growth can be very fast in some circumstances and the propagation process to obtain growth nutrients will enable the disease to spread to other healthy parts of the body. This process is aided by the blood and is particularly pervasive if the affected cells are near to the lymphatic glands (neck and groin). Known carcinogenic substances are classified under CHIP categories 1, 2 and 3.

EXAMPLES OF TYPES OF CANCER RELATIVE TO SPECIFIC SUBSTANCES

Asbestos

Asbestos fibres that enter the lungs may cause malignant mesothelioma of the pleura (thickening of the pleural lining that is a form of cancer). Occasionally, where the asbestos is ingested it may lead to a malignant mesothelioma of the peritoneum (the lining of the abdomen). Mesotheliomas have usually been growing for 10-12 years before they become clinically evident. The condition can be latent for 30 or more years, however life expectancy from the point of initial diagnosis may be as short as three to twelve months. The amphibole fibres in crocidolite (blue asbestos) and amosite (brown asbestos) carry the greatest risk of causing mesothelioma, but the serpentine fibres in chrysotile (white asbestos) can also cause mesothelioma, particularly if they contain tremolite. There is a trend that shows that deaths from mesothelioma are increasing; there are usually more than 1,000 per year and it this is predicted to rise to over 3,000 by 2020.

Research suggests that 50 per cent of asbestos sufferers, those with asbestosis, will also develop cancer of the lung or bronchus. In addition, there is an identified synergistic effect for asbestosis suffers that smoke. It is estimated that such people are at 100 times greater risk of contracting lung cancer than those that do not smoke who contract asbestosis.

Coal tar

Mineral oils and related products, tar bitumen diesel oil and by products of partial combustion of such substances (soot) have long been associated with skin cancer, particularly in males, cancer of the scrotum.

Chromium

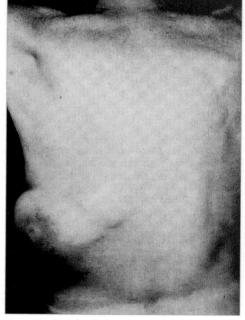

Figure B2-11: Mesothelioma. Source: *ABC of Work Related Disorders, BMJ Publishing Group.*

Chromium salts are used in the process of electroplating chromium metal onto steel components, such as vehicle trims and bathroom fitments. Exposure to chromium (hexavalent) has been proved to be a cause of lung cancer and linked to cancer of the prostate gland. An additional, common health effect of exposure to chromium is the destruction of the nasal membrane (septum), though not a cancer it is a significant health issue.

Wood dust

A major portion of airborne wood dust is contributed by particles larger than 10-µm size, which can be trapped effectively in the nasal passage. Nasal cancer is a significant hazard of woodworking and is particularly associated with hardwoods.

Mutagenic

DEFINITION OF MUTAGEN

Mutagenic substances are defined in CHIP as substances which may alter the body's deoxyribonucleic acid (DNA), in particular to reproductive cells and cause heritable genetic defects (mutations) in subsequent generations.

EXAMPLES OF SUBSTANCES FOUND IN THE WORKPLACE

Examples of substances which may impair fertility and result in mutations in subsequent generations are 2-Ethoxyethanol and plutonium oxide.

B2.2 - Main routes of attack on the human body

Main routes of entry of hazardous substances into the human body

The major *routes* of entry into the body by substances (including toxic, corrosive and dermatitic substances, dusts and fibres) and agents are:

- Eyes.
- Inhalation (nose).
- Skin pervasion.
- Injection.
- Ingestion via the gastro-intestinal tract (mouth).

This list represents the major routes of entry into the human body in their order of significance, inhalation being the most significant route as more harmful substances enter the body through this route than any other. Implantation is an additional, lesser, route of entry and is where any material, natural or artificial, is inserted into the body for medical purposes. Examples of implantation include hormone replacement therapy (HRT), replacement joints, cardiac pacemakers or breast implants.

Mucous membrane of eyes

Some substances are water soluble, i.e. they dissolve in water, for example, ammonia. The mucous membrane of the eye will absorb the ammonia forming ammonium hydroxide, an alkali, which will irritate and eventually destroy the tissue. Some substances will be absorbed by the mucous membrane and allow the substance to pass into the eye and then gain a route through the blood capillaries into the body. Some viruses and bacteria can gain access this way, e.g. the Brucella bacterium, which causes brucellosis, the Leptospira bacterium, which causes leptospirosis (Weil's Disease) and the Hepatitis B virus.

INHALATION

The most significant route of entry for harmful agents is via inhalation. It has been estimated that about 90% of industrial poisons are absorbed through the lungs.

The respiratory system consists of the windpipe or trachea which branches into the bronchi which supply the left and right lungs. The main bronchi divide into smaller bronchi which divide into smaller bronchioles. These small air passages branch further until they lead to the alveoli - of which there are perhaps 300 million in the lungs with a total surface area of approximately the size of a football pitch. These are small air-sacs arising at the ends of bronchioles. They lie on the lung's outer surface surrounded by a rich network of blood capillaries from the pulmonary artery. It is here that gas exchange, notably oxygen and carbon-dioxide, occurs and where substances that reach this area may also be transferred into the blood supply.

The size of particles that may enter the lungs by inhalation is important, they are measured in microns - a micron is one-millionth of a metre. The larger particles inhaled (in the region of greater than 10 microns) tend to only travel as far as the nose, smaller particles make their way past this point and enter the bronchi and bronchioles.

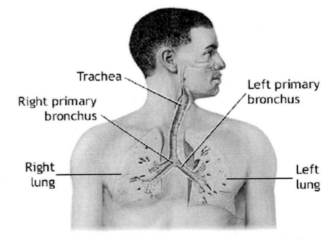

Figure B2-12: The respiratory system.   *Source: Ambiguous.*

Some of these particles are deposited in this respiratory section (between 5 and 10 microns) and the smaller particles (approx 5 microns and less) can enter the alveoli. The smallest particles (approximately 0.5 microns or less) are exhaled without settling.

INGESTION

Via the gastro-intestinal tract (GIT)

The alimentary canal which leads from the mouth to the anus can be considered as an extension of the skin. It may therefore be considered effectively "outside" the body. Chemicals can enter the GIT by, for example pipetting by mouth and eating, drinking or smoking in contaminated areas.

The passage of chemicals through the biological membranes can take place by various mechanisms such as passive and facilitated diffusion, active transport, filtration through the membrane pores, and by phagocytosis. The main site of absorption is in the small intestine and, to a lesser extent, the stomach (gut).

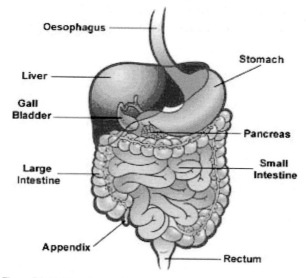

Figure B2-13: Digestive system.   *Source: STEM.*

SKIN PERVASION

The structure of the skin is detailed in the following figure.

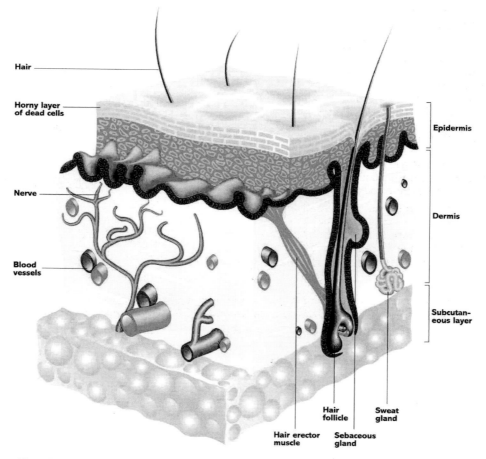

Figure B2-14: Skin layer.   *Source: SHP.*

Substances can be absorbed through the intact skin or they enter via cuts or abrasions, and enter through the eye. Solvents such as toluene and trichloroethylene can enter either accidentally or if used for washing the hands. These substances may have a local effect, such as de-fatting of the skin, or pass through into the blood system.

The absorption of organic based compounds directly through the epidermis, for example, chemicals like benzene, trichloroethylene and organic lead (e.g. tetraethyl lead used as a fuel additive) is known as *percutaneous absorption*. The direct effect on the skin results in a class of conditions known as dermatoses.

INJECTION

The outer layer of skin, when intact, will keep out most substances. However, if something sharp pushes through the external layer and into the bloodstream, a substance hazardous to health could be carried with it and then carried round the body. This is injection. Needles are usually associated with injection, but it could be anything sharp: broken glass, metal, wood splinters, all having the capability of pushing through the skin and carrying contaminants into the body.

THE SITES OF ABSORPTION OF HAZARDOUS SUBSTANCES INTO THE BLOODSTREAM

The process of entry of agents into the body is via **absorption.** Here the chemical agent diffuses across a biological membrane barrier from the site of absorption (e.g. the alveoli in the lungs) into the blood system. This process is influenced by factors such as the chemicals:

- Solubility.
- Small molecular size.
- Polarity (e.g. the likelihood of binding with the membrane).

The process of entry into the bloodstream can also occur by direct access via **cuts, damaged skin and injection**. This is where a chemical, or micro-organism is mechanically introduced below the epidermis. For example, "needle stick" injuries can occur where health workers accidentally puncture their skin with used syringes.

Once in the bloodstream many substances have the ability to cross the placental barrier and hence are absorbed by a developing foetus.

Lungs

The purpose of the lungs is gaseous exchange. Inhaled oxygen passes through the one-cell thick alveoli into the dense blood capillary network and is carried round the body to be used in the process of metabolism. Without oxygen metabolism could not take place and the body would die. A by-product of metabolism is carbon dioxide and this is carried to the lungs, exchanged for the oxygen and then expelled by the lungs by being exhaled.

If an airborne hazardous substance is inhaled, it may also take part in the gaseous exchange and therefore be absorbed into the body. These substances may be gases, vapours, water-soluble particles or respirable particles.

Carbon monoxide is more readily absorbed than oxygen, resulting in the carbon monoxide being carried round the body rather than oxygen. Carbon monoxide does not take part in metabolism so if there is not enough oxygen, the body will die; it is asphyxiated.

Absorption of harmful substances in the lungs is the most common route and process of entry into the body in the workplace. This involves harmful substances presented to the alveoli crossing the thin membrane between the lungs into the blood system via the capillary network.

Gut

Food is broken down by the chewing process, swallowed, passed down the oesophagus and into the stomach. The stomach contents are further broken down and churned into a soup-like consistency. Some absorption takes place through the stomach lining, but not much. Some chemicals are absorbed in the stomach, which is the basis for the design of some analgesics. Aspirin is absorbed in the stomach making it faster acting than if it had to travel further into the gastro-intestinal tract. However, the ability of the stomach to absorb certain substances means that toxic amounts may be absorbed accidentally, very quickly.

As the broken down food passes through the duodenum and into the small intestine (ileum), it gets broken down even further. Once in the small intestine, it passes over the cilia that line the intestine. The presence of the cilia means that there is a huge surface area for absorption to take place, and most of the absorption of the basic building blocks of food takes place here. Hazardous substances reaching this far may also be absorbed through the lining of the gut, taken away by the blood and carried round the body.

What is left at the end of the trip through the small intestine is passed into the large intestine (colon) where absorption of water takes place. This is another site where hazardous substances may be absorbed, along with the water.

Particles of lead for example can be absorbed after accidental ingestion, while bacteria may be absorbed in the gut when ingested with contaminated food.

Skin

The skin is a semi-permeable membrane, preventing most substances from entering. However, there are some substances that can be absorbed by intact skin. Tetra-ethyl lead (organic lead) is a substance readily absorbed by the skin. Once a substance passes through the skin, it can be carried round the body by the blood and may then head for its target organ(s) or be deposited in its target organ. The amount absorbed through the skin adds to the dose that has entered by other routes, for example, inhalation.

LOCAL AND SYSTEMIC EFFECTS

Local effects

Where a chemical has a direct effect on the lung it is termed a local effect.

For example, if the gas sulphur dioxide is inhaled, a dilute sulphurous acid forms on the lung lining causing irritation and constriction of the lung pipe work.

Systemic effects

Where a chemical enters via the lungs and affects the whole body, it is termed a systemic effect.

For example, if carbon monoxide is inhaled, it has no direct effect on the lungs; however it acts as a systemic poison because it replaces oxygen in the bloodstream thereby affecting cellular respiration.

Main routes and mechanisms of attack

Harmful substances, such as chlorinated hydrocarbons and fungal spores can directly attack the lung tissue, impair lung function (i.e. *local effects*) such as inflammation of the alveoli or pass through to the blood stream. Alternatively the effects may be experienced around the body (systemic effects), circulated via the blood stream and affecting target organs such as the liver.

In sensitised people, when the body is 'attacked' by allergens such as pollen, house mites and fungal spores, the muscles of the bronchi contract. This in turn restricts the amount of air that the lungs receive. This is known as bronchial asthma which can also be caused by occupational sensitisers such as di-isocyanates *(see later section on sensitisers)*. Exposure to many organic dusts, such as mouldy hay, can cause an inflammation of the alveoli known as *extrinsic allergic alveolitis*. An example of this is Farmer's lung, which occurs in response to the fungi which grows on mouldy straw and hay. These moulds thrive in warm damp conditions and outbreaks are most common in high rainfall areas. Symptoms include fever, head and muscle aches, and shortness of breath. Chronic exposure can lead to permanent scarring of the lung tissue. Similar conditions are bird fancier's lung (caused by bird excreta and bloom) and mushroom worker's lung caused by released spores.

TOXIC SUBSTANCES

Toxic substances may enter the body through the skin, by inhalation and ingestion. Skin and inhalation are the most common routes for such substances as benzene and trichloroethylene and similar solvents, and often they will cause local irritation or removal of skin fat (whitening of the surface) on contact, in addition they may be absorbed or penetrate through the skin and enter the blood stream. The agent will then travel through the body's system where often they will have an acute effect on organs such as the brain (e.g. narcotic) and a long term effect on organs such as bone marrow (leukaemia) and the liver (cirrhosis). Many toxic substances may be ingested. A notable example of a substance relating to this route of entry would be from the ingestion of a heavy metal, such as lead oxide, derived from handling lead roofing or flashing materials. Lead oxide may pass from the worker's hands to their food and be ingested.

CORROSIVE SUBSTANCES

(See earlier - common corrosive substances are acids and alkalis.) They have a local corrosive effect, on the skin, eyes, mucus and if inhaled the lungs. These substances will destroy body cells and regular contact at low level may result in dermatitis.

DERMATITIC SUBSTANCES

See earlier; by contact with the skin and forearms, dermatitic substances will have a local effect causing skin openings and laceration type wounds which are often quite debilitating and slow to heal. Often there is a high risk of biological infection. After recovery there is a possibility that an affected individual may become highly susceptible (sensitising dermatitis) to future contact, even at a level as low as a single molecule, with the rapid onset of the symptoms described earlier.

DUSTS AND FIBRES

Dust and fibres will normally enter the body by inhalation and affect the respiratory tract i.e. trachea, bronchus and the alveoli. The possibility for ingestion also exists and some process operators have developed cancer of the stomach/intestine through asbestos fibres being retained in the wall lining. Instances of cancer of the nasal passage, trachea and lungs are also associated with workers involved in the manufacture of furniture etc. from hard woods such as mahogany. Dusts such as coal and silica will cause a fibrotic effect (scarring of lung membrane), with resultant loss of lung functionality. Asbestosis, more commonly diagnosed as a lung disease, will result in scars which will propagate from the original point of contact with a chronic high risk of cancer developing.

DISTINCTION BETWEEN INHALABLE AND RESPIRABLE DUST

'Total inhalable dust' approximates to the fraction of airborne material which enters the nose and mouth during breathing and is, therefore, available for deposition in the body. **'Respirable dust'** approximates to the fraction which penetrates to the gas exchange region of the lung (the alveoli). These values are affected by such factors as rate of respiration and hygroscopicity.

The nose and mouth filter particles greater than about 10 microns in diameter. Those particles with a diameter between 10 microns and 5 microns tend to be deposited on the muco-cillary escalator in the bronchi and bronchioles. Particles of less than 5 microns are likely to reach and settle in the gas exchange region of the lung (the alveoli). Very small particles (less than about 0.3 microns diameter) exhibit random or Brownian motion and waft in and out of the alveoli much as a gas molecule would do. Thus:

- Total inhalable dust = particles with a diameter of about 10 microns or less.
- Respirable dust = particles with a diameter between about 5 microns - 0.3 microns.

In terms of shape and size, asbestos fibres with a diameter of less than 3 microns and a length to diameter ratio of **at least** 3:1 are thought to be the most damaging.

Target organs and target systems

CHEMICAL ENTRY AND TARGET ORGANS

Once chemicals have entered the bloodstream they are distributed at a rate which depends on:
- The rate of blood flow.
- The structure of the capillary wall and the cell membrane of the organ.
- The affinity of the tissue for the chemical.

Thus chemicals are stored or metabolised to a greater or lesser extent by the organs. Examples of storage include:

- Lead which replaces calcium in the long bones resulting in a structural weakness. The lead can later be released back into the bloodstream with toxic effects.
- Chlorinated hydrocarbons (such as ddt) which are stored in the body fat.

The primary metabolising organ is the liver which is the largest internal organ in the body. The absorbed material is passed to the liver via the hepatic portal vein. The liver is also provided with oxygenated blood via the hepatic artery. Within the liver these two blood supplies pass via a system of capillaries into liver lobules. Blood leaves the liver in the hepatic veins. The liver has some 500 metabolic functions including the detoxification of poisons.

Liver cells have the ability to regenerate after toxic damage by substances such as alcohol and chlorinated hydrocarbons; however chronic exposure can lead to cirrhosis. The general objective of **detoxification** is to make absorbed chemicals more water-soluble to render them less harmful and to aid secretion from the body. This is done via a series of metabolic reactions which are broadly classified into Phase 1 and Phase 2 reactions.

Phase 1 reactions are chemical reactions including:

- Oxidation.
- Reduction.
- Hydration.
- Hydrolysis.
- Dehalogenation.

Phase 2 reactions add a group to form a conjugate; for example:

- Glutathion conjugation.
- Glucuronidation.
- Sulphation.
- Acetylation.
- Amino acid conjunction.

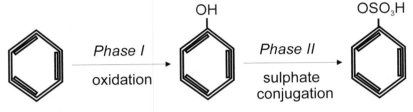

Figure B2-15: Benzene - phase I oxidation - phenol - phase II conjugation - phenyl sulphate.   *Source: Ambiguous.*

Other examples:
- After exposure to nickel, it is expelled in the urine (unchanged).
- After exposure to styrene, it is converted to mandelic acid which is expelled in the urine.
- After exposure to trichloroethylene, it is converted to trichloroacetic acid which is expelled in urine.

Sometimes this mechanism can make poisons as toxic or even more toxic. This is known as **bioactivation**. For example, 2-naphthylamine (or β-napthylamine) was used in the rubber and cable making industries as an anti-oxidant until the end of 1949 when they were withdrawn due to an excess of bladder cancers. 2-naphthylamine is changed by the liver into a bladder carcinogen:

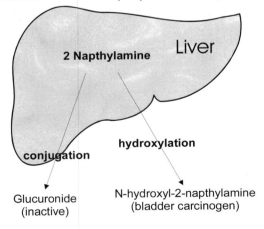

Figure B2-16: Liver (2-napthylamine).   *Source: Ambiguous.*

It should be noted that this only happens in humans and does not occur in laboratory rats for example.

The predominant route for excretion is via the kidneys, from which urine passes via the ureters into the bladder, and finally excreted via the urethra. Excretion via the digestive tract is also a major route (bile / faeces).

Substances can also be excreted via the lungs (particularly volatile substances like benzene) and in body fluids such as sweat, saliva, semen, breast milk and tears. These are, however, the minor routes.

The liver, kidneys and bladder are all susceptible to toxic substances because of the relatively high concentrations and long contact time - this makes them target organs.

Target organs   An organ of the human body on which a specified toxic material exerts its effect e.g. lungs, liver, brain, skin, bladder or eyes.

The following diagram illustrates some agents that target specific organs and systems in particular:

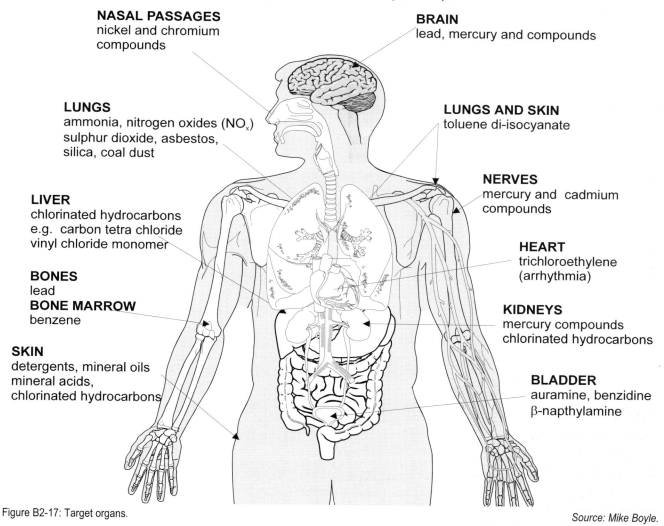

NASAL PASSAGES
nickel and chromium compounds

BRAIN
lead, mercury and compounds

LUNGS
ammonia, nitrogen oxides (NO_x) sulphur dioxide, asbestos, silica, coal dust

LUNGS AND SKIN
toluene di-isocyanate

NERVES
mercury and cadmium compounds

LIVER
chlorinated hydrocarbons e.g. carbon tetra chloride vinyl chloride monomer

HEART
trichloroethylene (arrhythmia)

BONES
lead
BONE MARROW
benzene

KIDNEYS
mercury compounds chlorinated hydrocarbons

SKIN
detergents, mineral oils mineral acids, chlorinated hydrocarbons

BLADDER
auramine, benzidine β-napthylamine

Figure B2-17: Target organs.

Source: Mike Boyle.

Common signs and symptoms of attack by hazardous substances

Common signs of workplace harm to health are:

Lungs:

Wheezing, shortness of breath, coughing (possibly with presence of blood), allergic asthma, with resultant, often permanent reduction in lung functionality.

Skin:

Reddening, cracking blisters common to dermatitis, often a chronic effect.

Nose and eyes:

Increased mucus, swelling and reddening, often acute effect on contact.

Gastro-intestinal tract:

Nausea and vomiting, resulting from ingestion of a substance.

THE BODY'S DEFENSIVE RESPONSES

The body's response against the attack by substances likely to cause damage can be divided into superficial (or external) defences and cellular (or internal) defences.

SUPERFICIAL DEFENCE MECHANISMS

1. Respiratory (inhalation)

Nose   On inhalation many substances and minor organisms are successfully trapped by nasal hairs, for example, the larger wood dust particles.

Respiratory tract   The next line of defence against inhalation or substances harmful to health begin here where a series of reflexes activate the coughing and sneezing mechanisms to forcibly expel the triggering substances.

Ciliary escalator   The passages of the respiratory system are also lined with mucus and well supplied with fine hair cells which sweep rhythmically towards the outside and pass along large particles. The respiratory system narrows as it enters the lungs where the ciliary escalator assumes more and more importance as the effective defence. Smaller particles of agents, such as some lead particles, are dealt with at this stage. The smallest particles, such as organic solvent vapours, reach the alveoli and are either deposited or exhaled.

2. Gastrointestinal (ingestion)

Mouth	For ingestion of substances the sense of taste can be a partial defence, by causing the person to spit the substance out. Saliva in the mouth provides a useful defence to substances which are not excessively acid or alkaline or in large quantities.
Gastrointestinal tract	Acid in the stomach also provides a useful defence similar to saliva. Vomiting and diarrhoea are additional reflex mechanisms which act to remove substances or quantities that the body is not equipped to deal with. This may give defence against systemic effects, though not direct effects like the burns caused by a corrosive agent.

3. Skin (absorption)

Skin	The body's largest organ provides a useful barrier against the absorption of many foreign organisms and chemicals (but not against all of them). Its effect is, however, limited by its physical characteristics. The outer part of the skin is covered in an oily layer and substances have to overcome this before they can damage the skin or enter the body. The outer part of the epidermis is made up of dead skin cells. These are readily sacrificed to substances without harm to the newer cells underneath. Repeated or prolonged exposure could defeat this. The skin, when attacked by substances may blister in order to protect the layers beneath. Openings in the skin such as sweat pores, hair follicles and cuts can allow entry and the skin itself may be permeable to some chemicals, e.g. toluene.

CELLULAR MECHANISMS

The cells of the body possess their own defence systems.

Scavenging action:	A type of white blood cell called macrophages attack invading particles in order to destroy them and remove them from the body. This process is known as phagocytosis.
Secretion of defensive substances:	Is done by some specialised cells. Histamine release and heparin, which promotes availability of blood sugar, are examples.
Prevention of excessive blood loss:	Reduced circulation through blood clotting and coagulation prevents excessive bleeding and slows or prevents the entry of germs.
Repair of damaged tissues:	Is a necessary defence mechanism which includes removal of dead cells, increased availability of defender cells and replacement of tissue strength, e.g. scar tissue caused by silica.
The lymphatic system:	Acts as a 'form of drainage system' throughout the body for the removal of foreign bodies. Lymphatic glands or nodes at specific points in the system act as selective filters preventing infection from entering the blood system. In many cases a localised inflammation occurs in the node at this time.

B2.3 - Toxicology

Introduction to toxicology

Toxicology is the study of the nature and effects of toxic substances, their detection and their treatment. A toxin is a substance which, when absorbed into the body, has the ability to cause harm by upsetting metabolic processes. There is no indication inherent in the term of the level of harm. It would be misleading to think of toxins as 'poisons', because wrapped up in the general meaning of poison is severe harm and death. All substances may be toxic in the right conditions. Water has the ability to evoke a toxic reaction, but the conditions required are not likely to be produced except in very unusual circumstances. In practice, the scope of the definition has been reduced to include only substances that evoke a toxic reaction under 'normal' conditions. The level of toxicity of a substance is a matter of dose, i.e. the amount that will do the harm considered, which is usually - death.

Toxicology is necessary for the body of knowledge and the categorization of substances used in the workplace to enable their safe use.

FACTORS AFFECTING TOXICITY

Duration of exposure

In humans, duration of exposure may be described as:

- **Short-term** - ranging from a few seconds to hours.
- **Long-term** - exposure over several months or years.

Long-term exposure can result in different effects than short-term exposure to the same chemical, due to:

- Repeated damage causing a different type of response.
- Accumulation of the parent chemical or metabolite in the body over a long period of time.

Interaction with other chemicals

Chemical exposure in the workplace involves more than one substance, in some cases a whole multitude of chemicals. Simultaneous exposure to two chemicals may alter the toxicity of one or both of the chemicals in one of several ways. The resulting effect may be: additive, synergistic, potentiation or antagonistic.

Additive effect

The combined toxic effect of two chemicals is equal to the sum of the individual effects of each chemical when given alone (1 + 3 = 4), for example:

- Xylene and MEK in paints and varnishes - narcosis.
- Organophosphorus insecticides - simultaneous exposure to two OP insecticides usually results in chlolinesterase inhibition which is additive.

Synergistic effect

The combined effect is greater than the sum of the effects of each chemical given alone (2 + 2 = "20"), for example:

- Carbon tetrachloride and ethanol - both chemicals are hepatoxic but in animal experiments total liver damage caused by both chemicals is greater than the sum of the individual effects.
- Smoking and asbestos - leading to elevated cancer risk.

Potentiation

The first substance has no toxic effect, but when simultaneous exposure occurs with a second chemical, the toxicity of the second chemical is enhanced (0 + 2 = "10"), for example:

- Isopropanol and carbon tetrachloride - isopropanol alone is not hepatoxic, but it increases the hepatoxicity of carbon tetrachloride.
- N-hexane and mek - mek increases n-hexane neuropathy.

Antagonism

The combined effect of two chemicals is less than the effects observed when each chemical is administered alone (1 + 3 = "2"), e.g.

- Paradoxon and phenobarbitone - the toxicity of pardoxon (organophosphate insecticide) is due to the parent compound (its metabolotes are less toxic). Pb, a microsomal enzyme inducer, increases its metabolism and therefore decreases is toxicity.
- Cadmium and zinc.
- Mercury and selenium.

Antagonistic interaction between two chemicals is the basis of antidotes.

Other factors affecting toxicity

Many other factors can alter the toxic affect of a chemical. Some examples are:

- **Species:** e.g. 2-naphthylamine causes bladder cancer in humans but not in rats.
- **Sex:** males may be more susceptible to some substances than females, e.g. chloroform in the mouse, or vice-versa.
- **Genetics:** some individuals are slow acetylators (deficient in acetyltransferase) affecting their ability to metabolise certain chemicals, e.g. isoniazid, leading to peripheral neuropathy.
- **Age:** children are particularly susceptible to the effects of lead because of a greater absorption (poor blood-brain barrier compared to adults).
- **Physical exercise:** may increase respiration rate and therefore inhalation of toxic vapours, for example.
- **Health:** detoxifying capacity of the liver may be compromised by, for instance, cirrhosis.
- **Diet:** animal experiments have indicated that tumour incidence, for instance, can be greatly affected by diet.

Toxicological evaluation

Defining hazard and risk

Hazard   -   potential of the chemical for causing harm (toxicity).

Risk   -   the likelihood that the harm will occur in a given situation.

The role of toxicology in occupational health

The following list provides some examples of how toxicological information may be applied in the field of occupational health:

1. Setting exposure limits.
2. Classification and labelling of chemicals.
3. Identifying harmful effects of chemicals - preparation of hazard data sheets.
4. Identifying thresholds of effects.
5. Identifying persons at risk.
6. Development of biological monitoring methods.
7. Understanding mechanisms of toxicity - predicting effects of new chemical.
8. Risks assessment for occupationally exposed humans.
9. Risk assessment for the public at large.

Legal requirements for the testing of new substances

NOTIFICATION OF NEW SUBSTANCES REGULATIONS (NONS 93) 1993

Introduction to NONS 93

Chemicals play a major part in all our lives: making clothing and consumer goods, controlling pests, increasing yields in agriculture, combating disease, making machinery run efficiently. Most chemicals have beneficial effects on our lives and can be made and used without harm. However, they can also have unintended harmful effects on people (workers, consumers or others just going about their everyday lives) and on the environment. A variety of legislation seeks to ensure that these possible harmful effects are avoided.

The UK chemical industry is the nation's fourth largest manufacturing industry and the UK manufacturing sector's number one export earner. The UK chemicals industry is also one of the largest in Europe.

NONS 93 and the seventh amendment directive (92/32/EEC)

NONS 93 implements part of a European Community (EC) Directive, commonly known as the Seventh Amendment Directive. The Directive is called this as it is the seventh time the EC's Dangerous Substances Directive (67/548/EEC), originally adopted in 1967, has been amended. NONS 93 replaces the Notification of New Substances Regulations 1982, as amended in 1986 and 1991.

The directive aims to protect people and the environment from the possible harmful effects of new substances and to create a 'single market' in new substances across the EC.

Substance

A substance in this case means a chemical such as sodium chloride (common salt). A preparation (i.e. a deliberate mixture of such substances) is not subject to these regulations, but one or more of its constituent parts may be.

New substance

A new substance is one which is not on a list called the European Inventory of Existing Commercial Chemical Substances (EINECS).

The single market

The Seventh Amendment is a single market directive. This means it has been adopted by the EC to lay down common trading requirements between EC Member States.

The Directive helps create this single market by ensuring that notification requirements are the same in all EC Member States and that a notification accepted in one Member State is valid for all of them; i.e. notification requirements are harmonised across the EC. This should save notifiers time and money and make trade between Member States easier. NONS 93 brings this into effect in the UK. Appendix 2 discusses the enlargement of the single market to include some members of the European Free Trade Association (EFTA).

Objective of NONS 93

NONS 93 aims to identify the possible risks posed to people and the environment from the placing on the market of new substances. It does this by obtaining information about them in a systematic way so that, if necessary, recommendations for control can be made.

Nons 93 requires those placing a new substance on the market to:

a. Notify to a competent authority their intention to place a new substance on the market.

b. Provide the competent authority with certain information on the substance.

c. (a) and (b) together comprise a notification.

Functions of the competent authority

The competent authority (CA) has a number of functions under the Regulations. These are concerned with the general running of the system. Most of the functions of the CA are stated as duties in the Regulations, as the notification system will only work efficiently and effectively if CAs carry out their functions within certain timescales.

Placing on the market

Placing on the market means making a substance available to another person. This includes selling it, lending it to someone else, passing it on, giving it away and importing it into the EC (i.e. control of the substance passes from one person to another).

The competent authority

The competent authority is the Health and Safety Executive (HSE) and the Department of the Environment (DoE) acting jointly.

The main functions of the competent authority are:

- Evaluating notification dossiers.
- Providing a risk assessment.
- Requiring additional information from notifiers where necessary.
- Advising on interpretation of the seventh amendment directive and NONS 93.
- Co-operating with other member state (CAS).
- Co-operating with the European Commission (CEC).

The functions of the CA and the role of the European Commission and other member state competent authorities are discussed in more detail in appendix 3 of NONS 93.

Confidentiality

In the interests of openness and the public's right of access to environmental information, certain information submitted by notifiers is available to anyone who asks for it. The information available is limited, however, as some information submitted by notifiers could give their competitors a commercial advantage if it were made available.

Risk and proportionality

The precise notification and risk assessment requirements in NONS 93 depend on the quantity of the new substance to be, or already, placed on the EC market and relate to the risks it is likely to pose. More information is generally required if the amount placed on the market is large than would be the case for small quantities.

In most cases the Regulations make it clear what a notification should contain. However, the competent authority will ensure, wherever possible, within the constraints of the Seventh Amendment, that the information required is proportional to the likely risk posed by the new substance. This means that for substances that can be demonstrated by the notifier to pose little risk, some elements of a notification may be considered by the CA to be unnecessary or unjustifiable (for example, in terms of animal welfare) or it may be possible to 'read across' data from an analogous substance.

Because of the constraints imposed by the Regulations and the Seventh Amendment, it will not normally be possible to alter the notification requirements at Level 1 and Level 2.

Substances that are placed on the market solely for 'simple transfers' (i.e. from one site to another only), in small quantities and which seem unlikely to have any hazardous properties may be seen by the competent authority as posing little risk. Notifiers of substances which may fall within this group are therefore advised to discuss the notification requirements with the competent authority before starting any testing. Notifiers of substances which were not notifiable prior to NONS 93 and have already been placed on the market, are also advised to discuss notification requirements with the CA prior to testing.

Where the competent authority has clear discretion under the Regulations (for example, where substances subject to research and development can be treated as having been notified) the information required will also be proportional to the risk.

The 'proportionality' approach outlined above should help reduce the resources spent on unnecessary tests, by industry in generating them and by the competent authority in evaluating them, and be beneficial in terms of animal welfare.

The competent authority's commitment to notifiers and the public

The CA appreciates the importance, both as part of the EC-wide system and to the chemicals industry, of carrying out its duties efficiently. The CA has therefore set itself standards in discharging these duties in a 'NONS Charter'. The Charter is set out in Appendix 4.

Important points from the NONS 93 charter

The CA will:

- Respond promptly and courteously to enquiries.
- Issue receipts within three days of receiving a notification dossier.
- Say whether a notification dossier is in compliance with regulations, normally within seven to ten working days.
- Clearly set out the reasons if a notification dossier is rejected.
- Maintain the confidentiality of certain information.
- Make non-confidential information available to the public on request.

Testing new chemicals for toxicity

Toxicity tests required in EU

According to the Notification of New Substances Regulations (NONS) 1993, new industrial chemicals are required to be tested on animals (mammals), known as in vivo testing or by using mammalian or non-mammalian cells, e.g. bacterial cells, known as in vitro testing in the following toxicity tests. Note: "in vivo" means in the body and "in vitro" means in glass.

Acute toxicity tests:	Acute oral toxicity (LD_{50}) or Acute dermal toxicity or Acute inhalation toxicity. Skin irritation. Eye irritation. Skin sensitisation.
Sub-acute toxicity tests:	28-day oral study or 28-day dermal study or 28-day inhalation study.
Mutagenicity tests:	In vitro non-mammalian cell assay: ■ Ames test - salmonella typhimurium reverse mutation assay. ■ In vitro mammalian cell assay. ■ Cytogenic test - chromosomal aberrations in CHO cells or human lymphocytes. In vivo mammalian cell assay: ■ Cytogenic test - chromosomal aberrations in bone marrow. ■ Micronucleus test - chromosomal damage in developing erythrocytes.
Additional tests:	(These are required if specific toxicity is indicated, e.g. carcinogenicity, and/or production of new substance reaches a specified quantity). Chronic 90-day toxicity test - oral/dermal/inhalation. Long-term carcinogenicity test. Reproductive toxicity tests.

CHEMICALS (HAZARD INFORMATION AND PACKAGING FOR SUPPLY) REGULATIONS 2002 (AND AS AMENDED)

NONS 93 is complemented by requirements set out in the Chemicals (Hazard Information and Packaging for Supply) Regulations 2002 (CHIP). CHIP Regulations 2002 requires suppliers of all chemicals, whether substances or preparations, of whatever quantity, to identify whether they are dangerous to humans and/or the environment. It also requires suppliers of dangerous chemicals to give adequate information to help those who use the chemicals to do so safely.

NONS 93 and CHIP Regulations 2002 provide a major advance in the systematic provision of information about chemicals to both the user and the regulator, and in the assessment of the risks from those chemicals. They provide the basis for the risk management of chemicals across the EC.

Classification and labelling of chemicals

New chemicals and existing chemicals which are hazardous should be classified and labelled on the basis of their physico-chemical properties and their toxicological properties. In the basis of toxicity tests a substance may be classified as follows:

Toxicity Test	Classification	Risk Phrase
Acute toxicity	Very toxic	R28/27/26
	Toxic	R25/24/23
	Harmful	R22/21/20
Skin irritation	Corrosive	R35/34
	Irritant	R38
Eye irritation	Irritant	R36/41
Skin sensitisation	Irritant	R43
Sub-acute toxicity	Toxic	R48
	Harmful	R48

Figure B2-18: Classification of chemicals.

Source: ACT.

Types of toxicity tests and their limitations

ANIMAL TESTING

The use of animals for testing to predict the effects of substances on humans is often of limited value unless the life form used has a physiology which is very close to that of humans (i.e. the primates). Rats and mice, for example might be chosen because the effects over many generations may be observed in a relatively short period (life cycle 2 years, but reproductive capability within 9 to 12 weeks of birth). However rats and mice do not retain urine within a bladder (unlike humans) so would not be useful to determine the chronic effects of cancer of the bladder in relation to humans. Over recent years public opinion has changed (historically, common testing procedures involved exposing rabbits to the effects of cigarette smoke exposure through inhalation and skin, eye contact with cosmetics)and animal testing in many countries is subject to strict codes and licensing.

AMES ASSAYS FOR TESTING MUTAGENICITY

This is a sensitive, cheap and quick technique which uses bacteria.

A common approach is to use a strain such as Salmonella typhimurium, mixed with a liver enzyme extracted from rats. The bacteria is then mixed with the suspect chemical and incubated for two days. The carcinogenicity of the substance is indicated by the number of mutations induced.

Again the information is limited because it may not always be possible to extrapolate to man. Evidently, biological organisms do not breathe 'like man' or see or digest 'like man' - hence many aspects of human body response cannot be compared like for like. Under CHIP, carcinogenic substances can be classified as:

Category 1	Substances known to be carcinogenic to man. There is sufficient evidence to establish a causal association between human exposure to a substance and the development of cancer.
Category 2	Substances which should be regarded as if they are carcinogenic to man. There is sufficient evidence to provide a strong presumption that human exposure to a substance may result in the development of cancer, generally on the basis of: ■ Appropriate long-term animal studies. ■ Other relevant information.
Category 3	Substances which cause concern for man owing to possible carcinogenic effects but in respect of which the available information is not adequate for making a satisfactory assessment. There is some evidence from appropriate animal studies, but this is insufficient to place the substance in Category 2. There are two sub-categories in Category 3: Substances which are well investigated but for which the evidence of a tumour-inducing effect is insufficient for classification in Category 2. Additional experiments would not be expected to yield further relevant information with respect to classification; Substances which are insufficiently investigated. The available data is inadequate, but raises concern for man. This classification is provisional; further experiments are necessary before a final decision can be made.

Figure B2-19: Classification of carcinogenic substances.

Source: ACT.

While many carcinogens have been recognised experimentally, only a small proportion have been clearly identified as human occupational carcinogens. Nevertheless, it was only through occupational carcinogenesis that some of the individual and groups of chemical carcinogens were first recognised.

LONG TERM TOXICITY TESTS

These tests are carried out to determine the chronic effects of new chemical substances in order to determine the socio economic impact of introduction into the workplace. The data is assessed by groups such as WATCH and ACT to determine dose exposure, levels relationships and assignment of occupational exposure limits.

Significance of LD_{50} LD_{90} LC_{50} and LC_{90}

DOSE / RESPONSE RELATIONSHIPS

Toxins have very different effects on organisms. They include the minimum level at which an effect is detectable; the sensitivity of the organism to small increases in dose; and the level at which the harmful effect (most significantly, death) occurs. Such factors are indicated in the dose-response relationship, which is a key concept in toxicology:

Dose-response relationship

"All substances are poisons; there is none which is not a poison. The right dose differentiates a poison and a remedy."

Figure B2-20: Quote - toxicology.

Source: Paracelsus (1493 - 1541).

Apart from the nature of the harm caused by a chemical, a key element in our ability to assess toxicity from animal studies or from human experience is the way the damage varies with the dose.

Definition of some terms

Dose: In some animal studies, this can be expressed as the amount administered (mg/kg bodyweight) via inhalation, oral or dermal routes with time. In humans, dose is the uptake of a chemical estimated from airborne measurements, biological monitoring or diet.

Dose-effect: Variation in the degree of effect with changing dose.

Dose-response: Proportion of the population that will demonstrate an effect or specified degree of effect, if graded, at a given dose. The dose-response relationship can be used to derive several values:

LD_{50}	Lethal dose killing 50% of the test animals; provides indication or relative toxicity of a substance and possible target organ(s).
LC_{50}	Lethal concentration of the contaminant in the atmosphere to be inhaled killing 50% of the test animals.
LD_{90}	Lethal dose killing 90% of the test animals.
LC_{90}	Lethal concentration killing 90% of the test animals.

No observed adverse effect level (NOAEL)

For some chemicals, the dose at which no measurable effect occurs; used when setting workplace exposure limits. For some chemicals (e.g. carcinogens) there may be no NOAEL.

THE FIXED DOSE PROCEDURE

Dose is the amount per unit body mass of toxin to which the organism is exposed.

Response is the resultant effect.

In order to define a close-response relationship we must specify the particular effect, i.e. death, and also the conditions under which the effect is obtained, i.e. length of time of administration of the dose. If we consider a specific example we can see that:

■ At low dose not all organisms will show a response, i.e. they all live.
■ At higher doses all organisms show a response, i.e. they all die.
■ In between there is a range of doses over which some organisms respond and others do not.

The toxicity of a substance is its potential to cause harm by reaction with body tissues. Measures of toxicity include lethal dose (LD_{50} and LD_{90}) and lethal concentration (LC_{50} and LC_{90}). The LD_{50} is the single dose of a substance, which when administered to a batch of animals under test kills 50% of them. It is measured in terms of mg of the substance per kg of body weight. Typical degrees of LD_{50} toxicity are:

Extremely toxic	1 mg or less	**Slightly toxic**	0.5 - 5 g
Highly toxic	1 - 50 mg	**Practically non-toxic**	5 - 15 g
Moderately toxic	50 - 500 mg	**Relatively harmless**	15 g or more

Figure B2-21: Degrees of LD_{50} toxicity.

Source: ACT.

In a similar way, the LC_{50} refers to an inhaled substance and is the concentration which kills 50% in a stated time. It should be appreciated that LD_{50} is not an exact value and in recent years there has been much discussion as to its usefulness and necessity in toxicology. The LD_{50} value may vary for the same compound between different groups of the same species of animal.

However, the value is of use in comparing how toxic a substance is in relation to other substances. The following table gives examples of LD_{50} values for a variety of chemical substances.

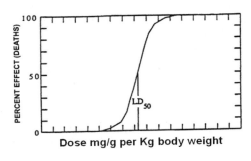

Figure B2-22: Dose / response curve. *Source: Ambiguous.*

The dose-response curve for any substance will be typically S-shaped. At first, the dose increase shows no ill effects. As soon as an effect is shown, i.e. death, the curve rises steeply. The increase in the dose from the first deaths to 50% of the test population dying is very small. The increase in the dose from 50% deaths to 90% deaths again is very small. Once the dose kills 100% of the animals, further dose increases make no difference.

Compound	LD50 (mg/kg)
Ethanol	10,000
DDT	100
Nicotine	1
Tetrodotoxin	0.1
Dioxin	0.001
Botulinus toxin	0.00001

Source: ACT.

Figure B2-22: Examples of LD_{50} values.

ED_{50} (effective dose for 50%) and TD_{50} (toxic dose for 50%) are related parameters which indicate the dose at which a biological response is likely. The effective dose is a pharmacological response where an effect can be seen, and the toxic dose is the toxic effect which causes damage, but does not kill. Comparison of ED_{50} with LD_{50} gives an indication of the margin of safety between the dose which causes the first identifiable effect and that which is fatal.

Testing for carcinogenic potential is more complex since there is no simple dose-response relationship. The toxicology of carcinogens is approached in a different way but still involves exposing laboratory animals (usually rats and mice) to the chemical by oral, inhalation or skin contact techniques.

There are also short-term predictive tests available which are considered to simulate potential carcinogenicity in man. They are called short term, in contrast to the usual lifetime studies in rodents which can take three to four years before a result is available.

Short term tests include:

- Those for mutation (Ames test).
- Tests for DNA damage.
- Tests for chromosomal damage.
- Tests for cell transformation.

Because of the extensive use of animals in carcinogenicity testing, there are at least 1,000 chemicals identified with this potential. However, not all chemicals which are carcinogenic in animals cause cancer in man, since there are wide differences in genetic constitution, metabolism and life span. It is essential, therefore, to interpret data on suspected carcinogens with great caution when making judgements in an occupational setting.

Chemical analogy

Chemical analogy is concerned with those properties of one chemical that are shared by another chemical or other chemicals. If one chemical has been tested and is known to have certain effects on the human body, then by analogy another chemical with shared properties will probably have the same effects. Chemical analogy is used when testing chemicals for categorisation purposes. The technique can save a lot of cost, effort and can enable categorisation decisions to be made more quickly. For example, any chemical which contains the benzene ring would be treated as a carcinogen until further knowledge showed anything different. In other words, the chemical would be considered Highly Toxic until proven otherwise.

B2.4 - Epidemiology

Epidemiological studies

Occupational health and hygiene are concerned with recognition, measurement, evaluation and control. Epidemiology is the science which forms the basis of the four stages. At its crudest, epidemiology may be said to be the elucidation of the cause having first observed the effects. For example, if a number of workers on a particular process are suddenly affected by dermatitis, i.e. the effect, it is likely that the cause is of occupational origin, possible a new raw material. However, the cause can often only be established in the light of current knowledge and understanding. **John Snow** (1813-1858) flew in the face of conventional wisdom when he suggested that cholera was due to contaminated water rather than airborne miasmas.

A semblance of the cause-effect relationship in occupational disease has been recognised since early times. **Hippocrates**, the father of medicine (born 460 BC), was probably among the first to recognise lead as a cause of colic; and **Pliny** (23-79 AD) describes mercurialism in writing of the diseases of slaves.

One of the greatest technical manuals ever written is *De Re Metallica* by **Agricola** (Georg Bauer), first published in Basle in 1556. He described and illustrated in detail the techniques and methods used by German mining engineers to win metallic ores and also covered aspects of occupational diseases (he was a medical doctor by profession). On miners in the Carpathian Mountains he comments:

On ventilation: "If a shaft is very deep and no tunnel reaches to it, or no drift from another shaft connects to it, or when a tunnel is of great length and no shaft reaches to it, then the air does not replenish itself. In such case it (the air) weighs heavily upon them (the miners), causing them to breathe with difficulty and extinguishing lamps. It is therefore necessary to install machines to enable the air to be renewed and for the miners to carry on their work."

On accidents: "The Burgomeister gives no one permission to enter the mines after blasting until the poisonous vapours are cleared."

On diseases of the lung: "If the dust has corrosive qualities, it eats away the lungs and implants consumption in the body. In the mines of the Carpathian Mountains, women are found who have married seven husbands, all of whom this terrible consumption has carried off to a premature death."

To protect miners against the effects of the dust, Agricola advised purification of the air by ventilation and the use of loose veils over their faces.

Paracelsus (1493-1541) published the first monograph devoted entirely to the occupational diseases of mine and smelter workers (*Von der Bergsucht und Anderen Bergkrankheiten, 1567*). Although he makes correct clinical observations, he then turns to alchemical theories to explain them: "The lung sickness comes through the power of the stars, in that their peculiar characteristics are boiled out, which settle on the lungs in three different ways: in a mercurial manner like a sublimated smoke that coagulates, like a salt spirit, which passes from resolution to coagulation, and thirdly, like a sulphur, which is precipitated on the walls by roasting".

If Hippocrates is the father of medicine then **Bernardino Ramazzini** (1633-1714) is the father of occupational medicine. His *De Morbis Artificum Diatriba* (1700) contains accounts of the occupational diseases suffered by miners of metals, healers by inunction, chemists, potters, tinsmiths, glass-workers, painters, sulphur-workers, blacksmiths, workers with gypsum and lime, apothecaries, cleaners of privies and cesspits, fullers, oil pressers, tanners, cheese-makers, tobacco-workers, corpse-carriers, midwives, wetnurses, vintners and brewers, bakers and millers, starch-makers, sifters and measurers of grain, stone-cutters, launderers, workers handling flax, jute and silk, bathmen, salt-makers, workers who stand for long periods, sedentary workers, grooms, porters, athletes, runners, singers, preachers, farmers, fishermen, soldiers, learner men, priests and nuns, printers, scribes and notaries, confectioners, weavers, coppersmiths, carpenters, grinders of metals, brick-makers, well-diggers, sailors and rowers, hunters, and soap-makers; in short, most of the important occupations of the day. As a result of his investigations he added an important question to the Hippocratic art, urging physicians to ask of their patients, "What is your occupation?". He also "urged physicians to leave their apothecaries shop, which is redolent with cinnamon and to visit the latrines where they may see the cause of ill-health".

Different types of study

MORBIDITY/MORTALITY STATISTICS

The relationship between occupational exposure to an agent and its associated diseases has been long established. In the 19th century, for example, felt hat makers showed symptoms of the effects on the central nervous system of the mercury salts used in the production process (hence the term 'as mad as a hatter). In the 20th century coal miners became disabled by respiratory problems due to the effects of coal dust on the lungs and painters have become unable to work in their chosen field due to occupational asthma. This recognition and measurement of the relationship between an occupation and susceptibility to a disease comes from two main sources:

Morbidity data is the incidence of a disease in a community or population. This may be triggered through statistics published by government and health agencies, by questioning the occupational group involved or through observation of medical practitioners treating such groups. Once a disease is suspected both the group in question and a control group are studied to see if there is a statistically significant causal relationship.

Mortality data is extracted from death certificates using the International Classification of Diseases Injuries and Causes of Death (ICD) coding system. In this country, mortality statistics are compiled under the auspices of the Office of Population Census and Surveys (OPCS) from data extracted from death certificates. The antecedent cause of death and the occupation of the deceased are recorded. This has obvious drawbacks for people who changed jobs since contacting a particular disease or who are retired.

Once occupational exposure to an agent has been shown to present a hazard to health it must be evaluated and exposure eliminated or controlled. The criteria for doing so will depend on exposure levels and effects. This may result in banning the substance from use completely, for example, the Control of Substances Hazardous to Health Regulations (COSHH) 2002 prohibits sand or other substance containing free silica from being used as an abrasive for blasting articles in any blasting apparatus due to the risk of silicosis.

CROSS SECTIONAL SURVEYS

The cross sectional survey is often used to assess the prevalence of acute or chronic health conditions in a population. The technique is used to measure exposure to risk and evidence of disease in groups, at the specific point in time of the survey. In a cross sectional survey a specific group is considered to see if a substance or activity is related to the health effect being investigated, e.g. drinking alcohol and its relation to cirrhosis of the liver. If a significant number of alcohol drinkers have cirrhosis at the time of survey it could support the hypothesis that cirrhosis is caused by drinking alcohol. It should be noted that it is not always possible to distinguish whether the exposure preceded or followed the disease, for example a person may have developed cirrhosis prior to starting to drink alcohol. It is an easy study to conduct as it identifies current health conditions and the exposure to the substance or activity has already occurred. As such, this type of study is less expensive to conduct than a cohort study. The main disadvantage of the cross sectional survey is that it may not necessarily confirm causes of health conditions, the best it can usually do is to identify possible associations of substances or activities and suggest case-control or cohort studies as a follow-up.

CASE CONTROL STUDIES

This method may be used to investigate, for example, the frequency of arc welders in a 'case' group who have respiratory problems or lung disease and compare them against a 'control' group drawn from the general population. It is quicker and less expensive than a cohort study and is often used as the first step in an epidemiological investigation, to see if there may be an association between a suspected cause and a known effect. It is also a useful method for investigating a disease of low prevalence as it enables their study without having to study thousands of people. Unfortunately, however, case-control studies are generally less informative than cohort studies and spurious associations may occur. The epidemiologist needs to ensure that the case group and the control group have things in common, other than their work situation. For example, if a case group of fifty arc welders exposed to welding fume is being studied with a control group of fifty office workers not exposed to welding fume, the results may show as:

This result would show there is a strong association with exposure to welding fume and respiratory problems, but cannot prove causation. This could also be a spurious association if the fifty arc welders were all heavy smokers and the office workers were not.

	50 welders	50 office workers
Respiratory problems	20	5
No respiratory problems	30	45

There are many variables that could affect the analysis. In addition, the results may not be considered valid if the number of subjects under study is not thought to be a large enough sample.

RETROSPECTIVE COHORT STUDIES

Retrospective cohort studies look back in time. In this situation the result (ill-health) is known, and the study tries to determine the cause. The 'cohort' is a number of individuals who have the health problem and who have been selected for study. The cohort may include individuals who have died as a result of the health problem being studied. Information is collected on the cohort's past lives and this is analysed to see what they had in common. If they all have, or had before they died, a respiratory problem, such as emphysema or lung cancer, the fact that they all spent some time working in the engineering industry would be of great interest.

This type of study is cheaper and quicker than a prospective cohort study. It allows the cohort to be selected purely on the basis of the ill-health condition of interest. Again, the number of individuals in the cohort will affect the validity of the results. Because it is a study of health conditions that have occurred, the epidemiologist does not have to wait for time to pass to gather the data necessary for the study. This is particularly useful when studying rare ill-health conditions, or chronic ill-health conditions that have a long latency period for their development. However, this type if study does have its limitations, there may be spurious associations made because the historic records analysed do not contain the full facts. Historic records may be very difficult to obtain, for example, a person's work record may not be available because the companies they worked for have gone out of business and/or no records were kept. In addition, the person's ill-health may not have been caused by work but by their lifestyle, and reliable information on lifestyle is not always available. Individuals being interviewed as part of the study sometimes have difficulty with their recall of facts or they may tell the epidemiologist what they think they want to hear.

PROSPECTIVE COHORT STUDIES

Prospective cohort studies look forward in time. They are considered the best method of obtaining epidemiological data, but they take a long time to conduct, a lifetime in some instances. The cohort, an identified group of people, is chosen and each individual is studied over time into the future. For example, the cohort may be a group of eight to ten year old children who use mobile telephones, who are being studied for any health conditions which may be associated with mobile telephone use. A further example may be a cohort made up of a group of workers using a chemical which has just come on to the market. The chemical will have gone through initial tests, and known information about the chemical would be made available in a health and safety data sheet, but the results of studying long term use of the chemical may change our knowledge of its effects. A prevalence of a particular health condition may be identified in the cohort group after years of use and as a result some of the data on the health and safety data sheet may have to be amended.

These studies take a lot of resources, in particular time. The study may experience difficulties over time, the people in the cohort may leave the work activity or not be involved with the chemical any more, because of career change or changing processes that cease its use in the workplace. Furthermore, they may not want to be involved in the study any longer or some may die from totally unrelated causes, such as car accidents. The cohort group may become depleted in numbers to the point that the results of the study will not be valid. In some cases the outcomes of the research may not be what the sponsor of the research hopes for, and the sponsor may chose to declare the results invalid. For example, a promoter of the use of mobile telephones might be carrying out research with the intent to prove that there are no ill-health effects associated with their use, but findings over time may suggest otherwise.

Application of epidemiological techniques to worker surveillance

Epidemiological disease studies will identify the result of causative agents on specific populations (work groups). Having determined the groups affected those involved in specific workplace activities may be observed and health screening may be carried out to determine instance of health injury at a stage ahead of it being irreversible or significant. Such techniques include lung functionality tests of miners, nasal and septum examination of electroplating process operators and blood testing of lead workers.

The results from health surveillance can be given to HSE who can collect and analyse the data, which can then be used to adjust the WELs in EH40. For example, when a number of bakery workers throughout the country developed respiratory problems and asthma, it gave force to the argument that flour dust is a respiratory sensitiser and led to a WEL being set.

Hazardous substances - evaluating risk

Learning outcomes

On completion of this element, candidates should be able to:

B3.1 Outline the factors which should be considered when assessing risks from hazardous substances.

B3.2 Describe Workplace Exposure Limits (WELs), how they are established, and the criteria for their application to the workplace.

Content

Relevant statutory provisions

Control of Substances Hazardous to Health Regulations (COSHH) 2002 (and as amended 2004)

Control of Asbestos Regulations (CAR) 2006

Control of Lead at Work Regulations (CLAW) 2002 (and as amended 2004)

This page is intentionally blank

B3.1 - Assessing risks

Occupations presenting exposure risks and typical chemical substances involved

The relationship between occupational exposure to an agent and its associated diseases has been long established. In the 19th century, for example, felt hat makers showed symptoms of the effects on the central nervous system of the mercury salts used in the production process (hence the term 'as mad as a hatter). Since the early 20th century coal mining has resulted in many miners developing severe debilitating respiratory illnesses due to the effects of coal dust on the lungs, and painters have become unable to work in their chosen field due to occupational asthma. This recognition and measurement of the relationship between an occupation and susceptibility to a disease comes from two main sources:

Morbidity Data: this is the incidence of a disease in a community or population.

Mortality Data: extracted from death certificates using the International Classification of Diseases Injuries and Causes of Death (ICD) coding system.

Once occupational exposure to an agent has been shown to present a hazard to health it must be evaluated and exposure eliminated or controlled. The criteria for doing so will depend on exposure levels and effects. This may result in banning the substance from use completely.

Source: ACT.

Specific obligations

CONTROL OF LEAD AT WORK REGULATIONS 2002

The **Control of Lead at Work Regulations (CLAW) 2002** aims to protect people at work exposed to lead by controlling that exposure. The Regulations, which are summarised below, apply to any work which exposes people to lead.

Exposure to lead must be assessed by employers so that they may take adequate measures to protect both employees and anyone else who may be exposed to lead at work. Once the level of exposure has been assessed, then adequate measures can be taken ranging from simple maintenance of good washing facilities through to the provision of control measures such as respiratory equipment and constant medical surveillance. The Regulations prohibit the employment of young persons and women of reproductive capacity from some manufacturing, smelting and refining processes **(specified in Schedule 1).**

WORK WITH LEAD

The Regulations apply to any work which exposes employees or others to lead. In practical terms, this means any work from which lead arises:

- In the form of lead dust, fume or vapour in such a way as it could be inhaled.
- In any form which is liable to be ingested such as powder, dust, paint or paste.
- In the form of lead compounds such as lead alkyls and compounds of lead, which could be absorbed through the skin?

Employers' duties under the 2002 Regulations extend to any other people at work on the premises where work with lead is being carried on.

Lead assessment

Before employers (or a self-employed person) can take adequate measures to protect people from lead at work, they need to know exactly what the degree of risk of lead exposure is. The level of risk dictates the measures to be taken. The employer's first duty, therefore, is to assess whether the exposure of any employee is liable to be significant. Exposure to lead is significant if any of the following criteria is satisfied:

(a) Exposure exceeds half the occupational exposure limit (OEL) for lead.

(b) There is a substantial risk of ingesting lead.

(c) There is a risk of the skin coming into contact with lead alkyls or any other substance containing lead in a form that can be absorbed through the skin, e.g. lead naphthenate.

The next step is to determine the nature and degree of exposure. The assessment must be made before the work is commenced and revised where there is a reason to suspect that it is incorrect.

The purpose of the assessment is to determine whether or not exposure to lead is significant. Where exposure is significant then the employer must, so far as is reasonably practicable, ensure the prevention or adequate control of exposure by means other than the provision of personal protective equipment (PPE). Where control measures are not sufficient by themselves and PPE is issued then it must comply with the PPE Regulations or be of a type approved by the Health and Safety Executive (HSE).

When deciding controls the employer must take reasonable steps to ensure that they are being used and employees are under a duty to make full and proper use of control measures, PPE or any other measures dictated by the Regulations.

ASBESTOS

Asbestos is a generic term for a number of silicates of iron, magnesium, calcium, sodium and aluminium which appear naturally in fibrous form. Asbestos is defined as any of the following minerals ... "crocidolite, amosite, chrysotile, fibrous anthophyllite, fibrous actinolite, fibrous tremolite and any mixture containing any of the said minerals".

The three common forms are often referred to by colour:

- Crocidolite, or "blue asbestos", because of its sky-blue appearance in the pure form,
- Amosite, a dirty grey/brown coloured fibrous mineral, also known as "brown" asbestos, and
- Chrysotile, known as "white asbestos", which in the pure form looks like dirty cotton wool.

The diseases associated with exposure to asbestos are: asbestosis, a form of fibrosis of the lung; cancer of the bronchus and of the linings of the chest, and abdominal cavities, the pleura and peritoneum.

Asbestosis is a form of progressive fibrosis of the lung occurring in those occupationally exposed to significant levels of asbestos. The disease may appear five to ten years from the commencement of exposure and is characterised by increasing and sometimes crippling shortage of breath with chest discomfort. In its later stages the disease is confirmed by chest X-ray, although changes in lung function may be detected earlier. Although persons in the community at large may have asbestos fibres in the lung, asbestosis is not known in the general community or among industrial populations exposed to very low doses of asbestos. Cancer of the bronchus may complicate asbestosis, most particularly in cigarette smokers. It is theoretically possible that very low doses of white asbestos (chrysotile) can cause bronchial cancer but in reality the risk to the community at large and to industrial workers not directly exposed is far too small to be measured in respect of a disease predominantly caused by cigarette smoking.

Mesothelioma, cancer of the pleura or peritoneum, is not necessarily associated with the presence of asbestosis or with cigarette smoking. It is probable that all forms of asbestos can cause mesothelioma but in practice the disease is mainly associated with exposure to blue asbestos (crocidolite) and to some extent to amosite (brown asbestos). It is probable that even exposure to low doses of these materials can precipitate mesothelioma. Even so, mesothelioma remains a relatively rare cancer, mainly found in those industrially exposed to crocidolite and to some extent in those living in the vicinity of premises where crocidolite was manipulated, e.g. shipyards and asbestos factories.

Asbestos cancers are characteristically of delayed onset; thus mesotheliomas rarely appear less than 20 years after exposure to blue asbestos or to amosite.

The relationship between exposure to very low doses of asbestos and disease remains uncertain, though the risk has probably been much exaggerated in recent years. Nevertheless, it remains important to find substitutes for asbestos wherever possible and to avoid disturbing or manipulating asbestos when community exposure, or exposure of industrial communities not otherwise at risk, may result. Blue and brown asbestos have been banned since 1985 and a ban on the use of white asbestos (chrysotile) since 1999.

THE CONTROL OF ASBESTOS REGULATIONS 2006

The **Control of Asbestos Regulations (CAR) 2006** bring together the three previous sets of Regulations covering the prohibition of asbestos, the control of asbestos at work and asbestos licensing.

The Regulations prohibit the importation, supply and use of all forms of asbestos. They continue the ban introduced in 1985 for blue and brown asbestos and in 1999 for white. They also continue the ban on second-hand use of asbestos products such as asbestos cement sheets and asbestos board and tiles, which includes panels that have been covered with paint or textured plaster containing asbestos.

The Control of Asbestos Regulations place emphasis on assessment to exposure; exposure prevention, reduction and control; adequate information, instruction and training for employees; monitoring and health surveillance. The regulations also clearly apply to incidental exposure.

Identification and assessment

Before any work with asbestos is started the employer must ensure a thorough assessment of the likely exposure is carried out. Such an assessment must identify the type of asbestos involved in the work, or to which the employees are likely to be exposed. The assessment must also determine the nature and degree of any exposure and the steps required to prevent or reduce the exposure to the lowest level reasonably practicable.

Assessments must be reviewed regularly and when there is reason to suspect that the original assessment is invalid or there is a significant change in the work to which the original assessment related. Assessments should be revised accordingly to take account of any such changes, etc.

Worker exposure must be below the airborne exposure limit (Control Limit). The Regulations have a single Control Limit for all types of asbestos of 0.1 fibres per cm^3. A 'Control Limit' (CL) is a maximum concentration of asbestos fibres in the air, averaged over any continuous 4 hour period, which must not be exceeded.

Short term exposures must also be strictly controlled. Worker exposure should not exceed 0.6 fibres per cm^3 of air averaged over any continuous 10 minute period using respiratory protective equipment (RPE) if exposure cannot be reduced sufficiently using other means.

Plan of work

Employers must also prepare a suitable 'plan of work' before any work involving asbestos removal from buildings, structures, plant or installations (including ships) is undertaken. Such 'plans of work' must be retained for the duration of the work. The 'plan of work' should address the location, nature, expected duration and asbestos handling methods involved with the work, and the characteristics of the protection and decontamination equipment for the asbestos workers and the protection equipment for any others who may be affected by such work.

The asbestos risk assessment and plan of work must be kept on site.

Notification

Under the Control of Asbestos Regulations 2006, anyone carrying out work on asbestos insulation, asbestos coating or asbestos insulating board (AIB) needs a licence issued by HSE unless they meet one of the exemptions:

- If employee exposure is sporadic and low intensity, i.e. the concentration will not exceed 0.6 fibres per cm^3 measured over 10 minutes; and exposure will not exceed the Control Limit; and the work involves short non-continuous maintenance activities. This latter stipulation will be where one person works with the materials for less than one hour in a seven-day period. The total time spent by all workers on the work should not exceed a total of two hours.
- The materials being removed have asbestos fibres firmly linked in a matrix, e.g. asbestos cement.
- Encapsulation or sealing of asbestos-containing materials which are in good condition.
- Air monitoring and control, and the collection and analysis of samples to find out if a specific material contains asbestos.

Even if a licence is not required the rest of the requirements of the Asbestos Regulations must still be complied with.

If the work is licensable, there are a number of duties:

- Notify the enforcing authority responsible for the site where the work is: HSE or the local authority, at least 28 days before work begins. A shorter time may be agreed by the enforcing authority, e.g. in emergencies. The notification should be in writing and the particulars are specified in Schedule 1.
- Designate the work area (see regulation 18 for details).
- Prepare specific asbestos emergency procedures.
- Pay for employees to undergo medical surveillance.

Information, instruction and training

Employees exposed to asbestos must be provided with adequate information, instruction and training to understand the risks associated with asbestos and the necessary precautions. Employees who carry out work in connection with the employer's duties under these Regulations should also be given adequate information, instruction and training to do their work effectively. Under Regulation 10, refresher training must also be provided.

Prevention or reduction of exposure

Wherever possible the employer must prevent exposure of asbestos to the employees. Where this is not reasonably practicable the employer must reduce the exposure to the lowest level reasonably practicable other than by using respiratory protective equipment. If the asbestos exposure is in connection with a manufacturing process or the installation of a product, then the prevention of such exposure should be achieved by the substitution of asbestos for a less harmful substance, where practicable. RPE, where used, must reduce exposure to as low as is reasonably practicable below Control Limits.

Any personal protective equipment (respiratory protective equipment and protective clothing) must comply with the health and safety requirements of any relevant design or manufacturing EC Directives applicable to such personal protective equipment and which are implemented in the UK.

Outline of the factors to be considered in the assessment of risks to health from chemical agents

ASSESSING RISKS

In addition to the general risk assessment required under Regulation 3 of the Management of Health and Safety at Work Regulations there are many pieces of legislation which require the assessment of risks to health from hazardous substances and agents. These include:

- COSHH Regulations 2002.
- CLAW Regulations 2002.
- CAR 2006.

Although these Regulations require assessments to be made of substances and agents hazardous to health, they do not specify the form they should take. In the most simple and obvious cases an assessment may not need recording as it can be readily explained. However, in most situations a record will be required in order to ensure compliance, accuracy and continuity.

MAKING AN ASSESSMENT

There are six major steps involved in making any assessment of hazardous substances:

1. The gathering of information about the substances, the work and the working practices, including how substances are used.
2. The evaluation of risks to health.
3. Deciding if any further precautions are required and what these will be.
4. Recording the assessment.
5. Providing information to those who are, or may be, at risk.
6. Deciding when the assessment needs to be reviewed.

THE FACTORS TO BE CONSIDERED IN AN ASSESSMENT

Any assessment must take into account:

1. The numbers exposed.
2. The risks to health.
3. How practicable it is to prevent exposure.
4. If prevention is not reasonably practicable, the frequency and duration of exposure.
5. Those steps needed to achieve adequate control of exposure.

Additionally the assessor must identify those actions needed to comply with specific regulatory requirements. For example, the COSHH Regulations 2002 have requirements relating to the:

1. Use of control measures.
2. Maintenance, examination and test of control measures etc.
3. Monitoring exposure in the workplace.
4. Health surveillance.
5. Information, instruction and training of persons exposed to hazardous substances.

Thus it is the likelihood, extent and consequence of exposure to the hazard that is important. Thus, if a substance or agent has little effect on an employee's health, because of its nature or because small quantities are used, it can be relatively straightforward to assess. Other substances and agents will require a great deal of effort in order to adequately control the risks to health and comply with the duties under specific legislation.

PARTICLE SIZE - TOTAL INHALABLE DUST AND RESPIRABLE DUST

'Total inhalable dust' approximates to the fraction of airborne material which enters the nose and mouth during breathing and is, therefore, available for deposition in the body (respiratory tract). 'Respirable dust' approximates to the fraction which penetrates to the gas exchange region of the lung. These values are affected by such factors as rate of respiration and hygroscopicity. The nose and mouth filter particles greater than about 10 μm in diameter. Those particles with a diameter between 10 μm and 5 μm tend to be deposited on the muco-cillary escalator in the bronchi and bronchioles. Particles of less than 5 μm are likely to reach and settle in the gas exchange region of the lung (the alveoli). Very small particles (less than about 0.3 μm diameter) exhibit random or Brownian motion and waft in and out of the alveoli much as a gas molecule would do. Thus:

Total Inhalable Dust = particles with a diameter of about 100 μm or less

Respirable Dust = particles with a diameter between about 5 μm - 0.3 μm

In terms of shape and size, asbestos fibres with a diameter of less than 3μm and a length to diameter ratio of *at least* 3:1 are thought to be the most damaging.

OCCUPATIONAL CARCINOGENIC HAZARDS

It is crucial that exposure to chemicals, which may be carcinogens are assessed. Some are known to be carcinogenic in certain forms and processes.

The following table shows some of the processes and agents associated with occupational cancer:

Industrial process	Type of cancer	Possible causative agents
Aluminium production	Lung, bladder	Pitch volatiles
Asbestos removal	Lung, pleura and peritoneum (mesothelioma)	Asbestos Fibres
Boot & shoe manufacture & repair	Nasal	Leather dust
Chemical Process Industry	Bone Marrow (Leukaemia)	Benzene
Coke Production	Lung	Polycyclic aromatic hydrocarbons
Furniture & cabinet making	Nasal	Hardwood dusts
PVC	Angio sarcoma of the liver	Vinyl chloride monomer
Chrome plating	Lung	Chromium (hexavalent)
Rubber industry	Bladder, leukaemia lymphomas	Various aromatic amines and solvents

Source: ACT.

Figure B3-1: Occupational cancer hazards.

Other chemicals and processes are known to cause severe health problems, although not necessarily cancer.

Examples of other occupational groups at risk:

Industrial process	Disease	Causative agents	Remarks
Cotton processing	Byssinosis	Cotton dust	Asthma like disease
Vehicle manufacture and repair (paint spraying)	Occupational asthma	Isocyanates	Sensitisation
Baking and milling	Occupational asthma	Flour dust	Sensitisation
Coal mines, foundries (fettling), stone masons (slate or granite),	Pneumoconiosis	Coal dust Silica	Chronic lung disease
Carpenters and electricians, builders, gas fitters, roofers, demolition workers, shipyard and rail workers, insulation workers.	Asbestosis pleural plaques thickening of pleura asbestos corns (calluses on hands)	Asbestos	Chronic lung disease (non-malignant but can turn lead to cancer / mesothelioma)
Mechanics Builders	Oil folliculitis, skin cancers (scrotum) Dermatitis	Greases, mineral oils, detergents and wet cement	Irritant contact
Hair dressers Health workers	Allergic contact dermatitis	Nickel, chromate, resins, hair dyes (phenols), Latex, formaldehyde and rubber additives	May cause respiratory sensitisation as well as dermatitic sensitisation

Source: ACT.

Figure B3-2: Occupational groups at risk.

INDIVIDUAL SUSCEPTIBILITIES

Although specific legislation will often have exposure standards, it should be remembered that susceptibility to a substance or agent could vary widely between individuals. Some individuals may tolerate excessive dose levels without apparent ill effect, whilst others might well show effects below the workplace exposure limit (WEL).

A further consideration when assessing risk is the susceptibility of groups of people. For example, the gender of persons exposed to hazardous substances can be relevant, as some substances can be more harmful to a specific sex. Mineral oil, for example, is associated with male cancer of the scrotum while women are thought to be more susceptible to fat soluble toxins due to their greater fat to lean body ratio. Other 'at risk' groups include:

1. Women of child bearing capacity - are at greater risk from exposure to teratogens (substances toxic for reproduction) and mutagens.

2. Atopic persons (i.e. those people who naturally suffer from asthma, eczema and hayfever) can be more susceptible to respiratory and skin irritants.

Factors which affect hazard/risk to individual

There are many factors which can determine the effects that chemicals can have on a particular individual. For example:

Chemical	Individual factors
Concentration	Gender
Exposure time	Age
Physical characteristics (e.g. form)	Body mass (size)
Solubility	Genetic makeup
Additive effects	Physical fitness and exercise
Synergistic effects	Health state
Other chemical reactions: potentiation or antagonistic effects.	Smoking / alcohol / drugs
	Diet

Figure B3-3: Chemical effects on particular individuals.

Source: ACT.

The form the substance takes will often dictate its route of entry into the body and the measures needed to protect against exposure. Remember that the assessment is of the process and a substance may have more than one state. Thus a volatile solvent can be present in both liquid and vapour forms.

Some substances can be more harmful to a specific sex. Mineral oil, for example, is associated with male cancer of the scrotum while women are thought to be more susceptible to fat soluble toxins due to their greater fat to lean body ratio. Other 'at risk' groups include:

1. *Age* - children have a less well developed blood-brain barrier and are therefore more susceptible to lead as a result of greater absorption.

2. *Physical fitness [Health Guidance Values (HGVs)]* - the uptake of atmospheric contaminants such as vapours can be increased due to an increased respiration rate.

3. *Health state* - the liver may be damaged by cirrhosis, for example.

Complex mixtures of chemicals may occur, such as welding fume. The effects of these can be difficult to assess as simultaneous exposure to two or more chemicals may alter toxicity in several ways. In additive effects the combined effects are equal to the sum of its parts. EH40 provides advice on assessing the effects of mixed exposures.

Other factors to consider include:

Potentiation is the effect where one chemical enhances the toxicity of a second. Cigarettes, for example, are thought to potentiate the cancer associated with asbestos - mesothelioma.

Synergism is where two or more, possibly dangerous, substances interact to make an even more hazardous substance. For example, two toxic substances - formaldehyde and hydrogen chloride combine together at normal temperature and pressure, to form bis (chloromethyl) ether (BCME). This is a chemical used in the production of ion exchange resin, a proven toxic human carcinogen causing lung cancer with a long term exposure limit of 0.001 ppm. This is 2000 times smaller than either of the limits for formaldehyde or hydrogen chloride.

Antagonism can be considered an opposite effect to that of synergism. This is where the combined effect of two chemicals is less than single exposure of each (cadmium and zinc, mercury and selenium). Antagonistic interactions between two chemicals are the basis for antidotes.

SENSITISATION

If a person is exposed to an allergen or some other substance recognised as foreign by the body's immune system this can lead to the process of sensitisation. About one third of the population is atopic - that is they are allergic to environmental sensitisers such as grass pollen, house dust mites and animal dusts. A similar substance-specific response can occur with substances such as:

- Di-Isocyanates.
- Flour and grain dust.
- Soldering flux / colophony fumes.
- Epoxy resin curing agents.
- Hard wood dusts (cedar, oak & mahogany).
- Welding fume.
- Gluteraldehyde.
- Platinum salts.

Note: respiratory sensitisers are denoted with the notation "Sen" and R42 or R43 in EH 40/year.

Sensitisation is substance specific with symptoms usually only occurring in response to that substance. It can occur to anyone and atopic people are not thought to be at any greater risk than non-atopics due to exposure to manufactured chemicals. The dose at which sensitisation occurs varies with time and concentration in a way that has not been fully established. Some substances can sensitise at below one millionth of a gram per cubic metre while for others the dose is considerably higher. Sensitisation is unpredictable with only about 5-25% of those exposed becoming sensitised. Once sensitisation occurs then it is irreversible unless the person does not come into contact with the agent. Symptoms can occur again if the person is re-exposed - even if several years have elapsed.

At the time of sensitisation the person will experience no apparent effects. However the body has recognised the sensitising agent as an antigen. Subsequent exposure to even very low levels of this substance leads to symptoms of:

Asthma - periodic attacks of wheezing, chest tightness and breathlessness resulting from constriction of the bronchi and bronchioles.

Rhinitis and conjunctivitis - runny or stuffy nose and watery or prickly eyes (akin to hay fever).

The most common effects in the short term are rhinitis and conjunctivitis (occasionally accompanied by dry coughs). If exposure to the sensitiser continues unchecked, then asthma may develop. Often symptoms occur immediately on or after exposure. Occasionally symptoms may not develop until hours after exposure during the evening or night. This may lead to difficulty in recognising the cause of the problem.

If exposure continues for a long time, then the symptoms can become progressively worse with increasingly severe attacks of asthma. Once asthma is established then attacks may be triggered by such things as tobacco smoke, cold air and physical exertion. Such attacks can continue for years after exposure to the sensitiser has ceased.

It has been estimated by the Labour Force Survey that 20,000 people believe they suffer from work-related asthma with a further 5,000 believing that their asthma has been made worse by work. The HSE has sponsored research into occupational asthma via a body known as SWORD (Surveillance of Work-related and Occupational Respiratory Disease). SWORD collects data relating to new occurrences of occupational asthma which is estimated to be at over 1,000 new cases each year. Researchers at SWORD believe that these statistics are the "tip of an iceberg" as the study only includes those sufferers examined by occupational health and chest physicians; this is therefore likely to be an under-estimate.

As described in the first section of this unit, in addition to respiratory sensitisers, skin sensitisation leading to allergic dermatitis can also occur.

MORPHOLOGY

When evaluating the risk, it is important to know how a substance may change in a process, which is morphology. The substance may be relatively harmless until mixed with another and then heated. What it morphs into may be extremely hazardous. For example, trichloroethylene degrades into phosgene in extreme heat. Trichloroethylene is hazardous, but phosgene though hazardous, presents a different risk.

B3.2 - Exposure limits for airborne contaminants

General philosophy and application of the various types of hygiene

THRESHOLDS OF EXPOSURE

Guidance Note EH40/year containing occupational exposure limits has been published since the late 1960s, first by Her Majesty's Factory Inspectorate and later their successors, the HSE. At first these limits were entirely based on data supplied by the American Conference of Governmental Industrial Hygienists (ACGIH) under a copyright agreement. The US Threshold Limit Values (TLVs) were published as guidance only. The UK started to evolve their own standards in respect of substances such as cotton dust and asbestos which differed from those set by the ACGIH. The differing needs of industry, the trades unions and government made the need for UK specific hygiene standards apparent.

The first UK standard was a Control Limit (CL) for asbestos which was followed by other substances. Less hazardous substances were assigned HSE Recommended Limits (RLs). The difficulty of assigning a 'safe limit' for substances like genotoxic carcinogens led to the setting up of the old framework of Occupational Exposure Limits (OEL) which encompassed both Maximum Exposure Limits (MELs) and Occupational Exposure Standards (OESs). The system has now streamlined into one type of OEL called Workplace Exposure Limits (WELs). These are listed in EH40, the document is regularly reviewed and generally reprinted each year.

Other hygiene standards

As with the UK, most standards do not claim to be absolute safety standards. The ACGIH say of their TLVs that:

"Threshold limit values refer to airborne concentrations of substances and represent conditions under which it is believed that nearly all workers may be repeatedly exposed day after day without adverse effect. Because of wide variation in individual susceptibility however, a small percentage of workers may experience discomfort from some substances at concentrations at or below the threshold limit: a smaller percentage may be affected more seriously by aggravation of a pre-existing condition or by development of an occupational disease".

Figure B3-4: Quote - ACGIH hygiene standards.   *Source: ACGIH.*

Another US body, the Occupational Safety and Health Administration (OSHA), say of their standard that:

"No employee will suffer material impairment to health or functional capacity even if such employee has regular exposure".

Figure B3-5: Quote - OSHS hygiene standards.   *Source: OSHA.*

This compares with the old Soviet Union which stated that "no detectable changes of any kind in a test Organisation should occur" in respect of exposure. The table below compares the USSR's approach with that of the US:

Contrasts in approaches to standard-setting in the USA and the former USSR (Calabrese, 1978)

USA	Former USSR
Minor physiological adaptive changes are permitted	Maximum allowable concentration will not permit the development of any disease or deviation from normal
Economic and technological feasibility are important considerations in the development of standards	Standards should be based entirely on health and not on technological and economic feasibility
Values are time-weighted averages	Concentrations are maximum values
Research emphasis is on pathology	Research emphasis is on nervous system testing
Except for carcinogens, goals of near zero exposure are not widely adopted	The goal is a level of exposure which does not strain the adaptive and compensatory mechanisms of the body

Figure B3-6: Contrasts of standard-setting in the USA and former USSR.

Source: ACT.

Clearly, the inference from the process shown above is that these standards must be intended for different purposes. The USSR standards were more stringent and were those which should be **aimed** at. ACGIH-type standards are pragmatic standards, **achievable now** by a reasonable employer and are potentially enforceable.

The real danger, with both the OESs in EH40 and with ACGIH Standards, is that users believe that they are set entirely on medical and scientific knowledge related to health and therefore afford **total** protection.

Meaning of terms

WORKPLACE EXPOSURE LIMITS (WEL)

Definition:

> "**Workplace exposure limit** for a substance hazardous to health means the exposure limit approved by the Health and Safety Commission for that substance in relation to the specified reference period when calculated by a method approved by the Health and Safety Commission, as contained in HSE publication **EH/40 Workplace Exposure Limits 2005** as updated from time to time."

Figure B3-7: Definition of WEL.

Source: The Control of Substances Hazardous to Health (Amendment) Regulations 2004 (which came into force on 17/01/05 and 06/04/05).

WORKPLACE EXPOSURE LIMITS TO DEFINE "ADEQUATE CONTROL"

EH40, which is published annually, contains the lists of Workplace Exposure Limits (WEL) for use with The Control of Substances Hazardous to Health Regulations (COSHH) 2002 (as amended 2005).

WELs are occupational exposure limits set under COSHH to protect the health of persons in the workplace. They are concentrations of airborne substances averaged over a period of time known as a Time Weighted Average (TWA). The two periods that are used are 8-hours and 15-minutes. The 8-hour TWA is known as an LTEL (long-term exposure limit), used to help protect against chronic ill-health effects. 15-minute STELs (short-term exposure limits) are to protect against acute ill-health effects such as eye irritation, which may happen in minutes or even seconds of exposure.

Where there are different exposures to a substance throughout the day, the 8 hour TWA of the inhaled substance can be expressed mathematically as follows:

$$\frac{C_1 T_1 + C_2 T_2 + C_3 T_3 + \dots C_n T_n}{8}$$

Where C_1 is the occupational exposure and T_1 is the associated exposure time in hours in any 24-hour period. When working out the 8 hour TWA, there may be no exposure for certain time periods such as the lunch break, other breaks and time spent on another job. This will reduce the TWA.

Some substances are not listed in EH40 because their use is prohibited, and some substances are listed, but certain uses are prohibited. COSHH regulation 4(1) states that those substances described in Column 1 of Schedule 2 are prohibited to the extent set out in the corresponding entry in Column 2 of that Schedule. An extract from schedule 2 is shown below:

	Description of substance	Purpose for which the substance is prohibited
1.	2-naphthylamine; benzidine; 4-aminodiphenyl; 4-nitrodiphenyl; their salts and any substance containing any of those compounds, in a total concentration equal to or greater than 0.1 per cent by mass.	Manufacture and use for all purposes including any manufacturing process in which a substance described in Column 1 of this item is formed.

2.	Sand or other substance containing free silica.	Use as an abrasive for blasting articles in any blasting apparatus.
3.	A substance - (a) containing compounds of silicon calculated as silica to the extent of more than 3 per cent by weight of dry material, other than natural sand, zirconium silicate (zircon), calcined china clay, calcined aluminous fireclay, sillimanite, calcined or fused alumina, olivine; or (b) composed of or containing dust or other matter deposited from a fettling or blasting process. Use as a parting material in connection with the making of metal castings.	Use as a parting material in connection with the making of metal castings.
4.	Carbon disulphide.	Use in the cold-cure process of vulcanising in the proofing of cloth with rubber.

Figure B3-8: Extract from Schedule 2.   *Source: Control of Substances Hazardous to Health Regulations (COSHH) 2002.*

COSHH states that exposure to hazardous substances should be prevented where it is reasonably practicable. Where this cannot be done by, for example changing the process, substituting it for something safer or enclosing the process, exposure should be reduced by other methods.

Regulation 7 (7) of COSHH states that control will be treated as adequate if:

(a) the principles of good practice for the control of exposure to substances hazardous to health set out in Schedule 2A are applied:

(b) any workplace exposure limit approved for that substance is not exceeded; and

(c) for a substance:

   (i) which carries the risk phrase R45, R46 or R49 (i.e. carcinogens), or for a substance or process that is listed in Schedule 1; or

   (ii) which carries the risk phrase R42 or R42/43 (i.e. respiratory sensitisers), or which is listed in section C of HSE publication *Asthmagen? Critical assessments of the evidence for agents implicated in occupational asthma,* exposure is reduced to as low a level as is reasonably practicable.

Total inhalable dust and respirable dust

'Total inhalable dust' approximates to the fraction of airborne material which enters the nose and mouth during breathing and is, therefore, available for deposition in the body (respiratory tract). 'Respirable dust' approximates to the fraction which penetrates to the gas exchange region of the lung. Where dusts contain components which have their own assigned occupational exposure limits, all the relevant limits should be complied with. Many cases of exposure can consist of a complex mixture of chemicals, such as a welding fume. The effects of these can be difficult to assess as simultaneous exposure to two or more chemicals may alter toxicity in several ways. In additive effects the combined effects are equal to the sum of its parts. EH40 provides advice on assessing the effects of mixed exposures.

SETTING OCCUPATIONAL EXPOSURE LIMITS

ACTS and WATCH

Workplace Exposure Limits are set on the recommendation of the Advisory Committee on Toxic Substances (ACTS) following assessment, by the Working on Action to Control Chemicals (WATCH), of the toxicological, epidemiological and other data. The committees have to consider at what concentration the limit should be set. Each substance is first reviewed by WATCH which considers what value should be recommended to ACTS. WATCH comes to a decision based on a scientific judgement of the available information on health effects and ACTS makes recommendations to the Health and Safety Commission (HSC).

WELs are derived by using the following criteria:

(i) The value would be set a level at which no adverse effects on human health would be expected to occur based on known or predicted effects. If this value is not identifiable with reasonable confidence then,

(ii) The value would be based at a level corresponding to what is considered to be good control taking into account the likely severity of health hazards and the cost and effectiveness of controls.

(iii) The WEL should not be set at a level where there is evidence of adverse effects on human health.

THE ROLE OF BIOLOGICAL LIMIT VALUES

Source: Reference Annual Publication EH40, Occupational Exposure Limits/Year.

Biological monitoring can be a very useful complementary technique to air monitoring when air sampling techniques alone may not give a reliable indication of exposure. The technique involves the measurement and assessment of hazardous substances or their metabolities in tissues; secretions excreta or expired air or any combination of these, in exposed workers. Measurements reflect absorption of a substance by all routes, including skin or gastrointestinal tract uptake following ingestion. The method is used where there is a reasonably well defined relationship between biological monitoring and effect; or where it gives information on accumulated dose and target organ burden which is related to toxicity. There are two types of biological monitoring guidance values:

Health Guidance Values is a health based guidance value set at a level at which there is no indication from the available scientific evidence that the substance is likely to be injurious to health. It is set where a clear relationship can be established between biological concentrations and health effects.

Benchmark Guidance Value is a hygiene-guidance value set at around the 90th percentile of available validated data, provided by a representative cross sectional study of workplaces with good occupational hygiene practices; it can therefore be achieved by the great majority of industry which employs good workplace practice. Biological monitoring guidance values (BMGVs) are non statutory and any biological monitoring undertaken in association with a guidance value needs to be conducted on a voluntary basis (with the informed consent of all concerned). BMGVs are intended to assist employers to ensure adequate control under COSHH. If the values are exceeded the employer should review current control measure since some workers may experience headaches and other symptoms at the benchmark value.

BMGVs are not an alternative or replacement for airborne occupational exposure limits.

Some examples of BMGVs from EH40 are listed in the following table:

Substance	Biological monitoring guidance values			
	Health guidance values	Sampling time	Benchmark guidance values	Sampling time
Carbon monoxide	30 ppm in end - tidal breath	Post shift		
Mercury	20 µmol / mol creatinine in urine	Random		
Glycerol trinitrate (nitroglycerine)			15 µmol / mol creatinine in urine	At the end of period of exposure. This may be mid shift or at the end of a shift
Xylene, o-, m-, p- or mixed isomers	650 mmol methyl hippuric acid / mol creatinine in urine	Post shift		

Figure B3-9: Examples of BMGVs .

Source: ACT.

Short and long term, time weighted exposure limits (LTEL, STEL)

Long-term and short-term exposure limits

LTEL   concerned with the total intake averaged over a reference period (usually 8 hours) and is therefore appropriate for protecting against the effects of long term exposure (chronic effects).

STEL   aimed primarily at avoiding the acute effects or at least reducing the risk of occurrence. Averaged over a 15-minute reference period.

EH40 is primarily concerned with airborne contaminants, which includes vapours, fumes and dusts. Certain substances listed have a skin annotation to denote that they can be absorbed through the skin. This warns that additional controls, in addition to respiratory protection, may be required.

Standards of exposure control expected for carcinogens, mutagens and asthmagens

Regulation 7(5) of COSHH sets out clear requirements for the control of carcinogenic and mutagenic substances:

7(5) where it is not reasonably practicable to prevent exposure to a carcinogen, the employer shall apply the following measures in addition to those required by paragraph 3, the risk reduction hierarchy -

(a)   Totally enclosing the process and handling systems, unless this is not reasonably practicable.

(b)   The prohibition of eating, drinking and smoking in areas that may be contaminated by carcinogens.

(c)   Cleaning floors, walls and other surfaces at regular intervals and whenever necessary.

(d)   Designating those areas and installations which may be contaminated by carcinogens and using suitable and sufficient warning signs.

(e)   Storing, handling and disposing of carcinogens safely, including using closed and clearly labeled containers.

The amount of a substance that is needed to produce sensitivity and lead to asthma varies considerably between individuals. In addition only a minority of individuals at risk will actually develop asthma. Once a person develops hypersensitivity as a result of exposure to a substance that causes asthma it is irreversible, however people develop symptoms of asthma at much lower levels than those which will cause hypersensitivity and if people are removed from exposure to the substance as soon as they start to develop symptoms, they are likely to make a complete recovery.

This page is intentionally blank

Hazardous substances - preventative and protective measures

Learning outcomes

On completion of this element, candidates should be able to:

B4.1   Explain the strategies used in the preventative and control of exposure to hazardous substances.

B4.2   Explain the specific strategy to be adopted when considering the control of exposure to carcinogenic substances.

B4.3   Describe the various types of Personal Protective Equipment (PPE) available for use with hazardous substances, their effectiveness, and the relevant specifications and standards to be met.

Content

Relevant statutory provisions

Control of Substances Hazardous to Health Regulations (COSHH) 2002 (and as amended)

Personal Protective Equipment at Work Regulations (PPER) 1992 (and as amended)

Control of Asbestos Regulations (CAWR) 2006

Control of Lead at Work Regulations (CLAW) 2002

This page is intentionally blank

ELEMENT B4 - HAZARDOUS SUBSTANCES - PREVENTATIVE AND PROTECTIVE MEASURES

B4.1 - Preventive and protective measures

Explanation of strategies relative to the concept of a hierarchy of control

HIERARCHY OF CONTROL

In the control of occupational health hazards many approaches are available, the use of which depends upon the severity and nature of the hazard. *The principal control strategies are outlined below.*

ELIMINATION

This represents an extreme form of control and is appropriately used where high risk is present from such things as carcinogens, where it is usually achieved through the prohibition of use of these substances. Care must be taken to ensure that all stock is safely disposed of and that controls are in place to prevent their re-entry, even as a sample or for research. If this level of control is not achievable then another must be selected.

Control at source

Quantity

A useful approach is to reduce the actual quantity of the substance presenting the hazard. This may be achieved by limiting the amount used or stored. It may be possible to use a more dilute form than is presently being used, for example, with acids. In the case of disposal it is possible to reduce the quantity by neutralisation.

Time

As a strategy this is usually linked to the above and forms the basis of occupational exposure limits, i.e. long-term exposure limits (8 hours time weighted average value) and short-term exposure limits (15 minutes weighted average value).

See also - 'change of work patterns to reduce length of exposure' below.

SUBSTITUTION

One substance for a less harmful substance

The substitution of a less toxic substance in place of a more highly toxic one, e.g. toluene for benzene, glass fibre for asbestos, is a frequently used technique. The use of vegetable oils to replace mineral oils (which may be carcinogenic) for metal machining processes, is another.

CHANGE OF WORK METHOD TO MINIMISE OR SUPPRESS THE GENERATION OF HARMFUL SUBSTANCES

A useful approach is to reduce the actual quantity of the substance which can become airborne; for example, prevention of large volumes of airborne vapours by use of a paint brush rather than an aerosol can of paint or paint spraying equipment. In the case of disposal of acids, the risk of acid burns or corrosion will be removed by neutralisation with a suitable alkali.

CHANGE OF WORK PATTERNS TO REDUCE LENGTH OF TIME OF EXPOSURE

As a strategy this is usually linked to the above and forms the basis of occupational exposure limits, i.e. long-term exposure limits (8 hours time weighted average value) and short-term exposure limits (15 minutes weighted average value). This is particularly relevant when considering shift patterns, where 12 hour shifts are common and the individual operators' work arrangements may need to be rotated, within a shift, to ensure 8 hours time weighted averages are not exceeded.

ISOLATION, ENCLOSURE AND SEGREGATION

Remote handling systems

Remote handling - for example the use of enclosed plant for the automated bottling of bleach.

Enclosure

This strategy is based on the containment of an offending substance or agent to prevent its free movement in the working environment. It may take a number of forms, e.g. glove boxes, pipelines, closed conveyors, laboratory fume cupboards.

Enclosure of process/plant - for example the processing of harmful substances such as isocyanides used in the production of isocyanates.

Segregation

Segregation is a method of controlling the risks from toxic substances. It can take a number of forms:

Distance - a relatively simple process where a person is separated from a source of danger by distance. For example, where herbicides are sprayed, others including members of the public are kept at a safe distance from the source.

Age - the protection of young workers (aged 16 to18 years) in certain trades, for example, working with lead. The Control of Lead at Work Regulations (CLAW) 2002 specifically excludes the employment of young persons working in lead processes.

Time - this is concerned with the restriction of certain hazardous operations to periods when the number of persons present is at its smallest, for instance at weekends. An example might be the spray painting of an Underground Railway Station Platform, when the system is closed from late evening until early morning.

Gender - there remains the possibility of sex linked vulnerability to certain toxic substances. It is a requirement of the Control of Lead at Work Regulations 1998 that female workers of child bearing age are excluded from lead exposure through work.

ENGINEERING CONTROL METHODS

Ventilation

Ventilation may be by natural or mechanical means. Extract ventilation is an important control strategy in the prevention of occupational disease from exposure to dusts, fumes, mists, vapours and gases. It is referred to as such in the Control of Substances Hazardous to Health Regulations (COSHH) 2002.

Local exhaust ventilation

Various local exhaust ventilation (LEV) systems are in use in the workplace, for example:

■ Captor hoods are used for welding and milling operations.
■ Receptor hoods, such as are used in fume cupboards and kilns.
■ High velocity low volume flow systems, for example, as used on a grinding tool.

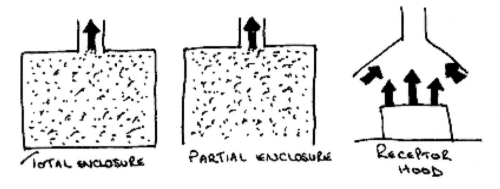

Figure B4-1: Receptor systems (hand drawn). *Source: ACT.*

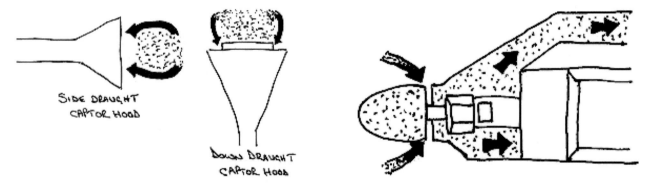

Figure B4-2: Captor systems (hand drawn). *Source: ACT.*   Figure B4-3: High velocity low volume system (hand drawn).*Source: ACT.*

COMPONENTS OF A BASIC SYSTEM

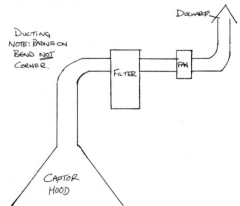

Figure B4-4: Components of a basic system (hand drawn). *Source: ACT.*

Remove contaminant at source so that its range of contamination is minimised. Removal is usually achieved by mechanical air handling. A typical local exhaust ventilation system consists of the following major parts:

Inlet - this is the collection point, e.g. hood, slot, booth, canopy, cabinet, or enclosure.

Ducting - to transport pollutants away from source. Ducting may contain bends, junctions, changes of section and dampers; it may be circular or rectangular in cross-section and be rigid or flexible.

Fan - the equipment that moves the air through the system. Occasionally, some other kind of air mover may be used, such as compressed air venturi.

Air Purifying Device/Cleaner - to prevent further pollution, e.g. dust filter, wet scrubber, or solvent recovery device.

- Particulate dust and fume collectors.
- Devices to remove mists, gases and vapours.

Discharge - to the atmosphere or a room, via a stack, diffuser, grille or open duct.

FACTORS THAT REDUCE A LEV SYSTEM'S EFFECTIVENESS

Efficiency

The efficiency of LEV systems can be affected by many factors including the following:

- Draughts.
- Capture hoods design (exhaust/extract hoods).
- Distance of capture point from the source.
- Damaged ducting.
- Unauthorised alterations.
- Process changes leading to overwhelming amounts of contamination.
- Incorrect hood location.
- Fan strength, air velocity achieved.
- Incorrect adjustment of fan.
- Too many bends in ducts.
- Blocked or defective filters.
- Leaving too many ports open.
- The cost of heating make up air.

It is vital that the pre and post ventilation contamination levels are determined and the required reduction should be part of the commissioning contract.

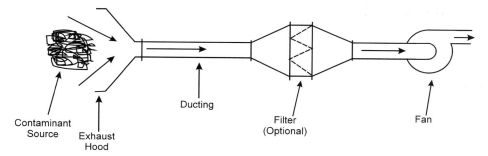

Contaminant Source   Exhaust Hood   Ducting   Filter (Optional)   Fan

Figure B4-5: Efficiency of a LEV.

Source: ACT.

Figure B4-6: Shows the size of fan and motor required for industrial scale LEV. *Source: ACT.*

Figure B4-7: Self contained unit which can be moved around the workplace. *Source: ACT.*

HOOD TYPE	DESCRIPTION
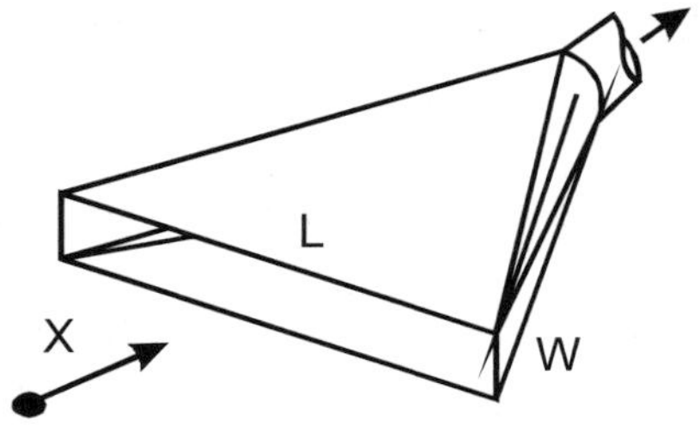	**SLOT**
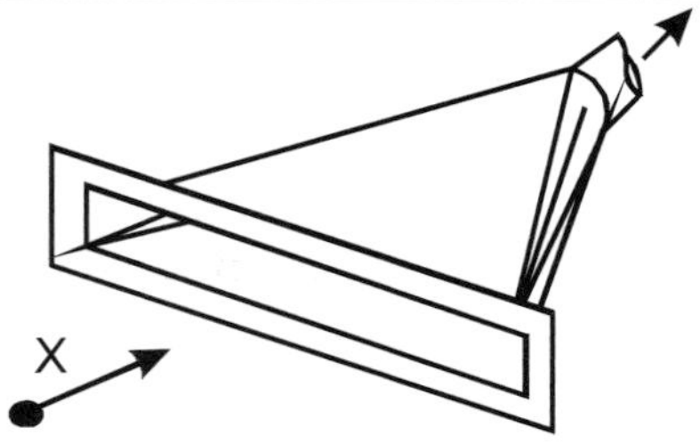	**FLANGED SLOT**
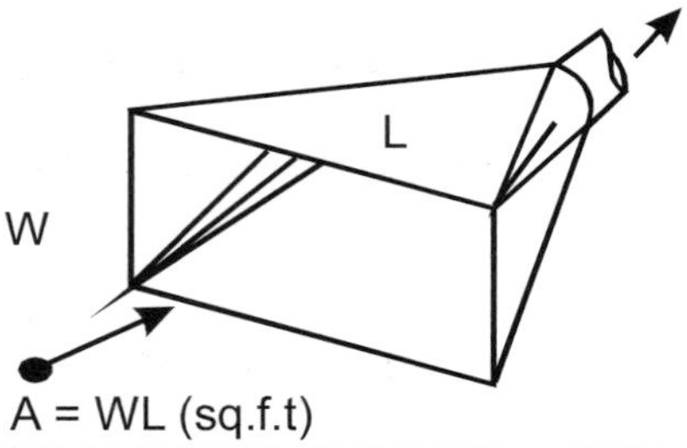	**PLAIN OPENING**
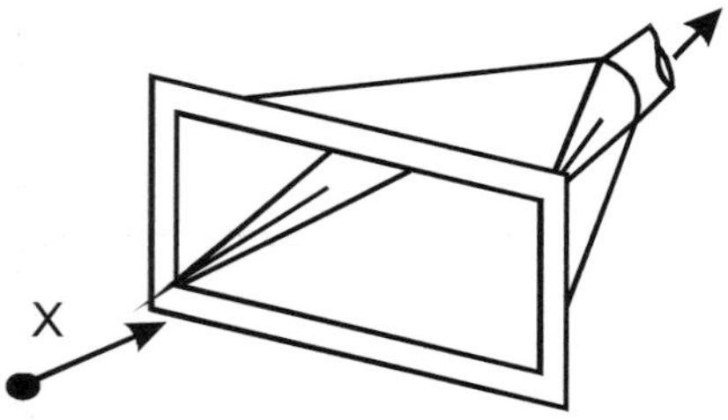	**FLANGED OPENING**
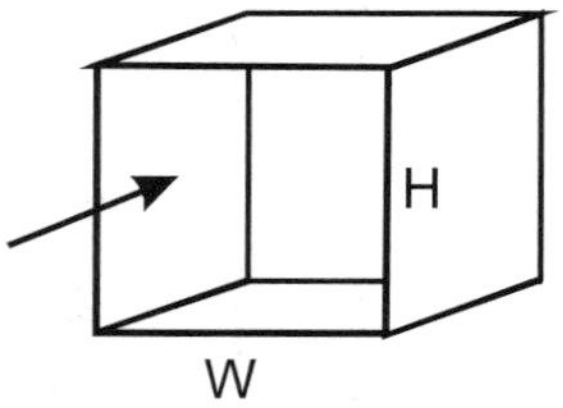	**BOOTH**
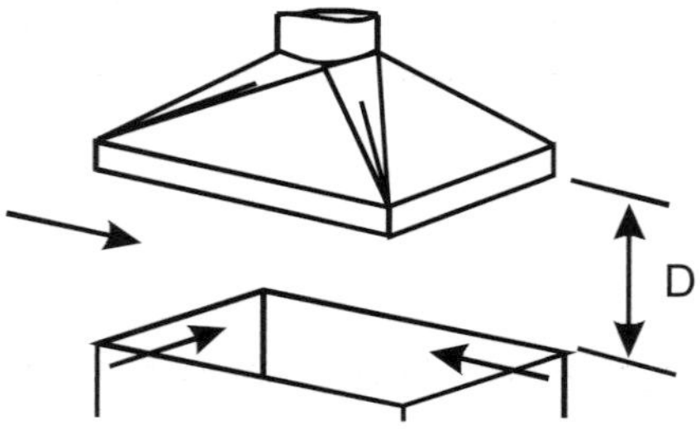	**CANOPY**

Figure B4-8: Hood types.

Source: Ambiguous.

Hood design

Basic rules of hood design:

Always	Never
Design hoods which confine or enclose the contaminant whenever possible.	Forget to provide adequate access for inspection and maintenance
Use canopy-type hoods for control of hot processes	Use canopy heads where operators must work over area
Position exhaust hoods to be whenever possible in line with normal contaminant travel	Design sharp-edged duct entries - low loss entries are always preferred.
Use flanges where possible - these should be one diameter but in excess of 150 mm	Assume all toxic gases and vapours are significantly heavier than air - additional ventilation at ground level may be required
Wherever possible, keep exhaust hood close to the contaminant source (extract volume is proportional to distance squared)	

Figure B4-9: Hood design - basic rules.

Source: ACT.

Ventilation system design

A correctly designed LEV system captures the containment concerned at, or very near to, its source before it can escape into the surrounding workroom environment.

Once captured, any contaminants are drawn through a duct until they are either:

■ Discharged directly to atmosphere.
■ Cleaned/filtered and then discharged to atmosphere.
■ Cleaned/filtered and then re-introduced into the workroom environment.

Any decisions as to which one of the above three options should be adopted for a particular contaminant must be based on the nature and toxicity of that substance.

In order to achieve the basic functions outlined above, a typical local extract system must consists of components illustrated in the following diagram:

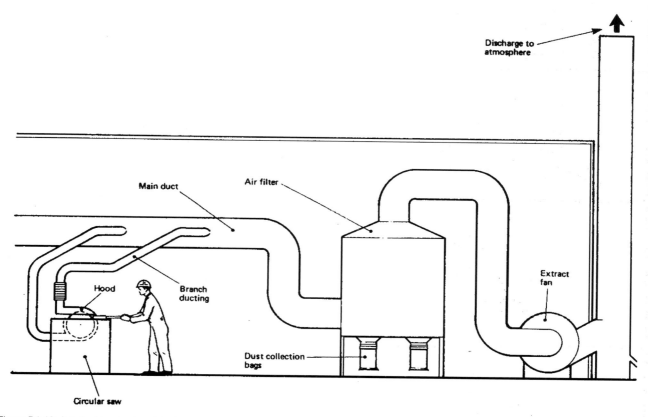

Figure B4-10: A typical local exhaust system.

Source: HSG37 HSE.

Capture hoods

The correct design of hoods (and slots) is essential if a local extract system is to function correctly, and effectively control contamination at source with the minimum of airflow and power consumption.

Effective control of a contaminant is achieved by first eliminating (or minimising) all air motion about the contaminated area, and then capturing the contaminated air by causing it to flow into the hood.

This airflow must be of a sufficiently high rate to ensure that the necessary capture velocity is maintained at all times.

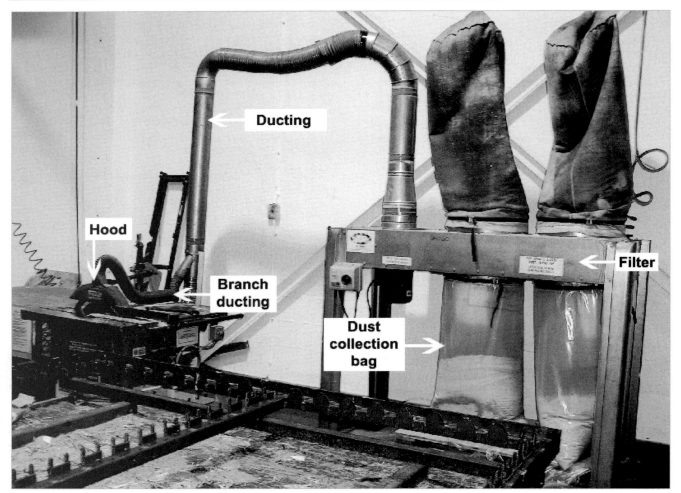

Figure B4-11: A typical local exhaust system.   *Source: ACT.*

Capture velocity

This is the velocity at any point in front of a hood necessary to overcome opposing air currents and to capture the contaminated air by causing it to flow into the hood. If the velocity drops below the capture velocity for the contaminant in question, control will be lost.

Actual values of capture velocity depend upon:

- The type of process involved.
- The characteristics of the contaminant.
- The mode of dispersion of the contaminant.
- The distance from the captor to the contamination.

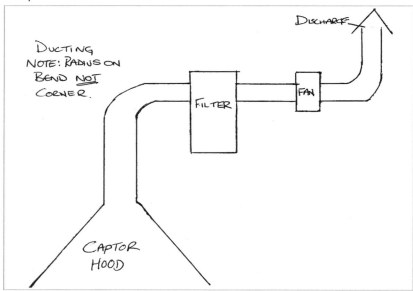

Figure B4-12: High volume captor system (hand drawn).   *Source: ACT.*

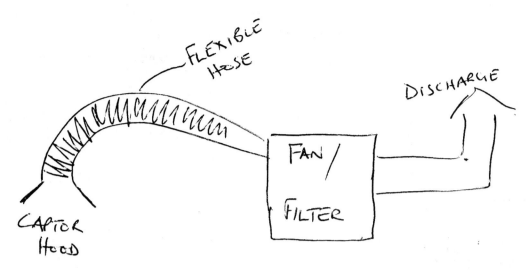

Figure B4-13: Low volume high velocity system (hand drawn).   *Source: ACT.*

Flange effects

Wherever possible, flanges should be provided on hoods to eliminate the tendency of drawing air from ineffective zones (behind) where no contaminant exists.

Increasing hood effectiveness in this matter will usually result in a 25% reduction in the airflow required to achieve contaminant capture.

As a general rule, the width of the flange around a hood is equal to the hood diameter, or side, but should not exceed 150mm.

Flanges are especially important when enclosure of the process is impracticable, as the airflow pattern in front of the hood must be such that the selected capture velocity is maintained in the zone of contaminant generation, conveying it into the exhaust hood opening.

Transport velocity

This is the minimum air velocity to move the contaminant in the air-stream the required distance through the system.

The velocity should be high enough to prevent settlement of the contaminant particles suspended in the airstream, but low enough to minimise duct losses and consequently fan power consumption. Thus if the transport velocity is not maintained, the particles will simply fall out of the airstream.

AIR CLEANING DEVICES

The type of air cleaning device to be used within a LEV system depends upon the nature of the contaminant.

Air cleaners

These are primarily used in air conditioning systems where large volumes of air with low resistance to airflow exist.

Particulate collectors

These are designed to extract large quantities of dust and fumes from the air where the concentration levels are far higher than an in-line filter could cope with. Examples of particulate collectors are:

- Wet collectors.
- Fabric filters.
- Cyclone filters.
- Electrostatic precipitators.

Mists, gases and vapours have a wide range of specialised devices and systems to remove them from the atmosphere, some examples of which are:

- Chemical absorption (scrubbers), e.g. acidic exhausts may utilise alkaline scrubbers.
- Condensation.

EXHAUST VENTILATION

Main points of consideration

The correct design is of vital importance to ensure adequate process control and minimum emission into the workplace.

Successful control of exposure of existing processes may well require modification of plant or layout to accommodate the design.

Consideration must be given to regulatory requirements and HSE guidance.

Ventilation systems must not introduce other problems (e.g. excess noise, explosion risk).

Successful control by ventilation may require a sound knowledge of processes, substances, plant, working methods and environment; and may require the application of more than one type of system:

- Mini   -   on-tool extract.
- Midi   -   local extract.
- Maxi   -   displacement / dilution.

Proper design of inflow systems for make-up air may contribute greatly to successful control.

The range of standard ventilation equipment is limited, but there is scope for reducing costs by the use of modular systems.

Process plant should be interlocked with ventilation equipment, and the latter should give warning of defective operation.

Minimum co-operation from operating management and workers should be expected. Unauthorised modification, especially by operators should be prevented. The design should not hamper work rate (i.e. not reduce bonus).

Ventilation systems should be designed to be reliable over a reasonable working life. Their quality should be no lower than that of the process plant itself.

REQUIREMENTS FOR INSPECTION

COSHH Regulation 9(2) a and schedule 4 set out requirements for inspection of LEV systems. A thorough examination and test must take place once every 14 months (more frequently for those processes listed in schedule 4). Records must be kept available for at least 5 years from the date on which it was made.

The majority of ventilation systems, although effective in protecting workers' health from airborne contaminants, can create other hazards. One of the main hazards that should be considered when designing LEV systems is that of noise reduction. Even if it has been considered as a design feature when establishing LEV systems, it should be monitored on a periodic basis.

DILUTION VENTILATION

This is referred to as general ventilation and involves using natural air movement through doors and windows or using fans and blowers mounted in the roof space to dilute any contaminated air, hence reducing or eliminating the airborne pollutants.

Dilution ventilation is a system designed to induce a general flow of clean air into a work area. This may be done by driving air into a work area, causing air flow around the work area, dilution of contaminants in the work area and then out of the work area through general leakage or through ventilation ducts to the open air. A variation on this is where air may be forcibly removed from the work area, but not associated with a particular contaminant source, and air is allowed in through ventilation ducts to dilute the air in the work area. Sometimes a combination of these two approaches is used. An example may be general air conditioning provided in an office environment. A particularly simple approach to providing dilution ventilation is to open a window and door and allow natural air flow to dilute the workplace air. This is not a reliable means of dealing with toxic contaminants and may be over-relied on in the construction industry. On its own it may prove inadequate but supported by respiratory protection equipment it may be acceptable for some substances.

Because it does not target any specific source and it relies on dispersal and dilution instead of specific removal, it can only be used with nuisance contaminants that are themselves fairly mobile in air. Dilution ventilation systems will only deal with general contamination and will not prevent contaminants entering a person's breathing zone. Local exhaust ventilation is the preferred means of controlling a person's exposure to substances.

Dilution ventilation may only be used as the sole means of control in circumstances where there is:

- Non toxic contaminant or vapour (not dusts).
- Contaminant which is uniformly produced in small, known quantities.
- No discrete point of release.
- No other practical means of reducing levels.

RESPIRATORY PROTECTIVE EQUIPMENT (RPE)

This remains a valid strategy as a "last resort" or as an interim control until a more satisfactory one can be established. It may be an essential secondary requirement also, to protect an individual from failure of the primary containment method; for example, failure of fume extraction when handling a toxic substance. It is unreasonable to expect employees to wear RPE with all its attendant problems when a better, more appropriate control may be implemented. A general approach to the selection of appropriate RPE must not only take account of the needs derived from the work to be done and the contaminant to be protected from but must include suitability for the person. This will include issues such as face fit and the ability of the person to use the equipment for a sustained period, if this is required. Every employee must use any respiratory personal protective equipment provided in accordance with the training and instructions that they have received. Where respiratory protective equipment (other than disposable respiratory protective equipment) is provided the employer must ensure that a thorough examination, and where appropriate testing, of that equipment is carried out at suitable intervals. *(More information in Section 4.3).*

PERSONAL PROTECTIVE EQUIPMENT (PPE)

Personal protective equipment (PPE) is a low level control and includes gloves, overalls, and eye protection. It is often in the form of a simple barrier between the user and the risk, for example, gloves and acid, and as such its effectiveness is subject to correct fit or adjustment. PPE is best used for low risk protection or as additional protection to safeguard against engineering control failure. It is important to determine the limitations of particular PPE before use. The main benefits include low cost and portability when considered against engineering strategies. *(See also - section 4.3).*

PERSONAL HYGIENE AND PROTECTION REGIMES

Personal hygiene and good housekeeping have an important role in the protection of the health and safety of the people at work. Laid down procedures and standards are necessary for preventing the spread of contamination. The provision of adequate washing / showering facilities is important to remove contamination from the body.

The provision of laundry facilities for overalls and PPE reduces the effect of contamination. Barrier creams and suitable hand protection are important considerations for chemical and biological risks.

Where personal hygiene is critical, for example, when stripping asbestos, a 'three room system' is employed. Workers enter the 'clean end' and put work clothes on, leaving by means of the 'dirty end'. When work has been completed they return by means of the 'dirty end', carry out personal hygiene and leave by means of the 'clean end'.

VACCINATION

Certain occupations, such as water treatment / sewage workers, medical profession, have a higher than average risk from some biological hazards. Staff from these occupations may need to be immunised against common high risks e.g. hepatitis B. Whilst vaccination can be an effective way of preventing ill-health as a result of exposure to biological agents, it is important that employers are aware of problems that can arise. In the first instance, vaccination is intrusive.

Employers need the permission of employees before adopting this method - this may not always be forthcoming. Secondly, it is possible that some people will suffer adverse effects from the vaccination. Finally, not all diseases are treatable by vaccination and, for those that are, vaccination might not be available.

HEALTH SURVEILLANCE

The Management of Health and Safety at Work Regulations (MHSWR) 1999, Regulation 6, deals with health surveillance and gives employers a duty to provide it where it is appropriate. Further details on health surveillance are contained in other Regulations e.g. COSHH. (Details can be found in the Approved Code of Practice schedule 6; extracts from the ACOP are given below).

Other than the cases stated in the COSHH schedule, surveillance may be appropriate where exposure to hazardous substances is such that an identifiable disease or adverse health effect may be linked to the exposure. There must be a reasonable likelihood that the disease or effect may occur under the particular conditions of work prevailing and that valid techniques exist to detect such conditions and effects.

The employer must keep records of surveillance in respect of each employee for at least 40 years. This requirement still applies where companies cease to trade, in which case the records must be offered to the HSE.

Substances for which health surveillance is appropriate		Processes
Vinyl Chloride Monomer (VCM).		In manufacturing, production, reclamation, storage, discharge, transport, use or polymerization.
Nitro or amino derivatives of phenol and of benzene or its homologues.		In the manufacture of nitro or amino derivatives of phenol and of benzene or its homologues and the making of explosives with the use of any of these substances.
1-Napthylamine and its salts Orthotolidine and its salts	Dianisidine and its salts Dichlorbenzidene and its salts	In manufacture, formation or use of these substances.
Auramine	Magenta	In manufacture.
Carbon Disulphide Disulpher Dichloride Benzene, including benzol	Carbon Tetrachloride Trichloroethylene	Process in which these substances are used, or given off as a vapour, in the manufacture of indiarubber or of articles or goods made wholly or partially of indiarubber.
Pitch		In manufacture of blocks of fuel consisting of coal, coal dust, coke or slurry with pitch as a binding substance.

Figure B4-14: Schedule 6 medical surveillance.

Source: COSHH AcoP.

DISCIPLINE

As a strategy it can take a number of forms; permits to work, authorised staff, standing instructions and signs such as no smoking. It is limited by one primary factor - human beings - consequently it is as vulnerable to things going wrong as people are at making errors and therefore cannot be relied on implicitly.

EMERGENCY AND SPILLAGE PROCEDURES

Regulation 13 of COSHH requires emergency and spillage procedures, as does Control of Major Accident Hazards Regulations (COMAH) 1999 for specific sites. For example, there could be a release of a gas such as chlorine, or a spillage of a liquid that is hazardous as a liquid, e.g. sulphuric acid, or a volatile liquid that quickly becomes a harmful vapour, e.g. trichloroethylene. The release of a substance may cause the WEL to be exceeded, both the STEL and the LTEL.

The procedures would have to involve protection of employees, others on site, neighbours, possibly the general public and the environment. For those on site, first aid and/or medical attention could be necessary.

Specific absorbent materials must be supplied for certain spillages and a means of disposing of them. Protection of ground water can be dealt with by bunding the container area in case of spillage and by protecting the drains. Respiratory protective equipment and other relevant PPE must be provided and the emergency team trained in the procedures.

Other considerations will be: cordoning off the area, warning alarms, means of calling out the emergency services, and cleaning up and possibly decontamination of the area to get things back to normal.

Causes of emergencies and spillages must be investigated and control measures devised to prevent recurrence. This may involve changing the way materials are brought on site, storage, the amount that is stored, ways of working, and the transport of materials off site.

B4.2 - Carcinogens

The COSHH Regulations 2002, Regulation 7 states specific requirements for carcinogens.

CONTROL OF EXPOSURE

Employer shall ensure that the exposure of employees to substances hazardous to health is either prevented or, where this is not reasonably practicable, adequately controlled.

So far as is reasonably practicable - as above, except to a carcinogen or biological agent where controls shall be by measures other than PPE.

Where not reasonably practicable to prevent exposure to a carcinogen by using an alternative substance or process, the following measure shall apply:

TOTAL ENCLOSURE

- Total enclosure of process.
- Use of plant, process and systems which minimise generation of, or suppress and contain, spills, leaks, dust, fumes and vapours of carcinogens.
- Limitation of quantities of a carcinogen at work.
- Keeping of numbers exposed to a minimum.

PROHIBITION OF EATING, DRINKING AND SMOKING IN CONTAMINATED AREAS

- Prohibition of eating, drinking and smoking in areas liable to contamination.
- Provision of hygiene measures including adequate washing facilities and regular cleaning of walls and surfaces.
- Designation of areas/installations liable to contamination and use of suitable and sufficient warning signs.

DESIGNATION AND CLEANING OF CONTAMINATED AREAS

In the event of failure of a control measure which may result in the escape of carcinogens, the employer shall ensure:

- Only those who are responsible for repair and maintenance work are permitted in the affected area and are provided with PPE.
- Employees and other persons who may be affected are informed of the failure forthwith, including the use of suitable warning signs in the affected area.

CLOSED AND LABELLED CONTAINERS

- Safe storage, handling and disposal of carcinogens and use of closed and clearly-labelled containers.
- If adequate control is not achieved, then employer shall provide suitable PPE to employees in addition to taking control measures.
- PPE provided shall comply with the Personal Protective Equipment Regulations (PPER) 2002 (dealing with the supply of PPE).
- For substances which have a workplace exposure limit (WEL), control of that substance shall, so far as inhalation is concerned, only be treated as adequate if the WEL is not exceeded or for carcinogens and respiratory sensitisers is reduced to as low a level as is reasonably practicable.
- Respiratory protection must be suitable and of a type or conforming to a standard approved by the HSE.

B4.3 - Personal protective equipment

The factors affecting the choice of personal protective equipment

PPE is the last resort, as it only protects the user, not the rest of the workforce. Also it may be cumbersome, uncomfortable and impair both mobility and dexterity.

Whatever control measures are used, they must be adequately maintained. Ventilation equipment must be tested regularly by a competent person. PPE must be maintained in an efficient state and replaced when worn out, time expired or damaged.

It is an employer's duty to provide Protective Clothing and/or Equipment when necessary and it is the employees' duty to wear, or use them when so required. PPE must be used when engineering controls are not adequate to reduce risk to an acceptable level. In general terms this will be when the provision and use are:

- A condition of a work permit.
- A requirement of a risk assessment.
- Where mandatory signs are displayed indicating the need to wear PPE.

In addition, the Personal Protective Equipment at Work Regulations (PPER) 1992 require that people, who are expected to work in the open air in low temperature or cold stores, should be provided with adequate and suitable protective clothing. PPE must be provided free of charge to employees, and the employer must provide training in use, care, limitations and maintenance.

SUPERVISION/MANAGEMENT CONTROLS

The PPER 1992 state the following:

- Ensure PPE is suitable for hazard and person.
- No PPE should be issued without adequate training/instruction.
- Issue, obtain signature and record.
- Set-up monitoring systems.
- Organise routine exchange systems.
- Implement cleaning/sterilisation.
- Issue written/verbal instructions, define when and where to use.
- Provide suitable storage.

There are several areas of special importance in respect of the provision, wearing and care of personal protective equipment. They include protection for ears, eyes, skin, whole body and lungs. This Element is concerned with PPE specifically with regard to:

- Respiratory protection.
- Eye protection.
- Skin protection.
- The degree of protection afforded.

Different types of respiratory protective equipment available

This equipment includes two main categories of respiratory protection:

1.   Respirators.

2.   Breathing Apparatus.

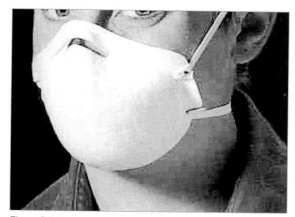

Figure B4-15: Paper filter respirator.   *Source: Haxton Safety.*

Figure B4-16: Mis-use of respirator.   *Source: ACT.*

Figure B4-17: Full face canister respirator. *Source: Haxton Safety.*

Figure B4-18: Breathing apparatus. *Source: Haxton Safety.*

THEIR APPLICATIONS AND LIMITATIONS

Respirators

Respirators filter the air breathed but do not provide additional oxygen. There are a number of types of respirator that provide a variety of degrees of protection from dealing with nuisance dusts to high efficiency respirators for solvents or asbestos. Some respirators may be nominated as providing non-specific protection from contaminants whereas others will be designed to protect from a very specific contaminant such as solvent vapours.

There are five main types of respirators:

1.   Filtering face piece.

2.   Half mask respirator.

3.   Full face respirator.

4.   Powered air purifying respirator.

5.   Powered visor respirator.

Advantages
- Unrestricted movement.
- Often lightweight and comfortable.
- Can be worn for long periods.

Limitations
- Purify the air by drawing it through a filter to remove contaminants. Therefore, can only be used when there is sufficient oxygen in the atmosphere.
- Requires careful selection by a competent person.

- Requires regular maintenance.
- Requires knowing when a cartridge is at the end of its useful life.
- Requires correct storage facilities.
- Can give a 'closed in' / claustrophobic feeling.
- Relies on user for correct fit/use etc.
- May be incompatible with other forms of personal protective equipment (PPE).
- Performance can be affected by beards and long hair, spectacles.
- Interferes with other senses, e.g. sense of smell.

Breathing apparatus

Breathing Apparatus provides a separate source of supply of air (including oxygen) to that which surrounds the person. Because of the self-contained nature of breathing apparatus it may be used to provide a high degree of protection from a variety of toxic contaminants and may be used in situations where the actual contaminant is not known or there is more than one contaminant.

There are three types of breathing apparatus:

1. Fresh air hose apparatus - clean air from uncontaminated source.

2. Compressed air line apparatus from compressed air source.

3. Self-contained breathing apparatus - from cylinder.

Advantages
- Supplies clean air from an uncontaminated source. Therefore, can be worn in oxygen deficient atmospheres.
- Has high assigned protection factor (APF). Therefore may be used in an atmosphere with high levels of toxic substance.
- Can be worn for long periods if connected to a permanent supply of air.

Limitations
- Can be heavy and cumbersome which restricts movement.
- Requires careful selection by competent person.
- Requires special training.
- Requires arrangements to monitor / supervise user and for emergencies.
- Requires regular maintenance.
- Requires correct storage facilities.
- Can give a 'closed in' / claustrophobic feeling.
- Relies on user for correct fit/use etc.
- May be incompatible with other forms of PPE.
- Performance can be affected by e.g. long hair.
- Interferes with other senses. e.g., sense of smell.

Selection

There are a number of issues to consider in the selection of respiratory protective equipment (RPE) not least the advantages and limitations shown above. One of the important factors is to ensure that the equipment will provide the level of protection required. This is indicated by the assigned protection factor given to the equipment by the manufacturers - the higher the factor the more protection provided. With a little knowledge it is possible to work out what assigned protection factor (APF) is needed using the following formula.

$$APF = \frac{\text{Concentration of contaminant in the workplace}}{\text{Concentration of contaminant in the face-piece}}$$

It is important to understand that this factor is only an indication of what the equipment will provide. Actual protection may be different due to fit and the task being conducted.

Use

Every employee must use any personal protective equipment provided in accordance with the training and instructions that they have received.

Maintenance

Where respiratory protective equipment (other than disposable respiratory protective equipment) is provided the employer must ensure that a thorough examination, and where appropriate testing, of that equipment is carried out at suitable intervals.

The significance of assigned protection factors

The PPER 1992, Regulation 4, states that PPE is to be used only after all other possible control measures have been considered or have been put in place.

To protect against dusts, vapours, particulates and dusts from inhalation, the type of PPE that is used is **respiratory protective equipment** (RPE).

Items of RPE have an **assigned protection factor (APF)**, decided on after research and testing by the manufacturer. Ten volunteers wear the RPE in laboratory conditions. The amount of contaminant in the atmosphere is measured and then, after a set period of time, the amount of contaminant in the face-piece is measured. The APF is the amount of contaminant in the atmosphere divided by the amount in the face piece. The APF will be a number such as 10 or 40, for example.

In practice, RPE does not fit the face as well in the workplace as it does in laboratory conditions because the worker may be bending and twisting during their normal work. A worker's face may be sweaty or greasy and in the case of a male may have facial stubble as the day progresses. For these reasons, a higher APF would be needed than the result of a mathematical formula would indicate.

Example:

Amount of airborne contaminant measured in the workplace = 20ppm.

Workplace exposure limit value (from EH40) = 2ppp.

Minimum theoretical APF required would be: 20/2 = 10.

A higher value of APF would be recommended to allow for real conditions.

The HSE use a scheme to identify the capabilities of various forms of RPE and provide advice on its selection and use.

Advice sheet	APF	Type of RPE
R1	4	■ filtering half-mask, EN 149 ■ filtering half-mask with valve, EN 405 ■ filtering half-mask without inhalation valves EN 1827 ■ half mask EN 140 and filter ■ full face mask EN136 and filter and ■ any of the above devices incorporating a low efficiency P1 particulate filter. *Caution: These are not suitable for use in confined spaces.*
R2	10	■ filtering half-mask, EN 149 ■ filtering half-mask with valve, EN 405 ■ filtering half-mask without inhalation valves EN 1827 ■ half mask EN 140 and filter ■ full face mask EN136 and filter ■ any of the above devices incorporating a medium efficiency P2 particulate filter, gas filter, or gas and P3 filter ■ powered hood model TH1 EN 146/EN 12941 and ■ power-assisted mask model TM1 EN 147/EN 12942. *Caution: These are not suitable for use in confined spaces.*
R3	20	■ filtering half-mask, EN 149 ■ filtering half-mask without inhalation valves EN 1827 ■ half mask EN 140 and filter ■ any of the above devices incorporating a high efficiency P3 particulate filter ■ full face mask EN136 and gas filter ■ powered hood model TH2 EN 146 / EN 12941 and ■ power-assisted mask model TM2 EN 147/EN 12942. *Caution: These are not suitable for use in confined spaces.*
R4	40	■ full face mask EN 136 and P3 filter ■ powered hood, helmet or blouse model TH3 EN 146/EN 12941 and ■ power-assisted full face mask model TM3 EN 147/EN 12942 *Caution: These are not suitable for use in confined spaces.*
R5	40	■ Fresh air hose BA EN 138/269 ■ compressed airline BA hood/helmet/visor LDH3 EN 1835 ■ constant flow compressed airline BA hood EN 270/271 or mask EN 139 or 12419 ■ constant flow compressed airline BA full face mask EN 139 and ■ constant flow compressed airline BA LDM3 mask EN 12419.
R6	2000	■ positive demand compressed airline BA with full face mask EN 139 and ■ positive demand full face mask self-contained BA (SCBA) EN 137.

Figure B4-19: COSHH Essentials: RPE guidance.

Source: HSE.

RPE is available in a wide range of varieties. They can be split into six basic types and two categories:

Category 1 - respirators

Particle filtering face pieces

These are commonly known as disposable facemasks. They have a relatively low filter breathing resistance but are easy to use and should be replaced at least at the end of every working period if not more frequently.

Mask & filter respirators

This type of respirator comprises a face piece connected to a suitable filter cartridge or canister for protection against particulates or chemicals. The face piece can just cover the mouth and nose (half mask/orinasal) or whole face (full-face mask). This type is not to be used in atmospheres containing less than 18% oxygen. It can take a great effort to breathe through the filters and they should be changed on a frequent basis. For these reasons the users require a high level of training and discipline.

Power assisted respirator

This is a similar type of respirator to the mask and filter variety. The main difference is that it is fitted with a battery-powered fan or blower, which draws the contaminated air through the filter and supplies clean air to the user. The fresh air can be ducted to the user via a visor or hood, or alternatively through to a full-face mask for a higher level of protection.

Category 2 - breathing apparatus

Compressed airline apparatus

Commonly known as Direct Line Breathing Apparatus (DLBA). This system uses an airline connecting the facemask to a supply of breathable air generated by a compressor. The type of compressor used should ideally be designed for this purpose and be of a non-oil type. The face mask/headpiece is supplied with air at pressure, which creates a positive pressure in the mask thus preventing the contaminants entering the breathing zone of the user.

Self contained open circuit air (BA)

The main difference between this variety and the compressed airline apparatus is that the supplied air is stored at 300 bar in cylinders mounted on the users back or on a portable trolley.

Self contained closed circuit air (BA)

This type uses a supply of air either in compressed, liquid or chemically bonded form usually held in a container within the apparatus. As it is a closed circuit the air is expelled and chemically cleaned or 'scrubbed' and mixed with a supply of clean air and thus can remain in use for longer periods of time.

Caution

BA systems are not for general use. They are expensive to purchase and require specialised training and health checks.

Prior to using or issuing RPE the following questions must be asked:

- Is it possible to control the hazard at source?
- Is the RPE designed to protect against the particular hazard?
- Will the RPE reduce the exposure to an acceptable level?
- Will it protect in practice?
- Have face fit tests been carried out and recorded?

- What training is required?
- Have provisions been made for cleaning, storage and maintenance?
- Does it increase exposure to any other hazards?
- Is it fully compatible with any other PPE issued?

The different types of eye and skin protection

EYE PROTECTION

When selecting suitable eye protection, some of the factors to be considered are:

Type and nature of hazard (impact, chemical, ultra violet (UV) light, etc.), type/standard/quality of protection, comfort and user acceptability issues, compatibility, maintenance requirements, training requirements and cost.

Figure B4-20: Eye and ear protection. *Source: Speedy Hire plc.*

Figure B4-21: Arc welding visor - UV reactive. *Source: ACT.*

Types	Advantages	Limitations
Spectacles	■ Lightweight, easy to wear. ■ Can incorporate prescription lenses. ■ Do not 'mist up'.	■ Do not give all round protection. ■ Relies on the wearer for use.
Goggles	■ Give all round protection ■ Can be worn over prescription lenses. ■ Capable of high impact protection. ■ Can protect against other hazards e.g. dust, molten metal.	■ Tendency to 'mist up' ■ Uncomfortable when worn for long periods. ■ Can affect peripheral vision.
Face shields (visors)	■ Gives full face protection against splashes. ■ Can incorporate a fan which creates air movement for comfort and protection against low level contaminants. ■ Can be integrated into other PPE e.g. head protection.	■ Require care in use, otherwise can become dirty and scratched. ■ Can affect peripheral vision. ■ Unless the visor is provided with extra sealing gusset around the visor, substances may go underneath the visor to the face.

Figure B4-22: Advantages and limitations of eye protection.

Source: ACT.

As you can see, there are several types of eye and face protector and it is important to select the correct type to give the required protection. Some of the hazards for which protection is required are:

- **Impact of solids** (Grade 1 face shield or goggles that are manufactured to the highest impact standard. Normal safety glasses are made to Grade 2 Impact Standard).
- **Ingress of liquid, dust or gas.** (Goggles or respirator required).
- **Splashes of molten metal.** (Face shield).
- **Exposure to glare / ultra-violet radiation.** (Face shield / lens filter).
- **Lasers.** (Special eye protection equipment required). The normal eye protection is no protection against some types of laser beams.

In all cases, Codes of Practice, Standards or Operational procedures will determine the type of protection required.

SKIN PROTECTION

Dermatitis is a major cause of absenteeism, accounting for over half of all working days lost through industrial sickness. It is an inflammatory skin condition (not infectious or contagious) caused by certain irritants contained in many industrial materials, or an allergy caused by dermatitic sensitisers. When other control measures have been used, but there is still a risk of skin exposure, skin protection will have to be used. The most likely exposure is to the hands and there are many types of protective gloves available. The type chosen will depend on the chemical the operator is exposed to and how much dexterity and feeling is necessary to carry out the task.

Latex gloves were once widely used as they allow dexterity and feeling, but latex rubber is both a dermatitic and a respiratory sensitiser. They have been replaced with nitrile, a man-made equivalent.

There are other hand and arm protective gloves and they should be chosen according to the chemical being handled. If the wrong ones are chosen, the chemical may pass directly through the glove and be held against the skin. The hands may also sweat, allowing the chemical to be more easily absorbed by the skin or to be held against the skin causing irritation or corrosion. Some gloves will break down very quickly if wrongly used with acidic or alkaline substances. The protective gloves manufacturer will advise on the correct type as will the catalogues they produce.

Protective gloves often have a powder inside for ease of pulling on and taking off, but unfortunately some users may have an allergic reaction to the powder, depending on the type of powder used.

The hands and arms can be protected with gauntlets, which reach high up the arm. Occasionally, whole body protection may be necessary where the substance can be absorbed through intact skin. These suits protect all the skin, but can be restrictive and hot.

In additions to personal protective equipment, barrier substances and skin cleansers could be used when contact is unavoidable. Barrier creams protect against either water soluble or solvent soluble irritants. To be effective the correct type must be used and it must cover the whole hand surface. After 2-3 hours it may need to be re-applied and it certainly will be necessary after washing. These creams are NOT effective against skin sensitisers (e.g. epoxy resin dermatitis). Also important, is the provision of adequate skin cleansers so as to not leave glues or resins to harden on the skin, and the use of after work creams may be necessary to replace some of the natural oil the skin has lost.

Specification and standards

The Personal Protective Equipment at Work Regulations apply unless there are more specific regulations that apply. Even where they do, regulation 5 requiring all PPE to be compatible always applies. Regulations which are more specific to the use of PPE include:

Control of Lead at Work Regulations (CLAW) 2002 which aim to protect people at work exposed to lead by controlling that exposure. PPE may be used to protect all routes of entry, i.e. protection from inhalation, ingestion and absorption through the skin.

Control of Asbestos Regulations (CAR) 2006

COSHH Regulations 2002,

These regulations are covered in more detail - see Relevant Statutory Provisions - Element B11.

This page is intentionally blank

Hazardous substances - monitoring and maintenance of control measures

Content

Relevant statutory provisions

Personal Protective Equipment at Work Regulations (PPER) 1992 (and as amended 2002)

Control of Substances Hazardous to Health Regulations (COSHH) 2002 (and as amended 2004)

Control of Asbestos Regulations (CAR) 2006

Control of Lead at Work Regulations (CLAW) 2002 (and as amended 2004)

This page is intentionally blank

B5.1 - Measurement of airborne contaminants

Monitoring and analysis of airborne particulate matter

The atmosphere which we breathe has a relatively fixed composition, 78.09% nitrogen, 20.95% oxygen, 0.93% argon, 0.03% carbon dioxide, insignificant amounts of neon, helium and krypton and traces of hydrogen, xenon, oxides of nitrogen and ozone which may be mixed with up to 5% water vapour. Any of these gases in a greater proportion than usual or any other substance present in the atmosphere may be regarded as a contaminant or as atmospheric pollution. One of the simplest ways to classify contaminants is by their physical state. There are three states of matter:

1. Gas.

2. Liquid.

3. Solid.

The physical state of a material is the one in which it exists at normal temperature and pressure.

(Source: www.safetyline, Hazardous Substances Management, Sampling of Airborne Contaminants).

Airborne particulate matter includes solid and liquid matter such as:

- Dusts.
- Fumes.
- Gases.
- Mists.
- Smokes.
- Bio-aerosols.

Exposure by inhalation of particulates is a major cause of occupational illness and disease.

There are four critical factors that may influence the health impact of airborne particulate matter - each of these four factors are interrelated.

- The nature of the dust in question.
- Particle size.
- Duration of exposure time.
- The airborne concentration of the dust in the breathing zone of the exposed person.

The worker's breathing zone is described by a hemisphere of 300mm radius extending in front of their face and measured from the mid-point of an imaginary line joining the ears.

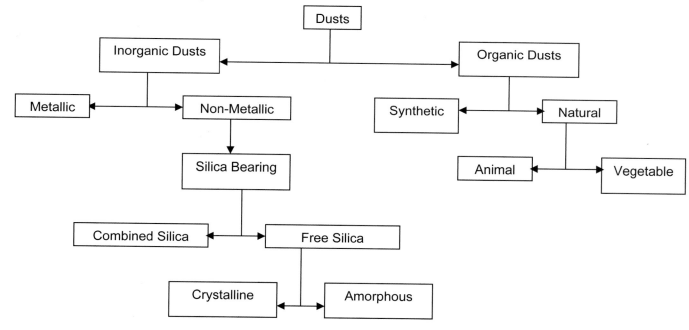

Figure B5-1: Classification for sampling and evaluating respirable dusts. Source: *www.safetyline, Hazardous Substances Management, Sampling of Airborne Contaminants (this figure is based on a similar diagram, which was adapted from a US Bureau of Mines Circular 8503, Feb. 1971 [Alpaugh, 1988, p.124]).*

Duration of exposure

This may be **acute** (i.e. minutes, hours, but usually no longer than a day or two at the most) or **chronic**, in that the duration of exposure may be measured in months or years, over a full working lifetime. Some airborne particulates may exert a toxic effect after a single acute exposure, e.g. beryllium. Other particulates may exert a toxic effect following a longer period of exposure, maybe several days to weeks, e.g. lead. Such exposures could be termed **sub-chronic**. Chronic lung conditions, e.g. mesothelioma, may follow prolonged exposure to crocidolite (blue asbestos).

Particle size

This is critical in determining where particulates will settle in the lung. Larger particles will settle in the bronchi and the bronchioles and will not tend to penetrate the smaller airways found in the alveolar region. These are termed *inspirable* particles. Those smaller particles that can penetrate to the gas exchange region of the lungs, the alveolus, are termed *respirable* particles. The term *inhalable* dust describes dust that is hazardous when deposited anywhere in the respiratory tree, including the nose and mouth.

Sampling strategies

ENVIRONMENTAL (ATMOSPHERIC) MONITORING

(Source: www.personnelzone.com, The Jeremy Stranks Column - Environmental Monitoring).

Environmental monitoring implies the continuous or intermittent sampling of air in the working environment with a view to detecting the presence of contaminants. Contaminants can take many forms such as gases, fogs, fumes, dusts and mists. Environmental monitoring can be undertaken on a long-term or short-term basis.

Short-term sampling techniques

Generally known as 'snap' or 'grab' sampling - taking an immediate sample of air from the workplace and passing it through a particular chemical agent which responds to the chemical being monitored.

Long-term sampling techniques

Instruments which are used for long-term sampling are broadly of two types - personal samplers and static sampling systems:

- *Personal samplers* - devices attached to the person and may take a number of forms, e.g. gas monitoring badges, filtration devices and impingers.
- *Static sampling systems* - sampling systems stationed in the work area. They sample continuously over a period of time, e.g. a working shift of 8 hours, or over longer periods if necessary. They operate using mains or battery-operated pumps. Long-term stain tube detectors are available for this purpose.

PRELIMINARY CONSIDERATIONS

The following must be considered when deciding an appropriate monitoring strategy.

Type of air contamination - this involves a review of the materials, processes and operating procedures being used within a plant, coupled with discussions with management and safety personnel. A brief 'walk-through' survey can also be useful as a guide to the extent of monitoring that may be necessary.

Hazard data sheets are also of use. When the background work has been completed it can then be decided what is to be measured.

Individuals affected - this will depend on the size and diversity of the group affected. The individuals selected must be representative, but selecting those with the highest exposure is a reasonable starting point. If the group is large then random sampling may have to be employed. The group should be made aware of the reason for sampling.

Approach to frequency of measurement - this will depend upon the hazard and whether it is acute or chronic and the control limits.

Technique for measurement - The particular sampling strategy, based on the hazard presented, is outlined in the following table:

Environmental measurements required to determine	Suitable types of measurement
Chronic hazard	Continuous personal dose measurement
	Continuous measurements of average background levels
	Spot readings of containment levels at selected positions and times
Acute hazard	Continuous personal monitoring with rapid response
	Continuous background monitoring with rapid response
	Spot readings of background contaminant levels at selected positions and times
Environmental control status	Continuous background monitoring
	Spot readings of background contaminant levels at selected positions and times
Whether area is safe to enter	Direct reading instruments

Figure B5-2: Sampling strategies.

Source: ACT.

When samples are collected for comparison with control limits, it is essential that the methods should achieve a high degree of reproducibility and specificity.

Sampling airborne particulates

(Source: www.safetyline, Hazardous Substances Management, Sampling of Airborne Contaminants).

There are two basic methods of sampling airborne particulates:

- Filtration sampling.
- Use of direct reading instruments.

Typically, a sampling train consists of:

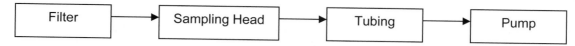

Figure B5-3: Typical sampling train.

Source: ACT.

Filters

The filter diameter, type and pore size will vary depending on the chemical being sampled and will be specified in the sampling method. An air sampling filter may contain millions of pores smaller than the diameter of a human hair (about 30 microns) or even cigarette smoke (about 0.5 micron). Pore size, like the filter itself, depends on the application requirements.

Sampling heads

A sampling head is a device that acts as a filter holder and which can be used to make a connection, via tubing, to the pump. Again the selection of the sampling head is determined by the nature of the airborne contaminant and the particle size range. These will be discussed later in this Element.

PEAK LEVEL AND STATIC MEASUREMENTS

Static sampling equipment

(Source: www.personnelzone.com, The Jeremy Stranks Column - Environmental Monitoring).

This form of equipment is located in the working area and samples continuously. Various devices are available:

- **Constant flow pump devices** - incorporates a pump which takes in a measured quantity of air on a continuing basis. For sampling dusts, selective filters are used; whereas, in the case of volatile substances, various absorbing media are used.
- **Long-term stain detector tubes** - these are linked to a constant flow pump and tube holder, sampling over an 8 hour period in most cases.
- **Direct monitoring devices** - include multi-gas detection and monitoring devices, which are capable of monitoring the concentrations of a number of gases at any one time. They incorporate a digital display and give an instant read out. In some cases, they can be linked to an alarm where a pre-determined concentration of a substance in air is exceeded.

Peak level measurements

The static measurements can either level out to a time-weighted average (TWA) generally over 8 hours, or can produce a graph which can be printed out to show the peak levels. This can indicate where the problem hours are, e.g. a particular time of day, which can then be investigated. This is useful where the peak levels are excursions past the occupational exposure level.

PERSONAL SAMPLING

Personal monitoring

The selective monitoring of high-risk workers, i.e. those who are closest to the source of contaminant generation is highly recommended. This approach is based on the rationale that the probability of significant exposure varies with distance from the source. If workers closest to the source are significantly exposed, then presumably, all other workers are also not significantly exposed and probably do not need to be monitored. Personal monitoring samples should be collected within the breathing zone and, if workers are wearing RPE, outside the face-piece. These samples represent the actual inhalation exposure or workers who are not wearing RPE and the potential exposure of workers who are wearing respirators. It is best to use pumps that automatically maintain a constant flow rate to collect samples, since it is difficult to observe and adjust pumps while wearing gloves, respirators and other PPE. Pumps should be protected with disposable coverings, to make decontamination easier. Personal monitoring may require the use of a variety of sampling media.

The most common system employed for personal monitoring is the adsorption of the material of concern on some suitable medium, followed by desorption and analysis. The adsorption can be carried out either actively by drawing air through the absorbent material using a pump or passively, by allowing natural diffusion to take place from the work area into a suitable medium within the measurement device; although as stated earlier, it is best to use pumps.

Personal sampling instruments

(Source: www.personnelzone.com, The Jeremy Stranks Column - Environmental Monitoring).

Gas monitoring badges

Incorporate a solid sorbent or impregnated carrier in a badge worn by the operator. Contact is by diffusion. The level of exposure is indicated by a change in colour or through analytical determination.

Filtration devices

These entail the use of a low flow or constant flow sample pump attached to the sampling head. The filter in the sampling head is located close to the operator's breathing zone.

Determination of the results by gravimetric analysis, solvent extraction, gas chromatography or atomic absorption.

Impingers

Air is bubble through the impinger (a glass bubble tube) which contains an appropriate absorbing medium. Impingers work in conjunction with a constant flow sample pump attached to the operator. Analysis is by gas chromatography or spectrophotometry.

Sorbent tubes

Incorporate a tube filled with two layers of solid adsorbent capable of completely removing chemicals from the air. The tube has breakable end tips and is inserted into a tube locator in the breathing zone of the operator. They operate in conjunction with a constant flow sample pump.

USE OF GUIDANCE NOTE HSG173

Guidance Note HSG173 "Monitoring strategies for toxic substances" was formerly published as EH42. This advises on the methodology to be used when investigating the nature, extent and control of exposure to substances hazardous to health. EH42 deals particularly with the monitoring of airborne contaminants.

It is possible to determine the scope of exposure without taking any measurements (i.e. deciding that exposure is under adequate control). Having identified the need to take measurements then a three stage strategy is advocated:

1. Initial appraisal.
2. Basic survey.
3. Detailed survey.

Depending on the results, these may be followed by:

■   Reappraisal.
■   Routine monitoring.

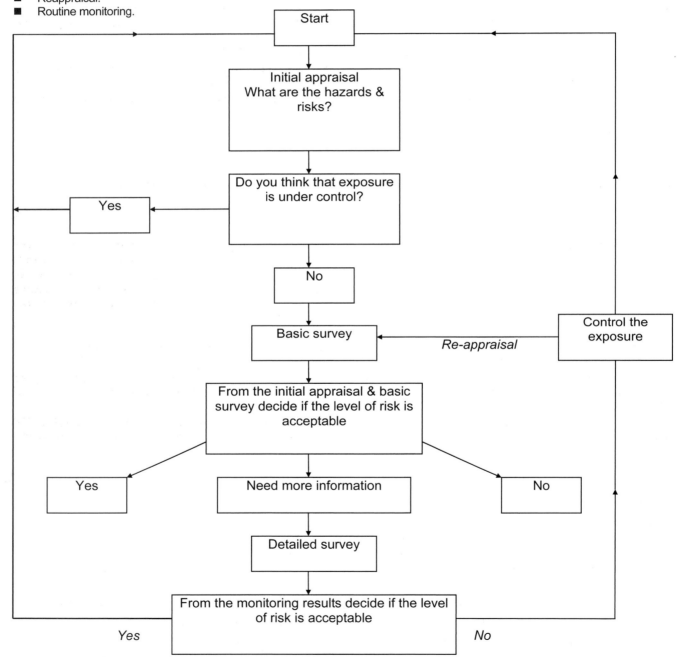

Figure B5-4: Monitoring strategy.   *Source: HSG173.*

Initial appraisal

The aim of the initial appraisal is to establish the need for, and the extent of exposure monitoring. This will give information about the extent of the hazards and the potential risks involved. It will also identify the need to obtain further exposure monitoring.

Information is gathered on the substance(s) that workers are exposed to and its hazardous and physical properties and airborne forms. Information will also be required about:

- The operations or processes where exposures are likely to occur.
- The number, type and position of the sources from which the substance may be released.
- Which groups of employees are most likely to be exposed.
- The duration and pattern of exposure.
- Working practices.
- The means by which releases of the substance are controlled.
- If respiratory protective equipment and/or other personal protective equipment are worn and its effectiveness.
- The occupational exposure limits (EH40), limits from other bodies or in-house standards for the substance involved.

This information can be obtained from a number of sources (e.g. labels; manufacturers' and suppliers' safety data sheets, HSE publications; technical literature from trade associations etc.)

Simple methods can then be used to determine the extent of the risk. Qualitative tests can aid this process; for example:

- Smoke tubes to highlight air movement under the influence of draughts, general and local exhaust ventilation systems.
- Use of a dust lamp (e.g. a Tyndall beam) which allows very fine airborne particles, which are invisible under normal light, to be seen.
- Smell can also be used as an indicator of contamination (this is, however, an unreliable method).

Based on the information collected during the initial appraisal it may be concluded that the level of exposure, by inhalation, is acceptable. Therefore it may not be necessary to carry out exposure monitoring if this is the case.

It should be borne in mind that levels of exposure to hazardous substances can change and the need for exposure monitoring should be reviewed as often as necessary.

Basic survey

A basic survey should be carried out if the initial appraisal suggests that:

- There is an exposure risk but the extent of the risk is uncertain.
- Major changes have been made to the process, procedures or control measures since the last assessment.
- Unusual or periodic operations are planned.
- A new process is being commissioned.
- A new WEL or in-house standard has been set.

The basic survey estimates personal exposure and provides an indication of the efficiency of process and engineering controls. Here "worst-case" situations should be considered, such as the 'dirtiest', or situations where exposed employees make the most complaints.

Before monitoring those employees should be identified who are likely to be at significant risk of exposure, together with the conditions which give rise to them. Semi-quantitative methods such as stain indicator tubes which give a rough numerical estimate of exposure can be used to estimate personal exposure. These semi-quantitative methods can be comparatively inexpensive and easy to use. Alternatively, more complex methods may have to be used which require specialist knowledge. For example:

- Computer exposure modelling.
- Organic vapour analysers such as photoionisation detectors, portable gas chromatographs and infra-red analysers.
- Validated laboratory based sampling and analytical techniques.

Simple measurements such as air velocity meters can be used to assess local exhaust ventilation systems to ensure that they are performing in accordance with the design specification. Also, the qualitative methods used in the initial appraisal can also be used again.

The basic survey may highlight defects and deficiencies in control strategies. Based on this and information gathered during the initial appraisal, you may conclude that the control of inhalation exposure is acceptable. If the conclusion is not certain, there are two alternatives:

- Carry out a detailed survey and take remedial action as necessary.
- Take direct action to control exposure.

Detailed survey

A detailed survey may be required when:

- The pattern and extent of exposure cannot be confidently determined by the basic survey.
- Highly variable exposure between employees doing similar tasks is discovered.
- Exposure to carcinogenic substances (risk phrase R45) or respiratory sensitisers (risk phrase R42) is involved.
- The initial appraisal and basic survey suggest that:
  - The time-weighted personal exposure may be very close to the WEL limits from another body or in-house standard.
  - The cost of additional control measures cannot be justified without evidence of the extent of exposure variability.
  - Undertaking major maintenance and one-off jobs such as plant decommissioning.

A detailed survey is likely to involve techniques already mentioned for the initial appraisal and basic survey. This will be in conjunction with more detailed monitoring of potential exposure to hazardous substances. A detailed survey is most suited to complex processes and will require an in-depth investigation of the process and its environment, for example:

- Procedures involved in the process.
- Work practices.
- Maintenance procedures including the type and frequency.
- Control measures in use and their suitability.
- Suitability and type of personal protective equipment provided.
- Previous monitoring results.
- Results of health surveillance programmes.
- Information, instruction and extent of training provided to those involved in the tasks/processes.

A detailed survey usually requires more specialist knowledge than an initial appraisal or basic survey. It is beyond the scope of this book to describe such a procedure in full, especially as detailed surveys vary with the situation in each workplace. For certain substances a detailed survey may need to include the use of biological monitoring.

REAPPRAISAL

Once remedial action identified by the survey(s) has been carried out the situation should be re-appraised. If the risks to health are judged to be high, additional exposure monitoring may be required. For example, when:

- Carcinogens are used.
- Patterns of exposure are very variable.

ROUTINE MONITORING

When the risk to employees has been adequately controlled, a routine monitoring programme may need to be set up in order to ensure that the control measures stay effective. This is mandatory under the processes listed at Schedule 5 of the COSHH Regulations (i.e. the continuous monitoring for vinyl chloride monomer and every 14 days for sprays given off from vessels during electroplating processes involving hexavalent chromium).

Routine monitoring can be time-consuming and expensive and it may be more cost-effective to invest in better control measures which reduce the:

- Need for expensive routine monitoring.
- The health risks.

Monitoring need not be complex as there are some simple and inexpensive instruments available which can provide information on the continued performance of control methods, for example:

- Smoke tubes.
- Dust lamps.
- Pressure sensing devices fitted to ventilation systems.

Routine monitoring results should be compared with those obtained from previous monitoring exercises. This allows progress to be monitored. However care should be taken to consider:

- The similarity of the processes and tasks monitored.
- Where and at what stage of the process the monitoring was carried out.
- The method of collecting and analysing the samples.

The frequency of routine surveys will vary. The nearer the measured exposure is to the WEL the more often monitoring will be required. A scheme for determining the frequency of routine monitoring is given in "BS EN 689

Workplace Atmospheres: Guidance for the Assessment of Exposure by Inhalation to Chemical Agents for Comparison with Limit Values and Measurement Strategy" (British Standard BS EN 689 1996).

Sampling heads

TYPES

Protected

Where size selection is important, as in inspirable dust sampling, a specific ***protected*** head is used. Two inspirable dust sampling devices are the multi-orifice (7-Hole) Sampler and the IOM Inspirable Dust Sampler. In particular the IOM Inspirable Dust Sampler is designed to overcome problems of sampler orientation or wind speed. The protected head is used in preference to the traditional ***open faced sampler*** which has a tendency to over-sample in environments where particulates of large sizes are present.

Figure B5-5: Multi-orifice (7-hole) sampler.   *Source: SKC Inc.*

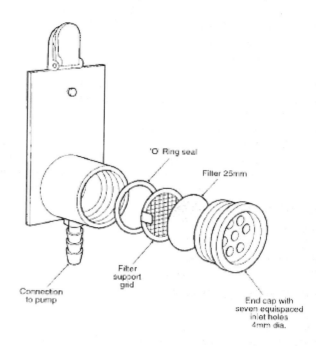

Figure B5-6: Multi-orifice (7-hole) sampler.   *Source: MDHS 14/3, HSE.*

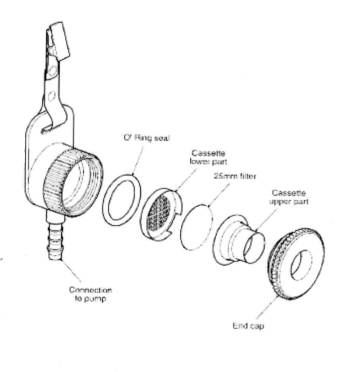

Figure B5-7: IOM inhalable sampler.   *Source: MDHS 14/3, HSE.*

Figure B5-8: IOM inhalable dust sampler.   *Source: SKC Inc.*

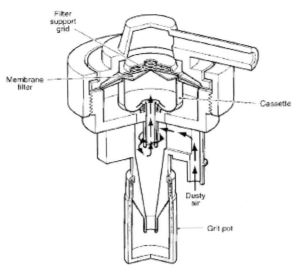

Figure B5-9: Cyclone respirable sampler.   *Source: MDHS 14/3, HSE.*   Figure B5-10: Cyclone sampling head.   *Source: SKC Inc.*

Cyclone

A *cyclone head* is used for respirable dust sampling.

Cyclones are designed to simulate the collection characteristics of the nose and mouth.

The cyclone is a particle size selector used in airborne particulate sampling and is named for the rotation of air within its chamber.

The cyclone functions on the same principle as a centrifuge: the rapid circulation of air separates particles according to their equivalent aerodynamic diameter.

The respirable particles collect on the filter while larger particles fall into the grit pot.

The cyclone/filter assembly is clipped onto the worker's collar or pocket as close to the breathing zone as possible, while the pump is attached to the worker's belt.

After activating the pump, the worker wears the apparatus throughout the entire sampling period.

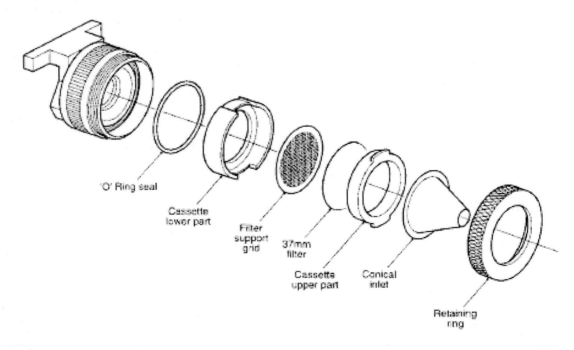

Figure B5-11: Conical inhalable sampler.   *Source: MDHS 14/3, HSE.*

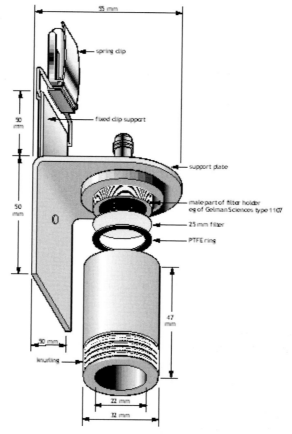

Figure B5-12: Cowl sampling head.   *Source: MDHS series No.59, HSE.*

Respirable dust and sampling efficiency curves

(Source: www.safetyline, Hazardous Substances Management, Sampling of Airborne Contaminants).

As mentioned previously, respirable dust refers to particles that settle deep within the lungs that are not ejected by exhaling, coughing or expulsion by mucus. Since these particles are not collected with 100% efficiency by the lungs, respirable dust is defined in terms of a sampling efficiency curve. These curves are sometimes referred to in terms of the 50% sampling efficiency or cut-point at a certain flow rate.

The term 50% cut-point is used to describe the performances of **cyclones** and other particle-size selective heads or devices. The 50% cut-point is the size of the dust that the device collects with 50% efficiency.

Particles smaller than the 50% cut-point will be collected with an efficiency greater than 50%.

Particles larger than the 50% cut-point will be collected with an efficiency less than 50%.

To reach world-wide consensus on the definition of respirable dust in the workplace, a compromise curve was developed with a 50% cut-point of 4 microns.

After sample collection, filters can be analysed by a variety of methods depending upon the chemical:

- Gravimetric - weighing the sample before and after collection.
- Atomic absorption/ICP - performing chemical analysis to determine specific compounds.
- Microscopic - counting individual fibres.

Cowl

(Source: HSE MDHS Series, No. 59, Man-Made Mineral Fibre Sampling).

An instrument used to sample fibres. This device is an open-faced filter holder fitted with an electrically conducting cylindrical cowl extending between 33 mm and 44 mm in front of the filter, and exposing a circular area of filter at least 20 mm in diameter. This type of holder is intended to protect the filter, whilst still permitting a uniform deposit. In correct use, the cowl will point downwards. A suitable design is shown in the diagram below. Flexible tubing is required to connect the filter holder to the pump, and a cap or bung for the cowl entrance to protect the filter from contamination during transport. The membrane filter must be of mixed esters of cellulose, of pore size 0.8 to 1.2μm, and 25 mm in diameter, with a printed grid. Flat-tipped metal tweezers of good quality are required for handling them. The pump must give a smooth flow and be capable of having its flow set to within 5%, and of maintaining the chosen flow rate through the membrane filter used to within ±10% during the period of sampling. For personal sampling, the pump must be light and portable, and a belt may be required if the pump is too large to fit in the worker's pocket.

MECHANISM OF OPERATION, CHOICE IN RELATION TO NATURE OF ATMOSPHERIC PARTICULATE, METHOD OF USE

Solid particulate sampling

Before any monitoring is carried out it is important to know the typical size of the particles to be studied. The table below illustrates the different sizes of particles from gas molecules up to very large grit particles.

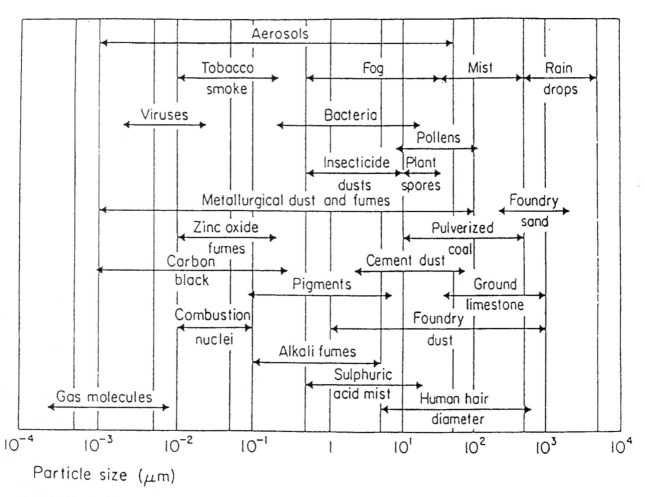

Figure B5-13: Particle size diagram. *Source: Ambiguous.*

Small particles of less than 10 microns (μm) have a slow falling velocity, and therefore any dust that is generated can remain in the atmosphere with little or no air movement. The particulate size of interest is the total inhalable dust and respirable dust. Measurement of these fractions is important to determine the type which exerts harmful effect on the three areas of the respiratory tract: the naso-pharynx, the trachea and bronchial tree and the pulmonary region. The COSHH Regulations 2002 define a 'substantial concentration of dust of any kind' as:

- 10 mg/m^3, as a time weighted average over an 8 hour period, of total inhalable dust.
- 4 mg/m^3, as a time weighted average over an 8 hour period, of respirable dust.

Note that this applies only to dusts not assigned an occupational exposure limit or classified as very toxic, toxic, harmful, corrosive or irritant which are already defined as hazardous substances. There are similar limits for both asbestos and lead.

Sampling of particulates

When samples are collected for comparison with control limits, it is essential that the methods should achieve a high degree of reproducibility and specificity. The methods referred to in this Element are expected to meet these requirements. Low cost, less precise procedures do have a place in sampling.

Classification of the methods that can be used are outlined in the diagram on the next page.

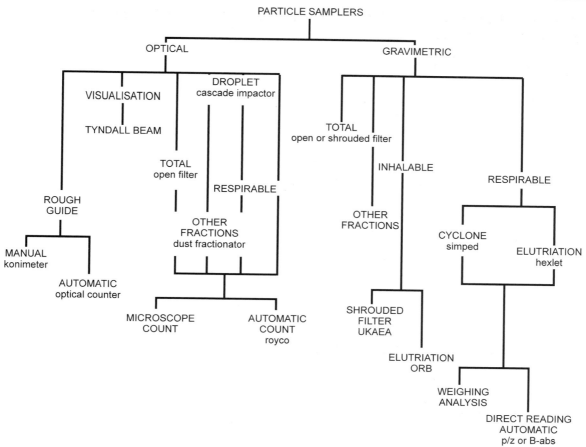

Figure B5-14: Classification of the methods for the sampling of particulates.

Source: Ambiguous.

There are three basic categories of dust:

- Respirable - under 10 microns in diameter.
- Thoracic - under 25 microns in diameter.
- Inhalable (inspirable) - under 100 microns in diameter.

Each type of dust exists in the air we breathe; the only difference between them is the diameter of the dust particle. The collection method varies, depending upon the type of dust to be evaluated.

Another key factor to consider in particulate (dust) monitoring is the filter selection. There are two types of filter: preweighed and matched weight. They can be made of polyvinyl chloride (PVC) or mixed cellulose ester (MCE). Generally, PVC filters are used for gravimetric analyses; they are more durable. However, MCE filters are used especially when testing for metals.

Preweighed filter analysis starts when the filters are equilibrated (consistent temperature and humidity) and weighed, or "tared". They are then placed in cassettes, sealed with colour-coded bands, and labelled with a unique identification number. After sampling, they are again equilibrated and post sampling weight is determined. The difference between the initial weight and the final weight is the number reported (along with the air volume sampled and the resulting mg/m3 calculation).

Preweighed filters are not good forever. You should avoid using any preweighed filters with a tare weight labelled more than six months old. Also, always try to return preweighed filters to the same lab that prepared them. Slight variations in analytical balances may affect your results. Blank filters in their cassettes should always be submitted when using preweighed filters. Blank filters are considered field blanks and help confirm the integrity of your samples during transport and storage.

Matched weight filters do not require the initial weighing, or "tare", step. A matched weight filter cassette contains two filters of equal weight, one on top of the other. During sampling, dust is collected on only the top filter; the bottom filter acts as a blank (equivalent to a preweight). Once back in the laboratory, both filters are weighed and the difference between them is the number you see on your report.

Total or nuisance dust sampling (30 microns or less) is performed by removing the plugs from the ports on the sampling cassettes to the air sampling equipment. Recommended sampling rates: of 1 to 2 litres per minute (Lpm) for a maximum of 133 litres.

When respirable dust (10 microns or less) is being evaluated, you will need to use a cyclone. This is a sampling device that excludes dust particles larger than the respirable size. Depending on the type of cyclone used, a two-or three-piece cassette may be needed, so make sure you check before ordering. Recommended sampling rates: of 1.7 Lpm or 2.2 Lpm (depending on the type of cyclone used), for a maximum of 400 litres.

A different type of sampler called the IOM has been designed to collect inhalable (inspirable) dust (100 microns or less) and offers an uncomplicated method of sampling and analysis. The moulded cassette has a 15-mm diameter inlet and is used with a standard personal sampling pump operating at 2 Lpm. Inside the tared cassette is a 25-mm PVC filter. Analysis is performed by post-weighing the entire cassette and filter, incorporating into the test results all particles collected during sampling, both on the filter and on the inside walls of the cassette.

Other tests can also be performed after gravimetric determination. Silica exposures can be evaluated by infrared (IR) or X-ray diffraction (XRD) techniques. Metals analyses may also be important. Ideally, samples for metals analyses should be collected on preweighed MCE filters. These filters are easily digested in acid, whereas at many times the PVC filters fail to digest completely.

The types of device for sampling vapours

PASSIVE AND ACTIVE DEVICES

Passive personal samplers

These are devices which collect a sample without the use of a pump. Gas is absorbed or adsorbed by the collecting medium at a rate of diffusion across a well-defined diffusion path. They rely upon a concentration gradient across a static layer of air, which is proportional to the concentration in the atmosphere outside the sampler. A passive sampler is attached close to the worker's breathing zone and the total exposure time is noted. Analysis of the sample gives the total concentration and from this the Time Weighted Average (TWA) can be calculated. Some passive samplers, like gas badges, are generally fitted to the lapel and change colour to indicate contamination.

The 2 main types of passive sampler are:

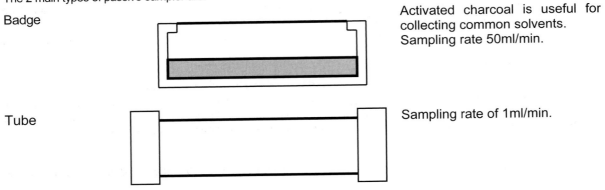

Badge

Activated charcoal is useful for collecting common solvents. Sampling rate 50ml/min.

Tube

Sampling rate of 1ml/min.

Figure B5-15: Types of passive samplers.

Source: ACT.

Passive samplers tend to be light, compact and easy to use. For this reason they are very well received by users amongst the workforce.

Active personal samplers

Active personal samplers are designed to be worn by the operator whilst carrying out their normal work routine. The sample device consists of a pump, fitted to a belt positioned at the waist. The pump is connected by a flexible tube to the collector which is attached near to the collar of the operator as close to the respiratory zone as possible. The collector may be a simple filter to collect dust or fibres or may be absorbent to collect vapours or gases. Analysis is carried out after completion of the work period.

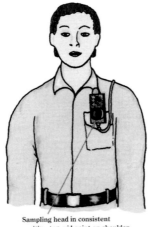

Sampling head in consistent position (eg mid point on shoulder seam)

Battery operated sampling pump

Figure B5-16: Example of an 'active personal monitoring sampler'.

Source: RoSPA OS&H.

ACTIVATED CHARCOAL TUBES AND PUMPS

Tubes

In these devices a powdered sample of solid with particle sizes in the range 0.1 - 1 mm is contained in a short glass or plastic tube. Charcoal is a suitable adsorbent for a very wide range of organic vapours and a short length of charcoal will effectively remove vapours from an air stream. Often two plugs of adsorbent material are used in the tube so that the presence of vapour on the second downstream plug indicates breakthrough and that the sample will be giving a low value. Solid adsorbents other than charcoal can be used in such devices, e.g. the porous polymers tenax and poropak Q. These alternative adsorbents are important for vapours which are so strongly adsorbed on charcoal that they cannot subsequently be easily desorbed for analysis.

After sampling, the tubes are sealed with plastic caps before the tube is sent for analysis. Obviously many variations in geometry and packing are possible. Larger amounts of adsorbent will enable larger concentrations of vapours to be assessed over longer time periods. Similarly, polar materials, such as silica gel, can be used in special applications for polar gases. The simplicity of the solid adsorbent sampling tube means that two or more of them can be used simultaneously with a simple splitting device so that the pump is pulling the same flow rate through two tubes mounted in a suitable adapter, enabling duplicate samples to be obtained.

In general, adsorbent tubes have more than sufficient capacity to sample organic vapours at their threshold limit value continuously for eight hours. Problems can sometimes occur where high humidity (> 90% RH) is present, when the adsorbent capacity can be reduced. Such limitations are indicated in the literature and by the manufacturer.

The sampling pump must operate consistently within a defined range to ensure accurate sampling is achieved. For gas and vapour determination a knowledge of the volume of atmosphere pulled through the sampler in a given time is essential, but variations in flow rate within that time are not important. In fact, very large variations in flow rate are admissible, provided the time over which the variations take place is small compared with the time over which variations in gas concentration take place. An accuracy of ± 5% in volume sampled is sufficient for most purposes.

It is important that the sampling technique selected for a particular application meets the following criteria:

1. It should have a known collection efficiency for the contaminant, which should be at least 75% with a reproducibility of ±5%.

2. It must provide sufficient material for analysis. If the contaminant is at its control limit, the amount collected, over the sampling period, should be at least five times the detection limit of the analytical technique used.

3. Collection of the sample should be compatible with the analytical technique and must ensure the minimum amount of degradation prior to analysis.

4. Sampling should involve the minimum of on-site preparation.

5. The sampling equipment and medium should not present a hazard to the wearer or the environment.

The sampling procedure selected should be as simple and straightforward as possible. It is advisable to have a written protocol which includes procedures for numbering and mounting the sampling head, testing for leaks, and handling and packing of the used sampling heads. Records of time of sampling, sampling period, flow rate, place and other relevant information must be kept.

Detector tubes

There are several different manufacturers of detector tubes, and it is most important that the literature provided with the pumps and tubes is strictly followed.

Types of tube construction:

1. Commonest is the simple stain length tube, but it may contain filter layers, drying layers, or oxidation layers.

2. Double tube or tube containing separate ampoules, avoids incompatibility or reaction during storage.

3. Comparison tube.

4. Narrow tube to achieve better resolution at low concentrations.

The above illustrates the main types of tubes. There are more variations and therefore it can only be re-emphasised that the manufacturer's operating instructions must be read and fully understood before tubes are used.

Pumps

There are four types:

1. Bellows pump.

2. Piston pump.

3. Ball pump.

4. Battery operated pump.

Never mix pumps and tubes of different manufacturers.

How to use tubes

- Choose tube to measure material of interest and expected range.
- Check tubes are in date.
- Check leak tightness of pump.
- Read instructions to ensure there are no limitations due to temperature, pressure, humidity or interfering substances.
- Break off tips of tube, prepare tube if necessary and insert correctly into pump. Arrows normally indicate the direction of air flow.
- Draw the requisite number of strokes.
- Immediately evaluate stain tube, unless manufacturers' operating instructions say otherwise. If there is any doubt when reading tube, always accept the higher figure.
- Remove tube and discard according to instructions. Many of the tubes are hazardous once opened (COSHH procedures will need to be considered as will disposal arrangements).
- Purge pump to remove any corrosive contaminants from inside the pump.

In terms of accuracy, manufacturers claim a relative standard deviation of approx. 20% or less, i.e. 1 parts per million (ppm) error in 5 ppm.

Long-term tubes

Detector tubes have been developed which indicate contaminant mass over extended periods of time. The tubes are designed for a flow rate of 10 - 20 ml/minute much lower than that of most short-term tubes which sample 100 ml in about 10 seconds. The total sample is also greater, up to 10 litres in 8 hours.

Direct reading instruments

Direct reading instruments were developed as early warning devices for use in industrial settings, where a leak or an accident could release a high concentration of a known chemical into the ambient atmosphere. Today, some direct reading instruments can detect contaminants in concentrations down to one part contaminant per million parts of air (ppm), although quantitative data are difficult to obtain when multiple contaminants are present. Some direct reading instruments are:

- **Combustible gas indicator (CGI)** - used to monitor combustible gases and vapours.
- **Flame ionisation detector (FID)** - used to monitor many organic gases and vapours.
- **Gamma radiation survey instrument** - monitors gamma radiation.
- **Portable infrared (IR) spectro-photometer** - used to monitor many gases and vapours.
- **Ultraviolet (UV) photo-ionisation detector (PID)** - monitors many organic and some inorganic gases and vapours.
- **Oxygen meter** - monitors oxygen.

ADVANTAGES

Direct reading instruments provide information at the time of sampling, enabling rapid decision making. Such instruments may be used to rapidly detect flammable or explosive atmospheres, oxygen deficiency, certain gases and vapours, and ionising radiation. The information provided by these instruments can be used to:

- Institute appropriate protective measures (e.g. PPE, evacuation).
- Determine the most appropriate equipment for further monitoring.
- Develop optimum sampling and analytical procedures/protocols.

DISADVANTAGES

- Usually detect and/or measure only specific classes of chemicals.
- Generally not designed to measure and/or detect airborne contaminants below 1 ppm.
- Many of the instruments that have been designed to detect one particular substance also detect others (interference) and consequently may give false readings.
- Direct reading instruments must be operated (and their data interpreted) by qualified individuals who are thoroughly familiar with the particular device's operating principles and limitations and who have obtained the device's latest operating instructions and calibration curves.

Stain tube (colourmetric) detectors

Colour change detectors; also called 'colourmetric' detectors. A piece of chemical detection equipment which incorporates an inert supporting material which is made to contain chemical reagents(s) that react in the presence of a target gas or liquid resulting in a specific colour change. These detectors may be either 'paper' or tubes. The sampling method may be either passive (diffusion/time) or via pump (volumetric). Intensity of colour change or length of stain (for tube) is directly related to gas concentration.

USE AND LIMITATIONS

A detector which has been designed to measure concentrations of specific gases and vapours; as outlined above, the compound inside the instrument reacts with the indicator chemical in the tube, producing a stain whose length or colour change is proportional to the compound's concentration. A limitation is that the measured concentration of the same compound may vary among different manufacturers' tubes. Another limitation is that similar chemicals can interfere, causing false readings. Also, whilst minimal operator training and expertise is required to actually use this piece of equipment, the greatest sources of error are: how the operator judges the stain's end-point and the tube's limited accuracy. The instrument may also be affected by humidity.

Dust monitoring (Tyndall beam)

BACKGROUND TERMINOLOGY

Colloid - a gel, or a combination of two or more substances so that very small particles of each are suspended throughout the others. The particles in a colloid are larger than a molecule but small enough to remain in suspension permanently and be homogeneous. The particles in a colloid are large enough to act as tiny mirrors and reflect or scatter light. If you pass a beam of light through a colloid, you can see the beam or the Tyndall Effect *(see below).*

The Tyndall Effect can also be visualised in air when sunlight comes in through a window and the dust and other particles can be seen floating in the air; however, the air molecules are too tiny to be seen.

THE TYNDALL EFFECT

Colloidal suspensions exhibit light scattering. A beam of light or laser, invisible in clear air or pure water, will trace a visible path through a genuine colloidal suspension, e.g. a headlight on a car shining through fog. When light is being reflected off smaller particles it allows you to actually see the light "beam." Low beams point downward toward the road and this allows more of the reflected light to hit the road with a smaller amount reaching your eyes. High beams pointing higher increase the amount of reflected light reaching your eyes. This is known as the Tyndall effect (after its discoverer, the 19th-century British physicist John Tyndall), and is a special instance of diffraction. The Tyndall beam is the light scattered by colloidal particles. Tyndall scattering occurs when the dimensions of the particles that are causing the scattering are larger than the wavelength of the radiation that is scattered.

You will not find the term "Tyndall effect" in a physics book. Tyndall noticed the effect but did not know how to explain it. The explanation was given by Gustav Mie in 1908. So the scattering of light by particles larger than the wavelength of the light is called "Mie scattering."

Very fine dust may not be visible to the naked eye so the Tyndall beam can be used in the workplace to show where the dust is, where it is escaping from and where it is at its worst. For example, dust escaping from the ducting in a local exhaust ventilation system used for removing fine hardwood dust from the process will show up in the beam.

USE AND LIMITATIONS

The Tyndall beam can be used as a first step to showing where the problem is and how much of a problem the dust is. Showing up the dust with the beam can give an idea of how much dust there is, but other methods must be used to give an exact amount. It is visual and does not involve a method of finding out the $mg.m^{-3}$ or the ppm of the dust. It does not measure the size of the particles, so methods of dust collection and laboratory analysis will be necessary to show if the dust is inhalable and what part of it is respirable.

The beam can be used by anyone with a small amount of training and after the initial purchase does not require extensive maintenance. They are also fairly sturdy.

Measurement principles

DUSTS

Gravimetric analysis using filtration technique

Points to consider:

- Pump selection.
- Fraction selection (total inhalable and respirable).
- Sampling rate and measurement.

The flow rate for personal sampling is normally 2 litres per minute. When high volume samples are taken, flow rates up to 100 litres pre minute are used.

- Sampling position.
- Gravimetric determination.

Pumps

A wide range of personal sampling pumps is now commercially available, most of which are small and light enough to be comfortably worn on the belt or carried in a pocket. Various pumping techniques are used, the most common are:

- Piston pumps.
- Rotary vane pumps.
- Diaphragm pumps.

Typical designs include a flexible cylinder which is alternately compressed rapidly and then allowed to expand slowly over a few seconds to draw atmosphere into it.

With most pumps used for sampling gases the flow rate can be varied over a range of pre-set values, generally between 10 ml/min and 200 ml/min. The techniques used for this include by-pass valves on rotary vane pumps, variable motor speeds on piston pumps and a range of standard orifices on compressed chamber pumps.

Piston and compressed chamber pumps:

The volume sampled is measured by counting the number of strokes during the sampling period. The volume sampled at each stroke is determined by the geometry of the pump and this technique is a very reliable method of measuring sampled volume. Compressed chamber pumps cannot be used for dust sampling.

Rotary vane pumps:

The volume sampled is then obtained by multiplying the flow rate by the time. It is necessary to measure the rate of flow through the pump, and this is often achieved with an integral flow meter. Variations in flow rate can occur due to malfunctions of the pump during the sampling time, although it is general practice to measure the flow rates at the beginning and end of the sampling period and assume that any variations between them have been linear during the sampling period.

Many airborne substances may cause potentially flammable atmospheres. It is for this reason that a sampling pump chosen should be of a suitable design to not be a source of electrical ignition. The battery capacity of the pump should be sufficient to cover the sampling time chosen and, in general, pumps should be capable of operating continuously for at least eight hours. Poor battery choice or quality may result in marked drops in sampling rates during the sampling period.

The sampling pump is the most expensive item in the sampling system and is probably the biggest source of error in hygiene monitoring. It is essential that it is serviced regularly. This servicing should include cleaning of the pump and relevant parts of the flow system and careful checks on battery capacity under sampling conditions.

Figure B5-17: Rotary vane pump.   *Source: SKC Inc.*

Filters

This is the most common form of measurement for dust concentrations. The process involves a known volume of air being drawn through a special filter or membrane by a pump.

There are a wide variety of filters available in various sizes ranging from 13mm (personal sampling) to 50mm diameter (static monitoring). The main filter types are:

Media	Advantages	Disadvantages
Cellulose fibre (paper)	Inexpensive and easy to handle	Absorbs water vapour
Glass Fibre	Inexpensive, high particle retention, low water vapour absorption	Sheds fibres easily, highly variable manufacturing tolerances
Silver	Low chemical interference (particularly X-ray diffraction) and low water vapour absorption	Expensive
Membrane (plastic)	Good optical properties under microscope and precise pore sized	Poor adhesion, high static, pores plug easily due to surface collection
PVC	Low chemical interference, low water vapour absorption and precise pore size (particularly silica IR)	Poor adhesion, high static, pores plug easily due to surface collection

Figure B5-18: Filters.

Source: ACT.

A filter can be part of a static sampler situated in a suitable place in the workroom, or alternatively it can be used in a special holder attached to a worker as close to the person's mouth/nose as possible. The filter is weighed prior to use and again after the end of the sampling period. The difference between the two weights represents the weight of dust collected. This, divided by the total volume of air which has passed through the filter, gives the average concentration of dust over the sampling period:

Weight gain in filter mg = concentration in mg/m^3

Total volume of air sampled m^3

Thus if air was drawn through the filter for 7 hours at a rate of 2 litres per minute and the weight increase of the filter is 0.9 mg then:

Total airflow = 2 x 60 x 7 = 840 litres = 0.84 m^3

Airborne concentration = 0.9 mg = 1.07 mg/ m^3

Total volume of air sampled is 0.84 m^3

If a membrane type filter made of cellulose acetate is used, it can be made transparent by adding a clearing fluid, allowing the dust to be examined under a microscope and the particles or fibres may be counted if necessary. This process is particularly important if fibrous matter such as asbestos is present.

Other filters can be chemically digested in order that the residues can be further examined by a variety of chemical means. Due to the variety of methods for analysing filters available, the appropriate filter must be chosen for the particular analysis. Weight in grams must be accurate to 5 decimal places, as air humidity can affect the weight of some filters, preconditioning may be required. When using personal samplers the level of respirable dust must be determined, a device such as a cyclone, *(see - head types - discussed earlier)* must be considered to separate respirable dust from non-respirable dust. The respirable dust is collected on a filter due to it being lighter than the non-respirable type. The filter holder can be chosen according to the analysis required. For example, a 7 hole UKAEA head for total airborne dust and a cyclone for respirable dust.

Chemical analysis

Samples that have been collected on a filter may be analysed using a variety techniques:

- Direct Weighing.
- Optical Microscopy for Fibre Counting (Asbestos).
- X-Ray Fluorescence Spectroscopy.
- Infra-Red Techniques.
- X-Ray Diffraction.
- Atomic Absorption.
- High Performance Liquid Chromatography (HPLC).

FIBRES

Microscopy

Microscopes can range in power from a simple single lens instrument (i.e. a magnifying glass) through to high-powered scanning electron microscopes and transmission electron microscopes capable of up to about five million times magnification. An optical or light microscope can magnify up to about 1,500 times and is used extensively for analytical work and medicine. The *compound light microscope* consists of:

- An eyepiece or viewing lens.
- A secondary lens in the body tube.
- An objective lens.
- An optical condenser that concentrates light (from a mirror or more usually a built-in illuminator).
- A stage which holds the specimen in place.

Microscope

Figure B5-19: Microscope.

Source: Corel Draw.

Phase contrast and interference types of microscope are types of light microscopes which have modified illumination and optical systems that make it possible for unstained transparent specimens to be seen clearly. Phase contrast light microscopy (PCLM) is a technique for revealing the structural features of microscope transparent objects with varying, but invisible differences in thickness, which result from varying differences in the phase of transmitted light. These phase differences are converted to visible intensity differences when part of the transmitted light has its optical path changed by about ¼ of a wavelength. They are very useful for the examination of living tissues and cells.

Asbestos fibre concentration is estimated by use of PCLM using the method described in (MDHS) 39/4 *"Asbestos fibres in air - Light microscope methods for use with the Control of Asbestos at Work Regulations"*. Accurate asbestos measurement is difficult to achieve because of the difficulty of fibre counting. Laboratories carrying out clearance tests and personal sampling must be accredited to EN 45001. Phase contrast microscopy is used to enhance the contrast between the fibre on the filter and the background. Although the type of fibre cannot be positively distinguished between asbestos and some other fibres such as gypsum and MMMF, an experienced analyst can comment on whether the fibres are visually consistent with asbestos. The microscope used is fitted with a Walton-Beckett graticule with a network of fine lines that can be viewed through the eyepiece. A sample is taken and mounted on a slide. The operator examines 100 fields or 200 fibres whichever occurs first. A respirable fibre is considered to be:

- ≥ 5 µm long.
- ≤ 3 µm in diameter.
- A length to diameter ratio of $\geq 3:1$.

Samples can also be examined using polarised light techniques in order to determine whether the fibres are crystalline, glass or mineral. Here two polarising filters can be used to distinguish visually identical crystals by highlighting their individual colour and tone patterns (known as their birefringence). A rotating polarising filter is positioned above the sample and one fixed below. Observing the optical properties of the sample can provide a unique identification for thousands of compounds. The sample's unique refractive indices, birefringence, and dispersion can all be quantitatively determined. A specific technique for fibres is described in MDHS 77 *"Asbestos in bulk materials - Sampling and identification by Polarised Light Microscopy (PLM)"*. Asbestos can also be positively identified using electron microscopy and energy dispersive x-ray analysis. The aim with these techniques is to eliminate non-asbestos fibres from the count. Test results given should include:

- The type(s) of asbestos identified.
- The sample number.
- The sample site.
- The sampling duration (in minutes).
- The flow rate (in litres per minute).
- The fibres counted.
- The number of graticule areas counted.
- The calculated result, expressed as fibres per millilitre of air (f/ml).
- The name of the analyst & date of analysis.

VAPOURS

Chemical analysis

Certain procedures may have to be performed on the adsorbed contaminant prior to analysis. For instance, a specific reaction may be carried out by adding reagents which produce a compound which can be estimated visually or spectrophotometrically. The simplest way of removing adsorbed vapour is to wash it off with a suitable solvent. For efficient removal, the partition of the vapour between the solid absorbent and washing solvent must lie heavily on the solvent side - otherwise excessive amounts of solvent will need to be used with undesirable dilution of the sample for analysis. Carbon disulphide is widely used, although care has to be exercised as this solvent is highly toxic and flammable. A convenient alternative for desorption is to heat the solid in a gas stream, so that the vapour is desorbed into the gas. The stream can then be analysed or the vapour can be re-trapped and flash heated and passed into a suitable analytical device. Solvent desorption dilutes the original sample and some losses can occur during 'wetting', but the resulting solution can be repeatedly analysed. No dilution occurs with thermal desorption, however the analyst must get the conditions right first time.

Analytical methods available include:

1. Gas Liquid Chromatography.

2. High Performance Liquid Chromatography.

3. Thin Layer Chromatography.

4. Spectrophotometry.

Standard methods

MDHS SERIES

Methods for the determination of hazardous substances (MDHS) guidance on analysis

The Methods for Determining Hazardous Substances (MDHS) are a specialised series of HSE publications that advise on the methods for monitoring exposure to various substances. Examples include:

MDHS No.	Substance	Method
17	Benzine in air	Laboratory method using charcoal adsorbent tubes, solvent desorption and gas chromatography
22	Benzine in air	Laboratory method using pumped porous polymer adsorbent tubes, thermal desorption and gas chromatography
36	Toluene in air	Laboratory method using pumped charcoal adsorbent tubes, solvent desorption and gas chromatography
38	Quartz in respirable airborne dusts	Laboratory method using infra red spectroscopy
39/4	Asbestos fibres in air	Light microscope methods for use with the Control of Asbestos at Work Regulations
56/2	Hydrogen cyanide in air	Laboratory method using an ion selective electrode
77	Asbestos in bulk materials	Sampling and identification by Polarised Light Microscopy (PLM)

Figure B5-20: MDHS Examples.

Source: ACT.

Chromatography

Chromatography (*writing in colour*) was first discovered in 1906 when a Russian Botanist (Mikhail Semenovitch Tswett) found that he could separate plant pigments, which were chemically similar, by washing them down a column of powdered limestone with a solvent. Each moved at a different rate because each differed in strength of adhesion to the powder. This resulted in the pigments separating into a series of bands, each of a different colour. With continued washing with the solvent (e.g. petroleum) the separated substances trickled out separately at the base of the column - one after the other. Chromatography was later developed as a method of separating, often complex, mixtures.

Gas liquid chromatography (GLC)

Gas liquid chromatography is a technique whereby solid and liquid samples are vaporised before introduction on to a packed column. The various components are separated out in a gas stream on the packed column where they are detected. This detection is normally carried out by flame ionisation (FID), thermal conductivity (TC), photo ionisation (PID), or electron capture (ECD). There are many thousands of compounds that can be detected by Gas Liquid Chromatography. The very sensitive detectors used allow the analysis of sub-microgram amounts of materials.

Atomic absorption spectrometry

Atoms absorb energy at the same frequency as they emit it. If a substance lies in a radiation path, its atoms will absorb certain of the energy quanta. This will produce dark lines or absorption spectra. This can then be analysed by a spectrometer. A sample in solution is atomised in a flame and the absorption of radiation by these atoms is measured. The degree of absorption is proportional to the quantity of the element within the solution. By also examining the absorption of known quantities of the substance (standard solutions) we can determine the actual concentration of the substance in the sample.

One common tool used in laboratory analysis is energy dispersive x-ray spectrometry (EDS). The analytical sample is placed in an electron microscope to which a (EDS) capability has been added. In the microscope, the bombardment by the energetic electron beam induces the emission of x-rays at energies which are characteristic of the elements present in the sample. The resultant EDS spectrum is analysed. The peaks indicate the presence of the associated element. The height of the peaks is related to the concentration of the element, so that quantitative elemental analysis is possible.

X-ray diffraction

A sample is exposed to an intense X-ray source. As the X-rays pass through a solid crystal they are diffracted according to the distance between the layers of the atoms. The diffraction pattern is then photographed and the spot densities and positions analysed. The spectrum produced will be characteristic of a particular compound.

B5.2 - Biological monitoring

Biological monitoring

Biological monitoring is concerned with finding out if there is the presence of a hazardous substance (or its metabolites) in the human body or if any damage has been done to the body by hazardous substances. While atmospheric monitoring is concerned with how much of a hazardous substance there is in the atmosphere that can be inhaled, biological monitoring finds out if the person has inhaled it and if it has done any harm.

There are several methods available: blood samples, urine samples, hair and nail samples, x-rays, lung function tests, breath samples, etc. Not all methods are available for choice. Some substances will only show up in the blood and some only by breath samples. Not all hazardous substances can be biologically monitored.

Advantages

- It allows for individual susceptibility. The atmosphere may contain a level below the WEL for the substance in question, but certain individuals may still show an uptake.
- It can show damage caused by an uptake from other routes of entry. The atmospheric measurement may be below the WEL, but some substances can go through intact skin. The person is inhaling very little, but may be absorbing it through the skin. It will cause damage in the body just the same.
- It can show changes in the body that can be reversed, rather than wait for damage to be obvious, which may be irreversible.
- It can check that the controls used are in fact working.
- It may show an uptake from more than just workplace exposure, which also could be seen as a disadvantage.

Disadvantages

- It can be invasive, such as taking blood samples.
- Some people worry that the samples will be used to find out more than just the presence of a workplace substance, e.g. drugs, HIV, HepB, and then the information may be used against them.
- These methods require a medically qualified person to carry them out and analyse the results.
- There are not that many methods to choose from.
- Not all hazardous substances can be measured in the body.
- A problem can show and may result in the employer spending a lot of resources finding the cause, when it is non-workplace exposure that is causing the measurable presence of the substance.

B5.3 - Monitoring and maintenance of control measures

Visual inspection of engineering controls

GENERAL POINTS

All control measures require monitoring and maintaining to ensure their effectiveness and efficiency. There are a number of reasons why this approach should be adopted.

- Statutory obligations.
- To comply with WELs.
- Provision of information to employees.
- Indicate the need for health surveillance.
- For insurance purposes.
- To develop in-house exposure standards.

Assessment can be divided into two types:

Initial commissioning assessment - to ensure design criteria has been achieved (before use).

Regular monitoring assessment - to ensure design parameters are still being met (in use).

LOCAL EXHAUST VENTILATION, ENCLOSURES, GLOVE BOXES

Visual inspection

A competent person (such as a suitable environmental safety and health professional) with appropriate knowledge and experience should inspect for any visual irregularities or defects that may be present. The equipment should be checked for damage, leaks or corrosion on any part or component and also all auxiliary supplies, such as electrical cabling and switching. It should be noted that the majority of components or sections of such equipment are often hidden from normal viewing; some contaminants present may also be invisible to the naked eye.

Dust lamp

By shining a powerful beam of light those dust particles within the respirable range, less then 10 micrometers, become visible to the naked eye. Although this does not indicate the exact quantity of dust present it does give a qualitative assessment. The lamp can be used near the capture source to indicate the effectiveness of LEV equipment at capturing the dust and to check for leaks along its path of travel. Commonly used types of lamp are either mains or battery powered. The mains operated type is fitted with a parabolic reflector unit, which allows fixed focusing to enable a parallel beam of light. They are fitted with reflectors which have safety glass screens attached. There is a range of bulbs available up to 2000 watts.

Battery operated versions are often easier to use and will provide a 12-volt output for approximately 60 minutes. They have output powers of between 100 to 250 watts.

Measurements for assessing performance of exhaust ventilation

METHODS AND EQUIPMENT FOR MEASURING CAPTURE VELOCITIES

There should be a standard procedure for determining the effectiveness of the LEV system in capturing a contaminant released outside of the ductwork, i.e. the **capture efficiency**. Such procedures should be used as part of the initial or periodic LEV system effectiveness test. The **'zone of capture'** is visualised by releasing smoke from a smoke tube around the intake to the LEV. At numerous points in the vicinity of the intake, velocity measurements are made.

The **capture velocity** is the air speed necessary to overcome opposing air currents and draw a contaminant into a hood or intake. Acceptable capture velocity depends on the mass of the particulate being captured, the prevailing air currents outside the hood, thermal properties of the contaminant and the velocity of the particulate or gas, relative to the hood flow.

Pre-requisite

Prior to the testing of a local LEV system, verification of the calibration and operability of the test equipment must be obtained; plus approval to enter the test area. As a precaution, potential hazards may be determined via a hazard evaluation conducted by a suitable environmental safety and health professional. Appropriate PPE must be provided.

Method

- **Assemble equipment** - air velocity meter, e.g. swinging vane anemometer and a measuring ruler.
- **Pre-testing inspection of equipment** - confirm the LEV system is operating; inspect the system, its associated ductwork and mechanical components for any obvious signs of damage. Do not test if the system is not operable or not of adequate integrity.
- **Evaluate and document the conditions surrounding the LEV system** - observe and record conditions in the work environment, e.g. windows open/shut; status of the room heating, ventilation and air-conditioning systems; traffic/movement of people/equipment around the system; permanent/temporary storage of equipment around the system.
- **Smoke tube** - release the smoke tube vapour/fume into the air in the vicinity of the duct intake; move the smoke release point to various locations around the duct opening until the zone of capture is visualised.
- **Initial evaluation velocity measurements by a suitable environmental safety and health professional** - determine appropriate sample locations to characterise the operation and LEV control of hazards; place the velocity-measuring meter's probe at various locations around the duct opening and record the reading at each point tested on an LEV Capture Velocity Form or suitable alternative. Compare results with the needed control velocity. Transfer the results to the LEV System Initial Evaluation Test Record or the LEV System Periodic Validation Test Record, if applicable.
- **Periodic validation velocity measurements by suitable environmental safety and health professional or technician** - procedure as above; then transfer the results to the LEV System Periodic Validation Test Record.
- Label/tag the LEV equipment noting the test date and name of person making the test.
- **Record keeping** - provide a copy of the an LEV Capture Velocity Form or suitable alternative to the Safety Co-ordinator, the Process/Operation and Exhaust System manager/owner and any other designated parties; original test report to be retained by the organisation responsible for the testing.

FACE VELOCITIES

There are three main instruments used for this measurement:

1. Swinging vane anemometer.
2. Rotating vane anemometer.
3. Hot wire anemometer.

During the measurement of face velocities all other equipment within the vicinity should be operated normally. The velocity should then be measured at a number of different collection points. By sub dividing the face area an accurate measurement drawn on a grid can then be taken. A mean value should be recorded as the average face velocity. If at any point the reading is significantly different from the mean reading further investigation should be made.

Swinging vane anemometer

This consists of a box containing a hinged vane. By mounting the vane on low friction bearings as air passes through the box it deflects the vane and a measurement can be achieved by reproducing the movement on a pointer which moves across a scale.

Rotating vane anemometer

This instrument has a series of light vanes mounted on radial arms, which rotate on a common spindle. As the spindle rotates it moves a set of counters on the instrument via a set of gears. This variety is not a direct reading instrument as the counter only records the linear air movement in a given period of time. However some of the more modern electronic versions can give continuous direct readings.

Hot wire anemometer

The Hot-Wire Anemometer is the most well known thermal anemometer, and measures a fluid velocity by noting the heat convected away by the fluid. The core of the anemometer is an exposed hot wire (usually made of platinum or tungsten) either heated up by a constant current or maintained at a constant temperature. In either case, the heat lost to fluid convection is a function of the fluid velocity.

By measuring the change in wire temperature under constant current or the current required to maintain a constant wire temperature, the heat lost can be obtained. The heat lost can then be converted into a fluid velocity in accordance with convective theory. Due to the tiny size of the wire, it is fragile and thus suitable only for clean gas flows.

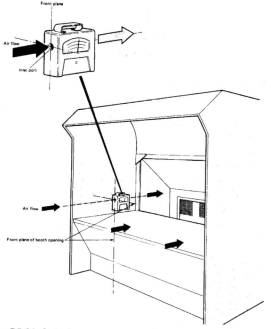

Figure B5-21: Swinging vane anemometer.   *Source: HSE - HSG173.*

TRANSPORT VELOCITIES

This is the speed at which air is transported through the ducting of a LEV system. It is usually measured in litres per minute or cubic metres per minute, depending on size of the system.

STATIC PRESSURES

Air inside a container presses outward creating pressure on the walls of the container. This is called the **Static Pressure**. This pressure exists even if the container has not been "pumped up". The pressure in this case is simply the Atmospheric Pressure.

The static pressure is an indicator of how much negative pressure the fans are creating and how effective they will be at drawing fresh air in through the inlets. An overly high static pressure can also indicate that there are not enough inlets in the LEV system.

Measurements are taken at various points along the ductwork, such as behind the fan and near the outlet.

When it is warm outside such as during the summer and the fans are running on or near their maximum speed the static pressure should be lower. In the winter the static pressure should be higher so that the air pulled through the inlets enters the LEV system faster, promoting thorough mixing of incoming air with the air already in the system.

Static pressure is measured using a **Pitot Tube** and is usually stated either in inches of water (H_2O) or in millimetres of water (mmH_2O). It is essentially a measure of the differential air pressure between the air pressures inside an application vs. ambient air pressure outside of an application, which for airflow calculation purposes is usually 0 (zero). There is an inverse relationship between airflow and static pressure. As the pressure differential rises, airflow drops.

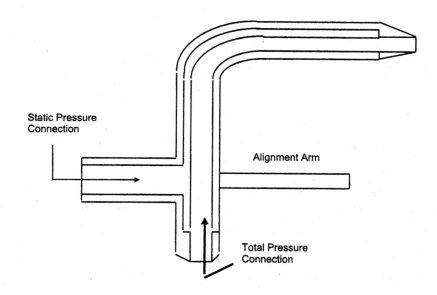

Figure B5-22: Pitot tube.

Source: ACT.

Statutory requirements

INSPECTION, EXAMINATION, TEST

Refer to HSG54: Maintenance, Examination and Testing of Local Exhaust Ventilation Equipment.

Use of LEV

Regulation 7 of COSHH Regulations 2002 requires that the exposure of employees to substances hazardous to health be either prevented or, where that is not reasonably practicable, be adequately controlled *(see also - HSE Guidance EH40)*. Schedule 3 of the regulation deals with the special provisions relating to biological agents. The regulation is supported by the COSHH Approved Code of Practice (paragraph 33) which lists ways in which control can be achieved and makes specific mention of enclosure, partial enclosure with LEV, LEV and sufficient ventilation.

Maintenance, examination and testing of LEV

Regulation 9 of COSHH Regulations 2002 requires that any control measure taken to comply with Regulation 7 must be maintained in an efficient state, in efficient working order, good repair and in clean condition. LEV systems should be examined and tested at least once every 14 months.

Regulation 9 also specifies that records shall be kept of the results of the tests including details of any repairs carried out as a result of the examinations and tests. These records shall be kept for at least five years.

There is a duty (Regulation 8) on the employee to use the LEV provided and report any defects observed.

Both COSHH Regulations 2002 and MHSWR 1999 require that those who carry out duties under these regulations should be competent to do so.

Other regulations

The MHSWR 1999 require an employer to make appropriate arrangements for the effective planning, organisation, control, monitoring and review of the preventative and protective measures, which includes LEV systems.

The Control of Asbestos Regulations (CAR) 2006 and The Control of Lead at Work Regulations (CLAW) 2002 also impose specific requirements for the provision of, and maintenance, examination and testing of LEV.

Furthermore, the Workplace (Health, Safety and Welfare) Regulations (WHSWR) 1992 also require the maintenance of general ventilation systems.

See also - Relevant Statutory Provisions - Element B11.

Biological agents

Learning outcomes

On completion of this element, candidates should be able to:

B6.1   Identify and describe the effects on the human body of the various types of biological agent found at work.

B6.2   Explain the assessment and control of risk from exposure to biological agents at work.

Content

Relevant statutory provisions

Control of Substances Hazardous to Health Regulations (COSHH) 2002 (and as amended)

This page is intentionally blank

ELEMENT B6 - BIOLOGICAL AGENTS

B6.1 - Biological agents and effects on the human body

Identification and evaluation

TYPES OF BIOLOGICAL AGENT

Most biological agents are micro-organisms, of which there are five basic groups:

1. Bacteria.

2. Rickettsiae and Chlamydiae.

3. Viruses.

4. Fungi.

5. Protozoa.

The micro-organisms considered in this Element are fungi, bacteria and viruses. Included in the term fungi are yeasts and moulds.

Micro-organisms can be:

- Saprophytic - they live freely on decaying matter.
- Parasitic - live in or on a living host (e.g. skin flora).
- Commensals - live in harmony with a host.
- Symbiotic - live in harmony for mutual benefit.
- Pathogenic - produce disease in the host.

The definition of biological agents, as set out in the Biological Agents Approved Code of Practice (ACOP), includes the general class of micro-organisms, and also cell cultures and human endoparasites, provided that they have one or more harmful properties that are specified in the definition.

Biological agents are classified into four hazard groups according to their ability to cause infection, the severity of the disease that may result, the risk that infection will spread to the community, and the availability of vaccines and effective treatment. These infection criteria are the only ones used for classification purposes, even though an infectious biological agent may have toxic, allergenic or other harmful properties, and some biological agents are not infectious at all. Although a non-infectious biological agent falls into group 1, substantial control measures may still be needed for it, depending on the harmful properties it has.

FUNGI

Fungus: any of a group of unicellular, multicellular or multinucleate non-photosynthetic organisms feeding on organic matter, which include yeast, moulds, mushrooms and toadstools. They are simple, parasitic life forms with more than 100 000 different species. Most are either harmless or positively beneficial to health. There are, however, a number of fungi that can cause sometimes fatal disease and illness in humans. For example, the cellulose fibres of cane-sugar after the sugar has been extracted, called bagasse, and used in the manufacture of fibreboard, was found to contain as much as 240 million fungal spores per gram.

Many fungi form minute bodies called spores, which are like seeds. The spores can be carried in air and, if they settle in a suitable location with nutrients available, they will grow.

Moulds: of the large group of fungi, they grow rapidly in moist conditions. Micropolyspora faeni is green-grey, dusty mould which grows on straw and hay. When handled, clouds of dusty spores are produced. The size of the spores is about 1 micron so when they are inhaled they penetrate to the alveoli.

Yeasts: are types of fungi which can cause infections of the skin or mucous membranes. The most important disease causing yeast is Candida Albicans, which causes candidiasis (thrush).

BACTERIA

These are a group of single-celled micro-organisms, some of which cause disease. They are commonly known as "germs" and have been recognised as a cause of disease for over a century. Most bacteria are harmless to humans and some are beneficial. The bacteria that cause disease are known as pathogens.

Bacteria were discovered by Antonj van Leewenhoek in the 17th century following the development of the microscope. In the 19th century, the French scientist, Louis Pasteur, established beyond doubt that they were the causes of many diseases.

Pathogenic bacteria are classified into three main groups, on the basis of shape: cocci (spherical); bacilli (rod-shaped); and spirochaetes or spirilla (spiral-shaped).

VIRUSES

These are the smallest known types of infectious agent. They are about one half to one hundredth the size of the smallest bacteria. It is debatable whether they are truly living organisms or just collections of large molecules capable of self-replication under very specific, favourable conditions. Their sole activity is to invade the cells of other organisms, which they take over to make copies of themselves. Outside living cells, they are totally inert. They do not carry out activities that are typical of life, such as metabolism. There are probably more types of virus than the number of types of all other organisms. They parasitise all recognised life forms, and while not all cause disease, many of them do.

Infections caused by viruses range from the common cold to serious diseases such as rabies, and can lead to the development of AIDS, and probably various cancers.

PRINCIPLES OF GENETIC MANIPULATION

Genetic engineering is a branch of genetics concerned, in its broadest sense, with the alteration of the inherited, genetic material carried by a living organism, in order to produce some desired change in the characteristics of the organism.

The application of science and engineering to the processing of materials by biological agents to produce goods and services is known as biotechnology, and the most controversial is genetic manipulation.

The main application so far has been to mass produce a variety of substances, i.e. proteins of various sorts that have uses in medical treatment and diagnosis.

If the gene responsible for synthesising a useful protein can be identified, and if it can be inserted into another cell that can be made to reproduce rapidly, then a colony of cells containing the gene can be grown. The colony will then produce the protein in large amounts.

This method has been used for producing the human hormones insulin and growth hormone, proteins such as factor VIII, which is used to treat haemophilia, and tissue plasminogen activator, used to dissolve blood clots.

Substances made this way are free of any risk of contamination with viruses such as HIV or the agent that causes Creutzfeldt-Jakob disease and are, therefore, safe to use in treatment.

The technique for this mass production of useful proteins by genetic engineering is called recombinant DNA technology. (DNA - deoxyribonucleic acid - the genetic material in cells that controls the manufacture of different proteins).

The technique is basically as follows: first of all a gene in the DNA of a cell that controls the manufacture of a certain useful protein is identified. Then, the gene is either extracted, or copied if the chemical structure can be identified. A recipient cell is chosen. Enzymes are used to split the DNA at a certain site and so produce a gap, and the gene is spliced into that gap.

The types of cell or organisms suitable for alteration are those that can be made to subsequently reproduce rapidly and indefinitely. The most popular have been the common intestinal bacterium *Escherichia Coli (E Coli)* and various yeasts, but cells of other organisms, including human cancer cells, have been used with success. The immortal HeLa cells derived from the malignant tumour which killed Henrietta Lacks are used in laboratories all over the world.

The bacteria, human cancer cells and other organisms can reproduce with ease and rapidity, and indefinitely, that is why they are used. The possibility of accidentally creating and liberating highly dangerous micro-organisms causes a great deal of concern, as does the possibility that they could colonise an exposed person following accidental inoculation. There is also the danger that the cells may produce high levels of hazardous proteins.

ENDOTOXINS, EXOTOXINS AND ENTEROTOXINS; MYCOTOXINS

Although toxin is often used interchangeably with poison, it refers strictly and specifically to poisonous proteins.

These poisonous proteins are produced by pathogenic (disease-causing) bacteria, for example *Clostridium tetani*, which causes tetanus. They are also produced by various animals, such as venomous snakes, and plants, such as the death cap mushroom.

Bacterial toxins are usually divided into three categories: endotoxins, exotoxins and enterotoxins.

Endotoxins - are released only from the inside of dead bacteria. The toxin is produced by the bacterium and held in the bacterial cell wall. It is only released on the death of the bacterium. Released endotoxins cause fever. They also make the walls of capillaries more permeable, causing fluid to leak into the surrounding tissue, sometimes resulting in a serious drop in blood pressure, a condition known as endotoxic shock.

Exotoxins - are released from the surface of live bacteria. The poison is released into the bloodstream, from where it causes widespread effects throughout the body. Exotoxins are among the most poisonous substances known. They are produced by certain types of bacteria, such as tetanus bacilli (bacilli are rod-shaped bacteria), which enter the body through a wound and produce an exotoxin that affects the nervous system to cause muscle spasms and paralysis, and diphtheria bacilli, which initially infect the throat, but release an exotoxin that damages the heart and the nervous system.

Infections by tetanus, diphtheria and some other bacteria that release life-threatening exotoxins can be prevented by immunisation with vaccines consisting of detoxified exotoxins. Treatment of such infections usually includes the administration of antibiotic drugs and an antitoxin to neutralise the exotoxin.

Enterotoxin - is the type of toxin that inflames the lining of the intestine, causing vomiting and diarrhoea. Staphylococcal food poisoning is caused by eating food contaminated with an enterotoxin produced by staphylococci bacteria; the toxin is resistant to heat and is therefore not destroyed by cooking. The bacteria themselves do not need to be alive or even present for this type of food poisoning to occur.

The severe intestinal purging that occurs in cholera is caused by an enterotoxin that is actually produced in the intestine by the cholera bacteria.

Mycotoxins - are produced by fungi. Mycotoxins can cause acute and chronic respiratory symptoms, such as mycobyssinosis in cotton workers.

The modes of transmission of disease and mechanisms of attack on the body

ROUTES OF ENTRY

The major routes of entry into the body by chemicals and agents are inhalation, ingestion, skin pervasion, injection and, to a lesser extent, implantation.

Fungi

Can cause disease in a variety of ways: the fruiting bodies of some soil living fungi contain toxins that can produce direct poisoning if eaten. Some fungi that infect food crops produce toxins that cause a type of food poisoning if eaten, for example, a fungus that grows on peanuts produces aflatoxin. Chronic aflatoxin poisoning is suspected of causing liver cancer. Inhaled spores of some fungi cause an allergic reaction in the lungs known as allergic alveolitis. Farmer's lung caused by spores from mouldy hay is an example of this. Some fungal spores are responsible for causing asthma and allergic rhinitis (hay fever). Some fungi are able to invade and form colonies in the lungs, in the skin, beneath the skin or in various tissues throughout the body. This can lead to conditions ranging from mild skin irritation to severe, sometimes fatal, widespread infection and illness.

Bacteria

Can enter the body through the lungs if droplets that are breathed, coughed or sneezed out by an infected person are inhaled. They can infect the digestive tract if contaminated food is eaten. Bacteria may be present in food at its primary source, brought to it by flies or from contamination on hands. Bacteria can enter the genito-urinary system. They can also penetrate the skin through various ways: through hair follicles, cuts and abrasions, and through deep wounds.

Bacteria cause disease because they produce toxins that are harmful to human cells. If they are present in sufficient quantity and the affected person in not immune, they will cause disease.

Some bacteria release endotoxins, which cause fever, haemorrhage and shock. Others produce exotoxins, which account for the damage done in diseases such as diphtheria, tetanus and toxic-shock syndrome.

Viruses

Gain entry to the body by all possible routes. They are inhaled in droplets; swallowed in food and liquids; passed through punctured skin on infected needles, in the saliva of feeding insects or rabid dogs; viruses are accepted directly by the mucous membranes of the genital tract and by the conjunctiva of the eye after accidental contamination.

Many viruses invade cells and multiply near their site of entry. Some enter the lymphatic vessels and spread to the lymph nodes. Some, such as the HIV virus, invade the lymphocytes (a type of white cell). Many pass from the lymphatics to the blood and are quickly carried to every part of the body. They may invade specific target organs, such as the liver, lungs, brain, and start to multiply. Some viruses travel along the nerve fibres to their target organs.

Viruses cause disease in a variety of ways:

- They can destroy or disrupt the cells they invade, causing serious illness if it is a vital organ.
- The response of the body's immune system may lead to fever and fatigue.
- Antibodies produced by the immune system may attach to viral particles and be circulated in the blood. The antibodies may then be deposited in various parts of the body causing inflammation and tissue damage.
- They may interact with the chromosomes of the host cells causing cancer.
- They may weaken the activity of the t-lymphocytes and so interfere with the immune system. The body's normal defences against a whole range of infections can be lost. This is how HIV works.

For further information, see also - Element B2, section 2.2.

The signs and symptoms of disease

FUNGI

Fungal infections can be broadly classified into superficial, subcutaneous and deep.

Superficial infections: affect the skin, hair, nails, genital organs and inside the mouth. The yeast Candida albicans causes thrush on the inside of the mouth and the genitals. Tinea, which includes ring-worm and athlete's foot, affects external areas of the body.

Subcutaneous infections: are those beneath the skin and are rare. The most common is sporotrichosis and could develop in a contaminated cut.

Deep infections: are those that affect internal organs: the lungs, aspergillosis can follow the inhalation of spores into the lungs, and more rarely, fungi can attack the liver, heart, bones, lymph nodes, brain or urinary tract. They are rare, but becoming more common. Some fungi are dealt with by the body's immune system and are a serious threat to people who have an immune deficiency disorder or are on immunosuppressant drugs.

Fungi are present all the time in the body and are prevented from multiplying through competition from bacteria. Fungal infections become a problem when people are taking antibiotic drugs, which destroy the bacterial competition.

BACTERIA

Bacteria cause disease because they produce toxins.

The first line of defence in the body against harmful bacteria are the substances hostile to the bacteria in the skin, respiratory tract, gastro-intestinal tract and genito-urinary system. The eyes have an enzyme in the tears and the stomach secretes hydrochloric acid.

If the bacteria break through these defences, two types of white blood cell attack them. Neutrophils engulf and destroy many of them and lymphocytes produce antibodies against them. Antibodies may remain in the blood for many years after an infection rendering further attacks mild or giving immunity. There are two types of immunity:

1. Active.
2. Acquired.

Active immunity comes about through surviving an infectious disease - although the attack may produce symptoms so mild as to pass unnoticed. Acquired immunity results from intentional exposure to infectious organisms (antigens) which have been altered to reduce the symptoms of the disease. This alteration is not enough to affect the production of antibodies needed to combat the more virulent form of the disease. As discussed earlier, allergies such as asthma and hayfever are caused by an over reactive response to antigens such as pollen. Here the allergen-antigen reaction damages the cell walls and produces histamine. This has two effects:

1. It increases the permeability of the small blood vessels causing seepage into the surrounding tissue and brings about spasm.
2. Causes swelling in certain groups of muscles (which include the bronchial tubes).

The former effect leads to irritation of the skin and eyes while the latter to asthma attacks in susceptible people.

VIRUSES

Viruses can severely interrupt the functions of the cells they invade, causing serious disease if the vital organs are affected. They cause a response in the immune system, which can lead to fever, fatigue or a disease process, or to inflammation and cell damage.

They can interact with the cell chromosomes and may cause cancer. Viruses may also weaken the immune system so the normal defences of the body against many diseases is lost.

The body's defence against viruses is the immune system, which will deal with most of them in time. However, with some viruses, the speed of the attack is such that serious damage or even death occurs before the immune system can adequately respond.

THE BODY'S DEFENCE MECHANISMS: SUMMARY

The main defence mechanisms against biological agents:

All routes of entry are available to micro-organisms and the main and sometimes only defence is the immune system. The immune system can be overwhelmed by the number of bacteria's or viruses that invade the cells and this can lead to severe illness and sometimes death.

Immune response: there are two types of immunity: active and acquired. Active immunity comes about through surviving an infectious disease - although the attack may produce symptoms so mild as to pass unnoticed. Acquired immunity results from intentional exposure to infectious organisms (antigens) which have been altered to reduce the symptoms of the disease. This alteration is not enough to affect the production of antibodies needed to combat the more virulent form of the disease. Anti-bodies are designed to destroy toxins and organisms invading the body. These invading organisms produce anti-body reactions which persist in some cases for a lifetime. Allergies such as asthma and hayfever are caused by an over-reactive response to antigens such as animal dander. Here the allergen-antigen reaction damages the cell walls and produces histamine. This has two effects:

- It increases the permeability of the small blood vessels causing seepage into the surrounding tissue and brings about spasm.
- Causes swelling in certain groups of muscles (which includes the bronchial tubes).

The former effect leads to irritation of the skin and eyes while the latter to asthma attacks in susceptible people.

Inflammatory response: this is the reaction of the body to injury caused by:

- Bacteria and viruses.
- Fungi, protozoa and worms.

The blood vessels in the affected area dilate so that the blood circulates more quickly and the skin appears red and feels hot. Soon the circulation at the centre of the damaged area slows down and white blood cells stick to the walls of the blood vessels and migrate to the damaged tissue. Here the white cells destroy invading organisms, remove any dead tissue and aid the process of repair. Anti-bodies also pass through the vessel walls to contain infection and, together with a substance known as fibrin, helps to contain the infection. Thus a thick cellular barrier is formed around the infected area.

DEFINITION OF ZOONOSE

Zoonoses are animal infections that may be transmitted to humans. The animal may or may not be ill or show any signs of infection.

Examples

There are many examples of zoonotic disease that are occupational: brucellosis, anthrax, cryptosporidosis, leptospirosis (Weil's disease), psittacosis, glanders, orf and ovine chlamydiosis.

Sources and symptoms of biological diseases

Brucellosis (alternative name: Undulant fever)

A zoonotic disease caused by a bacterium. Mainly found in cattle, goats and pigs. The Brucella bacterium includes three main species causing infection in humans. These are found in cattle, goats and pigs respectively (the latter two causing more serious illness). They are small aerobic bacteria easily killed by disinfectant, e.g. phenol, or pasteurisation. The organism does not produce spores but will survive drying and remain viable for long periods.

Symptoms

The symptoms are: lassitude, headache, muscular pain and drenching sweats especially at night.

In prolonged illness, the temperature pattern undulates.

The illness can be mild or severe with toxaemia.

Incubation period

1-3 weeks.

Transmission

Man is highly susceptible to brucellosis, but there is no evidence of person-to-person spread.

The reservoirs of infection are cattle (although no longer in the UK), goats and pigs. The bacteria are passed in the milk, and in the discharges when giving birth. The latter form a hazard to man and other animals in close proximity.

Humans become infected by:

- Consuming contaminated meat, milk or milk products.
- Inhaling organism.
- Contamination of mucous membranes with droplets.
- Direct inoculation into bloodstream.
- Through skin abrasions.

Risks

The highest occupational risk in UK is to slaughterers and packers handling infected carcasses (B Suis), but anyone is at risk whose work involves contact with...

- Infected bovine animals.
- Carcasses or untreated products.

- Laboratory specimens.

By reason of employment as:

- Farm workers.
- Veterinary worker.
- Slaughterhouse workers.
- Laboratory worker.
- Any other work relating to the care, treatment, examination or handling of such animals, carcasses or products.

Control

All workers at risk should be taught about risks and zoonotic disease and should wear:

- Eye and respiratory protection where splashing of fluids from animals is liable to occur at face height.
- Gloves to protect hands against skin cuts, bone cuts and scratches.

Anthrax (alternative name: Woolsorters' disease)

A zoonotic disease caused by a bacterium. The organism is a spore-forming bacterium, Bacillus anthracis, discovered by Pasteur in 1881.

The bacterium occurs primarily in animals. The spores can survive in the ground for many years. Transmitted by the handling of infected wool, hair, hides and skins or contact with infected soil. The spores enter via skin abrasions or by inhalation. They germinate in the body thereby releasing bacteria into the bloodstream causing serious systemic effects. Depending on the route of entry, symptoms will be either cutaneous pustules or pulmonary anthrax. Anthrax is often fatal and early diagnosis and treatment is vital.

Symptoms

Symptoms vary according to site of infection:

- Cutaneous pustule starts as small itchy pimple on forearm ...
  - Infection forms blisters and spreads.
  - Victim may become very ill.
  - If infection becomes systemic it results in death.
- Pulmonary anthrax ...
  - Symptoms flu-like.
  - Again, can become systemic with fatal results.

Early diagnosis and treatment are crucial.

Incubation period

2 - 7 days.

Transmission

The handling of infected wool, hair, hides and skins can release spores into the atmosphere so that they will be inhaled. Thus spores enter the body via broken skin or alveoli. They germinate in the body and bacteria enter the bloodstream, causing serious systemic symptoms.

The reservoir of infection is spore-contaminated land, the spores having been deposited from body fluids containing the bacteria. Spores live for many years in the environment. Grass-eating animals become infected during grazing or by eating infected foodstuffs.

Person-to-person spread is rare. Human cases are caused by infection, e.g. abraded skin.

Guidance Note EH23 of HSE highlights the following sources of infection:

- Imported goat hair, wool, horse or camel hair imported from Asia or Middle East.
- Animal hides and skins from Africa, Asia, Central and South America.
- Sacks or packing materials in contact with infected cargoes.

Risks

Workers in the following occupations are most at risk:

- Wool, hide or skin handling/manufacturing of goods using these.
- Meat trade.
- Handling bonemeal.
- Handling contaminated sacks.
- Farming.
- Dockers.
- Lorry drivers.

Control

Main methods of prevention include:

- Use of proper protective clothing.
- Mechanical handling techniques.
- Ventilation of dusty processes.
- Providing training in the above.
- Training persons at risk in knowing/recognising early signs of disease.
- Getting prompt treatment in cases of infection.
- Exhibiting Anthrax Cautionary Notices (F410 HSE).
- Distributing Anthrax Card MS (B).

Cryptosporidiosis

A zoonotic disease caused by a parasite. Cryptosporidiosis is now recognised as an important opportunistic infection, especially in immuno-compromised hosts. Members of the genus *Cryptosporidium* are parasites of the intestinal tracts of fishes, reptiles, birds, and mammals. *Cryptosporidium* isolated from humans is now referred to as *C. parvum.* *Cryptosporidium* infections have been reported from a variety of wild and domesticated animals, and in the last six or seven years literally hundreds of human infections have been reported, including epidemics in several major urban areas in the United States.

Cryptosporidium is a small parasite, measuring about 3-5 µm. It lives on (or just under) the surface of the cells lining the small intestine, reproduces asexually, and oocysts are passed in the faeces. Transmission of the infection occurs via the oocysts. Many human infections have been traced to the contamination of drinking water with oocysts from agricultural "run-off" (i.e., drainage from pastures), so it is considered zoonotic.

In most patients infected with cryptosporidiosis the infection causes a short term, mild diarrhoea, and often individuals may not seek medical treatment, and the infection may subside on its own. In persons with compromised immune systems, this parasite can cause a pronounced chronic diarrhoea; in severe cases the infected individual may produce up to 15 litres/day of stools, and this may go on for weeks or months. Whilst, such an infection may not be fatal, it can exacerbate other infections common in immuno-compromised hosts.

Leptospirosis (Weil's Disease)

A zoonotic disease caused by a bacterium. Caused by bacteria Leptospira, spiral shaped bacteria of which there are various species (serotypes).

Survival of the organism is encouraged by warm surroundings; therefore the preponderance of cases in UK is between July and December. It survival depends on protection from direct sunlight: so it survives well in:

- Water courses and ditches protected by vegetation.
- 15 days or more in soil.
- Poorly in badly polluted water or water with pH below 7.
- Is not possible in salt water (which kills it).

Symptoms

Symptoms vary according to serotype but include:

- Liver damage including jaundice.
- Kidney failure.
- Meningitis.
- Conjunctivitis.
- Flu-like illness.

Incubation period

4-19 days, usually around 10 days. Illness lasts between a few days and 3 weeks.

Transmission

Rodents represent the most important reservoir of infections, especially rats (also gerbils, voles, field mice). Other sources of infection are dogs, hedgehogs, foxes, pigs, cattle. These animals are not necessarily ill, but carry leptospires in kidneys and excrete it in urine. Man is not a natural host. Transmission from person to person is rare (though possible). Infection can be transmitted:

- Directly via direct contact with blood, tissues, organs or urine.
- Indirectly by contaminated environment.

Infection enters through:

- Broken skin or mucous membrane.
- By inoculation, e.g. animal bites or accidental laboratory infection.
- By handling infected animals.
- By inhalation of aerosolised leptospires, e.g. following urination of cow in dairy.

Risks

Mortality is normally low, but risk increases with age. Following illness, immunity lasts for years. Workers in the following occupations are most at risk:

- Water and sewage work.
- Farming, e.g. rat contamination of foodstuffs and infestation of farm buildings during winter inhalation of leptospira when cows urinating in dairy - there is probably a massive under-diagnosis in this group where illness is either less severe (so the patient does not call the doctor) or fatal (but not recognised as the cause of death).
- Water sports and leisure activities - activities more likely in summer when water more polluted.

Control

This disease can be controlled by:

- Effective and continued rodent control.
- Wearing protective clothing e.g. rat-catcher, sewer worker.
- Sensible, basic health and hygiene precautions, e.g. protection of cuts and removal of contamination.
- Training to ensure GP is advised of person's occupation or possible exposure to assist early diagnosis.

Carrying Leptospirosis information card. This is a zoonotic disease caused by bacteria Leptospira, spiral shaped bacteria of which there are various species (serotypes).

(Source: www.adam.com/A.D.A.M.Inc).

E. coli

A bacterial infection. E. coli enteritis is an inflammation of the small intestine caused by a type of bacterial gastroenteritis, escherichia coli bacteria.

Symptoms

The symptoms result from toxins and/or bacterial invasion into the intestine. The incubation period is 24 to 72 hours:

diarrhoea that is acute and severe, both bloody and non bloody.

- Stomach cramping.
- Gas.
- Vomiting (although rare).
- Loss of appetite.
- Abdominal pain.
- Fever.

In adults, the infection is usually not severe, but in children and infants, the infection frequently requires hospitalisation, and in some cases is life-threatening. Certain types of E. coli infection (usually caused by the Escherichia coli) are associated with hemolytic uremic syndrome, an acute disease characterized by destruction of the red blood cells, drastic decrease in the platelets, and acute kidney failure. Infection is often associated with recent travel to an area endemic for E. coli, or exposure to untreated or contaminated water.

Legionnellosis/Legionnaires' Disease

An infection caused by a bacteria found in water. This is an a type of pneumonia caused by Legionella pneumophila (of which there are over 20 species and 120 serogroups).

It is an occupational disease for those who maintain water systems, though not for the passer-by infected from a cooling tower. The organism is ubiquitous in water and frequently present in water cooling systems and domestic hot water systems. Large workplace buildings are therefore susceptible to infected water systems, especially hotels and hospitals. It is a particular hazard in hospitals, where there are many people with naturally reduced defences.

The organism is widespread in the environment, and is readily recovered from rivers, lakes, streams, ponds and soil. It needs certain conditions to multiply, e.g. presence of sludge, scale, algae, rust and organic material plus a temperature of 20-50^{0}C.

Symptoms

The symptoms are:

- Aching muscles, headaches, fever followed by cough.
- Confusion, emotional disturbance and delirium may follow the acute phase.
- Fatality rate about 12% in the UK.

There are no distinguishing clinical or radiological features. Diagnosis is based on identifying specific antibodies.

Incubation period

2-10 days.

Transmission

Victims become infected by inhaling the organism in contaminated water aerosols. Smoking, age and alcohol may increase susceptibility.

There is no risk of person-to-person spread.

Risks

The greatest risks are from:

- Showers.
- Air conditioning sprays.
- Water cooling towers.
- Recirculating water cooling systems.

Control

Where clusters of cases occur, identification of the source of infection is easier. Many individual cases have arisen having been contracted in a hotel abroad - Italy, Spain and Portugal.

Careful commissioning, adequate maintenance, routine cleaning of systems and use of biocides are requirements for all installations *(see also - HSE Guidance Note EH48).*

The hazard can be controlled by:

- Proper design of water systems (being aware of features which may contribute to outbreak).
- Chlorination of water to concentration 2-4 ppm.
- Heating water to 55 - 60^{0}C and above.

Hepatitis

A disease caused by a virus. Hepatitis is inflammation of the liver. There are a number of types of hepatitis, the B variety being the most serious. Hepatitis is caused by a virus and is passed from human to human

Hepatitis A is spread by ingesting the virus from the faeces of an infected person, from food or water contaminated by the faeces of a contaminated person or from eating raw or undercooked shellfish harvested from contaminated water.

Hepatitis B is caused by a virus (HBV) which is very resilient in that it remains viable for weeks in the environment, it is resistant to common antiseptics and is not affected by boiling for less than thirty minutes.

The hepatitis B antigen can be found in blood, stool, urine, tears, saliva, sweat, bile and seminal fluid. It can persist for many years after an illness, so a person who has recovered may still be a carrier.

Symptoms vary, but typically the sequence is: flu-like illness with aches and pains in the joints, general tiredness, anorexia, nausea and high fever, jaundice and the liver enlarged and tender.

The primary risks are through contaminated blood, aerosol or droplet transmission. Because HBV can be carried in all body fluids, it is easily spread from person to person by exchange of body fluids in which the infectious agent is present. The disease is therefore spread by: sexual contact, injection or injury with contaminated needles, tattooing, dentistry, non-sexual intimate contact such as sharing a toothbrush, contact or infusions with contaminated blood products, and perinatal spread from infected mother to baby at birth.

10% of cases go on to become chronic carriers, possibly with serious liver diseases or liver cancer. Return to full health may take 6-12 months.

Workers most at risk are those in health care: hospital personnel, dentists, laboratory staff, domestic staff, teachers, prison officers, ambulance staff, police and customs officers. Intravenous drug abusers are also seriously at risk.

Workers who are responsible for keeping streets, parks and toilets clean are at risk from discarded needles.

Control measures include: destroying the virus by bleach, halogens such as chlorine, fluorine, iodine, or autoclaving. All materials and utensils must be disinfected, PPE should be worn and disposable gloves must be worn for examination of patient, blood taking, etc.

Hepatitis B is classified as a Class III biological agent - an agent that can cause human disease, might be a hazard to workers, and for which an effective vaccine exists.

Hepatitis B is a reportable disease.

Occupational groups at risk are health care workers, dentists, laboratory workers, custodial and emergency service workers.

Control measures include disinfection of hands and PPE. Disposable gloves must be worn for examination of the patient, blood taking, etc.

HIV

A viral infection. HIV (Human Immuno-deficiency Virus) is a virus which attacks the body's immune defence mechanism. The virus is not recognised by the immune system because its structure mimics a blood sugar which is not recognised as invasive. It is a delicate virus that does not live for very long outside the body. It is unlikely to survive, for example in old discarded needles. Contamination is more likely from direct contact with blood or other bodily fluids, or from blood samples freshly taken.

HIV is the infection which, through progressive destruction of specific immune cells (CD4 cells) leads to AIDS. Opportunistic infections, specific malignancies, HIV wasting or HIV encephalopthy are part of a complex case definition which comprise the Acquired Immuno Deficiency Syndrome. HIV is a sexually transmitted and bloodborne virus (BBV). This means it can be transmitted by unprotected sexual intercourse or by routes similar to other BBVs, i.e. shared needle use by injecting drug users, or mother to child transmission before, during or after (via breast milk form an infected mother to her child) the birth of the child. In countries that can afford anti-retroviral therapies the progression to AIDS is not inevitable and the patterns of survival have been fundamentally changed by these drugs. However, there is currently no cure and patients need to continue on therapy. There is currently no effective vaccine although much research is going on to seek to develop one.

Occupational transmission could be needlestick injuries during the taking of blood samples and other sharps injuries when dealing with the samples. Dentists, doctors, surgeons, nurses, other care workers, professions involved with drug users: prison warders, police, social workers, are just some of the occupations at risk.

AIDS

As mentioned above, Acquired Immune Deficiency Syndrome (AIDS) is caused by the HIV, which attacks the body's immune defence mechanism. The virus can be found in most infected body fluids and is passed from human to human. It is delicate and easy to kill by heat and chemicals. It lives for only a short time outside its host.

Symptoms

Some people who contract HIV experience very strong symptoms, but others experience none at all. Those who do have symptoms generally experience fever, fatigue, and, often, rash. Other common symptoms can include headache, swollen lymph nodes, and sore throat. These symptoms can occur within days or weeks of the initial exposure to the virus during a period called *primary or acute HIV infection.* Because of the non-specific symptoms associated with primary or acute HIV infection, symptoms are not a reliable way to diagnose HIV infection.

Testing for HIV antibodies is the only way to identify infection. The HIV antibody test only works after the infected person's immune system develops antibodies to HIV.

Aspergillosis (or Farmer's lung)

This disease is caused by *Aspergillus*, a fungus, which can affect the body in various ways. It is a saprophyte, that is, it grows on material which is not alive. Bread or jam left to the open air for a few days will grow a variety of microbes among which will be *Aspergillus fumigatus* (grey-green in colour) or *Aspergillus niger* (black).

There are three different interactions of the fungus with the human body and some species produce toxins.

Aspergillus can be found growing harmlessly in various parts of the body such as the outer ear, lungs or the gut. The fungus does not invade the tissues, but grows on the outer surface or in the cavities. It seems to do no great harm.

Invasive disease

The normal human body seems able to resist invasion by *Aspergillosis*. However, if the fungus reaches an area of the body not normally exposed to infectious agents, for example, the eyeball or the valves of the heart, it will grow. An invasive disease, where it grows in the tissues, is very serious. As a fungus it will not be affected by antibiotics and there is no vaccine. If an eye becomes infected by a piercing injury, it will usually have to be removed. Systemic disease is usually fatal.

Allergy

Aspergillus forms spores which are about three microns in diameter. When material that contains the fungus, such as hay or straw, is disturbed, the spores are released. It has been estimated that a farm worker moving mouldy hay could inhale a million spores a minute. The spores penetrate the lungs causing a typical asthma. The allergic reaction is known as allergic alveolitis, where there is thickening of the alveoli walls preventing gaseous exchange.

Toxins

Some kinds of *Aspergillus* produce toxins. *Aspergillus flavus* grows on peanuts and other materials and produces aflatoxin, which produces fatal poisoning in stock animals, and can cause cancer. Storage under proper conditions prevents growth of this fungus.

Aspergillus is extremely widespread in the environment, therefore elimination is not possible. The spores can reach the affected site by inhalation, ingestion, contact with a body surface or use of contaminated surgical instruments or materials. The fungus will infect those whose defences are defective in some way: people with AIDS, or diseases which reduce immunity, for example cancers or alcoholism, and those whose treatment suppresses immunity.

Control can be achieved by proper storage, and where mouldy material is handled, good ventilation and respiratory protective equipment.

Biological sensitisation

If a person is exposed to an allergen or some other substance recognised as foreign by the body's immune system this can lead to the process of sensitisation. About one third of the population is atopic - that is they are allergic to environmental sensitisers such as grass pollen, house dust mites and animal dusts. A similar substance-specific response can occur with fungi and moulds.

Sensitisation can occur from inhaling small particles of fish protein. Tiny particles of prawns or shrimps can become airborne when they are being shelled by hand and particles of fish are released when trout and salmon are being gutted and de-boned.

The dose at which sensitisation occurs varies with time and concentration in a way that has not been fully established. Some substances can sensitise at below one millionth of a gram per cubic metre while for others the dose is considerably higher. Sensitisation is unpredictable with only about 5-25% of those exposed becoming sensitised. Once sensitisation occurs then it is irreversible. The only help is if the person does not come into contact with the agent. Symptoms can occur again if the person is re-exposed - even if several years have elapsed.

At the time of sensitisation the person will experience no apparent effects; however the body has recognised the sensitising agent as an antigen. Subsequent exposure to even very low levels of this agent leads to symptoms of:

Asthma: with periodic attacks of wheezing, chest tightness and breathlessness resulting from constriction of the bronchi and bronchioles;

Rhinitis and conjunctivitis: runny or stuffy nose and watery or prickly eyes (akin to hay fever).

The most common effects in the short term are rhinitis and conjunctivitis (occasionally accompanied by dry coughs). If exposure to the sensitiser continues unchecked, then asthma may develop. Often symptoms occur immediately on or after exposure. Occasionally symptoms may not develop until hours after exposure during the evening or night. This may lead to difficulty in recognising the cause of the problem.

If exposure continues for a long time, then the symptoms can become progressively worse with increasingly severe attacks of asthma. Once asthma is established then attacks may be triggered by such things as tobacco smoke, cold air and physical exertion. Such attacks can continue years after exposure to the sensitiser has ceased.

It has been estimated by the Labour Force Survey that 20,000 people believe they suffer from work-related asthma with a further 5,000 believing that their asthma has been made worse by work. The HSE has sponsored research into occupational asthma via a body known as SWORD (Surveillance of Work-related and Occupational Respiratory Disease). SWORD collects data relating to new occurrences of occupational asthma which is estimated to be at over 1,000 new cases each year. Researchers at SWORD believe that these statistics are the "tip of an iceberg" as the study only includes those sufferers examined by occupational health and chest physicians. This is likely therefore to be an under-estimate.

As described in the first section of this unit, in addition to respiratory sensitisers, skin sensitisation leading to allergic dermatitis can also occur.

Aspergillus is a mould or fungi that can cause respiratory sensitisation. As previously discussed, the mould is present in hay that has been packed when slightly damp. When dried out and moved the fungal spores become airborne and can be inhaled. The allergic effect is in the alveoli region of the lungs where there is swelling from fluid in the tissue. This causes the sufferer to have difficulty with breathing. The symptoms become progressively worse at each subsequent exposure. Aspergillus causes Extrinsic Allergic Alveolitis, otherwise known as Farmer's Lung.

B6.2 - Assessment and control of risk

Biological risks

OCCUPATIONAL GROUPS AT RISK

Occupational groups at risk of illness through biological agents are many and varied:

- Health care workers, dentists, laboratory workers, custodial and emergency service workers, police, fire ambulance, paramedics, street cleaners who may come into contact with contaminated needles and other sharps that could be contaminated with the Hepatitis B virus and/or HIV.
- Farm workers and others who may be involved with feeding animals may come into contact with aspergilla.

- Anyone who handles animal hides may come into contact with anthracis, i.e. dock workers, leather tanning workers, carpet makers.
- Workers in contact with cooling towers, showers or other areas where water may form an aerosol may inhale droplets contaminated with Legionella.
- Anyone who works with animals is at risk from a zoonotic disease: vets, veterinary nurses, abattoir workers, grooms.
- Laboratory workers who work with any of the biological agents.
- Workers who come into contact with rats or areas in which rats have been: sewer workers, warehouse workers, farmers, operatives in the food industries, and cleaners who may come into contact with Leptospira.
- Farm workers who drink unpasteurised milk may be at risk from Brucella.

INTENTIONAL WORK

Where the work intentionally involves biological agents, for example, with the development of vaccines or purposely infecting animals for research, the employer must ensure an assessment of the risks to health is carried out. This will involve knowing the group that the agent belongs to and ensuring the controls are appropriate to that group. If the agent is modified so it is more hazardous than the named agent on the Approved List (approved by the HSC), it should be classified as though it were in a higher group.

OPPORTUNISTIC INFECTION

Infection may develop from work, where the biological agent is present by chance or is present because that is the environment in which it exists. For example, an employee does not have to work with the Leptospira bacterium to become infected. It may be present in the working environment because that is the habitat of the rats that carry the bacteria. The possible presence of biological agents that can cause infection must be part of the risk assessment, e.g. the presence of Legionella where water may be atomised.

Opportunist infection may occur in vulnerable people, i.e. people who are taking immuno-suppressant drugs. Where the immune system is suppressed by drugs such as steroids, it cannot fight off the bacteria and viruses that attack. Also, anti-biotics taken for certain infections will kill off the friendly bacteria and allow other pathogens to attack. For example, following a course of anti-biotics, the depletion of the friendly bacteria will allow the fungus Candida albicans to attack and cause infection, i.e. thrush. Normally, Candida albicans is present, but the friendly bacteria keep it in check.

These are all issues that need to be considered in the biological agents' risk assessment.

The role of diagnostic laboratories

For most of the attacks on the body by biological agents, the body responds with the immune system. This, in the majority of cases, works very well, but occasionally the system becomes overwhelmed. The body develops flu-like symptoms and unless other infections are considered, the usual treatment for flu will be followed: keep warm, rest, plenty of fluids. However, if it is a different pathogen causing the illness and it goes on unchecked, damage could occur to the major organs of the body, e.g. the liver from HBV, or death could result. Where the possibility of certain pathogens are present or where it is known they are present, a sample of blood could be sent off to the diagnostic laboratory to identify the particular pathogen and then decide on the course of action. The quicker the diagnosis, the more likely the treatment will work.

Workers in diagnostic laboratories are in the position of working with a wide range of pathogens and need strict control measures so they do not become infected.

THE ROLE OF RISK ASSESSMENT

Assessment and control strategies

Biological agents are classified according to the level of risk of infection:

Group 1 - unlikely to cause human disease;

Group 2 - can cause human disease and may be a hazard to employees; it is unlikely to spread to the community and there is usually effective prophylaxis or treatment available;

Group 3 - can cause severe human disease and may be a serious hazard to employees; it may spread to the community, but there is usually effective prophylaxis or treatment available;

Group 4 - causes severe human disease and is a serious hazard to employees; it is likely to spread to the community and there is usually no effective prophylaxis or treatment available.

Risk assessment must be carried out according to the general requirement of regulation 6 of the COSHH Regulations 2002. If the work to be carried out exposes employees to any biological agent, the employer must take into account the group into which that agent is classified. *See also - Relevant Statutory Provisions - Element B11 - COSHH, Schedule 3 (Regulation 7) Biological Agents.*

An assessment should include consideration of:

- The biological agents that may be present.
- What hazard groups they belong to.
- What form they are in, e.g. may form spores or cysts that are resistant to disinfection, or in the development cycle a form may be dependent on an intermediate host.
- The diseases they may cause.
- How and where they are present and how they are transmitted.
- The likelihood of exposure and consequent disease (including the identification of susceptible workers, e.g. Immuno-compromised).
- Whether there can be substitution by a less hazardous agent.
- Control measures and minimisation of numbers exposed.
- Monitoring procedures.
- Health surveillance.

The selection of control measures for biological agents should take into account that there are no exposure limits for them. Exposure may have to be reduced to levels that are at the limit of detection.

If exposure cannot be prevented, then it should be controlled by the following measures, which can be applied according to the results of the assessment:

- Keep as low as possible the number of people exposed or likely to be exposed.
- Design work processes and engineering controls to prevent or minimise the release of biological agents into the workplace.
- Display the biohazard sign and any other relevant warning signs.
- Draw up plans to deal with accidents involving biological agents.
- Specify appropriate decontamination and disinfection procedures.
- Arrange the means for safe collection, storage and disposal of contaminated waste, including safe and identifiable containers, after suitable treatment where necessary.
- Arrange for the safe movement of biological agents within the workplace.
- State procedures for taking, handling and processing samples.
- Provide collective protection where possible and individual protection otherwise, e.g. PPE.
- Provide vaccines for those not immune.
- Provide washing and toilet facilities.
- Prohibit eating, drinking, smoking and the application of cosmetics in the workplace.

There are special control measures for health and veterinary care facilities and for laboratories, animal rooms and industrial processes. **(See the end of this Element for an extract taken from General COSHH ACOP/Carcinogens ACOP/Biological Agents ACOP - Control of Substances Hazardous to Health 2002).**

Controls for intentional work should be chosen from these lists, with the minimum containment level being: level 2 for handling Group 2 biological agents, level 3 for Group 3 and level 4 for Group 4.

Level 2 is the minimum for laboratories which do not intentionally work with biological agents, but handle materials where there exists uncertainties about the presence of a Group 2, 3, or 4 biological agents. Level 3 or 4, where appropriate, should be used in unintentional work if the employer knows or suspects such a containment level is necessary.

Implementing risk control measures

RISK CONTROL MEASURES IN RELATION TO THE HIERARCHY OF CONTROL

In the control of occupational health hazards many approaches are available, the use of which depends upon the severity and nature of the hazard. The principal control strategies are outlined below.

ERADICATION/ELIMINATION

This involves the eradication or elimination of a hazard by design or specification and consists of hazard prevention and control features.

This represents an extreme form of control and is appropriately used where high risk is present. It is usually achieved through the prohibition of use of these substances or not carrying out the work that involves their use. However, if the work with the micro-organisms is intentional, it would not make sense to eliminate them. Care must be taken to ensure that discarded stock is safely disposed of and that controls are in place to prevent their re-entry, even as a sample or for research. If this level of control is not achievable then another must be selected.

REDUCED VIRULENCE

During research, pathogens may be genetically modified to be less virulent and still allow the research to continue. For example, Salmonella typhimurium (which causes gastro-enteritis) could be made less virulent, but still have the necessary properties to be used in the Ames Test for signs of a substance having mutagenic properties. However, if the virulent properties are the purpose of the research, then this control is not suitable.

CHANGE OF WORK METHOD TO MINIMISE OR SUPPRESS GENERATION OF AEROSOLS

Aerosols or finely suspended droplets containing pathogens may become airborne. The best way to suppress or minimise aerosols is to change the work method so aerosols are not produced or if they are, they are contained. Aerosols carrying micro-organisms can also be scrubbed (passed through water and disinfectant or biocide curtains to kill the pathogens). Local exhaust ventilation can be used to remove the aerosol at source. Processes such as aeration are used in effluent treatment and it is usual to have remote positioning for this treatment.

ISOLATION AND SEGREGATION

If a biological agent cannot be eliminated or replaced, another option is to enclose it completely to prevent harm to workers, e.g. handling substances in a glove box. A dedicated room away from the general work area with its own air movement and ventilation system, completely isolated from all other systems could also be used. Any accidental loss of containment within the room would not then have an impact on the general working area.

A relatively simple process is to restrict the numbers exposed to the hazard. This technique is used when dealing with highly infectious diseases either in patient treatment or for purposes of research. The fewer the people who come into contact, the better. The ones who are allowed to work with the infectious patient may also be protected by vaccine, where one exists.

CONTAINMENT/ENCLOSURE

This strategy is based on the containment or enclosure of an offending agent to prevent its free movement in the working environment. It may take a number of forms, e.g., pipelines, closed conveyors, laboratory fume cupboards.

VENTILATION

Ventilation may be by natural or mechanical means. Extract ventilation is an important control strategy in the prevention of occupational disease from exposure to biological agents..

Reg 7(1) of the COSHH Regulations 2002, states:

"Every employer shall ensure that the exposure of his employees to substances hazardous to health is either prevented, or where this is not reasonably practicable, adequately controlled".

Depending upon the severity of the hazard and nature of the workplace, the employer must introduce some form of control measures.

HEPA filters

High Efficiency Particulate Air (HEPA) filters are available to be used as a positive pressure clean air re-circulating system in clinics, waiting rooms, hospital emergency rooms and other confined areas or as a partial or complete exhausting system to create a negative pressure isolation room for possible use with patients known or suspected of having tuberculosis, SARS or other infectious diseases.

Designs are available with powerful motor/blower which can deliver up to 800 cubic feet per minute (CFM) or 1360 m3/hr to provide a large number of room air changes per hour to minimize the spread of airborne diseases to patients and healthcare workers.

When used as a negative pressure unit, the air passing through the HEPA filter may be cleansed of 99.99% of particles as small as 0.3 micron.

SHARPS CONTROL

Biological agents can be passed directly into the body by injection. They can be injected by needles or other sharp objects, which form part of the work equipment. Injection can also occur when glass gets broken and is handled. Careful disposal of sharps is necessary to prevent accidental injection. Sharps containers should be provided and used so needles and syringes are not left lying about.

Care must be taken when dealing with the possibility that someone may come into contact with discarded needles. Needle stick injuries can give rise to infections by agents such as hepatitis B, hepatitis C, HIV, malaria and syphilis. A recent study has identified 22 causing agents which could be transmitted by means of sharps.

Sharps should be handled as little as possible and disposed of in a special container, which should be lidded.

IMMUNISATION

How vaccines work

Disease causing organisms have two distinct effects on the body. The first effect is very obvious; we feel ill, exhibiting a variety of symptoms such as fever, vomiting and diarrhoea. The disease-causing organism also induces an immune response in the infected host. As the response increases in strength over time, the infectious agents are slowly reduced in number until symptoms disappear and recovery is complete.

The host recovery occurs because the disease causing organisms contain proteins called "antigens" which stimulate the body's immune response. The main effect of antigens is to cause the body to produce proteins called "antibodies." The proteins bind to the disease causing organisms and cause dysfunction and eventual destruction. At the same time, "memory cells" are produced in an immune response. Memory cells are cells which remain in the blood stream, sometimes for the life span of the host, ready to initiate a quick protective immune response against subsequent infections with the particular disease causing agent which induced their production. This response is often so rapid that infection doesn't develop and the host is unaware.

Vaccines exist for protection against some of the occupational diseases caused by biological agents, but certainly not all. There is a vaccine available that offers some protection against Hepatitis B and one for Leptospira, but that is not always available.

There are a number of vaccines available for those who intentionally work with certain bacteria and viruses, such as the TB vaccine and protection against malaria.

DECONTAMINATION AND DISINFECTION

Should be carried out according to COSHH Regulations 2002. For example, decontamination and washing facilities and disinfection should be carried out for all containment levels, i.e. 2, 3 and 4. **(See also - Relevant Statutory Provisions - Element B11 - extract taken from General COSHH ACOP/Carcinogens ACOP/Biological Agents ACOP - COSHH 2002).**

Protective clothing and personal protective equipment may need to be decontaminated and disinfected as will equipment that is used. All surfaces: walls, floors, ceilings, tables, ventilation ducts may also need to be dealt with. Changing areas and showering facilities will need decontamination and disinfection, and regular swabs taken to ensure the cleaning is working.

NOTIFICATION REQUIREMENTS TO HSE

Unless notification has been made under the Genetically Modified Organisms (Contained Use) Regulations, then notice of at least 20 working days must be given of an intention to use for the first time, an agent or agents from a particular group other than Group 1. The actual agents should be identified if they are listed as:

Any Group 3 or 4 agent.

The following Group 2 agents:

- Bordetella pertussis.
- Corynebacterium diphtheriae.
- Neisseria meningitidis.

The above requirements do not apply if an employer only provides a diagnostic service and will not involve a process likely to propagate, concentrate or otherwise increase the risk of exposure to that agent.

It is also necessary to inform HSE if any Group 4 biological agent is to be consigned to different premises. This should be at least 30 days in advance.

The role of specific biological control measures

EFFLUENT AND WASTE DISPOSAL (CONTROLLED)

Should be handled according to the containment measures for health and veterinary care facilities, laboratories and animal rooms and the containment measures for industrial processes listed in COSHH Regulations 2002. *(See also - Relevant Statutory Provisions - Element B11 - extract taken from General COSHH ACOP/Carcinogens ACOP/Biological Agents ACOP - Control of Substances Hazardous to Health 2002).*

PERSONAL HYGIENE MEASURES

Personal hygiene to prevent spread of disease will require segregation of domestic and work clothing and, as a minimum, regular hand washing (prescribed technique for a minimum of 30 seconds). Normally workers will use an apron which is impervious and disposable. Where it is necessary to take increased precautions it may be necessary to shower, before and at the end of a shift or exposure period. Eating, drinking smoking should not be allowed in exposed areas.

PERSONAL PROTECTIVE EQUIPMENT

Where personal protective equipment (including protective clothing) is provided to meet the requirements of COSHH relating to biological agents, the employer must ensure that it is: properly stored in a well defined place; checked and cleaned at suitable intervals; and repaired or replaced before it is used again if it is found to be defective.

If there is a possibility that PPE may be contaminated by biological agents, it should be removed on leaving the work area and kept apart from uncontaminated clothing and equipment. Contaminated equipment should be decontaminated and cleaned or destroyed.

BIOHAZARD SIGNS

COSHH Regulations 2002 Part IV Biohazard sign specify:

"The biohazard sign required by Regulation 7(6) (a) shall be in the form shown below ..."

Figure B6-1: Biohazard sign.

Source: Stocksigns.

BASELINE TESTING AND HEALTH SURVEILLANCE

This is necessary to assess employees' immunity before or after vaccination. If there is an indication that infection has occurred, then it may be appropriate to take specimens in order to attempt to isolate infectious agents. If someone shows signs of illness which could be due to exposure at work, then others who may have been exposed should be placed under surveillance.

People may show a susceptibility to microbial allergens and immunological testing may show which agents are responsible. All workers exposed to respiratory sensitisers of biological origin should be under surveillance. The level of surveillance should be related to the risk identified in the risk assessment.

EXAMPLES OF CONTROL MEASURES IN AN OCCUPATIONAL CONTEXT

Hospitals

There are two main issues which hospitals and clinics need to manage effectively:

- Patient infection.
- Patient staff cross infection.

Hygiene standards should be such that the cross infection of patients and staff is prevented or kept to a minimum. Patients will often be at risk from everyday illness such as the common cold which will be introduced on a daily basis from both staff and visiting members of the public. It is very difficult to protect against the introduction of such common infections for the general patient population. High risk patients are therefore segregated from the general population into isolation wards. Here precautions are taken to ensure both patient and staffs are segregated to prevent cross infection. A number of procedures are used depending on the risk factors. From basic hygiene, washing of hands, equipment, such as stethoscope and thermometers issued on personal patient basis, when dealing with the medium risk level. Where there is potential for significant risk additional safeguards may be required in addition to hygiene or equipment issue. With highly virulent infections, it may be necessary to have sealed wards, with airlock access and negative pressure air supply. Staff may be required to wear bio body suits (staff wear total protection with a controlled air feed line). Provision of suitable (stainless steel work surfaces, tiled floors, walls etc.) cleanable surfaces, rigorous sterilisation programme and swab testing following cleaning.

(See also - Relevant Statutory Provisions - Element B11 - extract taken from General COSHH ACOP/Carcinogens ACOP/Biological Agents ACOP - Control of Substances Hazardous to Health 2002).

Laboratory work

There are many factors to consider when scaling up production from the laboratory to commercial quantities. A bacteriological process, such as yeasts, moulds and fungi used in a fermentation process, may not be suitable for scaling up if it presents a major health risk to workers and the general public. While these may be controllable on the small scale, the problems associated with their large scale use can mean such a substantial investment in containment and other safety equipment that the process would be uneconomic.

An additional factor to take into account is the plant may be expected to run for long periods of time, which does not usually happen in the laboratory. Most experiments are carried out using glass (in vitro) and are usually carefully monitored and controlled. Many reaction vessels are made from materials such as mild or stainless steel, which can corrode and become difficult to decontaminate. This can be mitigated by the use of steel clad with titanium or glass-lined metal reaction vessels. These provide a corrosion resistant surface, which is relatively easy to clean when decontamination is necessary. Ease of decontamination can be critical where only small amounts of product are required; the same vessels may be used for several processes thereby necessitating frequent cleaning. While laboratory experiments are usually closely monitored, this is more difficult in large-scale production.

(See also - Relevant Statutory Provisions - Element B11 - extract taken from General COSHH ACOP/Carcinogens ACOP/Biological Agents ACOP - Control of Substances Hazardous to Health 2002).

Animal houses

Containment measures as with hospitals will be dependent on the risk; good guidance is provided in the in the COSHH ACOP Part II, Containment measures for health and veterinary care facilities, laboratories and animal rooms.

(See also - Relevant Statutory Provisions - Element B11 - extract taken from General COSHH ACOP/Carcinogens ACOP/Biological Agents ACOP - Control of Substances Hazardous to Health 2002).

PART II - CONTAINMENT MEASURES FOR HEALTH AND VETERINARY CARE FACILITIES, LABORATORIES AND ANIMAL ROOMS

Containment measures	Containment levels		
	2	3	4
The workplace is to be separated from any other activities in the same building.	No	Yes	Yes
Input air and extract air to the workplace are to be filtered using HEPA or equivalent.	No	Yes, on extract air	Yes, on input air and double on extract air
Access is to be restricted to authorised persons only.	Yes	Yes	Yes, via air-lock key procedure
The workplace is to be sealable to permit disinfection.	No	Yes	Yes
Specified disinfection procedures.	Yes	Yes	Yes
The workplace is to be maintained at an air pressure negative to atmosphere.	No, unless mechanically ventilated	Yes	Yes
Efficient vector control, e.g. rodents and insects.	Yes, for animal containment	Yes, for animal containment	Yes
Surfaces impervious to water and easy to clean.	Yes, for bench	Yes, for bench and floor (and walls for animal containment)	Yes, for bench, floor, walls and ceiling
Surfaces resistant to acids, alkalis, solvents, disinfectants.	Yes, for bench	Yes, for bench and floor (and walls for animal containment)	Yes, for bench, floor, walls and ceiling
Safe storage of biological agents.	Yes	Yes	Yes, secure storage
An observation window, or alternative, is to be present, so that occupants can be seen.	No	Yes	Yes
A laboratory containing its own equipment.	No	Yes, so far as is reasonably practicable	Yes
Infected material, including any animal, is to be handled in a safety cabinet or isolator or other suitable containment.	Yes, where aerosol produced	Yes, where aerosol produced	Yes (Class III cabinet)
Incinerator for disposal of animal carcases.	Accessible	Accessible	Yes, on site

In this Part of this Schedule, 'Class III cabinet' means safety cabinet defined as such in British Standard 5726: Part I: 1992, or unit offering an equivalent level of operator protection as defined in British Standard 5726: Part I: 1992.

PART III - CONTAINMENT MEASURES FOR INDUSTRIAL PROCESSES

Containment measures	Containment levels		
	2	**3**	**4**
1. Viable micro-organisms should be contained in a system which physically separates the process from the environment (closed system).	Yes	Yes	Yes
2. Exhaust gases from the closed system should be treated so as to -	Minimise release	Prevent release	Prevent release
3. Sample collection, addition of materials to a closed system and transfer of viable micro-organisms to another closed system, should be performed as to -	Minimise release	Prevent release	Prevent release
4. Bulk culture fluids should not be removed from the closed system unless the viable micro-organisms have been -	Inactivated by validated means	Inactivated by validated chemical or physical means	Inactivated by validated chemical or physical means
5. Seals should be designed so as to -	Minimise release	Prevent release	Prevent release
6. Closed systems should be located within a controlled area -	Optional	Optional	Yes, and purpose-built
biohazard signs should be posted;	Optional	Yes	Yes
access should be restricted to nominated personnel only,	Optional	Yes	Yes, via air-lock
personnel should wear protective clothing;	Yes, work clothing	Yes	Yes, a complete change
decontamination and washing facilities should be provided for personnel	Yes	Yes	Yes
personnel should shower before leaving the controlled area;	No	Optional	Yes
effluent from sinks and showers should be collected and inactivated before release;	No	Optional	Yes
the controlled area should be adequately ventilated to minimise air contamination;	Optional	Optional	Yes
the controlled area should be maintained at an air pressure negative to atmosphere;	No	Optional	Yes
input and extract air to the controlled area should be HEPA filtered;	No	Optional	Yes
the controlled area should be designed to contain spillage of the entire contents of closed system;	Optional	Yes	Yes
the controlled area should be sealable to permit fumigation.	No	Optional	Yes
7. Effluent treatment before final discharge.	Inactivated by validated means	Inactivated by validated chemical or physical means	Inactivated by validated physical means

This page is intentionally blank

Physical agents 1 - noise and vibration

Learning outcomes

On completion of this element, candidates should be able to:

B7.1 Explain the basic physical concepts relevant to noise, its effects on the individual and the assessment and control of exposure.

B7.2 Explain the basic physical concepts relevant to vibration, its effects on the individual and the assessment and control of exposure.

Content

Relevant statutory provisions

Control of Noise at Work Regulations (CNWR) 2005

Control of Vibration at Work Regulations (CVWR) 2005

This page is intentionally blank

B7.1 - Noise

Physics

DEFINITION OF NOISE

Any signal that does not convey useful information. Noise is also defined as unwanted sound. Some sounds can cause annoyance or stress and loud noise can cause damage to the ear.

BASIC CONCEPTS

Sound

Sound may be defined as variations in **pressure** through any medium (air, water) which can be detected by the human ear.

Wavelength

- **Wavelength (λ)** - is the distance covered during one complete cycle (i.e. the distance between wave peaks).

The relationship between wavelength and frequency is described by the formula:

$$\text{Wavelength} = \frac{\text{speed of sound}}{\text{frequency}}$$

Thus, as the speed of sound in air at normal temperature is 344 metres per second. A frequency of 20 Hz = a wavelength of 17 m and 20 kHz = 0.017 m.

The loudness of a sound is related to the amplitude of the pressure change. The larger the pressure change, the louder the sound.

The **intensity** of a sound describes the rate of flow of sound energy which is measured in watts per square metre (W/m^2). Thus high intensity sound has more energy than low intensity sound.

The highest sound intensity that does not produce a sensation of pain is about one watt per square metre - the threshold of pain. The lowest sound intensity that the ear can perceive, at a frequency of 1000 Hz, is one million millionth of a watt per square metre (1×10^{-12} W/m^2) - the threshold of hearing. Thus the range of 'normal intensity is: 1/1,000,000,000,000 - 1 W/m^2

The 12 orders of magnitude difference between the highest and lowest levels of intensity represents a vast, unmanageable scale (a million). This range equates to a pressure range of between 20 micropascals (µPa) to 20 Pa. In most industrial situations sound pressures constantly change, thus the average sound pressure measured by SPL meters is the root mean square or **rms** value.

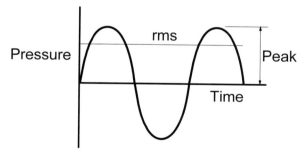

Figure B7-1: rms and peak levels of a sound wave.

Source: ACT.

Amplitude

Amplitude is important in the description of a wave phenomenon such as light or sound. In general, the greater the amplitude of the wave, the more energy it transmits (e.g., a brighter light or a louder sound).

Frequency

Frequency (f) - the number of cycles that the wave travels per second, or Hertz (Hz). The normal range of human hearing is 20 - 20,000 Hz in a young healthy adult. Sound may be of a single frequency (i.e. a pure tone such as a tuning fork) but are usually a complex mixture of frequencies. **Broad band noise** is the term often used to describe industrial noise because it contains a wide mixture of frequencies.

Intensity

Intensity (W/m^2) - describes the rate of flow of sound energy. High intensity sound has more energy than low intensity sound. Intensity is measured in watts per square metre (W/m^2).

Pitch

The frequency of the sound is related to **Pitch**. High frequency sound such as that caused by steam escaping from a valve would be described as high pitch whereas low frequency noise like that emitted from a passing lorry or bus would have a low pitch.

THE DECIBEL (dB)

Is the unit used to measure the loudness of sound. It is one tenth of a Bel (named for A. G. Bell), but the larger unit is rarely used. The decibel is a measure of sound intensity as a function of power ratio, with the difference in decibels between two sounds being given by $dB = 10 \log_{10}(P_1/P_2)$, where P_1 and P_2 are the power levels of the two sounds.

A-WEIGHTING (dB (A))

The human ear can hear sound over a range of frequencies, from 20 Hz up to approximately 20000 Hz (20 kHz). However, the ear does not hear the same at all frequencies; it naturally reduces (attenuates) low frequencies and very high frequencies. To take account of the response of the ear measured sound levels are usually 'A weighted'. 'A' weighted is a weighting added to a noise meter reading (by electronic filters) to represent the way the ear hears sound of different frequencies, hence the term dB (A). The majority of measurements are made in terms of dB (A), although there are other weightings that are used in some circumstances.

The range of frequencies that we encounter is often divided into Octave Bands. 'A' noise can be measured in each octave band and these levels can be used when assessing the attenuation of hearing protectors, or when diagnosing noise problems.

THE APPLICATION OF THE BASIC CONCEPTS OF SOUND PHYSICS TO THE EVALUATION OF OCCUPATIONAL NOISE

The significance of logarithmic scales

In order to make the scale more manageable, the logarithmic **Bel** (B) scale was devised. 1 Bel represents a change in sound energy corresponding to tenfold change in energy. Thus logarithms to the base 10 are used ($\log_{10}$) which is denoted by the term log. If the threshold of hearing is taken as the basis for the scale (i.e. as a reference value) then the sound pressure level (in Bels) will equate to:

$$SPL = \log(P^2_{rms} / P^2_{ref}) \, B$$

where P_{rms} is the measured intensity; and

P_{ref} is the reference intensity (20 μPa or 2×10^{-5} Pa)

The Bel forms too narrow a scale, i.e. it would only be 0, 1, 2, 3, …12 for the range of human hearing. For a more useful range the Bel is divided into 10 parts to give the decibel (dB). This makes the range 0 – 120. In order to convert the above equation to dB, it becomes:

$$SPL = 10 \log(P^2_{rms} / P^2_{ref}) \, dB \qquad \text{under the rules of logarithms, taking out the square terms this becomes:}$$

$$SPL = 20 \log(P_{rms} / P_{ref}) \, dB$$

Thus the threshold of hearing:

$$SPL = 20 \log(2 \times 10^{-5} / 2 \times 10^{-5}) \, dB = 20 \log(1) \qquad \textbf{\textit{= 0dB}}$$

as the log of 1 = 0, the threshold of pain (about 20 Pa):

$$SPL = 20 \log(20 / 2 \times 10^{-5}) \, dB \qquad \textbf{\textit{= 120 dB}}$$

An increase of three decibels, anywhere along the scale, denotes a **doubling** of intensity. The human ear is, however, a poor SPL meter. One would expect that upon doubling the sound pressure one would double the loudness. However, this is not the case. To obtain a subjective doubling of the loudness, the sound pressure level needs to be increased by about 10 dB.

The normal, young, healthy human ear can detect sound in a range of between 20 Hz to 20,000 Hz. The ear is most sensitive to frequencies of between 1000-4000 Hz. This varies from individual to individual but corresponds to about 120 dB (or 20 Pa). Above and below these frequency limits the sound intensity of the threshold of hearing changes. *(See - figure B7-2)*

The threshold at 100 Hz is some 100 times greater, i.e. 20 dB, than the threshold at 1000 Hz. If a low frequency (say 100 Hz) sound and a middle frequency sound (say 1000 Hz) of equal intensity were played alternately the low frequency would sound much quieter.

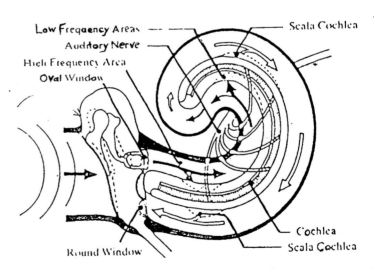

Figure B7-2: The propagation of sound in a healthy ear.   *Source: Ambiguous.*

The ear is most responsive to sound energy in the middle frequencies (say 500 Hz to 4000 Hz). Sounds of higher and lower frequencies need to have more energy in them before the ear can detect them.

The A weighting curve shown in the following diagram mimics the sensitivity of the human ear. The ear is less sensitive to low frequency sound and is non-linear in its assessment of loudness. As previously indicated, the ear is most sensitive to sounds around 5,000 Hz.

Most measurements of sound are made with instruments that attempt to respond in a similar way to the human ear. Measurements with meters which have this type of frequency response are said to be 'A'-weighted. The measured noise levels are given the abbreviation **dB (A)**.

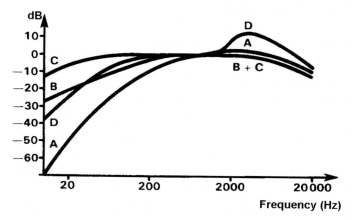

Figure B7-3: 'A', 'B', 'C' and 'D' weighting curves.   *Source: Ambiguous.*

Other terms used include dB (B) and dB(C) and dB (Lin):

dB(B)   not so much weighting (attenuation) at low frequencies as dB (A), sometimes used to measure music noise with a 'bass' beat.

dB(C)   weighting only at very low and high frequencies, used to measure 'peak' noise. This should not be used for measuring peak noise levels which have energy components at both the high and low frequency ends of the spectrum (0-20 Hz and greater than 15 kHz).

dB(Lin)   no weighting at all, also used to measure 'peak' noise.

Note that the "D" scale was previously used in aircraft noise measurements.

It is important to note that the use of the term dB indicates an unweighted linear measurement which is sometimes denoted by the term dB (Lin); however, this is not strictly necessary. The expression "dB" should not be substituted for dB (A).

Addition of combined sounds (equal and unequal)

Calculating the effects of combined noise levels can be achieved by using the rules of logarithms. An increase of three decibels represents a doubling in intensity. Thus if *two* machines, each producing 84 dB (A), are switched on then the expected noise level for a worker would be:

84 dB (A) + 84 dB (A) = 87 dB (A)

If *four* of these machines are switched on then the intensity will increase to:

87 dB (A) + 87 dB (A) = 90 dB (A).

Although this technique can be used for direct multiples (i.e. 2, 4, 8, 16 etc.), it cannot be used to calculated the intensity of say 3, 5, or 6 machines. This can be calculated by first converting to Bels - (e.g. 84 dB (A) = 8.4 Bels), and then using the formula:

SPL   = $\text{Log} (10^s \times n)$ B (A)

where s is the noise level and n is the number of equal intensity level sources.

The noise level for five of these machines (84 dB (A) each) can be calculated by:

SPL   = $\text{Log} (10^{8.4} \times 5)$ B (A)
             =   9.099 B (A)
             =   91 dB (A)

Where there are noise sources of differing levels, then this can be calculated using the formula:

SPL = $\text{Log} (10^{s1} + 10^{s2} + 10^{s3} + \ldots 10^{sn})$

where sn = the noise level in bels.

Thus if four machines produce noise levels at a worker's position of 91 dB(A), 93 dB(A), 89 dB(A) and 86 dB(A) respectively when each is operated in turn with the other three switched off then the calculated noise level would be:

SPL = $\text{Log} (10^{9.1} + 10^{9.3} + 10^{8.9} + 10^{8.6})$ B (A)
        = 9.648 B (A)
        = 96.48 dB (A)
        = 96.5 dB (A)

NOISE RATING CURVES

Source: Safety at Work, Fourth Edition, J Ridley.

There are a standard series of Noise Rating (NR) Curves which are stylised forms of the loudness response curves. These NR curves are often used as a criterion for noise control, and as such are internationally accepted. Other criteria may also be encountered such as NC curves (Noise Criteria used in the USA).

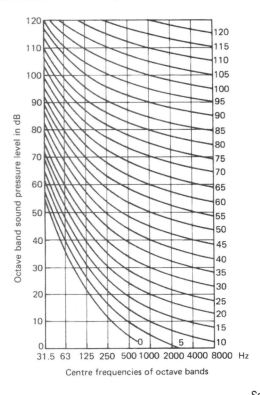

Figure B7-4: Noise rating curves.

Source: Safety at Work, Fourth Edition, J Ridley.

Sound pressure levels measured in octave bands are compared with the curves from which a noise rating (NR) is obtained. The higher frequencies, where the ear is more sensitive, are given heavier noise ratings than the lower frequencies. For example, 30 d(B) on the 4000Hz frequency has an NR of 35, while 30 d(B) on the 250Hz band has an NR of 20. There are European agreed Acceptable NRs, which should not be exceeded and are read off the 1000Hz band (see opposite).

45	General office
50	Office with business machines
60	Light engineering works
70	Heavy engineering works

Effects

PHYSIOLOGICAL EFFECTS OF EXPOSURE TO HIGH NOISE LEVELS

Acute and chronic effects

Causes of deafness include:

1. Sensorineural loss caused by such factors as:

- *Congenital deafness* - associated with the mother's exposure to rubella, flu and some drugs during pregnancy.
- *Ototoxic drugs* - e.g. some antibiotics such as streptomycin, anti-rheumatic drugs and diuretics.
- *Presbycusis* - the normal decline of hearing sensitivity at the higher frequencies as a person ages.

2. Conductive loss such as earwax, blocked Eustachian tube and ruptured ear drum.

3. Central deafness whereby the hearing mechanism is in good condition but the brain does not recognise sounds.

The acute effect of exposure to very high noise levels is acoustic trauma. This involves sudden damage caused by exposure to a burst of very high energy noise (e.g. bomb blasts) which can cause physical rupture of the eardrum and displacement of the ossicles.

4. Occupation deafness can be categorised into two main types which are based on acute and chronic effects respectively:

- *Temporary threshold shift (TTS).* Short periods of exposure to excessive noise levels produce varying degrees of inner ear damage which is initially reversible. This auditory fatigue is known as 'temporary threshold shift' (*TTS*). As its name implies, this type of exposure produces an elevation of the hearing threshold which progressively reduces with time after leaving the excessively noisy environment. The time taken to recover from the temporary threshold shift may be anything from a few minutes to days depending upon the degree of exposure.
- *Permanent threshold shift (chronic).* Permanent damage, known as 'noise induced hearing loss' (*NIHL*), occurs when exposure to excessive noise continues over a long period of time.

The full relationship between temporary threshold shift and noise induced hearing loss is not fully understood. It is possible for a person with noise induced hearing loss to be affected by temporary threshold shift due to exposure to noise but the degree of temporary threshold shift is reduced by the extent of the noise induced hearing loss.

Both the temporary threshold shift and the permanent noise induced hearing loss are frequency dependent insofar as the greatest loss generally occurs at frequencies about one half to one octave higher than the frequency of the noise source. However, noise induced hearing loss generally occurs first in the 4000 Hz octave band. This is commonly known as the *"4k dip"*. If exposure continues over a number of years, the hearing loss at 4000 Hz increases along with losses in lower octave bands. Not everyone develops the same hearing loss when exposed to the same noise. Similarly, not everyone has the same level of threshold - anything up to 20dB deviation from the accepted standard has been noted.

Other conditions are also associated with excessive noise. *Tinnitus* is the internal presence of sound in the ear and may have a number of causes including ear infections and exposure to excessive noise. Sufferers of NIHL often complain of a high-pitched tinnitus, usually intermittent at first, becoming continuous in up to 20% of cases. Tinnitus produces 'phantom' noise in the ear of varying degrees of seriousness.

People with NIHL can also display symptoms of a condition known as loudness *recruitment* whereby the person cannot hear sounds below a certain level and, when sounds rise above this level, 'normal' hearing is suddenly restored and the listener turns the volume down or asks the speaker not to shout.

Damage to the hearing can result in reduced social interaction and a feeling of isolation by the person affected. Medical science cannot currently replace a cochlea and technology such as surgical implants and hearing aids are extremely poor substitutes for normal hearing as they merely magnify sound without correcting distortion. In essence, even relatively moderate hearing damage, can lead to a significant drop in the sufferer's quality of life and all reasonable steps should be taken to prevent impairment.

HEARING LOSS IN AN INDIVIDUAL

Audiometry

Role

Audiometry is a technique for evaluating the degree of hearing loss or impairment over the range of frequencies most necessary for normal conversation (4-6 kHz). For industrial purposes audiometry can be used for the early detection and the assessment of the degree of noise induced hearing loss. Perhaps a less obvious advantage to audiometry is that it can identify those whose individual differences mean that they are not adequately protected even below the action levels.

Principles

The subject is placed in a booth which is soundproof in order to mask ambient noise. Headphones are fitted and tones, which are generated by an audiometer, are played in sequence to each ear in turn. The audiometer generates pure tones at 0.5, 1, 2, 3, 4, 6 and 8 kHz at intensities which are increased in 5 dB steps until the subject responds by pushing a button. The reaction is recorded and a graph generated. Hearing levels from -10 dB to over 90 dB can be recorded.

For obvious reasons it is necessary to ensure that readings are not affected by factors such as earwax and other obstructions, a heavy cold or from temporary threshold shift due having been exposed to high levels of noise.

Measurement and assessment of exposure

INSTRUMENTATION AND MEASUREMENT OF NOISE

Types

Terminology:

Daily Personal Noise Exposure $L_{EP,d}$

Equivalent Continuous Sound Level L_{eq}

L_A	'A' weighted sound pressure level, dB (A).
L_C	'C' weighted sound pressure level, dB(C).
L_{WA}	'A' weighted sound power level, dB (A).
Octave band	a band of frequencies, Hz.

The sound level meter

Noise is measured using a *sound pressure level* meter which works in simple terms by converting pressure variations into an electric signal. This is achieved by capturing the sound with a microphone, pre-amplification of the resultant voltage signal and then processing the signal into the information required dependent on the type of meter (e.g. 'A', 'B', 'C', or 'D' weighting, integrating levels, fast or slow response). The microphone is the most important component within the meter as its sensitivity and accuracy will determine the accuracy of the final reading. Meters can be set to fast or slow response depending on the characteristics of the noise level. Where levels are rapidly fluctuating, rapid measurements are required and the meter should be set to fast time weighting.

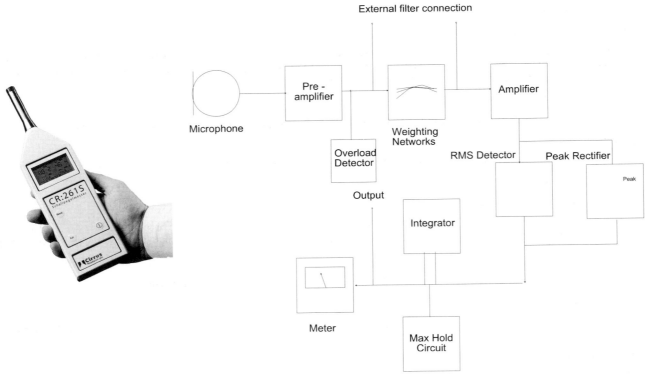

Figure B7-5: Sound level meter.
Source: Cirrus Research plc.

Figure B7-6: The basic integrating sound level meter.

Source: ACT.

There are 4 basic classes of sound level meter:

Type 0   Very accurate meter designed for use as a laboratory reference standard. Has a high standard of tolerance over a wide frequency range. Not generally used in the 'field'.

Type 1   Used in laboratories or in the field where high precision is required.

Type 2   General field meter.

Type 3   Basic level indicator which could be used to establish if noise limits were being exceeded. The least accurate type of noise survey meter.

The instrument used for noise surveys should be at least a type 2 (or class 2) sound level meter and should meet at least Class 2 of BS EN ISO 61672-1:2003. Sound level meters should be calibrated using a portable acoustic calibrator which should also be at least class 2. All batteries must be checked before during and after each measurement session. Laboratory calibration should be carried out within the previous two years.

Meters are used to measure the:

- **Sound pressure level (L_p)** - the intensity of sound at a given moment in time at a given position (i.e. the instantaneous level) an unweighted linear measurement db (Lin).
- **Equivalent continuous sound level (L_{Aeq})** - an average measure of intensity of sound over a reference period usually the period of time over which the measurement was taken. Measured in db (A). As the intensity and spacing of the noise levels usually vary with time, an integrating meter is used. This meter automatically calculates the L_{Aeq} by summing or integrating the sound level over the measurement period.
- **Peak pressure level** - under the Control of Noise at Work Regulations the peak exposure limit value is 140 dB(C-weighted). Some sound level meters produce peak pressure values for impulsive noise or where a fast time weighting reading exceeds 125 dB (A).

A basic instrument used for noise surveys should be an integrating sound level meter capable of taking readings at:

- A weighted L_{eq}.
- C-weighted maximum peak sound pressure to above 140 dB(C).

An octave band analysis feature together with C-weighted L_{eq} would be needed to assess ear protection and noise control measures. See later section on frequency analysis.

Ideally, **Sound Level Meter** readings should be taken at the subject's ear without any extraneous reflections from the operator, the meter itself or the subject's body. The meter should be either held at arm length or, ideally, mounted on a tripod. In practice mounting on a tripod is rarely achievable in a typical workplace where the subject is moving around - the character of the noise changing as he/she does so. The operator must therefore try to minimise this by careful positioning of the microphone so as to have a clear path between the (appropriate) subject's ear and the source of the noise(s). Due to the physical layout of the workplace or the hazards present this 'ideal' positioning may not be possible. In these cases personal dosimetry may have to be considered

Methodology

Measurement equipment

Draw up a list of required equipment and check batteries, operation and other aspects of the equipment beforehand. Also prepare any necessary power cables, replacement recording paper, pens, batteries and other supplies, and any necessary equipment such as tripods, measures, timers, cameras, writing utensils, field note, transceivers, etc.

Documents

In order to record measurement points and other information at the site, prepare site documents based on maps, etc.

Other

Discuss personnel deployment and measurement processes amongst personnel beforehand.

Precautions in measurement

Records prior to measurement

Record the date and time of measurement, location, weather conditions, personnel names, microphone height, measurement range, frequency compensation of the noise level meter, paper feed speed of the level recorder, and model and manufacturer of equipment.

Wind effect

When measuring noise outdoors, attach a wind prevention screen to the microphone of the noise level meter.

Measurement site

Select a location that is not effected by reverberated sound or subjected to magnetic fields, vibrations, or extreme temperatures or humidity.

Measurement period

Select a time that background noise is stable and there are no other sources possibly effecting measurements. Where the problem source is stable, measurement need last only 2 - 3 min. However, if 'A'-weighted sound pressure level fluctuates greatly, measure for 250 sec or more. If there is background noise from traffic or other source, measure for the aforementioned duration in a period in which those effects are not noticeable. Especially when recording, the longer the recording, the better.

Range setting

Get an idea of A-weighted sound pressure level prior to measurement and then set the full scale with some leeway that accounts for the full measurement time.

With shock signals, the peak of the waveform can go off the scale even though the needle reading (measured value) may not, therefore it is necessary to keep an eye on the overload warning lamp that lights when a waveform peaks. This same precaution is needed for the audio recorder and not just the measuring equipment.

Keeping records during measuring

Using one's own sense of hearing, distinguish between the target sound and other noise and make a record to that effect on the recording paper during measurement. If the measurement environment changes during measurement, record the change in status, the time it occurred and other related information on the recording paper. For example, if a machine stops or someone passes in front of the noise level meter, make a note of the change in status and the time it happened on the recording paper.

Instructions to others

Warn others beforehand not to make sounds while recording noise.

Measurement point records

Differentiate recording points by numbers or other means and mark them on the prepared documents beforehand. Also include the distance from the source, walls, etc. In order to verify the measurement point after measurement, take photographs of the site.

Communications during measurement

If the boundary area cannot be seen from the source, station one person at the source to monitor operation and another person at the measurement point, with the two communicating by transceiver. If a large peak or other special event is detected at the measurement point, the person at the measurement should contact the person monitoring the source and record any useful information that can be reported.

Calibration

When undertaking measurements of noise it is of course essential that the measurement equipment is working properly though the means available to the user to check this are limited. The regular calibration of such equipment is therefore an important requirement though the costs involved can be high. Furthermore it is both inconvenient and undesirable to have measurement equipment away for calibration for long periods of time. Typically, test signals stored on a compact disc are played using a CD player, into an Interface Unit. The interface unit's output provides an electrical signal that is substituted for the measurement microphone on a sound level meter. BS 7580 - Specification for the verification of Sound Level Meters, specifies a limited but sufficient range of tests to verify the accuracy of the measurement instrumentation at various intervals. As a general requirement the standard recommends that verification shall be performed at least every two years. The majority of the test procedures are carried out with an electrical signal substituted for the measurement microphone with a series of test signals being used to assess the performance of the sound level meter in respect of noise, linearity, frequency weightings, time weightings, peak response, RMS accuracy, time averaging, pulse range, sound exposure level and overload indication.

Many of the test signals used to assess performance are complex and are certainly not available to the majority of people involved on a day-to-day basis with the measurement of sound. The test for RMS accuracy for example requires that a reading obtained from a continuous 2kHz sinusoidal signal be compared with that obtained from a sequence of tone bursts consisting of 11 cycles of a 2kHz sine wave repeated 40 times a second and with an amplitude 6.6 dB higher than the continuous signal.

Calculation of $L_{EP,d}$

The daily personal noise exposure is a measure of the noise energy (noise dose) a person receives over the working day (8 hours). $L_{EP,d}$ is numerically the same as the equivalent continuous sound level (L_{eq}) measured over a full shift and normalised to 8 hours. It is the measure of the true average level over 8 hours calculated from the energy dose received over a full working day.

The person carrying out the survey should take representative readings which reflects the operator's working day including the various positions and tasks that he or she will undertake (i.e. 'A' weighted L_{eq} readings). Once these fractional exposures have been taken, then the $L_{EP,d}$ can be determined by either calculation, nomograms or HSE's noise exposure ready reckoner.

Calculating fractional exposures:

Step 1   Determine the fractional noise exposure values (*f*) for each noise exposure, using the formula:

$$f = \frac{t}{8} \, anti \log\left[0.1(L - 90)\right]$$

where t = exposure time in hours

L = 'A' weighted L_{eq}

Step 2   Add together the fractional exposure values to give a total fractional exposure, f_T

Step 3   Determine the daily noise exposure given by:

$L_{EP,d} = 90 + 10 \log f_T$

Example: A person works at a machine for 2 hrs 15 minutes per day. The 'A' weighted L_{eq} is measured at 102 dB(A). The remainder of the day is spent in an area which is below 70 dB(A) - this is low enough to be ignored.

Calculation			
	1	Convert dB(A) to B(A) =	10.2 B(A)
	2	Convert to antilog =	1.58×10^{10}
	3	Multiply by t (duration in hours) =	3.57×10^{10}
	4	Divide by 8 =	4.46×10^{9}
	5	Convert to log =	9.65
	6	Multiply by 10 =	96.5
		LEP,d =	96.5 dB(A)

Note: where there are multiple levels, sum the values for each exposure at step 3.

For exposures at different levels: the HSE ready-reckoner (calculation table) provides a simple way of working out the daily personal noise exposure of employees, based on the level of noise and duration of exposure. Noise exposure points can be used to help prioritise the noise control programme by showing which tasks contribute the most to the overall noise exposure. Tackling these first will have the greatest effect on reducing the personal noise exposure.

The following ready-reckoner (calculation table) and examples have been taken from HSE Guidance on Regulations *Controlling Noise at Work: L108.*

An employee has the following typical work pattern: 5 hours where a 'listening check' suggests the noise level is around 80 dB; 2 hours at a machine for which the manufacturer has declared 86 dB at the operator position (a listening check suggests this is about right); 45 minutes on a task where noise measurements have shown 95 dB to be typical.

	Noise level	Duration	Notes	Exposure points
	80	5 hours	No column for 5 hours, so add together values from 4 and 1 hour columns in row corresponding to 80dB.	16 + 4 = 20
	86	2 hours	Directly from table	32
	95	45 minutes	No column for 45 minutes, so add together values from 30 and 15 minute columns in row corresponding to 95dB.	65 + 32 = 97
			Total noise exposure points	149
			$L_{EP,d}$	86 to 87 dB

Sound pressure level, L_{Aeq} (dB)	Duration of exposure (hours)								
	¼	½	1	2	4	8	10	12
95	32	65	125	250	500	1000		
94	25	50	120	240	400	800		
93	20	40	80	160	320	630		
92	16	32	65	125	250	500	625	
91	12	25	50	100	200	400	500	600
90	10	20	40	80	160	320	400	470
89	8	16	32	65	130	250	310	380
88	6	12	25	50	100	200	250	300
87	5	10	20	40	80	160	200	240
86	1	8	15	32	65	130	160	190
85		6	12	25	50	100	125	150
84		5	10	20	40	80	100	120
83		4	8	16	32	65	80	95
82			6	12	25	50	65	75
81			5	10	20	40	50	60
80			4	8	16	32	40	48
79				6	13	25	32	38
78				5	10	20	25	30
75					5	10	13	15

Total exposure points	Noise exposure $L_{EP,d}$ (dB)
800	94
630	93
500	92
400	91
320	90
250	89
200	88
160	87
130	86
100	85
80	84
65	83
50	82
40	81
32	80
25	79
20	78
16	77

The pattern of noise exposure gives an $L_{EP,d}$ of between 86 and 87 dB. The priority for noise control or risk reduction is the task involving exposure to 95 dB for 45 minutes, since this gives the highest individual noise exposure points.

Figure B7-7: Noise exposure points - Worked example of daily exposure.

Source: HSE, Reducing Noise at Work, L108.

Weekly noise exposure ready-reckoner

The weekly noise exposure level ($L_{EP,w}$) takes account of the daily personal exposures for the number of days worked in a week (up to a maximum of seven days). It may be calculated using the formula given in Schedule 1 Part 2 of the Regulations (CNWR).

	$L_{EP,d}$	Day	Notes	Exposure points
	80	1, 2, 5	Work in general area away from major noise sources.	32 + 32 + 32 = 96
	86	3	Work along side others, including work adjacent to a major noise source.	130
	92	4	Work on equipment that constitutes a major noise source.	500
			Total noise exposure points	726
			$L_{EP,w}$	86 to 87 dB

Daily noise exposure, $L_{EP,d}$	Points							Total exposure points	Weekly noise exposure, $L_{EP,w}$
	Day 1	Day 2	Day 3	Day 4	Day 5	Day 6	Day 7		
95	1000	1000	1000	1000	1000	1000	1000	5000	95
94	800	800	800	800	800	800	800	4000	94
93	630	630	630	630	630	630	630	3200	93
92	500	500	500	500	500	500	500	2500	92
91	400	400	400	400	400	400	400	2000	91
90	320	320	320	320	320	320	320	1600	90
89	250	250	250	250	250	250	250	1300	89
88	200	200	200	200	200	200	200	1000	88
87	160	160	160	160	160	160	160	800	87
86	130	130	130	130	130	130	130	630	86
85	100	100	100	100	100	100	100	500	85
84	80	80	80	80	80	80	80	400	84
83	65	65	65	65	65	65	65	320	83
82	50	50	50	50	50	50	50	250	82
81	40	40	40	40	40	40	40	200	81
80	32	32	32	32	32	32	32	160	80
79	25	25	25	25	25	25	25	130	79
78	20	20	20	20	20	20	20	100	78

Figure B7-8: Weekly noise exposure - Worked example based on HSE table.

Source: HSE, Reducing Noise at Work, L108 and ACT.

In this example the workers work pattern varies significantly during the week and although the worker is exposed to significant noise levels on one of the days when considered as a weekly exposure this is a lot lower. Again the priority for noise control or risk reduction is the tasks on day 4 involving exposure that leads to an $L_{EP,d}$ of 92, since this gives the highest individual noise exposure points.

Observations, methods and results together with details of the instruments used should be accurately recorded. Noise survey reports should be kept at least until the next assessment is made. The survey should be repeated whenever:

- Audiometry results indicate that controls are not working.
- New machinery is introduced.
- Workplace layout and/or processes are redesigned.
- Changes in working patterns occur.

Modifications to machinery are made.

Calculation of Leq

Used to describe noise whose level varies with time. L_{Aeq} is defined as the A-weighted energy average of the noise level, averaged over the measurement period. It can be considered as the notional continuous steady noise level which would have the same total A-weighted acoustic energy as the real fluctuation noise measured over the same period of time. Thus to maintain the L_{Aeq} when the sound pressure level is doubled (increased by three decibels) exposure must be halved.

Noise levels vs. exposure times for an equivalent noise level (L_{Aeq}) of 90 dB(A)	
87	16 hours
90	8 hours
93	4 hours
96	2 hours
99	1 hours
102	0.5 hours
105	0.25 hours

Figure B7-9: Calculation of Leq.

Source: ACT.

Use of frequency analysis

Complex noise can be analysed by examination of its frequency spectrum. This consists of a value of sound pressure level for each frequency or frequency band (i.e. a section of the frequency spectrum). For the purposes of examining industrial noise these bands have a bandwidth of one octave. An octave band is a band where the highest frequency is twice the lowest frequency. The band is denoted by its centre frequency. For example the 1 kHz octave band includes all frequencies between the ranges 707-1414 Hz:

- Lowest frequency (Hz): 707.
- Centre frequency (Hz): 1000.
- Highest frequency (Hz): 1414.

Thus industrial noise can be analysed by carrying out a frequency (or octave) band analysis. Here the components of the noise source are measured (in dB) at eight frequency bands centred at 63Hz, 125Hz, 250Hz, 500 Hz, 1 kHz, 2 kHz, 4 kHz and 8 kHz. The purpose of carrying out such a frequency band analysis is to assess the suitability of ear protection.

Background noise

Background noise may be defined as background sound that is apparent in the room other than the noise source being assessed, stemming from many possible sources such as heating, ventilation, the air-conditioning system, other equipment in the room, exterior sources such as traffic, aircraft noise or neighbours.

When measuring a noise source such as a machine, the level of background noise can have an influence. Obviously the background noise must not be greater (or drown out) than the noise level of interest. For practical purposes the sound pressure level (SPL) of the background noise must be at least 3 dB less than the SPL of interest. A correction level may, however, be required to ensure accuracy. This can be achieved by:

1. Measure total noise with the source running (e.g. a machine).

2. Measure the background noise with the source switched off.

3. Calculate the difference between 1 and 2 above. If this is less than 3 dB then the background noise is too high for accurate measurement. If between 3 and 10 dB then a correction is necessary. No correction is necessary if the difference is greater than 10 dB.

4. Use the chart shown to find the correction factor. The x-axis is the difference value found in step 3. The y-axis gives the correction value.

5. Subtract the correction value from the total reading at step 1. This gives the noise level of the source.

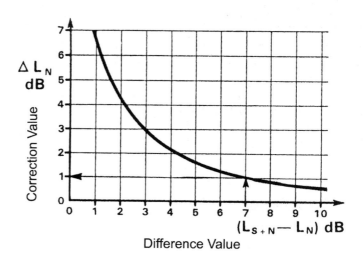

Figure B7-10: Chart for measuring the sound level under conditions of high background noise.
Source: Measuring sound, Brüel and Kjaer.

Effects

Sound is received by the external ear and transmitted along the ear canal, setting the tympanic membrane (the ear drum) in motion. This motion is transmitted via the middle ear bones (the ossicles) to the inner ear, a liquid-filled cavity of complex shape lying within the bony structure of the skull. The ossicles consist of three bones known as the 'hammer', 'anvil' and 'stirrup' which provide a threefold mechanical amplification of the sound. This causes the liquid in a portion of the inner ear, known as the cochlea, to vibrate. The cochlea contains membranes and hair cells which are very sensitive to this vibration. These generate electrical impulses when appropriately stimulated. The impulses are transmitted via the auditory nerve to the brain, where they are decoded into what we recognise as the sensation of sound.

It should be realised that the cochlea can respond to both air conduction (the chain of events described above) and to bone conduction where the sound directly vibrates the skull or the ear canal walls, which in turn stimulate the cochlea. For a person with normal hearing, bone conduction sensitivity is much lower than its corresponding air conduction sensitivity although both paths make a contribution to the overall sound. In practice, this means that even if the auditory canal was completely blocked (and the head enclosed in an acoustic shield), the ear would still receive some sound.

NOISE SURVEYS

Planning and approach

The first step in conducting a noise survey is to establish the extent of individual exposure. Factors can include:

- The identity of employees/persons employed in the area.
- Shift patterns and lengths.
- Working positions.
- Time in positions over the working day/shift.
- Overall noise levels.

The second step is to observe the types and characteristics of the noise within the area and the contributions made by each source (e.g. machine). This may involve switching individual sources on and off and/or observing the effects of different operations on the noise characteristics. This observation will allow the assessor to decide on the type of sound level meter required and form the basis of later recommendations.

Representative measurements should then be taken at each of the identified operator positions. The (calibrated) meter should be positioned as close to the operator's ear as possible with the microphone directed towards the source avoiding any shielding effect or reflections. The aim is to measure the individual's exposure, therefore the meter should follow the operator's head as he or she moves. As previously stated, enough measurements need to be taken in order to accurately estimate the operator's personal daily exposure. Full and accurate details should be noted as measurements are taken.

Figure B7-11: Sound level meter with truck. *Source: Cirrus Research plc.*

The details required would include:

- Noise sources.
- Sound pressure level L_{Aeq}.
- Exposure times.
- Fractional exposures *(for calculating daily noise exposures see the ready-reckoner).*
- Peak SPL dB(C).
- Determining noise exposure

Interpretation and evaluation of results

A noise survey should convey clear, unambiguous, information to the intended recipient who may not be conversant with the terms used. Essential information should include:

- The workplace, areas, jobs or people assessed.
- Measurement locations and durations and any noise control measures being used at the time.
- Daily personal noise exposures ($l_{ep,d}$) where they are above the lower action level.
- Peak noise exposures where they are above the peak action level.
- The sources of noise.
- Any further information necessary to help comply with the reduction of noise exposure.
- The date of assessment.

Additional information which may be added are:

- Details of instruments used - including serial numbers, details of field calibration checks and the dates they were calibrated.
- Detailed field readings and the people, tasks and conditions that readings were taken.
- A detailed plan of the survey area including indications of people and their workstations together with exposure times.
- Details of work patterns where employees move between areas.
- The assessment of and recommendations for existing or new ear protectors as appropriate (i.e. from octave band analysis).
- Recommendations for action.

NOISE ASSESSMENTS

Planning and approach

There is a clear distinction between a noise survey and noise assessment. The former, as outlined above, is essentially a record of noise levels in a noisy area. The purpose of a noise assessment, as required by Regulation 5 of the Control of Noise at Work Regulations (CNWR) 2005, is to:

■ Identify whether people are at risk from noise exposure causing hearing damage.
■ Determine the level of risk, by quantifying daily or weekly personal noise exposure levels.
■ Identify priorities for action in noise reduction or protection.

This demonstrates that an employer has considered:

■ All the factors relating to the risks from noise exposure.
■ The steps which need to be taken to achieve and maintain adequate control of the risks.
■ The need for health surveillance.
■ How any further action plan for noise reduction or protection will be implemented.

An employer is required to conduct a noise assessment when any employee is likely to be exposed to noise at or above the lower exposure action value identified in the Control of Noise at Work Regulations 2005.

Factors to be considered include:

■ Level, type and duration of exposure.
■ Employees or groups of employees whose health is at particular risk, such as those with pre-existing conditions, young people and pregnant women.
■ Any effects from the interaction between noise and the use of toxic substances at work.
■ Any effects from the interaction between noise and vibration.
■ Indirect effects resulting from the interaction between noise and audible warning signals, such as the masking of warning signals by the noise environment or any hearing protection worn.
■ Information supplied by the manufacturers of work equipment.
■ Availability of alternative equipment with lower noise emission.
■ Extension of exposure to noise at the workplace beyond normal working hours, including overtime, rest or lunch breaks.
■ Appropriate information obtained following health surveillance, indicating if noise induced hearing loss is developing.
■ Availability of personal hearing protectors with adequate attenuation characteristics.

The assessment must be conducted by a person with the appropriate level of competence in noise assessment.

Interpretation and evaluation of results

From the noise assessment report the employer should be able to develop an action plan including the immediate measures needed to control noise exposure and the introduction of noise control measures. A strategy would include:

■ Engineering control of existing noisy machines.
■ Modifications to noise transmission paths.
■ Changes in methods of working.

■ The provision of ear protection.
■ Information, instruction and training.
■ Health surveillance.

The noise assessment must be reviewed and updated regularly as part of the employer's ongoing noise-risk management and control programme. Reports should be kept readily available for as long as they are relevant to the premises and to the staff who work there - and at least until the next assessment has been completed. An update will be required if there are any significant changes to the workplace, plant or processes, working hours and after the implementation of noise control measures. In any event, a regular review should be planned to ensure continued effectiveness.

EXPOSURE LIMIT VALUES AND ACTION VALUES

Regulation 4 of The Control of Noise at Work Regulations (CNWR) 2005 sets out the definition of 'daily average noise exposure' as the time weighted average of the levels of noise to which a worker is exposed over an 8 hour working day, taking account of levels of noise and duration of exposure and including impulsive noises. The exposure action values are the levels of exposure to noise at which the employer is required to take certain actions.

	Lower exposure action values	Upper exposure action values	Exposure limit values
Daily or weekly personal noise exposure (A-weighted)	80 dB	85 dB	87 dB
Peak sound pressure (C-weighted).	135 dB	137 dB	140 dB

Figure B7-12: Noise exposure values.

Source: CNWR 2005.

Under regulation 4 of CNWR 2005 if the noise levels in the workplace vary greatly from day to day, then the employer can choose to use weekly noise exposure levels instead of daily noise exposure levels. This is only likely to be appropriate where daily noise exposure on one or two days is at least 5dB higher than other days, or the working week comprises three or fewer days of exposure. Weekly noise exposure level means the average of daily noise exposure levels over a week and normalised to five working days. When using weekly averaging, there must be no increase in risk to health. It is not acceptable to expose employees to very high noise levels for one day without providing hearing protection when using weekly averaging.

Lower exposure action value

Where the daily or weekly exposure level of 80 dB(A) or a peak sound pressure level of 135 dB(C) is likely to be exceeded the employer must make hearing protection available upon request and provide the employees and their representatives with suitable and sufficient information, instruction and training.

This shall include:

- Nature of risks from exposure to noise.
- Organisational and technical measures taken in order to comply.
- Exposure limit values and upper and lower exposure action values.
- Significant findings of the risk assessment, including any measurements taken, with an explanation of those findings.
- Availability and provision of personal hearing protectors and their correct use.
- Why and how to detect and report signs of hearing damage.
- Entitlement to health surveillance.
- Safe working practices to minimise exposure to noise.
- The collective results of any health surveillance in compiled in a form in a format which prevents those results from being identified as relating to a particular person

Upper exposure action value

Where the daily or weekly exposure level of 85dB(A) or a peak sound pressure level of 137 dB(C), the upper exposure action value, is likely to be exceeded the employer - shall provide employees with hearing protection.
In addition the employer will:

- Ensure that the area is designated a hearing protection zone, fitted with mandatory hearing protection signs.
- Ensure access to the area is restricted where practicable.
- So far as reasonably practicable, ensure those employees entering the area wear hearing protection.

The employer must ensure that workers are not exposed to levels above an exposure limit value or if one is exceeded immediately reduce exposure below that level, investigate the reasons and modify measures to prevent a reoccurrence.

Exposure limit value

The exposure limit values are the levels of noise exposure which must not be exceeded. When assessing exposure to ensure limit values are not exceeded, the effect of personal hearing protection provided to the employee can be taken into account. This will depend on the attenuation provided by the hearing protection, it appropriateness for the type of noise and protection use and maintenance.

PERSONAL SAMPLING AND DOSIMETRY

Figure B7-13 Dosemeter microphone.
Source: Controlling noise at work L108 HSE.

The dosemeter

An alternative means of measuring noise, especially where a person is highly mobile or working places where access for measurement is difficult, is a personal sound exposure meter or dosemeter. Dosemeters should therefore only be used in one of two preferred positions (shoulder or head mounted), worn or clipped to the clothing. People selected to wear dosimeters must be given appropriate instruction to ensure results are valid, which includes not interfering with the microphone or instrument during the course of measurements, and limiting their own speech as much as possible as an individual's own voice should not be included in an assessment of their daily personal noise exposure.

Dosemeters do not meet the design specifications for Type 1 Sound Level meters because of the position of the dosemeter. This affects the accuracy of the reading, which will be reduced by reflections from the body. The degree of error will depend on the position of the microphone and the nature and direction of the sound.

Dosemeters should be fitted with an overload indicator, which is triggered when the sound has exceeded the range of the meter. When this happens the level is not integrated and consequently the dose reading will be inaccurate. Readings taken when the overload indicator is triggered should be discarded. Unfortunately the overload indicator can be tripped by factors other than excessive work-place noise. For example:

- Microphone impact including blowing into or shouting into the microphone.
- Momentary tampering (e.g. sudden removal of the microphone cable from the body of the instrument).
- Close proximity of an airline to the microphone.
- Close proximity to a radio transmitter.

Dosemeters are used to measure the total noise dose received over the measurement period, which can be then used to calculate the daily personal exposure level. However for reliability the measurement period is normally several hours, preferably an entire shift to reduce inaccuracies. If a shorter period is sampled than care must be taken to ensure that the result is representative of the full shift exposure. This will require an understanding of the tasks performed and the cycle of those tasks.

One limitation of dosimetry is that while the instrument records the accumulated dose over the measurement period it will not give any information about the causes (sources) of the noise. This will require a separate noise survey investigation.

In addition, any result obtained will only be representative of the role conducted by that individual. Identification of a number of individuals to create a representative sample across all employees affected by exposure to noise will be required

Figure B7-14: Dose badge
personal noise dosemeter.
Source: Cirrus Research plc.

Finally, dosimetry relies on the co-operation of both the subject and co-workers. If the work is not carried out normally or tampering occurs then the readings may be of little value. Training and supervision is needed to minimise this 'novelty' effect. Even so supervision could be so time consuming as to become impracticable. The expense and time consuming nature of personal dosimetry taken together with the limitations outlined above means that they should only be used when other techniques are unsuitable.

Controls

THE PRINCIPLES OF NOISE REDUCTION AND THEIR APPLICATION TO THE CONTROL OF OCCUPATIONAL NOISE

Transmission

Typical applications

Machine feet, pumps, mezzanine installations.

Technique

Mounting motors, pumps, gearboxes and other items of plant on rubber bonded cork (or similar) pads can be a very effective way of reducing transmission of vibration and therefore noise radiated by the rest of the structure. This is particularly the case where vibrating units are bolted to steel supports or floors. However, a common error with the use of these pads is for the bolt to "short-circuit" the pad, resulting in no isolation. Additional pads must be fitted under the bolt heads as shown below. There are many types of off-the-shelf anti-vibration mounts available, for instance rubber/neoprene or spring types. The type of isolator that is most appropriate will depend on, among other factors, the mass of the plant and the frequency of vibration to be isolated.

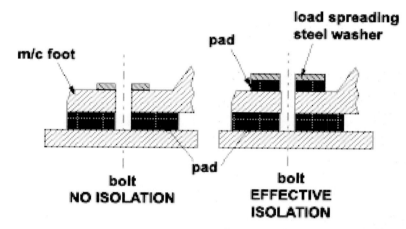

Figure B7-15: Noise control.

Source: www.hse.gov.uk/publications/10 top noise control techniques.

Reflection

Materials which are mainly porous in order to dissipate the sound energy, are normally applied to surfaces to eliminate sound reflection and reduce reverberant noise build-up within an enclosed space. They are, for example, applied to the internal surfaces of equipment casings and noise enclosures for this purpose.

Absorption

The principle of sound absorption is to reduce the amount of reflected energy by transforming it into some form of energy other than vibrational energy. Typically friction rubbing within the material converts the sound energy into heat.

Porous materials through which air can pass are often good sound absorbers. Thin layers of material will only absorb high frequencies, whereas thicker layers will absorb over a much larger frequency range. Absorbent materials are not usually effective for frequencies below 100 Hz.

Porous materials, that are good thermal insulators, are usually good absorbers; examples include visco-elastics, mineral wool and foam.

In rooms with hard materials on the floor, walls and ceiling any noise from machines that reaches these surfaces will be reflected back into the room. (A reverberant sound field will be created). This effect can be reduced by the use of absorbent material.

Covering the ceiling with sound absorbent material will give a reduction of up to 8 dB at distances away from the source. Near the source levels will not be changed.

Covering the walls and ceiling may give up to a 5 dB reduction.

Absorbent on the walls and ceiling near the operator will reduce local reflections and may give a noise reduction of a few dB for people near the source.

Damping

Typical applications

Chutes, hoppers, machine guards, panels, conveyors, tanks.

Technique

There are 2 basic techniques:

- Unconstrained layer damping where a layer of bitumastic (or similar) high damping material is stuck to the surface.
- Constrained layer damping where a laminate is constructed.

Constrained layer damping is more rugged and generally more effective. Either remanufacture steel (or aluminium) guards, panels or other components from commercially available sound deadened steel or buy self adhesive steel sheet. The latter can simply be stuck on to existing components (inside or outside) covering about 80% of the flat surface area to give a 5 - 25 dB reduction in the noise radiated (use a thickness that is 40% to 100% of the thickness of the panel to be treated).

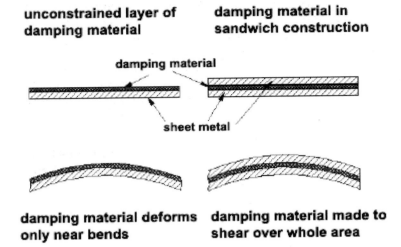

Figure B7-16: Noise damping.

Source: www.hse.gov.uk/publications/10 top noise control techniques.

Limitations: the efficiency falls off for thicker sheets. Above about 3mm sheet thickness it becomes increasingly difficult to achieve a substantial noise reduction.

THE INFLUENCE OF SOUND REDUCTION INDICES AND SOUND ABSORPTION COEFFICIENTS

Defined as 'A set of values measured by a specific test method to establish the actual amount of sound that will be stopped by the material, partition or panel when located between two rooms.'

A material's sound absorbing properties are expressed by the sound absorption coefficient, α, (alpha), as a function of the frequency. α ranges from 0 (total reflection) to 1.00 (total absorption).

DESIGN SPECIFICATIONS

Examples

Where a noise problem is evident then it can be dealt with in several ways including designing workplaces for low noise emission.

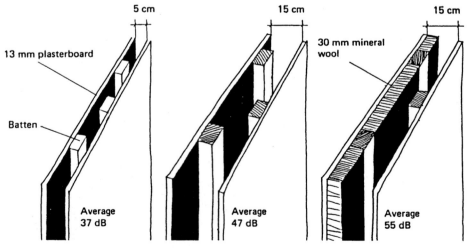

Figure B7-17: Attenuation of partitions.

Source: Ambiguous.

Designing workplaces for low noise emission

This involves the limitation of noise exposure by choice of design, layout and materials used. For example, use of absorption in the roof to reduce reflected noise. The choice of materials will be dictated by the noise levels generated in the workplace and the data shown in the tables above. The evaluation of noise control techniques to remedy specific problems.

Control at source

Relocation

Noise reduction can be achieved by moving the noise source away from areas where people are working. Moving the noise source to an adjacent room will also create a reduction in sound. In other cases, when noise is not emitted equally in all directions, turning it round can achieve significant reduction. Similarly, noisy exhausts should be directed away from workers and discharged further away by the use of a flexible hose.

Redesign

Noise is generated by vibrating surfaces and fluids. If this vibration can be reduced or eliminated then so will the noise. Possible changes in design that will aid this process are:

- Cushioning impact with plastic or nylon surfaces.
- Replacing metal gears with nylon or belts.

- Stiffening structural parts.
- Using mesh instead of sheet metal.

- Replacing rigid pipework with flexible materials.
- Using large diameter fans that run at low speed. This will move the same amount of air as small fast running fans but will do it quieter.
- Similarly, using large diameter, low pressure ducting.
- Streamlining ducting to avoid turbulence. This will have the added benefit of increasing efficiency.

Maintenance

Vibrated noise can be reduced by adopting a programme of regular maintenance. Regular maintenance will ensure that:

- Worn or badly fitting parts are replaced.
- Loose parts are secured.

- Rotating and moving parts are balanced correctly.
- Moving parts are well lubricated.

Along transmission path

Isolation

Positioning an elastic element (e.g. rubber mount etc.) in the path of vibration can isolate a noise radiating area from a vibration input.

Barriers

In some situations noise levels, at a distance from the source, can be reduced by the use of noise barriers. Screens and barriers place an obstacle in the noise transmission path. Barriers work on the principle of increasing the effective distance between the noise source and the receiver and elimination of the line-of-sight sound path. The effectiveness of the barrier will depend on the frequency of the sound. At low frequencies barriers will give little or no noise reduction. Barriers are not effective in reverberant sound fields or for people working close to the source. These limitations mean that they are best used in conjunction with other reduction techniques.

Enclosure

Acoustic enclosures are widely used in industry, but are not suitable for machines that need to be accessed frequently. This will include most workshop machines. An enclosure is simply a sound resistant cover fitted over a noise source. If a machine is enclosed with the operator, the operator is likely to be exposed to an increased sound level. Typically enclosures can be used with machines like pumps, compressors and conveyors. Enclosures can be full or partial depending on the machine.

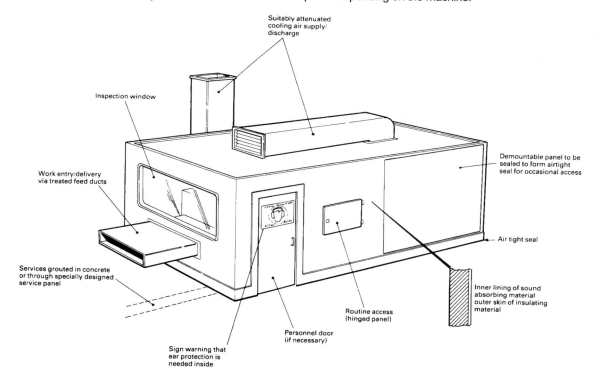

Figure B7-18: Noise enclosure.

Source: HSE, Reducing Noise at Work, L108.

At receiver

Acoustic havens

The employees can also be enclosed in a noise refuge which is an acoustically designed enclosure which has been designed with regard to ergonomic factors such as seating and is properly ventilated.

Where barriers are used indoors, covering the ceiling with absorbent material should be considered in order to prevent reflections.

In some situations it may be necessary to enclose a machine or process. For an enclosure to provide adequate attenuation the following steps should be taken:

- The enclosure should be built with a material such as brick, metal or wood and should not contact any holes.
- Doors and inspection hatches must be made to fit tightly.
- The inside of the enclosure should be lined with a sound absorbent material such as mineral, wool or foam rubber etc.
- If openings are required for ventilation or material input / output they should have some form of sound attenuation fitted.
- Gaps for services (cables, pipes etc.) should be sealed.
- To prevent the transmission of vibration, the machine should be vibration isolated from the enclosure and the floor.
- All services to the machine must have flexible connections.

Ear protection (passive and active)

Active noise control or noise cancelling is an electronic system that relies on the principle that two sounds of equal amplitude but reversed phase will cancel each other out. A microphone is used to capture the sound which is digitally processed to produce cancelling sounds via a loudspeaker.

Active noise reduction (ANR) protectors use an electronic sound cancelling system to reduce noise. This is particularly effective at low frequencies (50-500 Hz) where normal ***(passive)*** protectors are least effective.

Electronic hearing protection can be divided into two main categories: products intended to improve short range communications in noisy environments, and products intended to provide entertainment during work or play. Terms like Noise Cancelling Ear Muffs and/or Active Ear Muffs are sometimes used to describe this type of product. However, the technology used is not noise cancellation but rather different compression and filtration techniques.

TYPES OF HEARING PROTECTION

Ear plugs

These are designed to fit into the outer portion of the ear canal and remain in position without any external fixing device. They may be made of rubber, plastic or similar resilient materials, in a variety of designs, and generally in a number of sizes to help obtain a good fit. They can be corded or be fitted with a neckband to prevent loss (and to aid monitoring). Designs intended for permanent, reusable (i.e. used a few times) or one-use disposable types. Disposable earplugs are usually made from organic wadding and impregnated with wax or some other binder. Where applicable, the correct size required should be determined by a competent person. Custom moulded plugs, which can offer high levels of comfort, can be individually moulded to a person's ear. Semi insert (using a head-band) ear protectors rely on pressure of the band to maintain a seal. This can be useful for those spending short times in ear-protection zones.

Correctly selected earplugs have good attenuation characteristics at both high and low frequencies, and do not hinder the use of head protection or eye and face protection. It is also more difficult to see if earplugs are being worn thereby increasing the need for observant supervision to ensure their use. Earplugs are more effective in attenuating high frequencies than low.

Prolonged contact with the ear canal may cause a skin reaction particularly when plugs are dirty. Accordingly, care must be taken to clean them after use. People suffering from ear infections, discharges or irritation should be referred to a doctor. The rules are summarised as follows:

- Disposable ear plugs should only be used.
- Reusable, washable types, should be cleaned in accordance with manufacturer's instructions.
- Reusable plugs should be checked for suppleness and softness.
- Ear plugs should not be handled unless hands are clean.
- Ear plugs should be used only by the person they are issued to.
- Adequate supplies of disposable/replacement plugs must be kept available.

Ear defenders, muffs and pads

These are cups, frequently made of light metal or plastic and filled with sound absorbent material. To ensure a light comfortable fit around the ear, muffs are lined with a pad of elastometric material or a 'sausage like' roll filled with a high viscosity liquid (glycerol, Vaseline, etc.). This lining acts as an effective seal and helps damp vibration on the muffs. This type of 'over the ear' protector is either suspended in caps which are sized for proper fit or supported by head band similar to that used for ear phones. The latter type provides a universal fit, and is particularly suitable for intermittent wear. Headbands for standard muffs come in a variety of designs. Usually these are worn over the head or under the chin.

Many safety helmets incorporate a fitting for attaching ear defenders which will have different characteristics than a standard earmuff. They can be uncomfortable in hot conditions. This can be affected by:

- Weight of muffs.
- Headband pressure.
- The size of the muff cup.

Muffs give better attenuation at high frequencies than low, and average attenuation of frequencies under 1000 Hz which is usually lower than with plugs. In addition, they may be heavy and cumbersome and interfere with the use of head, eye and face protection.

Spectacle wearers and people with long hair may also have difficulty in ensuring a good seal around the ear thereby reducing their effectiveness. Muffs are more expensive than plugs. The advantage with muffs is that they are highly visible and therefore easily monitored. In addition communication equipment can be fitted - however this must not present a new noise hazard.

Other types

Level dependant, or amplitude sensitive, protectors are available. These come in two types - electronic and mechanical (carefully designed air ducts) designs. Both vary the level of protection given with varying levels of sound pressure. These are useful because they allow good communication in quieter areas.

Flat frequency response protectors are available where the ability to hear high frequency sounds is important (e.g. musicians). These give similar attenuation across the whole spectrum whereas most protectors provide greater attenuation at high frequencies than they do at low.

Dual protection

At extreme noise levels a combination of both muffs and ear plugs may be required to provide effective attenuation. This is likely at an $L_{EP,d}$ of 115 dB(A) or where peak pressure levels exceed 160 dB (particularly if there is substantial noise at low frequencies under ~500 Hz). Where this is the case manufacturer's data must be obtained for the muff and plug combination. It cannot be assumed that the attenuation provided by the combination is simply the sum of the components.

ATTENUATION DATA

There are three principal methods for estimating sound pressure levels when ear protectors are worn (as defined by BS EN 24869-2:1995). These are:

- **Octave band -** The most accurate prediction method - however it requires the measurement of the octave band spectrum. It is the most complicated method of calculating the effective A-weighted sound pressure level (SPL) at the ear.

- **HML (high, medium, low) -** Three values H, M and L, (e.g. H31, M27, L24) supplied by the manufacturer of the ear protector, are used with two simple measurements of SPL (A-weighted and C-weighted average sound pressure levels). This is the preferred method where the octave-band spectrum is not available.

- **SNR (single number rating) -** The SNR value is used with a single measurement of SPL (C-weighted average sound pressure level).

The HSE Noise at Work guidance gives example of all three methods. The preferred method, octave band analysis, is considered below.

Octave band analysis

Thus industrial noise can be analysed by carrying out a frequency (or octave) band analysis. Here the components of the noise source are measured (in dB) at eight frequency bands centred at 63Hz, 125Hz, 250Hz, 500 Hz, 1 kHz, 2 kHz, 4 kHz and 8 kHz. One must then apply correction factors to convert readings to d(B)A (i.e. to mimic the sensitivity of the human ear).

Octave -band frequency	Hz	63	125	250	500	1k	2k	4k	8k
A-weighting correction	dB	-26.2	-16.1	-8.6	-3.2	0	+1.2	+1.0	-1.1

Figure B7-19: Octave band analysis.

Source: ACT.

The purpose of carrying out such a frequency band analysis is to assess the suitability of ear protection. There are many types and models of ear protection available giving a wide range of protection levels needed for the variety of industrial situations. The protection given by any hearing protector will depend on both the fit and the frequency of the noise. Manufacturers supply mean attenuation test data gained from measurements taken from a variety of subjects with differently shaped heads and a range of frequencies. If this mean (average) test data were used 'as is' then only 50% of the population would receive the protection assumed. For this reason the data is corrected by subtracting one standard deviation. This gives an *assumed protection* or *assumed attenuation* which takes greater account of testing inaccuracies, variations in manufacturing and the differences in the physiology of each individual ear. The aim when providing ear protectors is to ensure that the noise is attenuated sufficiently without 'over-protecting' the operator thereby impairing communication.

The assumed protection of any given hearing protector is calculated by first measuring the frequency band pressure levels which contribute to the overall sound pressure level. This is known as a frequency (or octave) band analysis. Levels are usually measured at 63, 125, 250, 500, 1k, 2k, 4k and 8k Hz centre frequencies for each band. These measurements can then be converted by graphical means or by calculation into assumed protection levels using supplier's data. Some noise instruments/calculators programmed with the common models of hearing protectors carry out this function automatically. In essence the calculation involves:

- Calculating the A-weighted noise level.

- Calculating the assumed attenuation of the ear protector.

- Calculating the noise level at the ear (wearing the ear protector).

An example calculation is as follows. A worker is exposed to 103.2 dB(A). Octave band analysis shows that this comprises 90, 92, 94, 94, 96, 98, 96, 94 dB respectively and the supplier's data for the ear protector is as shown in the chart over the page:

Octave -band frequency	Hz	63	125	250	500	1k	2k	4k	8k
Band pressure level	dB	90	92	94	94	96	98	96	94
A-weighting correction	dB	-26.2	-16.1	-8.6	-3.2	0	+1.2	+1.0	-1.1
Weighted band noise level (1)	dB(A)	63.8	75.9	85.4	90.8	96	99.2	97	92.9
Mean attenuation	dB	7.4	10.0	14.4	19.6	22.8	29.6	38.8	34.1
Standard deviation	dB	3.3	3.6	3.6	4.6	4.0	6.2	7.4	5.2
Assumed protection value (2)	dB	4.1	6.4	10.8	15.0	18.8	23.4	31.4	28.9
Assumed protection level Lines (1)-(2)	dB(A)	59.7	69.5	74.6	75.8	77.2	75.8	65.6	64.0

The sum of the assumed protection levels (in bels) in the last row can be added:

$$= Log(10^{5.97} + 10^{6.95} + 10^{7.46} + 10^{7.58} + 10^{7.72} + 10^{7.58} + 10^{6.56} + 10^{6.40})$$

$$= 8.239 \text{ B(A)}$$

$$= 82 \text{ dB(A)}$$

Figure B7-20: Example calculation.   Source: ACT.

The 'A'-weighted total noise level at the ear fitted with the ear protector considered is assumed to be 82 dB(A). Thus the ear protector gives a reduction of around 21 dB(A). Obviously this assumed protection can only be provided if the protectors fit properly and they are correctly used.

FACTORS AFFECTING DEGREE OF PROTECTION IN PRACTICE VERSUS THEORETICAL PROTECTION

Personal protective equipment is only viable if:

- It is compatible with other PPE (e.g. glasses, safety helmets).
- They are correctly fitted (e.g. no interference with ear muff seals, ear plugs inserted and fitted correctly).
- They give sufficient protection with regard to the type and characteristics of the noise (i.e. they must offer protection to at least below the second or peak action levels and, in order to avoid giving limited protection, must give an assumed protection of at least 5dB(A)).
- *Real world* attenuation is considered. Practical work situations can result in about 5 dB less than predicted by manufacturer's average attenuation data. With ear plugs this can be up to 18 dB - mainly due to poor fitting.
- They are hygienic, comfortable to use and do not provoke a toxic reaction in the wearer.
- They are suitable for the working environment (e.g. traceable types in the food industry).
- Protectors are used all the time in noisy areas *(see - example in table - below)*.

Example: An operator is working in a noisy environment with a continuous sound pressure level of 113 dB(A) and wears ear protectors capable of 30 dB(A) reduction:

Percentage of time protector is worn	Time worn during an 8 hour day	Actual noise reduction / dB(A)
0%	Not worn	-
50%	4 hours	3
75%	6 hours	6
87%	7 hours	9
95%	7 hours 30 minutes	12
97%	7 hours 45 minutes	15
97.9%	7 hours.50 minutes	16.6
99%	7 hours 55 minutes	18.5
99.6%	7 hours 58 minutes	23
99.82%	7 hours 59 minutes	25.5
100%	8 hours (all day)	30

Figure B7-21: Efficiency of ear muffs.   Source: ACT.

See also - Relevant Statutory Provisions - Element B11 - for further information.

ROLE OF HEALTH SURVEILLANCE

Regulation 9 of the CNWR 2005 states that if a risk assessment indicates a risk to the health and safety of employees who are, or are liable to be, exposed to noise, then they must be put under suitable health surveillance (including testing of their hearing). The employer must keep and maintain a suitable health record. The employer will, providing reasonable notice is provided; allow the employee access to their health record.

Where, as a result of health surveillance, an employee is found to have identifiable hearing damage the employer shall ensure that the employee is examined by a doctor. If the doctor or any specialist to whom the doctor considers it necessary to refer the employee to considers that the damage is likely to be the result of exposure to *noise*, the employer shall:

- Ensure that a suitably qualified person informs the employee accordingly.
- Review the risk assessment.
- Review any measure taken to comply with the regulations.
- Consider assigning the employee to alternative *work.*
- Ensure continued health surveillance.
- Provide for a review of the health of any other employee who has been similarly exposed.

Employees must, when required by the employer and at the cost of the employer, present themselves during *working* hours for health surveillance procedures.

The results of health surveillance will be expressed as audiograms, the principles of which are outlined in previous section.

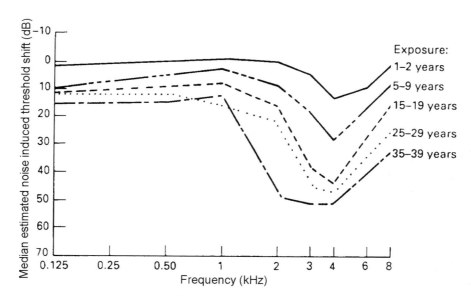

Figure B7-22: Audiogram.

Source: Ambiguous.

The 'normal' subject will show an almost horizontal line high up on the chart with a slight dip at high frequencies depending on the subject's age (presbycusis). A flat audiogram curve lower down on the chart indicates a similar hearing loss at all frequencies (indicative of conductive loss). The classic pattern of industrial deafness is the four-K-dip. This is the dip or notch centred on the 4 or 6 kHz region which become larger as the years of exposure progress.

B7.2 - Vibration

Physics

BASIC CONCEPTS

Displacement, velocity, amplitude, frequency and acceleration for oscillating particles

The units used for vibration are similar to those of noise. These are:

- Frequency measured in Hertz (cycles per second); of frequency, equal to 1 cycle per second. The term is combined with metric prefixes to denote multiple units such as the kilohertz (1,000 Hz), megahertz (1,000,000 Hz), and gigahertz (1,000,000,000 Hz).
- Displacement measured in metres.
- Acceleration - the rate of change of velocity in metres per second squared (ms^{-2}).
- Amplitude.

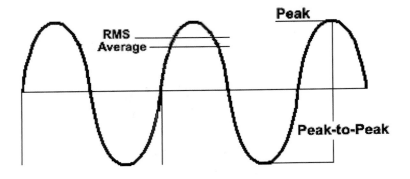

Figure B7-23: Frequency.

Source: Ambiguous.

Peak Amplitude (Pk) is the maximum excursion of the wave from the zero or equilibrium point.

Peak-to-Peak Amplitude (Pk-Pk) is the distance from a negative peak to a positive peak. In the case of the sine wave, the peak-to-peak value is exactly twice the peak value because the waveform is symmetrical, but this is not necessarily the case with all vibration waveforms, as we will see shortly.

Root Mean Square Amplitude (RMS) is the square root of the average of the squared values of the waveform. In the case of the sine wave, the RMS value is 0.707 times the peak value, but this is only true in the case of the sine wave. The RMS value is proportional to the area under the curve -- if the negative peaks are rectified, i.e., made positive, and the area under the resulting curve averaged to a constant level, that level would be proportional to the RMS value.

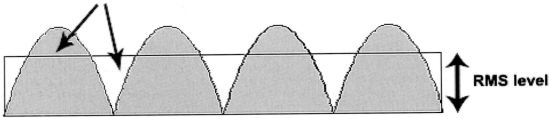

Figure B7-24: RMS level.

Source: Ambiguous.

The RMS value of a vibration signal is an important measure of its amplitude. As mentioned before, it is numerically equal to the square root of the average of the squared value of amplitude. To calculate this value, the instantaneous amplitude values of the waveform must be squared and these squared values averaged over a certain length of time. This time interval must be at least one period of the wave in order to arrive at the correct value. The squared values are all positive, and thus so is their average. Then the square root of this average value is extracted to get the RMS value.

Most mechanical vibration found in the workplace is not simple sinusoidal or pure harmonic motion. From hand-held tools the signal is complex, being composed of many frequencies at varying amplitudes, thus requiring averaging, such as 'root mean square' levels over a known frequency bandwidth. Scientists have found difficulty expressing vibration intensity, especially the acceleration unit (ms^{-2}). At low frequencies around 1Hz, experienced in large ships and in semi-submersible oil exploration structures, amplitude (displacement) of several metres is required to generate appreciable acceleration. At frequencies around 30-60Hz coinciding with the firing frequencies of pneumatic rock drills or chipping hammers, high acceleration peak values of around $1000ms^{-2}$ are generated with amplitudes of the order of fractions of millimetres.

Effects

SIGNIFICANCE OF AMPLITUDE AND FREQUENCY OF VIBRATIONS ON COMFORT LEVELS

- 0.3 Hz   Motion sickness.
- 1-2Hz   Relaxing.
- 3-4Hz   Whole body.

- 5-8Hz   Interference.
- 10Hz   Face and cheeks.
- 20Hz   Tingling.

The sensory and psycho-physiological response to vibration for the human subject depends to a marked degree on *resonance*, defined as the tendency of the human body (or parts of it) to act in concert with externally generated vibration. The impinging vibration may be amplified by as much as a factor of four. For vertical vibration in the region of 4 to 8Hz, man's 'whole body', mainly upper torso, may be in resonance and thus most susceptible to the harmful effects of vibration. At this frequency there will be the maximum mechanical vibration energy transfer between the source and the body, with an actual amplification of the incoming vibration signal. The characteristic frequencies and the amplification factors will be determined by the mass, the elasticity and the damping of the organ (e.g. head approximately 25Hz, eyeball 30-60Hz and the hand 50-150Hz - see the figure below).

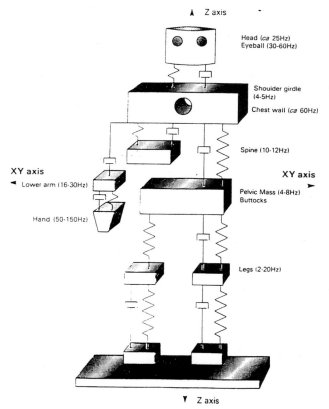

Figure B7-25: Simplified mechanical system representing the human body.

Source: Ambiguous.

Occupational exposure to vibration may arise in a number of ways, often reaching workers at intensity levels disturbing to comfort, efficiency, health and safety. There are two routes of vibration energy transmission. In the case of whole body vibration it is transmitted to the worker through a contacting or supporting structure which is itself vibrating, e.g. a ship's deck, the seat or floor of a vehicle (tractor or tank), or a whole structure shaken by machinery (e.g. in the processing of coal, iron ore or concrete), where the vibration is intentionally generated for impacting. By far the most common route of entry to the human body is through the hands, wrists and arms of the subject - so called segmental vibration or hand arm vibration (HAV), where there is actual contact with the vibrating source. Examples in industry include the use of pneumatic drills, electrically-driven rotary tools, chain saws and the use of grinding and abrading tools.

ILL-HEALTH EFFECTS AND CONDITIONS PRODUCED BY

Whole body vibration

The human response to whole body vibration (WBV) transmitted through vehicle seats in trucks, farm vehicles, or heavy equipment earth movers, or through ships and aeroplanes depends primarily on resonance within the frequency range 1 to 20Hz, predominantly in the vertical of Z axis mode. Unlike segmental vibration, whole body vibration is a general stressor impinging on all the body organs. The non-specific physiological response is an increase in heart rate, cardiac output and oxygen uptake. If, however, the vibration is intense (up to 50ms^{-2}) gross mechanical interference with the haemodyamics of both central and peripheral blood flow will result. The principal resonance of a human subject vibrated in the Z axis occurs around 5Hz. Rough riding vehicles over uneven terrain could therefore disturb cerebral blood flow in drivers resulting in decreased work performance. The most common problem associated with whole body vibration is, however, back pain and in particular lower back pain.

Such signs as cerebral oedema and generalised debilitating effects, conveyed through the central nervous system, have been described by investigators in the Soviet Union. Displacement of intervertebral discs has been reported, associated with the vibration from off-road trucks, farm tractors and earth moving vehicles. It is, however, difficult to establish clear cause and effect relationships. This is because many of the surveys reported poor ergonomic design factors, adverse working environments, fatigue and non-specific stress factors. Even harder to establish are the causes of conditions such as abdominal pain, digestive problems, urinary difficulties, prostatitis, visual disorders, vertigo, headaches and sleeplessness. Discretion, therefore, is required to establish a direct link with vibration especially since many of the behavioural/performance field studies to date have not been controlled under strict epidemiological, statistical conditions.

Studies carried out under laboratory conditions attempting to simulate military environments such as jet aircraft cockpits or navy vessels use young, physically fit military subjects who may not represent a typical factory worker. In these laboratory studies sinusoidal vibration has been used, a condition which does not represent the variety of conditions found in the workplace. Occupational health physicians are aware that long distance coach drivers and truck drivers are more prone to many of the above ailments but they have not been able to establish vibration as the cause due to the number of confounding variables present -bad posture, irregular dietary habits and the ever increasing stress of driving on crowded roads. To rectify this, studies carried out by NIOSH, Cincinnati in 1974-1976 on 3205 long distance truck drivers and 1448 interstate bus drivers concluded that the combined effects of body posture, postural fatigue, dietary habits and whole body vibration contributed to a significant excess of venous, bowel, respiratory, muscular and back disorders compared to three control groups - office workers, the general population and air traffic controllers. The studies also showed that rest periods and their distribution throughout the work day played a complex role in the overall performance.

Segmental vibration

The specific effects of intense vibration transmitted to the hands and arms by vibrating knobs or controls are long term damage to soft tissues, bones and joints. Thickening of the skin and underlying tissues probably explains **Raynaud's phenomenon or hand-arm vibration syndrome** or **HAVS** (one of which is commonly known as vibration white finger) seen in experienced work people who use vibrating hand tools. The recent compensation award of £125,000 to 7 former miners combined with the later agreement by the government to pay about £500 million to over 30,000 former miners suffering from HAVS indicates the scale of the problem.

The symptoms are progressive and there is no cure or treatment currently available. After a latent period, the fingers 'throb' particularly on cold, wet and windy mornings. This is followed by intermittent tingling and numbness with the fingers going white or blanching. Continued exposure results in a steady deterioration in symptoms with sufferers experiencing spasm, 'dead finger' and painful 'hot aches'. Fingers can also become blue (cyanotic' due to lack of circulation). This seems to occur in response to a change in metabolic demand in the fingers induced, for example, by temperature change. It seems that the blood vessels are unable to dilate rapidly enough or at all or because of thickened tissues which then become anoxic. The medical effects are as follows:

- Vascular changes in the blood vessels of the fingers.
- Neurological changes in the peripheral nerves.
- Muscle and tendon damage in the fingers, hands, wrists and forearms.
- Suspected bone and joint changes.
- Damage to the autonomic centres of the central nervous system in the brain influencing the endocrine, cardiac, vestibular and cochlea functions (not proven).

The classification of HAVS was formerly carried out using the Taylor-Pelmar classification - however this is being replaced by the **Stockholm Workshop** scale.

Classification of HAVS using the Stockholm Workshop scale:

1 Vascular component*

Stage	(Grade)	Description
0		No attacks.
1V	(mild)	Occasional attacks affecting only tips of one or more fingers.
2V	(moderate)	Occasional attacks affecting distal and middle (rarely also proximal) phalanges or one or more fingers.
Stage	(grade)	Description.
3V	(severe)	Frequent blanching attacks affecting all phalanges of most fingers.
4V	(very severe)	As in Stage 3 but with trophic skin changes in fingertips.

Figure B7-26: Vascular component.   *Source: ACT.*

2 Sensori-Neural Component*

Stage	Description
0_{SN}	Vibration exposed. No symptoms.
1_{SN}	Intermittent or persistent numbness with or without tingling.
2_{SN}	As in 1_{SN} with reduced sensory perception.
3_{SN}	As in 2_{SN} with reduced tactile discrimination and manipulative dexterity.

Figure B7-27: Sensori-neural component.   *Source: ACT.*

* The staging is made separately for each hand. Grade of disorder is indicated by the stage (as above) and the number of affected fingers on each hand e.g. 'Stage/Hand/No. of digits'.

The condition appears to be most common with low frequency vibrations; however it has been known to occur at frequencies up to 1500 Hz. Examples of at risk activities include:

- The use of hand-held chain saws in forestry.
- The use of hand-held rotary tools in grinding or in the sanding or polishing of metal, or the holding of material being ground, or metal being sanded or polished by rotary tools.
- The use of hand-held percussive metal-working tools, or the holding of metal being worked upon by percussive tools in riveting, caulking, chipping, hammering, fettling or swaging.
- The use of hand-held powered percussive drills or hand-held powered percussive hammers in mining, quarrying, demolition, or on roads or footpaths, including road construction.
- The holding of material being worked upon by pounding machines in shoe manufacture.

Provided the source of vibration is stopped early in stage 2 then circulation may improve; however it is debatable whether the neurological symptoms can improve. Sufferers are therefore encouraged to change their jobs.

IDENTIFICATION OF GROUPS OF WORKERS AT RISK

Workers may be exposed to HAVS when operating hand-held power tools such as road breakers or when holding materials being worked by machines such as pedestal grinders. The most well known health effect is vibration white finger, but other effects include damage to sensory nerves, muscles and joints in the hands and arms.

Drivers of some mobile machines, including certain tractors, fork lift trucks and quarrying or earth-moving machinery, may be exposed to WBV and shocks which are associated with back pain. Other work factors, such as posture and heavy lifting, are also known to contribute to back problems for drivers and the relative importance of WBV is not clear at present.

Measurement assessment of exposure

MEASUREMENT OF VIBRATION

The accelerometer

The electrical output from a piezo-electric crystal (accelerometer) mounted on the handle of the work-piece is fed into a vibration analyser with computer facilities attached. The signal is 'weighted', a requirement of all the existing *vibration standards.* As with noise the acceleration level may be given in decibels (dB) or as acceleration in metres per second squared [ms^{-2}]. An acceleration of 1 ms^{-2} corresponds to 120 dB, and 10 ms^{-2} to 140 dB. For field measurements instruments are now available giving direct readings, the signal being fed from a directly-mounted accelerometer. This instrumentation is valuable for controlling the vibration levels in the workplace and for testing new tools before issue to employees. The vibration *dose* is the product of both the level of vibration (intensity) and the exposure time working the tool.

Figure B7-28: Miniature triaxial accelerometer.
Source: www.noise-and-vibration.co.uk.

Figure B7-29: Force balance accelerometer.
Source: www. vibration.shef.ac.uk.

EXPOSURE STANDARDS FOR VIBRATION

The Council of Ministers and the European Parliament adopted a joint text for a Physical Agents (Vibration) Directive regarding exposure of workers to the risks arising from vibration on 21 May 2002.

The Directive was published in the Official Journal of the European Communities on 6 July 2002 (L177 Vol 45, p12) as Directive 2002/44/EC on the minimum health and safety requirements regarding the exposure of workers to the risks arising from vibration. The Directive requirements were enacted in the UK as The Control of Vibration at Work Regulations 2005, made under the Health and Safety at Work Act (HASAWA) 1974.

EXPOSURE LIMIT VALUES AND ACTION VALUES

Regulation 4 of The Control of Vibration at Work Regulations (CVWR) 2005 states the personal daily exposure limits and daily exposure action values normalised over an 8-hour reference period. The exposure action values(EAV) are the daily amount of exposure to vibration above which the employer is required to take certain actions. The greater the exposure level, the greater the risk and the more action employers will need to take to reduce the risk.

	Daily exposure action value (EAV)	Daily exposure limit value (ELV)
Hand-arm vibration	2.5 m/s^2 A(8)	5 m/s^2 A(8)
Whole body vibration.	0.5 m/s^2 A(8)	1.15 m/s^2 A(8)

Figure B7-30: Vibration exposure values.   *Source: CVWR 2005.*

Exposure limit value

The exposure limit values (ELV) are the maximum amount of vibration an employee may be exposed to on any single day, which must not be exceeded. The Regulations allow a transitional period for the limit value until July 2010. This only applies to work equipment already in use before July 2007. The exposure limit value may be exceeded during the transitional period as long as you have complied with all the other requirements of the Regulations and taken all reasonably practicable actions to reduce exposure as much as you can.

When assessing exposure to ensure limit values are not exceeded, the effect of personal protection provided to the employee can be taken into account. This will depend on the attenuation provided by the protection, its appropriateness for the type of vibration protection, use and maintenance requirements.

Regulation 5 of CVWR 2005 requires the employer to make a suitable and sufficient assessment of the risk created by work that is liable to expose employees to risk from vibration. The assessment must observe work practices, make reference to information regarding the magnitude of vibration from equipment and if necessary measurement of the magnitude of the vibration.

Consideration must also be given to the:

- Type and duration of use.
- Effects of exposure, exposures limit / action values.
- Effects on employees at particular risk.
- Effects of vibration on equipment and the ability to use it, manufacturers' information.
- Availability of replacement equipment.
- Extent of exposure at the workplace (e.g. rest facilities), temperature.
- Information on health surveillance.

The risk assessment should be recorded as soon as is practicable after the risk assessment is made and reviewed regularly.

Controls

Regulation 6 of CVWR 2005 states: that the employer must seek to eliminate the risk of vibration at source or, if not reasonably practicable, reduce it to as low a level as is reasonably practicable. Where the personal daily exposure limit is exceeded the employer must reduce exposure by implementing a programme of organisational and technical measures. Measures include the use of other methods of work, ergonomics, maintenance of equipment, design and layout, rest facilities, information, instruction and training, limitation by schedules and breaks and the provision of personal protective equipment to protect from cold and damp.

Measures must be adapted to take account of any group or individual employee whose health may be of particular risk from exposure to vibration.

Protective measures are the only means of protecting people who work with vibrating machinery. The following controls should be considered.

CONTROL MEASURES IN RESPECT OF WHOLE BODY VIBRATION FOR OCCUPATIONS SUCH AS FARMERS, CONSTRUCTION WORKERS AND DRIVERS

Although no single technique is best for all situations, the following guidelines will be helpful in most instances:

- Reduce whole body vibration by driving vehicles with suspension seats that have appropriate vibration-damping characteristics.
- The work schedule should be examined to reduce vibration exposure either by alternating with non-vibration work or avoiding continuous vibration by, for example, scheduling ten minute breaks every hour.
- Carry out a detailed ergonomic assessment of hazardous tasks. This should include duration and frequency of the task.
- Training of all exposed employees on the proper use of tools and the minimisation of exposure.
- Establish a routine health surveillance programme.

CONTROL MEASURES IN RESPECT OF SEGMENTAL VIBRATION FOR OCCUPATIONS SUCH AS THOSE HANDLING VIBRATING TOOLS

It is the combined responsibility of the employer and the tool manufacturer to reduce vibration levels on hand tools to safe limits. Foremost in this drive have been the chain saw manufacturers. Sweden and Finland have succeeded in reducing the relevance of Hand Harm Vibration Syndrome (HAVS) from 50-60% to 5-10% of the workforce in their forestry operations. Some progress has been made with pneumatic, percussive drills and chipping hammers. At present guidance suggests that a maximum usage time of 30 minutes per day is allowed for tools with a hammer action and 2 hours per day for those with a rotary action. The EC Machinery Directive (89/392/EEC) requires that instructions for hand-held portable machinery should indicate whether or not the operator will be subjected to vibrations where the accelerations exceeds 2.5 ms^{-2}. In addition, the:

> "discomfort, fatigue and psychological stress faced by the operator must be reduced to a minimum taking ergonomic principles into account."

Figure B7-31: Quote - ergonomic principles.

Source: CVWR 2005.

Protective measures are the only means of protecting people who work with vibrating machinery. The following controls should be considered:

- The need for such machinery should be reviewed so as to eliminate unnecessary operations.
- Consideration should be given to the automation of processes.
- The vibration characteristics of the hand tools in the works should be assessed and reference made to the BSI and ISO guidelines.
- The work schedule should be examined to reduce vibration exposure either by alternating with non-vibration work or avoiding continuous vibration by, for example, scheduling ten minute breaks every hour.
- Carry out a detailed ergonomic assessment of hazardous tasks (e.g. breaking asphalt with a road breaker). This should include duration and frequency of the task.
- Development of a purchasing policy to include consideration of vibration and, where necessary, vibration isolating devices.
- Training of all exposed employees on the proper use of tools and the minimisation of exposure.

- Establish a routine health surveillance programme.
- Tools should be maintained to their optimum performance thereby reducing vibration to a minimum (e.g. the bearings of grinders).
- Wearing gloves is recommended for safety and for retaining heat. They will not absorb a significant fraction of the vibration energy which lies within the 30-300hz range. There is also the danger that the absorbent material used in glove manufacture may introduce a resonance frequency and therefore the total energy input to the hands may be increased (Bednall, Health and Safety Executive 1988). There have been recent reports of patented composite materials that, when moulded into hand-grips and fitted onto vibrating power tools, reduces vibration by 45%.
- The greater the coupling (hand and tool interface), the more energy enters the hand. Increasing grip force increases the coupling. There are working techniques for all tools and the expertise developed over time justifies an initial training period for new starters.
- Operators with established HAVS should avoid exposure to cold and thus minimise the number of blanching attacks. Operators with *advanced* HAVS who are *deteriorating* (as measured by annual medical checks) should be removed from further exposure. The medical priority is to prevent finger tip ulceration (tissue necrosis).

Finally, regard to the redesigning tools, rescheduling work methods, or automating the process - a continuous review should be maintained until such time as the risks associated with vibration are under control. As with any management system, the controls in place for vibration should include audit and review.

HEALTH SURVEILLANCE

Regulation 7 of CVWR 2005 states that health surveillance must be carried out if there is a risk to the health of employees liable to be exposed to vibration. This is in order to prevent or diagnose any health effect linked with exposure to vibration. A record of health shall be kept of any employee who undergoes health surveillance. The employer shall, providing reasonable notice is given, provide the employee with access to their health records and provide copies to an enforcing officer on request.

If health surveillance identifies a disease or adverse health effect, considered by a doctor or other occupational health professional to be a result of exposure to vibration, the employer shall ensure that a qualified person informs the employee and provides information and advice. The employer must ensure they are kept informed of any significant findings from health surveillance, taking into account any medical confidentiality. In addition the employer must also

- Review risk assessments.
- Review the measures taken to comply.
- Consider assigning the employee to other work.
- Review the health of any other employee who has been similarly exposed and consider alternative work.

This page is intentionally blank

ELEMENT B7 - PHYSICAL AGENTS 1 - NOISE AND VIBRATION

Physical agents 2 - radiation and the thermal environment

Learning outcomes

On completion of this element, candidates should be able to:

B8.1   Outline of basic physics of ionising and non-ionising radiation.

B8.2   Outline the effects of exposure to non-ionising radiation, its measurement and control.

B8.3   Outline the effects of exposure to ionising radiation, its measurement and control.

B8.4   Outline the effects of extremes of temperature, its measurement and control.

Content

Relevant statutory provisions

Ionising Radiations Regulations (IRR) 1999

Workplace (Health, Safety and Welfare) Regulations (WHSWR) 1992 (and as amended 2002)

This page is intentionally blank

B8.1 - Radiation physics

Basic concepts

Radiation is a form of energy. The types of radiation are grouped and labelled according to the amount of energy they have. Some of these forms of energy are transmitted by waves called electromagnetic waves. The distance between wave peaks is the "wavelength". The number of wave peaks passing a given point in one second is the "frequency." The higher the peaks, the greater the frequency, the more energy they carry. The more energy they carry, the greater the harm they can do to the human body.

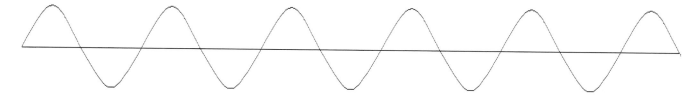

Figure B8-1: Wavelength.

Source: ACT.

Radiation can be arranged according to its frequency or wavelength into a series called the **electromagnetic spectrum**. This is represented by the following diagram (not to scale):

wavelength (m)	10^{-10}				10^{-5}		10^{0}
Gamma rays	X-rays	Ultra-violet	Visible	Infra-red	Microwaves	Radiowaves
frequency (Hz) 10^{24}			10^{15}			10^{6}

Figure B8-2: Electromagnetic spectrum.

Source: Ambiguous.

The part of the spectrum with greatest energy is where the Gamma rays and the X-rays are. They are so powerful that they will remove the electron from the atom, which is called ionisation. These powerful rays are known as ionising radiation. The radiation from the lower energy part of the spectrum: Ultra-violet (UV), Visible light, Infra-red (IR), Microwaves and Radiowaves, do not contain enough energy to ionise and are therefore known as non-ionising radiation. Radiation can therefore be classified in terms of its energy into two types: *ionising* and *non-ionising*. There is also a type of ionising radiation that is not electromagnetic waves, but is particulate. The particles of ionising radiation are known as Alpha (α), Beta (β) and Neutron radiation. There are others, but consideration of them is beyond the scope of the syllabus.

THE TYPES OF NON IONISING RADIATION, ORIGINS AND SOURCES

Non-ionising radiation is used in lighting, heating, lasers, sterilisation, sunbeds, radar, television, radio and electric power lines. Low frequency electromagnetic radiations are also emitted by a wide variety of products at home and in the workplace, from photocopiers to power lines, household appliances, e.g. microwave ovens, and mobile phones to radios and computers.

Non-ionising radiation is defined as that which is unable to produce electrically charged particles (ions). This is because it has insufficient energy to remove an orbital electron when it interacts with atomic structures such as atoms or molecules.

There are several categories of non-ionising radiation defined according to its wavelength:

Radiation	Wavelength
Ultra-violet (UV)	100 - 400 nm
Visible light	400 - 750 nm
Infrared (IR)	750 - 10^{3} µm (1 mm)
Microwave & Radio frequency	1 mm - 100 m

Figure B8-3: Radiation wavelengths.

Source: ACT.

Ultraviolet radiation (UV)

Ultraviolet (UV) radiation has a wavelength of between 100 to 40 nm. This part of the spectrum is further subdivided into three bands according to wavelength.

Region	Wavelength nm
UV-A	380 - 320
UV-B	320 - 290
UV-C	290 - 200

Figure B8-4: UV radiation wavelengths.

Source: ACT.

UV is produced:

■ From very hot bodies (e.g. electric arcs, sunlight).
■ By an electric discharge through gases.

Visible light

Visible wavelengths 400 - 750 nm are usually of low hazard. Retinal thermal injury and retinal photo-chemical injury from chronic exposure to blue-light can occur.

Light is that part of the electromagnetic spectrum visible to the human eye. In common with the rest of the electromagnetic spectrum it is a form of energy which has the characteristics of wave motion. It can therefore be described by its wavelength (colour) and its amplitude (intensity). Our eyes are sensitive to a range of wavelengths from ~ 400 nanometres (the blue end) to ~ 700 nm (red).

The basic unit of light is the lumen, which is used to measure the total output (luminous flux) of a light source. Illuminance is measured in lux, which is defined as one lumen illuminating 1 square metre of surface area. The brightness or luminance of a surface is measured in candela.

Infrared (IR)

Of or relating to the range of invisible radiation wavelengths from about 750 nanometers, just longer than red in the visible spectrum, to 1 millimetre, on the border of the microwave region.

IR is widely found throughout industry with high temperature sources ranging from furnaces (e.g. glass and foundries), arc lamps, radiant heaters and welding. As with ultraviolet radiation it is further subdivided into sub groups (e.g. IR-A with a wavelength of 900 nm to 1400 nm). The proportion of radiation with wavelengths below 1500 nm increases as the temperature rises. For example:

■ At 1000°c ~5% of energy is at wavelengths below 1500 nm.
■ At 2000°C the value is 40%.

This is important as the most damaging wavelengths for organs, such as the eyes, are below 1400 nm.

Microwaves and radio frequency radiation

As previously mentioned, radio frequency and microwave radiation are both forms of energy called electromagnetic radiation.

Radiofrequency or radiowaves have a range of frequencies and wavelengths. Very High Frequency (VHF) radiowaves are used for TV and FM radio. Medium Frequency (MF) radiowaves are used for AM radio. Radiofrequency is used in heat sealers and glue driers.

Microwaves are actually just radiowaves of higher frequencies. Microwaves are used for radar and satellite communications, for telephone and TV transmissions, for microwave ovens, and for diathermy in medical clinics.

Microwaves are the name given to radiation between the Infrared and radio region, with wavelengths typically in the 1mm to 10cm range. One classification of the Microwave region has three sectors:

1. Millimetre wavelengths   0.1-1 cm.

2. Microwave radio, radar   1-10 cm.

3. Radar   10-100 cm.

Another classification is given as:

< 3 cm   Microwaves are absorbed in the outer surface of the skin.

3-10 cm   Microwaves penetrate more deeply into the skin.

10-200 cm   Microwaves penetrate deeply with the potential to damage internal organs.

> 200 cm   The body is thought to be transparent to these microwaves.

The greatest danger lies with the 10-20 cm microwaves, as deep tissue heating may occur without the warning sensation of heat.

Lasers

Laser stands for the *"Light Amplification by the Stimulated Emission of Radiation"*. Atomic electrons are stimulated to produce photons which are have the same wavelength and are precisely in step so that the peaks and troughs exactly match in a coherent way. Stimulation is encouraged by the trapping of this radiation so that further emissions occur within a resonant cavity. Here the radiation bounces back and forth, stimulating emissions in the desired way before the light escapes. This 'coherent' light possesses the ability to carry information and can have a high energy density.

The wavelength of the radiation emitted by a laser may be in the invisible ultra violet or infra red (heat) regions or in the visible (light) region of the electromagnetic spectrum. The output radiation is related directly to the chemical composition of the substance which is used at the heart of the laser (lasing medium) to generate the beam. Lasers are generally referred to in terms of their lasing medium, e.g. helium/neon, argon, carbon dioxide, ruby etc. The output beam may be a continuous emission and is called continuous wave (CW) or a pulse or series of pulses and this beam characteristic is also used when describing a laser. As the wavelength of the laser beam may well be outside the visible region, it is called laser radiation rather than laser light.

Unlike other sources of optical radiation the laser produces radiation at a specific wavelength (monochromatic). Because the laser generally produces an almost parallel beam of radiation the intensity will not fall off with the square of the distance as in the case of conventional radiation sources. Reflections, even from dark surfaces, are also hazardous because the beam does not lose energy by divergence.

Lasers, depending on their power can be used, for example to cut metal, cut body tissue during surgery, laser printing and in laser pens and pointers. They are classified according to their power.

THE TYPES OF IONISING RADIATION, ORIGINS AND SOURCES

Types of ionising radiation

Ionising radiation is produced by unstable atoms. Unstable atoms differ from stable atoms because they have an excess of energy or mass or both.

Unstable atoms are said to be radioactive. In order to reach stability, these atoms give off, or emit, the excess energy or mass. These emissions are called radiation. The kinds of radiation are electromagnetic and particulate (i.e. mass given off with the energy of motion).

(Source: HSE/Radiation).

Ionising radiation occurs as either electromagnetic rays (such as X-rays and gamma rays) or particles (such as alpha and beta particles). It occurs naturally (e.g. from the radioactive decay of natural radioactive substances such as radon gas and its decay products) but can also be produced artificially. Everyone receives some exposure to natural background radiation.

Ionising radiation is used in medicine for diagnosis and treatment, nuclear power, radiography, gauges, safety signs, smoke detectors, sterilisation of medical appliances, archaeological dating, baggage inspection, research and teaching.

The most common types of ionising radiation are:

Name	Symbol	Type
Alpha	α	Particulate.
Beta	β^-	Particulate.
Neutron		Particulate.
X-ray		Electromagnetic.
Gamma	λ	Electromagnetic.

Figure B8-5: Common types of ionising radiation.

Source: ACT.

Note that other types of radiation, such as positrons (β^+), thermal neutrons, fast neutrons and protons, exist but are beyond the scope of this Element.

Ionising radiation may be defined as electromagnetic or particulate radiation, which has sufficient energy to cause ionisation. Ionisation is where an electron is removed from an atom causing that atom to become electrically charged.

Alpha particles

Alpha particles are comparatively large, travel short distances in dense materials, and can only just penetrate the skin. The principal risk is through ingestion or inhalation of a source of alpha particles, which might place the material close to vulnerable tissue; when this happens the high localised energy effect will destroy tissue of the organ/s affected.

Beta particles

Beta particles are much faster moving than alpha particles. They are smaller in mass than alpha particles, but have longer range, so they can damage and penetrate the skin. Whilst they have greater penetrating power than alpha, beta particles are less ionising and take longer to effect the same degree of damage.

Neutrons

Neutrons are emitted during certain nuclear processes, e.g. nuclear fission. Neutrons have great penetrating power. Their particular characteristics are made use of in meters for measuring the moisture content of soil.

Gamma rays

Have great penetrating power. Gamma radiation passing through a normal atom will sometimes force the loss of an electron, leaving the atom positively charged; this is called an ion.

X-rays

X-rays are produced by sudden acceleration or deceleration of a charged particle, usually when high-speed electrons strike a suitable target under controlled conditions. The electrical potential required to accelerate electrons to speeds where X-ray production will occur is a minimum of 15,000 volts. X-rays are very similar in their effects to gamma rays. X-rays and gamma rays have high energy, and high penetration power through fairly dense material. In low-density substances, including air, they may travel long distances.

The most familiar examples of ionising radiation in the workplace are in hospitals, dentist surgeries and veterinary surgeries where X-rays are used extensively. X-ray machines are used for security purposes at baggage handling points in airports. In addition, Gamma rays are used in non-destructive testing of metals, say, welds in pipelines and also in food processing factories for measuring the contents of sealed tins.

PARTICULATE AND NON-PARTICULATE TYPES OF IONISING RADIATION, ORIGINS AND SOURCES

Particulate radiation

Alpha and beta particles are produced as a result of radioactive decay. When this happens a new element is produced and radiation is emitted by the atom.

Non-particulate radiation

Gamma radiation is produced when an energetic or 'excited' nucleus loses excess energy. This may result from the ejection of α and β^- particles which means that both alpha and beta radiation may be accompanied by the release of gamma rays. Gamma rays are packets of energy which posses a characteristic wavelength similar to, but shorter than, X-rays. When a particle passes through a heavy atom it transfers a quantity of energy to that atom which is then emitted in the form of X-rays (which are less energetic than gamma rays). An X-ray machine works by bombarding a dense material with high speed electrons. High voltage (greater than 5 kV) equipment such as radar has the potential to produce parasitic X-rays.

The amount of radiation produced is governed by the number of disintegrations occurring per second, the so-called *activity*. In general, this depends on two things: the speed with which atoms decay (i.e. how unstable they are) and the number of radioactive atoms present (i.e. the amount of material). The SI unit of activity is the **Becquerel (Bq)**. 1 Bq equals 1 disintegration per second *(see units of radioactivity section below)*.

The speed with which radioactive decay takes place varies from one substance to another and is characterised by the so-called radioactive *half-life*. The *half-life* of the radioactive material is defined as the time taken for activity in the form of emission of particles and energy to be reduced by one half. Therefore half the nuclei originally present having changed into a different type. After two half lives the radioactivity will be one-quarter of the original value. Half-lives for different radioactive elements can range from fractions of a second to millions of years. The more unstable the element the shorter the half-life. Examples of half-lives are:

Element	Half life
Uranium 235	718 million years
Caesium 137	30 years
Strontium 90	50 days
Radon 216	4.5×10^{-7} seconds

Figure B8-6: Examples of half-lives.

Source: ACT.

Uses and applications

Nearly 90% of average annual radiation doses are from non-occupational sources such as foodstuffs, building materials and radon (particularly in granite areas such as Cornwall). About 87% of the average radiation exposure in the UK comes from natural, rather than man made, sources. Ionising radiation is used widely throughout the working environment. The most obvious place is in the nuclear industry; however it is also used for non-destructive testing (NDT), security equipment, in smoke detectors and for a variety of medical purposes.

The following table gives some common sources:

Equipment / Device	Application - Notes
Radiography (X-rays)	Medical, security and NDT
Ionisation effect smoke detectors	Mainly alpha radiation. Widespread use at home and at work. Optical and photo-electric detectors are non-radioactive.
Thickness gauges, flow gauges and level gauges.	Penetrating radiations (e.g. gamma rays) needed to highlight differences in flow, level, thickness.
Moisture/density gauges	Used in portable devices. Contain two radioactive sources.
High voltage systems	Over 5,000v may produce X-rays. Should be designed/shielded to prevent this.
Radioactive materials	Radioactive tracer isotopes used for medical purposes; very dense depleted uranium used for weight in aircraft and yachts as well as for military purposes; thoriated alloys used in high performance magnesium alloys (e.g. for aircraft engines).
Luminous dials, gauges and markers.	Used in older equipment - some luminous paints etc. are very active and long lived.

Figure B8-7: Common sources of radiation.

Source: ACT.

ROLE OF THE INTERNATIONAL COMMISSION FOR RADIOLOGICAL PROTECTION

The International Commission on Radiological Protection was founded in 1928 to advance for the public benefit the science of radiological protection. The ICRP provides recommendations and guidance on protection against the risks associated with ionising radiation, from artificial sources as widely used in medicine, general industry and nuclear enterprises, and from naturally occurring sources. These reports and recommendations are published four times each year on behalf of the ICRP as the journal *Annals of the ICRP.*

ROLE OF THE NATIONAL RADIOLOGICAL PROTECTION BOARD / HEALTH PROTECTION AGENCY

The National Radiological Protection Board (NRPB) was created by the Radiological Protection Act 1970.

The statutory functions of NRPB are:

- By means of research and otherwise, to advance the acquisition of knowledge about the protection of mankind from radiation hazards.
- To provide information and advice to persons (including Government Departments) with responsibilities in the United Kingdom in relation to the protection from radiation hazards either of the community as a whole or of particular sections of the community.

The NRPB was also given the power to:

- Provide technical services to persons concerned with radiation hazards.
- Make charges for such services, and for providing information and advice.

The Health Protection Agency's (HPA) role is to provide an integrated approach to protecting UK public health through the provision of support and advice to the NHS, local authorities, emergency services, other Arms Length Bodies, the Department of Health and the Devolved Administrations. The Agency was established as a special health authority (SpHA) in 2003.

In 2005, the Agency was established as a non-departmental public body, as the National Radiological Protection Board (NRPB) merged with the HPA SpHA. Radiation protection as part of health protection incorporated in its remit of the new Radiation Protection Division.

Advisory groups
- Advisory Group on Non-Ionising Radiation (AGNIR).
- Advisory Group on Ionising Radiation (AGIR).
- Radiation, Risk and Society Advisory Group (RRSAG).

B8.2 - Non-ionising radiation

Effects

THE ACUTE AND CHRONIC PHYSIOLOGICAL EFFECTS OF EXPOSURE TO NON-IONISING RADIATION

Optical radiation

Optical radiation is another term for light, covering ultraviolet (UV) radiation, visible light, and infrared radiation. For example, overexposure to ultraviolet and blue 'light' can cause common sunburn, photokeratitis ('welder's eye'/'arc eye') and burning of the retina or cornea.

The greatest risks to health are probably posed by:

- UV radiation from the sun. Exposure of the eyes to UV radiation can damage the cornea and produce pain and symptoms similar to that of sand in the eye. The effects on the skin range from redness, burning and accelerated ageing through to various types of skin cancer.
- The misuse of powerful lasers. High-power lasers can cause serious damage to the eye (including blindness) as well as producing skin burns.

Ultraviolet

Ultraviolet (UV) radiation has a relatively low penetrating power and its biological effects are restricted to the surface organs such as the skin, the eyes and the lining of the mouth arising from certain dental procedures. Certain drugs, such as diuretics, oral contraceptives, anti-diabetic drugs and some antibiotics can magnify the effects of UV due to their photosensitising properties.

Target organs at risk are the eyes, hands and buccal lining of the mouth.

A summary of UV effects on biological systems:

	UV wavelength
Bactericidal	200 - 300 nm
Keratitis	250 - 310 nm
Erythema	240 - 275 nm
	290 - 310 nm
Carcinogenesis	290 - 310 nm
Skin Pigmentation	270 - 650 nm

Source: ACT.

Figure B8-8: UV effects on biological systems.

Ultraviolet radiation can be measured using a variety of instruments such as photoelectric cells, photo-conductive cells, photo-voltaic cells or photochemical detectors. Most instruments also use a filter system.

The skin

A significant amount of UV radiation in range 290 - 320 nm is absorbed into the epidermis. While a small amount of UV radiation may be beneficial, because it allows for the formation of vitamin D_3 by the skin, excessive amounts can affect cellular metabolism.

Acute effects are reddening of the skin (erythema) or sunburn. This is also caused by Sunlight in 290 - 320 nm region. Mild sunburn shows erythema a few hours after exposure while longer exposure causes thickening of the skin (oedema), blistering, burning, tenderness and irritation of skin. The skin has a delayed protection mechanism called melanogenesis (i.e. suntan).

One chronic effect of continued exposure to UV radiation is premature ageing due to a decrease in the skin's elasticity. Although UV can only penetrate the superficial layers of the skin, it causes damage to both RNA and DNA molecules which can lead to cutaneous tumours that may be malignant (skin cancer).

The eye

Most damage to the eye is thought to occur at the 210-315 nm range. Excessive exposure leads to:

- Photokeratitis (inflammation of the cornea).
- The induction or promotion of cataracts (the lens of the eye becomes opaque).
- Damage due to an acceleration of the normal ageing of cells in the retina.

Cornea

Ultraviolet radiation of wavelengths shorter than 300 nm (actinic rays) can damage the corneal epithelium. This is most commonly the result of exposure to the sun at high altitude and in areas where shorter wavelengths are readily reflected from bright surfaces such as snow, water, and sand.

'Arc eye' or 'welder's flash' is a type of photokeratitis. There is a latent period of a few hours (about 6-12 hours) between exposure and the onset of symptoms. Symptoms begin with pain akin to 'grit in the eyes'. There is an aversion to bright light. The conjunctiva and cornea become inflamed. The severity of condition depends on duration, intensity and wavelength of UV radiation exposure. The symptoms normally abate after ~ 36 hours and permanent corneal damage is unusual provided that the corneal tissue has time to recover. The eye tends to become more sensitive to UV radiation after repeated exposure.

UVA can penetrate the cornea and is absorbed by the aqueous humour and in the lens, which may produce a harmless, transient fluorescence - chronic exposure may lead to yellowing of the lens.

Lens

Wavelengths of 300-400 nm are transmitted through the cornea, and 80% are absorbed by the lens, where they can cause cataractous changes.

Epidemiologic studies suggest that exposure to solar radiation in these wave lengths near the equator is correlated with a higher incidence of cataracts.

They also indicate that workers exposed to bright sunlight in occupations such as farming, truck driving and construction work appear to have a higher incidence of cataract than those who work primarily indoors.

Experimental studies have shown that these wavelengths cause changes in the lens protein, which lead to cataract formation in animals.

Visible light

Visible light has a spectrum of 400-750 nm. If the wavelengths of this spectrum penetrate fully to the retina, they can cause thermal, mechanical, or photic injuries.

Thermal injuries/retinal thermal injuries

They are produced by light intense enough to increase the temperature in the retina by 10-20^{0}C.

Lasers used in therapy can cause this type of injury. The light is absorbed by the retinal pigment epithelium, where its energy is converted to heat, and the heat causes photocoagulation of retinal tissue.

Mechanical injuries

They can be produced by exposure to laser energy from a Q-switched or mode-locked laser, which produces sonic shock waves that disrupt retinal tissue.

Photic injuries/retinal photo-chemical injury

They are caused by prolonged exposure to intense light, which produces varying degrees of cellular damage in the retinal macula without a significant increase in the temperature of the tissue.

Sun gazing is the most common cause of this type of injury, but prolonged unprotected exposure to a welding arc can also damage the retinal macula. There may be permanent decrease in visual acuity.

The intensity of light, length of exposure, and age are all-important factors. Older people are more sensitive; also those who have had cataract surgery because filtration of light by the lens is impaired.

Infrared

Two different effects can be identified from infrared (IR) radiation. These are:

1. Effects on the thermo-regulatory system by the radiant energy absorbed (e.g. heat stress).
2. Effects on specific organs, particularly the skin and eyes.

The skin responds to IR radiation by vasodilation; however chronic exposure produces pigmentation. Skin temperatures above 45°C cause burns.

High doses of IR radiation can cause acute pain through damage to the cornea. Blood vessels grow into the normally clear cornea and it become opaque due to the ulcers caused by burning. A delayed effect can occur due to the cumulative effects of IR exposure.

"La cataracte des verriers" (glassblower's cataract) is an example of a heat injury that damages the anterior lens capsule among unprotected artists. Denser cataractous changes can occur in unprotected workers who observe glowing masses of glass or iron for many hours a day. Potters may also be exposed to this type of radiation.

Another important factor is the distance between the worker and the source of radiation. In the case of arc welding, infrared radiation decreases rapidly as a function of distance, so that farther than 1 metre away from where welding takes place, it does not pose an ocular hazard anymore, but ultraviolet radiation still does. That is why welders wear tinted glasses and surrounding workers only have to wear clear ones.

Wavelength	Effect
> 1500 nm	Radiation is absorbed by water in surface layers of skin where energy is dissipated as heat - thermoregulatory system.
900 - 1400 nm	Causes cataracts (clouding of the transparent lens of the eye).
1000 - 1400 nm	Causes permanent damage to the lens. A significant proportion of the energy is transmitted by the cornea and penetrates the eye.
1300 nm	The skin is transparent to this radiation.

Figure B8-9: Infrared radiation effects.

Source: ACT.

Remember: the most damaging wavelengths for organs, such as the eyes, are below 1400 nm.

Microwaves and radio frequency radiation

Electromagnetic radiation can interact with objects (or people) in three different ways. The energy waves can pass through an object without being changed, like light through a window. It can be reflected, like light off a mirror, or it can be absorbed and cause the object to heat up, like a pavement in the sun.

The health hazards of electromagnetic radiation are related only to the absorption of energy. The effects of absorbed energy depend on many different factors such as its wavelength and frequency, its intensity and duration. Different materials also absorb energy differently.

When microwaves or radiowaves are absorbed by body tissues, localized or spot heating can occur. The increased temperature can damage tissues, especially those with poor temperature control such as the lens of the eye.

Cataracts, clouding of the lens of the eye, may occur at the very high energy levels encountered close to radiating radar antennas. Heat damage to tissues is caused by high levels of exposure for short periods of time.

The health effects of low levels of exposure to radiowaves or microwaves for long periods of time are much harder to find and to prove. Some scientific studies show health effects from long-term, low level exposure, other studies do not.

The following list includes health effects which some researchers suspect may be related to excessive radio frequency/microwave exposure:

- Psychological changes, e.g., insomnia, irritability, mood swings.
- Depression.
- Headaches.
- Nervous system abnormalities.
- Hormonal changes.
- Miscarriages and birth defects.
- Male Infertility.
- Altered immunity.
- Leukaemia.

Of course, many of these health effects are relatively common, and most people having these problems have NOT had excessive exposure to radio frequency/microwave radiation.

Safety and health precautions

Employers who have people working around devices which produce radio frequency/microwave radiation need to be sure that those devices are properly shielded to prevent leakage of radiation. Safety information regarding proper use and shielding of those devices can usually be obtained from owner/operator manuals and manufacturers.

Radio frequency sealers and heaters have been among the major sources of employee exposure to radio frequency/microwave radiation. When these machines are used, employees should use mechanical or electrical devices that allow them to stay as far away form the source of radiation as possible. Whenever possible, these sealers should be turned off when not being used. Maintenance and adjustment of this type of equipment should be performed only by trained technicians and only when the machines are turned off.

Warnings should be posted to keep everyone away from the source of radiation except for those workers who are absolutely essential to performing the job.

People who are regularly exposed to significant levels of radiofrequency/microwave radiation should have pre-employment and annual physical exams. The doctors should pay careful attention to the eyes to look for cataracts, to the nervous system for any abnormalities, to the blood to detect any early evidence of leukaemia, and to the reproductive system to detect any abnormalities. Information concerning the frequency and intensity of the radiation exposures and duration of exposures should be provided to the physician.

In work areas where there is known or suspected to be significant amounts of radio frequency/microwave radiation present, specialists should measure the amounts of radiation present. If excessive radio frequency/microwave radiation is detected, modifications in the workplace should be made to reduce radiation exposure of workers. Afterwards, additional measurements should be made to determine if the radiation exposure has been reduced.

Microwave cooking ovens

Microwave ovens used for heating food, when used in accordance with manufacturer's instructions, do not expose personnel to microwave radiation.

Microwave ovens do not need to be included in an employer's Hazard Communication program.

Lasers

Effects on the eye

The fact that eye damage may result from exposure to high levels of ultra violet, visible and infra red radiation (optical radiation) has been discussed in the previous sections.

Once damaged the retina cannot be repaired and the cells will not regenerate. This damage can be caused naturally by staring into the sun which would cause a level of retinal illumination about a million times greater than normal. A 1mW continuous wave visible laser can give an order of magnitude higher than the direct viewing of the sun.

The type of eye damage depends on the particular tissue affected, which in turn depends on the ocular transmission characteristics of the type of laser used. Both the far infra red (1400 nm - 1 mm) and far ultra violet (200 - 295 nm) radiation will affect only the cornea at the front of the eye where they will be absorbed. Near ultra violet radiation (295 - 400 nm) will penetrate some depth into the eye as far as the lens, whereas the near infra red (700 - 1400 nm) and all visible radiation (400 - 700 nm) will penetrate to the retina.

Near infra red lasers pose a particular hazard, as they cannot be perceived, although they enter the eye and are focused onto the retina. Both visible light and near infra red radiation is focused onto a very small spot (~ 10 µm diameter) on the retinal surface.

Effects on the skin

Because there is no focusing effect, the skin is more resistant to damage when irradiated than the eye. Acute exposure to laser radiation from Class 4 lasers may give rise to skin damage which may range from mild erythema (skin reddening) through to deep burns (tissue charring).

EXAMPLES OF WORKPLACE OCCURRENCES AND APPLICATIONS

Ultraviolet

Major workplace sources are incandescent lamps, gas discharge lamps (including fluorescent lights and xenon arc lamps) and industrial UV lasers. UV radiation is also used in several dental procedures. Outdoor workers are exposed to the sunlight, which contains ultraviolet rays. This natural exposure to UV radiation has increased in recent years due to environmental factors such as ozone depletion.

Other workplace sources are:

- The sun - meaning those who work outdoors are at risk of exposure.
- Curing with UV (e.g. inks, coatings on floor & wall coverings, timber panels, fibre optics, etc.).
- UV sources in photocopiers and laser printers.
- Lasers.
- Back lights.
- Welding.
- Germicidal lamps.

UV radiation reflects off water, sand, snow, concrete or any light-coloured surface. It also increases in intensity with altitude.

UV radiation can cause cheilitis, which is the inflammation, cracking, and dryness of the lips. Groups prone to this include seamen, agricultural workers and arc welders.

Another occupational group at risk from UV exposure are dentists and dental technicians. This is due to certain dental procedures such as the hardening of fillings used for cavities (photopolymerisation of methacrylates). In this process each tooth typically requires 250 seconds of exposure to UVA 350 - 380 nm at a high power density.

Visible light

Workplace sources:

- Lasers.
- Spotlights.
- Welding arcs.

Visible light is not normally a problem, but where intense (e.g. in lasers) can potentially cause damage to the cornea and retina of the eye. It can also cause cataracts. Another effect is that pulsing or stroboscopic light can cause fits in susceptible people.

Infrared

Infra-red is a component of radiant heat, therefore a factor in foundries & smelters. Other workplace sources are:

- Lasers.
- Molten glass.
- Infrared lamps.
- The sun.

Steel workers have been recorded as developing cataracts 15-20 years after first exposure. A link has been established between the effects of industrial exposure and ageing with many workers developing cataracts over the age of 60.

Microwaves and radio frequency radiation

This type of radiation is produced by radio/television transmitters. It is used industrially for induction heating of metals and is often found in intruder detectors.

Since the discovery that microwaves have the ability to heat, numerous attempts have been made to capitalize on this phenomenon for commercial applications. As the consumer's personal experience with residential microwave ovens has shown, the primary drawback of microwave heating is its inability to heat materials in a uniform manner, leaving hot spots that damage the item being heated and cold spots where the item is unheated or unprocessed. As a result, previous attempts to employ microwaves in commercial processes requiring uniform heating have been unsuccessful and extremely costly.

Often used mainly as a source of heat or in the communications industry:

- TV, FM radio & radar transmitters.
- Mobile communications (mobile telephones, 'CB' radios, walkie-talkies).
- Dielectric heaters for plastic sealing, glue curing, particle & panel board production.
- Induction heaters for hardening, tempering, forging, etc.
- Plastic welders.
- Microwave ovens.

Lasers

The light beam produced by most lasers is pencil-sized, and maintains its size and direction over very large distances; this sharply focused beam of coherent light is suitable for a wide variety of applications. Lasers have been used in industry for cutting and boring metals and other materials, and for inspecting optical equipment. In medicine, they have been used in surgical operations. Lasers have been used in several kinds of scientific research. The field of holography (holograms) is based on the fact that actual wave-front patterns, captured in a photographic image of an object illuminated with laser light, can be reconstructed to produce a three-dimensional image of the object.

Lasers have opened a new field of scientific research, nonlinear optics, which is concerned with the study of such phenomena as the frequency doubling of coherent light by certain crystals. One important result of laser research is the development of lasers that can be tuned to emit light over a range of frequencies, instead of producing light of only a single frequency. Work is being done to develop lasers for communication; in a manner similar to radio transmission, the transmitted light beam is modulated with a signal and is received and demodulated some distance away. Lasers have also been used in plasma physics and chemistry.

(For examples of industrial applications of lasers see matrix in "Controls" section).

Measurement

MEASUREMENT OF POWER DENSITY

Exposures are based on power density measurements (milliwatts per square centimetre).

Power density of solar radiation

The sun is the source of heat and energy for the earth. The solar output on the earth is called the power density. The power density of the sun's radiation on the surface of the earth is approximately 1.4 kW/m^2. This value varies slightly throughout the year but by no more than 0.1 percent. One reason for this variation is the changing earth-sun distance. This distance varies by about six percent throughout the year, causing the power density to range from about 1.308 kW/m^2 to 1.398 kW/m^2. The power density also varies with the 11-year cycle of sunspots. In the 1980s, scientists discovered that the total amount of solar radiation ebbs or rises in synch with the increase or decrease of sunspots during this cycle. During the peak of the cycle, hundreds of dark spots cover the surface of the sun with bright regions giving off extra radiation. During the minimum, the sunspots disappear, causing the sun's energy to decrease by about 0.1 percent. Furthermore, the energy the sun gives off, and hence the power density on the earth, will keep on changing with time because, as the sun evolves, its total radiation output varies. The power density 4.5 billion years ago would be smaller than that today since the sun's brightness has increased by roughly 30 percent.

Today, by measuring the power density, there is evidence that suggests that the sunlight hitting the earth is slightly brighter than that twenty five years ago. It has been reported that the intensity of solar radiation has increased. If such speculation is true, it raises the possibility that the global warming experienced over the past few years can be attributed to the variances in solar output.

BIOLOGICAL EFFECT

When radiation passes through a biological material, most of the energy deposited (>99%) goes into production of heat. The resulting rise in temperature is very small; therefore you are not going to suffer ill-health effects from the thermal energy, and in fact you are not even going to feel it.

The biological effects of the types of non-ionising radiation are discussed above under each of the type headings.

EXPOSURE STANDARDS

Ultraviolet radiation is absorbed by oxygen in the air to produce ozone, which has an OES of 0.1 ppm. Even below this level it may cause smarting of the eyes.

Restrictions on exposure to electric and magnetic fields are covered by NRPB guidelines. The International Commission on Non-ionising Radiation Protection (ICNIRP) has also published guidelines.

In the electromagnetic fields, the limits are there mainly to protect against the body heating. This is in terms of 'specific absorption rate' (SAR).

The NRPB guidelines give a whole body SAR restriction of 0.4 W kg^{-1}, localised exposure in the head and trunk restricted to 10 W kg^{-1} and in the limbs 20 W kg^{-1}. Although there is no specific legislation on this, HSE would consider compliance with these restrictions as fulfilling the general duty of care on the operators of equipment that generate electromagnetic fields.

Controls

EXPLANATION OF ASSESSMENT OF RISKS

The risk of being damaged by non-ionising radiation is dependent on the power of the radiation, i.e. the frequency of the waves. It also depends on the likelihood of coming into contact with the radiation, the number of people exposed and the presence of any vulnerable people. Ultra violet radiation is the most powerful of the non-ionising radiations. As with other forms of energy, the controls should be based on time, distance and shielding.

EXAMPLE OF PROTECTIVE MEASURES IN RELATION TO UV

Protection against over-exposure to UV may be achieved by a combination of:

1. Engineering control measures.
2. Administrative control measures.
3. Personal protection.

Engineering control measures

The use of engineering controls can provide physical shielding against the effects of radiation. In addition to well designed equipment, appropriately sited to minimise exposure, the following can be used reduce exposure.

- Containment - sealed housings; screened areas using partitions or curtains.
- Use of interlocks.
- Elimination of reflected UV radiation by use of non-reflective surfaces.
- Use of barriers to ensure a safety factor distance (inverse square law).

Administrative control measures

The use of administrative controls can reduce individual's exposure to radiation, by controlling the proximity and time of any interaction between an individual and radiation.

- Limitation of access.
- Hazard awareness training and use of hazard warning signs, lights etc.
- Limitation of exposure time.
- Safe maintenance procedures.

Personal protection

Protection of the skin - cover exposed areas, i.e. backs of hands, face, neck and forearms. Protective gloves are suitable for hands (e.g. PVC). Forearms protected by long sleeves made from poplin or flannelette. Some barrier creams contain a UV filter but their effectiveness depends on an adequate film thickness.

Protection of eyes - is normally achieved through the use of eye and face protectors (glasses, goggles, shields and helmets. Most standard ophthalmic lenses offer a degree of UV attenuation (e.g. sunglasses and spectacles). This is achieved through the incorporation of UV absorbing additives such as iron oxides into the glass used for lenses or by the addition of reflective coatings. The degree of protection achieved is however variable depending on factors such as the material the lens is made from, its thickness, the tints used and the radiation wavelength (e.g. UV-A, UV-B). Standards for goggles, spectacles or face shields offering protection in welding or similar operations are specified in a series of standards including:

- BS EN 169:1992 - general transmittance requirements and recommended use.
- BS EN 170:1992 - specification for ultraviolet filters.
- BS EN 171:1992 - specification for infrared filters.

Time, distance and shielding will protect against the range of non-ionising radiations. Complete enclosure will shield, as will screens. Other shielding could be the use of PPE: goggles with a filter, sunglasses, and skin covering. Suntan creams and lotions can be used to filter out the harmful effects of UV. Clothing and screens will protect against IR, for example for foundry workers. Total enclosure by design, for example, a microwave oven, which incorporates an interlock device that will only allow the oven to work with the door shut, will protect against tissue damage from microwaves.

Reducing the time of exposure will help to prevent skin damage.

The further the distance radiation has to travel, the more likely it is to lose its harmful energy. The further away the person is from the source, the less likely the energy will be enough to do any harm.

IDENTIFICATION OF HAZARDS CLASSIFICATION OF LASERS (EN 60825-1)

All lasers should be labelled with their class and appropriate warnings.

Class	Characteristics
Class 1	Inherently safe laser products. Safety is achieved either due to their low power or by their total enclosure, e.g. laser printers, CD players.
Class 1M	Either a highly divergent beam or a large diameter beam, therefore only a small part can enter the eye. Harmful if viewed through magnifiers, e.g. fibre optic communication systems.
Class 2	Maximum output of 1 milliwatt (mW), wavelength between 400 and 700 nm. Damage to eye prevented by blinking and averting the head, an instinctive response. Repeated deliberate exposure is not safe. e.g. laser pointers and barcode scanners.
Class 2M	Either a highly divergent beam or a large diameter beam, therefore only a small part can enter the eye, limited to 1mW. Harmful if viewed through magnifiers or for long periods, e.g. civil engineering applications: level and orientation instruments.
Class 3R	Higher powered than classes 1 and 2. Max output of 5mW, exceeds max permissible exposure and can cause eye injuries. This class replaces the former 3A and lower part of 3B, e.g. some laser pointers and some alignment products for home improvement work.
Class 3B	Output power of 500 mW (half a watt). Cause eye damage from direct beam and reflections. Extent of injury depends on radiant power entering eye and duration of exposure, e.g. lasers for physiotherapy treatment and research lasers.
Class 4	Output greater than 500 mW with no upper restriction. Cause injury to eye and skin and a fire hazard e.g. lasers in displays, laser surgery and cutting metals.

Figure B8-10: Laser classes and appropriate warnings.

Source: ACT.

Outline of associated controls

Many chemical and physical hazards other than laser radiation can be found in the laser area that must also be adequately controlled:

Electrical equipment and systems
- Always be aware of the high risk of injury and fire in laser operations because of the presence of electrical power sources.
- The installation, operation, and maintenance of electrical equipment and systems must conform to the standards stated in the EN 60825.

Lighting
- Adequate lighting is necessary in controlled areas.
- If lights are extinguished during laser operation, provide control switches in convenient locations or install a radio controlled switch.
- When natural light is not sufficient for safe egress from a laser area during an electrical power failure, install emergency lighting.
- A laser operation may involve ionizing radiation that originates from the presence of radioactive materials or the use of electrical power in excess of 15 kV.
- Microwave and radio frequency (RF) fields may be generated by laser systems or support equipment.
- Do a hazard assessment to evaluate the hazards before starting an operation.

B8.3 - Ionising radiation

Effects

INJURIES DUE TO IONISING RADIATION

X-rays, beta rays, and other radiation sources in adequate doses can cause ocular injury.

Lids

The eyelid is particularly vulnerable to x-ray damage because of the thinness of its skin. Loss of lashes and scarring can lead to inversion or eversion (entropion or ectropion) of the lid margins and prevent adequate closure.

Conjonctiva

Scarring of the conjonctiva can impair the production of mucus and the function of the lachrymal gland ducts, thereby causing dryness of the eyes.

Lens

X-ray radiation in a dose of 500-800 R. directed toward the lens surface can cause cataracts, sometimes with a delay of several months to a year before the opacities appear.

EFFECTS OF EXPOSURE TO IONISING RADIATION

Ionising radiation can by definition remove orbital electrons from atoms causing them to become electrically charged. When this occurs in a living cell, various types of damage may occur. This ranges from direct interference the cell's operation and reproduction when molecular chains are broken within the DNA structure. Ionisation can also cause the formation of highly reactive groups of atom called free radicals. These cause harm because of the undesirable chain chemical reactions they cause. With quite low doses of radioactivity no effect may occur but higher doses can cause molecular changes relating to the cells structure and function. Changes can affect the cell in a number of ways:

- Complete recovery.
- Loss of reproductive capability (cell division is prevented).
- Genetic changes (mutations).
- Cell death.

The clinical symptoms of this can take the form of radiation sickness, cataracts or the development of cancer in the longer term.

Effects can be classified as somatic and genetic:

Somatic effects - effects evident during the lifetime of the exposed individual.

Genetic effects - effects apparent in the descendants of the exposed individuals.

Potential health effects

The effects on the body of exposure to ionising radiation will depend on the type of radiation, the frequency and duration of exposure. Acute effects will include nausea, vomiting, diarrhoea and burns (either superficial skin burns or deep, penetrating burns causing cell damage). Long term (chronic) effects such as dermatitis, skin ulcers, cataracts and cancers can also be expected.

Acute exposure

Early effects of a single acute dose (apparent within 60 days of exposure) vary from slight blood changes, for exposures between 0.25 and 1 Sv, to death, which is the probable outcome of exposures exceeding 6 Sv.

Delayed effects may occur some time after recovery from early effects. They include loss of hair and temporary or permanent infertility.

Late effects such as leukaemia may occur many years after the exposure, their probability increasing as the dose increases.

Chronic exposure

Practically all occupational radiation involves chronic exposures, i.e. small weekly doses (e.g. < 1 mSv) occurring over many months or years. Somatic effects of an accumulated chronic exposure are less serious than those of an equivalent acute exposure.

In a lifetime of occupational exposure without any observable effect, an individual's total dose can be large enough so that an equal dose given in a few hours would be seriously disabling or fatal.

From chronic exposures there are no delayed effects and the probability of late effects is minimal. If chronic occupational doses are within the International Commission on Radiological Protection (ICRP) dose limiting recommendations, the probability of late effects is so small that it has not been possible to establish whether any such effect exists.

The biological effects of radiation can also be defined as either *stochastic (random)* or *non-stochastic*:

Stochastic effects - are those for which the probability of the effect occurring, rather than its severity, is a function of dose (e.g. cancer, genetic effects). There is no threshold dose below which a stochastic effect will certainly not occur.

Non-stochastic effects - are those for which the severity of the effect varies with dose and for which a threshold may therefore exist (e.g. cataracts of the lens of the eye, damage to blood vessels, impairment of fertility).

Summary of effects

The following flow chart summarises the biological effects:

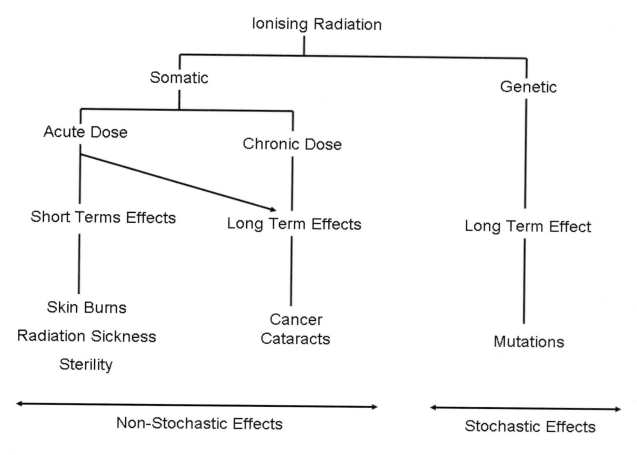

Figure B8-11: Biological effects.

Source: ACT.

EXAMPLES OF WORKPLACE OCCURRENCES AND APPLICATIONS

Nuclear industry

The nuclear industry includes nuclear fuel fabrication, nuclear power generation, nuclear fuel reprocessing, radioactive waste (treatment, decommissioning, storage and disposal) and research.

Non-nuclear industry

- Industry (e.g. radiography).
- Medicine/Dentistry (e.g. diagnostics & treatment).
- Research (e.g. biological research).
- Teaching (e.g. schools & undergraduate).
- Sterilisation (e.g. food & medical products).
- Measurement (e.g. thickness and levels).
- Security (e.g. airport personnel).

Measurement

When scientists measure radiation, they use different terms depending on whether they are discussing radiation coming from a radioactive source, the radiation dose absorbed by a person, or the risk that a person will suffer health effects (biological risk) from exposure to radiation.

The employer should make an assessment of the work being, or to be, carried out in any particular area.

- The areas should be designated as ***controlled*** if, after consulting the Radiation Protection Advisor, it appears to be necessary to set up special procedures for persons in the area, whether for routine procedures or for accidents, in order to prevent significant exposures and in any event if ***persons are likely to receive more than 6mSv per year***.
- Any area where the employer finds it necessary to keep conditions under review to check if the area should be designated as controlled, or if the area is such that ***persons may receive more than 1mSv per year***, should be designated as ***supervised***.
- An area should also be designated as controlled if there is significant risk of spreading radioactive contamination outside the working area.

- Controlled areas should be physically demarcated or suitably delineated.
- Signs should be displayed in controlled and supervised areas to indicate that the area is controlled and they should also provide information about the nature and risks of the radiation sources.

Persons entering a controlled area should either be classified or be entering in accordance with 'written arrangements' designed to ensure that doses will not exceed, in cases of persons over 18, levels which would otherwise require the persons to be classified. In the case of other persons the relevant dose limit is applicable.

- Units of radioactivity.

SI units and prefixes

The International System of Units ('System Internationale' [SI]) for radiation measurement:

	Radioactivity	**Absorbed dose**	**Dose equivalent**	**Exposure**
Common Units	curie (Ci)	Rad	rem	roentgen (R)
SI Units	becquerel (Bq)	gray (Gy)	sievert (Sv)	coulomb/kilogram (C/kg)

Figure B8-12: International systems of units for radiation measurement.   Source: Guidance for Radiation Accident Measurement.

Following is a list of prefixes and their meanings that are often used in conjunction with SI units:

Multiple	**Prefix**	**Symbol**
10^{12}	Tera	T
10^9	Giga	G
10^6	Mega	M
10^3	Kilo	k
10^{-2}	Centi	c
10^{-3}	Milli	m
10^{-6}	Micro	μ
10^{-9}	Nano	n

Figure B8-13: SI prefixes.   Source: Guidance for Radiation Accident Measurement.

Most scientists in the international community measure radiation using the SI, a uniform system of weights and measures that evolved from the metric system. However, in the USA, the conventional system of measurement is still widely used.

Different units of measure are used depending on what aspect of radiation is being measured. For example, the amount of radiation being given off, or emitted, by a radioactive material is measured using the conventional unit *curie* (Ci), named for the famed scientist Marie Curie, or the SI unit *Becquerel* (Bq). The radiation dose absorbed by a person (that is, the amount of energy deposited in human tissue by radiation) is measured using the conventional unit *rad* or the SI unit *gray* (Gy). The biological risk of exposure to radiation is measured using the conventional unit *rem* or the SI unit *sievert* (Sv).

MEASURING EMITTED RADIATION

When the amount of radiation being emitted or given off is discussed, the unit of measure used is the conventional unit Ci or the SI unit Bq.

A radioactive atom gives off or emits radioactivity because the nucleus has too many particles, too much energy, or too much mass to be stable. The nucleus breaks down, or disintegrates, in an attempt to reach a nonradioactive (stable) state. As the nucleus disintegrates, energy is released in the form of radiation.

The Ci or Bq is used to express the number of disintegrations of radioactive atoms in a radioactive material over a period of time. For example, one Ci is equal to 37 billion (37×10^9) disintegrations per second. The Ci is being replaced by the Bq. Since one Bq is equal to one disintegration per second, one Ci is equal to 37 billion (37×10^9) Bq.

Ci or Bq may be used to refer to the amount of radioactive materials released into the environment. For example, during the Chernobyl power plant accident that took place in the former Soviet Union, an estimated total of 81 million Ci of radioactive cesium (a type of radioactive material) was released.

RADIATION DOSE

When a person is exposed to radiation, energy is deposited in the tissues of the body. The amount of energy deposited per unit of weight of human tissue is called the *absorbed dose*. Absorbed dose is measured using the conventional *rad* or the SI *Gy*. Biological damage does not just depend on the absorbed dose. It also depends on the type of radiation. For example, one Gy of α radiation in tissue can be much more harmful than one Gy of β radiation.

The rad, which stands for radiation absorbed dose, was the conventional unit of measurement, but it has been replaced by the *Gy (Gray)*. One Gy is equal to 100 rad.

DOSE EQUIVALENT

This refers to radiation dose to the whole body or single organ that has been adjusted to make it equivalent in risk of cancer to the amount of dose from gamma radiation that would cause the same risk of cancer. The weighting factor for γ radiation, X-rays and β particles is set at 1. For α particles it is set at 20. The equivalent dose is expressed in a unit called the sievert (Sv). The measurement is usually in millisieverts (mSv), the mSv being a thousandth of a Sv.

Measuring biological risk

A person's biological risk (that is, the risk that a person will suffer health effects from an exposure to radiation) is measured using the conventional unit *rem* or the SI unit *Sv*.

The equivalent dose is used to quantify the **effective dose**. This is the sum of the equivalent doses to the exposed organs and tissues weighted by the appropriate tissue-weighting factor. The effective dose is also expressed in sieverts.

THE USE OF IONISATION CHAMBERS (GEIGER COUNTER)

Radiation cannot be detected by human senses. A variety of instruments are available for detecting and measuring radiation. The most common type of radiation detector is a Geiger-Mueller (GM) tube, also called a Geiger counter.

Geiger counters measures alpha, beta, gamma, and x-radiation; they can:

- Monitor personal radiation exposure.
- Monitor an area or perimeter.
- Detect radiation leaks and contamination.
- Ensure regulatory compliance.
- Monitor changes in background radiation.
- Demonstrate principles of nuclear physics.
- Check for radioactive minerals in the earth.

SCINTILLATION DETECTORS

(Source: www.imagine.gsfc.nasa.gov).

A popular method for the detection of gamma-rays involves the use of crystal scintillators. The general description of a scintillator is a material that emits low-energy (usually in the visible range) photons when struck by a high-energy charged particle. When used as a gamma-ray detector, the scintillator does not directly detect the gamma-rays. Instead, the gamma-rays produce charged particles in the scintillator crystals which interact with the crystal and emit photons. These lower energy photons are subsequently collected by photomultiplier tubes (PMTs).

When gamma-rays pass through matter, they can undergo three basic processes:

- Compton scattering.
- Photoelectric absorption.
- Pair production.

Each of these processes can create high-energy electrons or anti-electrons (positrons) which interact in the scintillator as charged particles. By adding up the energy collected in the surrounding photomultiplier tubes, we can determine the energy of the gamma-ray detected.

Scintillators can be made of a variety of materials, depending on the intended applications. The most common scintillators used in gamma-ray detectors which are made of inorganic materials are usually an alkali halide salt, such as sodium iodide (NaI) or cesium iodide (CsI). To help these materials do their job, a bit of impurity is often added. This material is called an 'activator'. Thallium and sodium are often used for this purpose. So one often sees detectors described as NaI(Tl), which means it is a sodium iodide crystal with a thallium activator, or as CsI(Na), which is a cesium iodide crystal with a sodium activator.

Inorganic scintillators have been used as gamma-ray detectors aboard many space-based missions to observe sources of cosmic gamma-radiation. These missions include:

- The Compton Gamma-Ray Observatory (CGRO).
- The first High Energy Astrophysical Observatory (HEAO-1).
- The Rossl X-Ray Timing Explorer (RXTE).

The GLAST Gamma-Ray Burst Monitor will use 12 NaI scintillators and 2 bismuth germanate (BGO) detectors to cover the entire sky and be sensitive to gamma-rays between a few keV and 25 MeV.

FILM BADGES

Film badges are a form of dosimeter used to monitor dosage of ionising radiation. The film badge is an established, accurate method for reporting dose, used in medical practices such as dental offices and veterinary clinics, as well as universities and hospitals that utilize X-rays. Film badges provide accurate detection based on dose assessment methodology; they are slim and lightweight and can be worn on the body or extremities. The film packet is sealed to shield the sensitive material from light-induced exposure and is encased in a specially designed moulded plastic holder. The multi-filter system is designed so that radiation will reach the exposed film after penetrating the five different filter areas: open window (OW), aluminium (Al), copper (Cu), lead/tin (Pb/Sn), and plastic (Pl). A complex algorithm is deployed to analyze the results of these filter areas and report dose.

Badges give radiographers a way of determining the total radiation exposure for a period of time. Radiation exposed film turns black when it is developed. Plastic, aluminium, cadmium and/or lead filters in the holder for the film packet allow determination of types of radiation and its approximate energy. Lead filters out low energy radiation so that the film records only high energy radiation exposure under the lead filters. Plastic filters out most beta particles. Aluminium and cadmium filter out different energies of X-rays as well as beta particles. Cadmium converts neutrons into gamma radiation so that the neutron exposure may be measured. Unfortunately, film also detects heat and mechanical damage so the film dosimeters must be handled carefully.

THERMOLUMINESCENT DOSIMETERS (TLD)

The thermoluminescent dosimeter badges contain small pieces of material such as lithium fluoride or manganese sulphate which absorb the radiation in such a fashion that some of the electrons in the material remain in excited or high energy states for a long time. When the thermoluminescent dosimeter materials are heated, they release light in quantities related to their radiation exposure. The materials can be reused, are relatively rugged and give reliable information over long periods of time. Also, the badges are generally smaller than film badges.

Thermoluminescent (TL) means emitting light when heated. In brief, the mechanism of TL is as follows:

When a strong energy source (such as ionising radiation) hits a TL material, electrons are freed from some atoms and moved to other parts of the material, leaving behind "holes" of positive charge. Subsequently when the TL material is heated, the electrons and the "holes" re-combine, and release the extra energy in the form of light. The light intensity can be measured, and related to the amount of energy initially absorbed through exposure to the energy source.

Controls

UK RADIATION PROTECTION LEGISLATION

The *Ionising Radiation Regulations (IRR) 1999* are the principal set of UK radiation protection regulations and are essential reading for those involved in radiological protection, and radiation employers who work (or intend to work) with ionising radiations.

The *Ionising Radiations (Medical Exposure) Regulations (IRMER) 2000*, together with IRR 1999 implement the basic measures for the health protection of individuals against dangers of ionising radiation in relation to medical exposure. The Regulations impose duties on those responsible for administering ionising radiation to protect persons undergoing medical exposure whether as part of their own medical diagnosis or treatment or as part of occupational health surveillance, health screening, voluntary participation in research or medico-legal procedures.

The *Justification of Practices involving Ionising Radiations 2004* introduce the international radiological protection principle of generic "justification" of classes of practices involving exposure to ionising radiation. They are designed to weigh the health detriments of such practices against economic, social or other benefits. The regulations should not impose any new significant compliance burden on small users because they will have previously had to obtain site-by-site justification under RSA 1993 *(see below)*. Innovative practices belonging to a new class or type of practice are likely to be made by the larger users - justification will then be valid after due process under the regulations (and will then be valid for all users).

The *Radioactive Substances Act (RSA) 1993*. Essential reading for those involved with the use of radioactive materials and sources, and who accumulate and dispose of radioactive waste in the UK. This is another principal piece of legislation for UK radiation protection.

The *Radiation (Emergency Preparedness and Public Information) Regulations (REPPIR) 2001* implement basic safety standards for the protection of the health of workers and the general public against the dangers arising from ionising radiation and impose requirements for that purpose on operators of premises where radioactive substances are present (in quantities exceeding specified thresholds). Most small users do not need to worry about compliance with REPPIR since their holdings of radioactive materials is likely to be less than the set threshold limits. That said, there could be circumstances where a small user holds a large radioactive source in an irradiator which no longer has a valid 'special form' certificate.

The *Radioactive Material (Road Transport) Regulations (RM(RT)) 2002* are divided into 14 Parts and broadly follow the sequence of the IAEA Regulations of 1996. They make provisions concerning the transport in Great Britain of radioactive material by road and detail transport limits, packaging requirements and labelling.

DESCRIPTION OF RADIOLOGICAL LIMITS

Classes of persons to whom dose limits apply - from IRR 1999

Employees of 18 years of age or above

1. For the purposes of regulation 11(1), the limit on effective dose for any employee of 18 years of age or above shall be 20 mSv in any calendar year.

2. Without prejudice to paragraph 1 -

    (a) the limit on equivalent dose for the lens of the eye shall be 150 mSv in a calendar year;

    (b) the limit on equivalent dose for the skin shall be 500 mSv in a calendar year as applied to the dose averaged over any area of 1cm2 regardless of the area exposed;

    (c) the limit on equivalent dose for the hands, forearms, feet and ankles shall be 500 mSv in a calendar year.

Trainees aged under 18 years

3. For the purposes of regulation 11(1), the limit on effective dose for any trainee under 18 years of age shall be 6 mSv in any calendar year.

4. Without prejudice to paragraph 3 -

    (a) the limit on equivalent dose for the lens of the eye shall be 50 mSv in a calendar year;

(b) the limit on equivalent dose for the skin shall be 150 mSv in a calendar year as applied to the dose averaged over any area of 1 cm2 regardless of the area exposed;

(c) the limit on equivalent dose for the hands, forearms, feet and ankles shall be 150 mSv in a calendar year.

Women of reproductive capacity

5. Without prejudice to paragraphs 1 and 3, the limit on equivalent dose for the abdomen of a woman of reproductive capacity who is at work, being the equivalent dose from external radiation resulting from exposure to ionising radiation averaged throughout the abdomen, shall be 13 mSv in any consecutive period of three months.

Other persons

6. Subject to paragraph 7, for the purposes of regulation 11(1) the limit on effective dose for any person other than an employee or trainee, including any person below the age of 16, shall be 1 mSv in any calendar year.

7. Paragraph 6 shall not apply in relation to any person (not being a comforter or carer) who may be exposed to ionising radiation resulting from the medical exposure of another and in such a case the limit on effective dose for any such person shall be 5 mSv in any period of 5 consecutive calendar years.

8. Without prejudice to paragraphs 6 and 7 -

    (a) the limit on equivalent dose for the lens of the eye shall be 15 mSv in any calendar year;

    (b) the limit on equivalent dose for the skin shall be 50 mSv in any calendar year averaged over any 1 cm2 area regardless of the area exposed;

    (c) the limit on equivalent dose for the hands, forearms, feet and ankles shall be 50 mSv in a calendar year.

ALARA/ALARP principle

The ALARA/ALARP principle is the requirement to keep radiation doses as low as is reasonably achievable / practicable. The ALARP principle allows a measure of discretion to be observed and takes into account social and economic factors. It does not mean that doses below laid down statutory limits are acceptable. It does mean that whatever the dose rate to which people are exposed, steps should be considered, and taken if reasonable to do so, to restrict the dose to the lowest reasonably practicable.

DEFINITION OF CLASSIFIED PERSON

In relation to the Ionising Radiations Regulations (IRR) 1999, a classified worker is one who is likely to receive a dose in excess of 6 mSv (millisieverts) a year, or an equivalent dose which exceeds 3/10 (three tenths) of any relevant dose limit. An equivalent dose is the absorbed dose X (multiplied by) a quality factor (which depends on where in the body the absorption occurred).

A classified worker must have medical surveillance, dose limits modified for overexposure, overexposure investigated and notified to the HSE.

PRACTICAL CONTROL OF EXTERNAL RADIATION

External radiation hazards are those from sources outside the body such that there is no possibility of these entering into the body as particulate contamination. In general such sources can be shut off, removed or a person can leave an area in which they arise.

There are three general guidelines for controlling exposure to ionising radiation: minimising exposure time, maximising distance from the radiation source, and shielding yourself from the radiation source.

Time

Time is an important factor in limiting exposure to the public and to radiological emergency responders. The shorter the period of time one stays in a radiation field, the smaller the dose he or she will receive. The maximum time to be spent in the radiation environment is given as the exposure time. The exposure time can be calculated using the following equation:

Exposure Time = Dose Limit/Dose Rate.

Because of this time factor, it is very important to carefully plan the work to be done prior to entering the radiation environment. Working as quickly as practicable once there, as well as rotating personnel who are in the radiation area, also will help minimise exposure of individuals.

Distance

Distance can be used to reduce exposures. A dramatic reduction in effective dose can be obtained by increasing the distance between you and the radiation source. The decrease in exposure rate as one moves away from the source is greater than one might expect. Doubling the distance from a point source of radiation decreases the exposure rate to 1/4 of its original value. This relationship is called the inverse square law. The word inverse implies that the exposure rate decreases and the distance from the source increases. Square suggests that this decrease is more rapid than just a one-to-one proportion.

Radiation exposure levels decrease as distance from a non point source increases, but not in the same mathematical proportions as the inverse square law suggests.

In radiological emergencies where the radiation exposure rates are very high, some shielding may be necessary.

Shielding

Shielding is the placement of an "absorber" between you and the radiation source. An absorber is a material that reduces the number of particles or photons travelling from the radiation source to you. Alpha, beta and neutron radiation can all be stopped by different thickness of absorbers. There is no absorber shield that can stop all gamma rays. Instead, introduction of a shield of a specified thickness will reduce the radiation intensity by a certain fraction. Addition of more shielding will reduce the intensity further.

Recommendations for shielding procedures should involve careful comparison of the exposure reduced by the shielding with the exposure added due to increased time required to shield the area.

Shielding material can include barrels, boards, vehicles, buildings, gravel, water, or whatever else is immediately available.

PRACTICAL CONTROL OF INTERNAL RADIATION

Internal radiation hazards can occur where it is possible for radioactive materials to be taken into the body from contamination on articles or from airborne contamination. This may be by inhalation, ingestion, through the skin or thorough a break in the skin. Once inside the body such contamination will continue to irradiate the person until it has been excreted, decayed away or otherwise removed.

The internal hazard is minimised by limiting the intake of contaminated air and drinking water, and the consumption of contaminated foods. Breathing apparatus will be required if the atmosphere is contaminated and whole body protection to prevent entry through the skin. Lead lined clothing can form a barrier against ionising radiation.

Eating, drinking, smoking and the application of cosmetics should not be allowed in areas where unsealed radioactive sources are used. A high standard of cleanliness and decontamination procedures should be adhered to. Any breaks in the skin must be covered with a suitable protective material.

ROLE OF THE RADIATION PROTECTION ADVISER

The Ionising Radiations Regulations (IRR) 1999 require that radiation employers shall consult with suitable Radiation Protection Advisers (RPAs) for the purpose of advising them on the observances of the IRR 1999. The radiation employer appoints in writing one or more suitable RPA defining their scope. An RPA is an individual who meets the HSE criteria of competence by achieving NVQ Level 4 in Occupational Health and Safety with the appropriate Radiological Protection Units or having a Certificate awarded by an HSE recognised assessing body.

Qualified person

These are persons given the tasks of carrying our or supervising tests on radiation monitoring equipment and authorising the records of such tests as specified under the IRR 1999, Regulation 19.

ROLE OF THE RADIATION PROTECTION SUPERVISOR

A radiation employer is required to appoint one or more Radiation Protection Supervisors for the purpose of securing compliance with the Regulations in respect of work carried out in any area subject to 'local rules for work in controlled or supervised areas'. Their area of work needs to be defined and they must be trained so that they understand the requirements of legislation and local rules insofar as they affect their area of work. They also need to understand the reasons for the precautions that need to be taken in their area of work and they should command the respect of those they supervise.

B8.4 - Thermal environment - extremes of temperature

Effects

UNIT OF HEAT

The basic unit of heat is the joule (J). This is a very small quantity of heat. A typical small electric fire gives out 1000 J every second.

It is more convenient to talk about the *rate* of heat emission i.e. joules per second (J/s) which is the watt (W). (1 kW is 1000W).

THE MAIN EFFECTS OF WORKING IN HIGH AND LOW TEMPERATURES AND HUMIDITIES

The body

All warm blooded animals need to maintain the temperature of their body within a narrow range. In human beings this means that we need to maintain a core body temperature of around 37°C (normal limits range from 36.4°C to 37.2°C).

The body creates heat during the process of metabolism. Foodstuffs (proteins, carbohydrates and fat) are assimilated by the body and their energy released in the form of heat. This heat production is influenced by environmental conditions such as temperature and humidity and balanced by control mechanisms such as sweating and shivering which attempt to maintain the core body temperature within the normal range. The control centre in the base of the brain responsible for this regulation is the hypothalamus. When the function of the hypothalmus is affected by fever, for example, then overheating results which can lead to fatal heat-stroke if left untreated.

Active muscles metabolise food faster than muscles at rest, giving off more heat in the process, thus physical activity increases body temperature. If body temperature is too high for the hypothalamus to balance by sweating then biological function can become impaired leading to cellular damage. If the body temperature is too low, the rate at which foodstuffs are metabolised decreases; therefore the amount of heat energy produced is less.

Regulatory mechanisms

Body temperature is regulated by the rate at which the skin radiates heat and by the evaporation of water vapour (perspiration). Perspiring (or sweating) is the evaporation of water combined with various salts in the body through special glands and pores in the skin. This is similar to panting which is the evaporation of water vapour through pores in the mouth.

The radiant process occurs through vasodilatation. Skin temperature is raised due to an increase in blood flow. If this process is insufficient then the blood vessel size is increased further in order to induce sweat which, in turn, is evaporated. A further increase in temperature will occur which leads to the process of sweating. Excessive sweating can lead to muscle fatigue followed by cramps and pains due to the loss of body salts (the water/salt balance). Overheating can lead to a range of health effects ranging from heat oedema (e.g. swelling ankles) through to heat stroke which can lead to coma and death. These are summarised as:

Condition	Remarks
Heat oedema	Swelling.
Heat syncope	Blood vessels dilate.
Cramps	Water/salt balance affected.
Hidromeiosis	Sweat glands cease to function.
Prickly Heat	Blocked sweat glands, sweat escapes into the dermis.
Anhydrosis	Excess radiant heat.
Heat hyper-pyrexia	Raised body temperature (39-40°C) first stage of heat stroke.
Heat stoke	Body temperature up to 42°C - signs of neurological failure leading up to coma.

Figure B8-14: Human body regulatory mechanisms.   *Source: ACT.*

When the body is cold then the blood vessels in the skin contract and the muscles under the skin vibrate (shiver) in an attempt to generate heat and maintain the core temperature. Extreme cold or lowering of body temperature can lead to numbness, frost bite and hypothermia which is defined as a fall in body temperature to below 35°C.

Environmental parameters

It is a common experience that we can regulate our body temperature to remain fairly constant despite the surrounding air temperature and other sources of radiated heat and cold provided that exposure is neither too extreme nor too prolonged. The efficiency of the body's cooling and heating mechanisms can be affected by a number of environmental factors. The main factors are:

- Air velocity/wind speed;
- The type and amount of clothing worn.
- The mean radiant temperature (i.e. the temperature of the surroundings).
- The humidity of the surrounding air (which affects the rate of sweat evaporation).
- The work rate.
- Air temperature.

The rate of heat transfer between a body and its surrounding environment depends upon heat exchange from the above factors in four ways:

Conduction - when body is in contact with (i.e. touching) objects e.g. bare feet on the floor or arm on table.

Convection - when heat is transferred by a current of moving air. It depends on the difference between the temperature of the skin and the air temperature and the rate of air movement.

Radiation - depends on the surface temperature of the skin combined with the mean radiant temperature of the surroundings. If the surroundings contain a source of high radiant heat such as a furnace, then heat will be transferred to the relatively cooler body from the furnace.

Evaporation - depends on the perspiration (or sweat) on the skin, and its rate of evaporation which, in turn, depends on air temperature, air velocity and relative humidity.

The contribution of each of the above mechanisms to heat loss, in average thermal comfort conditions, is about:

- Radiation   -   45%.
- Convection   -   30%.
- Evaporation   -   25%.
- Conduction   -   Negligible.

TYPICAL WORK SITUATIONS LIKELY TO LEAD TO THERMAL DISCOMFORT

(Source: WorkCover NSW September 2001).

Source of heat or cold

Working conditions which expose employees to heat or cold:

- Work in direct sunlight (e.g. bitumen laying, construction). The risks increase when combined with high temperatures, high humidity and low air movement.
- Work requiring high physical work rate in humid conditions (e.g. laundries, kitchens).
- Work in cold weather (e.g. horticulture, power line maintenance). The risks increase when combined with low temperatures, wet and windy conditions.
- Plant which becomes hot (e.g. ovens, dryers, furnaces) or cold (e.g. freezers).
- Workplace with inadequate control or ventilation.

Nature of work undertaken

A risk assessment should consider how the work being done interacts with (or generates) hot or cold conditions:

- Work in close proximity to sources of heat or cold (e.g. metal forging).
- Work in hot conditions (e.g. smelter, boiler room, asbestos removal) requiring protective clothing that inhibits loss of body heat.
- Work in cold conditions where loss of body heat may affect function (e.g. occupational driving, garden maintenance in wet weather).
- The interaction of other hazards with hot or cold conditions (e.g. work in confined spaces, where limited ability to move about could increase the effects of heat or cold.

Duration of exposure to heat or cold

Risks to health and safety will be influenced by the length of time workers are exposed to heat or cold:

- Work activity requiring prolonged physical exertion in high temperatures or high humidity.
- Work activity requiring prolonged physical inactivity in low temperatures or wet conditions.

Work in hot or cold environments

Hazard	Typical exposures	Possible effects
High air temperature	Outdoor physical work in hot weather (e.g. road construction). Indoor physical work in a hot working environment (e.g. foundry, bakery).	Discomfort, sweating, flushed skin, fatigue, dizziness, muscle cramps, nausea, vomiting, dehydration, and excessive or erratic pulse. **Severe exposure:** heat stroke, hyperthermia, loss of consciousness, death.
Low air temperature	Prolonged exposure to low air temperatures while wearing clothing inadequate for cold conditions. Outdoor work in cold weather, indoor work in cold environments.	Discomfort, shivering, loss of motor co-ordination, slurred speech. **Severe exposure:** irrational behaviour, frostbite, hypothermia, loss of consciousness, death.
Humidity	Work with plant or processes, which generate humidity (e.g. brick curing, steam presses).	Discomfort, flushed skin, sweating, fatigue, headaches, dizziness, nausea, vomiting, excessive or erratic pulse. **Severe exposure:** collapse, heat stroke, hyperthermia.
Air movement (high)	Prolonged outdoor activity in cold, wet and windy conditions, work in wet clothing in cold wind.	(In cold conditions) discomfort, shivering, cold-related illnesses. **Severe exposure:** hypothermia, loss of consciousness.
Air movement (low)	Work in enclosed area with inadequate ventilation during hot weather.	(In hot conditions) discomfort, flushed skin, sweating, fatigue, headaches, dizziness and excessive or erratic pulse. **Severe exposure:** nausea, vomiting, collapse, heat stroke.
Radiant heat	Exposure to UV radiation from the sun, exposure to radiant or conducted heat from plant (dryer, oven, furnace) or processes such as smelting, molten metals.	Discomfort, sweating, fatigue, dizziness, nausea and vomiting, radiation burns to exposed skin. **Severe exposure:** severe burns, heat stroke, collapse, loss of consciousness.

Figure B8-15: Exposures to heat and cold and possible effects.   *Source: WorkCover NSW September 2001.*

Measurement

HUMAN BODY/THERMAL ENVIRONMENT PARAMETERS AND OUTLINE OF INSTRUMENTATION

Surrounding temperature

A thermometer is most commonly used to measure temperature. In its most basic form, the **mercury-in-glass type**, it consists of a uniform diameter glass capillary that opens into a mercury filled bulb at one end. The assembly is sealed to preserve a partial vacuum in the capillary. If the temperature increases, the mercury expands and rises inside and the resulting temperature may then be read on an adjacent scale. Mercury is most commonly used to measure ordinary temperature ranges - however for more diverse ranges substances such as alcohol and ether are used.

A wide variety of devices are used as thermometers. The primary requirement is that one easily measured property, such as the length of the mercury column, should change markedly and predictably with changes in temperature. The variation of that property should also stay fairly linear with variations in temperature. A unit change in temperature should lead to a unit change in the property to be measured at all points of the scale.

The electrical resistance of conductors and semi-conductors increases with an increase in temperature. This phenomenon is the basis of the **resistance thermometer** in which a constant voltage, or electrical potential is applied across the thermistor or sensing element. For a thermistor of a given composition the measurement of a specific temperature will induce a specific resistance across the thermistor. This resistance is measured by a galvanometer and becomes the measure of the temperature.

Various thermistors made of oxides of nickel, maganese, or cobalt are used to sense temperatures between -46 and 150°C (-50° and 300°F). Similarly, thermistors employing other metals and alloys are designed to be used at higher temperatures. With proper circuitry, the current reading can be converted to a direct digital display of the temperature.

Very accurate temperature measurements can be made using **thermocouples** in which a small voltage difference (measured in mV) arises when 2 wires of dissimilar metals are joined to form a loop, and the 2 junctions have different temperatures. To increase the voltage signal, several thermocouples can be connected in series to form a thermopile. Since the voltage depends on the difference of the junction temperatures, one junction must be maintained at a known temperature; otherwise an electronic compensation circuit must be built into the device to measure the actual temperature of the sensor.

Thermistors and thermocouples often have sensing units less than a ¼ cm in length, which permits them to respond rapidly to temperature changes and also makes them ideal for many biological and engineering uses.

Humidity

This is the moisture content of the atmosphere. In the atmosphere there is always some moisture present in the form of water vapour; however the maximum amount depends upon the air temperature. The amount of vapour that will saturate the air increases with a rise in temperature:

- At 4.4°C, 454kg (1000lbs) of moist air contains a max. of 2kg of water vapour.
- At 37.8°C, 454kg of moist air contains a maximum of 18kg of water vapour.

The level of discomfort is high when the atmosphere is saturated with water because the evaporation of perspiration, with its attendant cooling effect, is impossible.

The term 'absolute humidity' is used to describe the weight of water vapour contained in a particular volume of air and is expressed in pounds of water per pound of dry air.

Relative humidity (RH) is the ratio between the actual vapour content of the atmosphere and the vapour content of air at the same time saturated with water vapour. If the temperature of the atmosphere rises and there is no change in the vapour content of the atmosphere, the absolute humidity remains the same but the relative humidity is lowered. The following 2 values are important in order to calculate the RH at any particular air temperature:

1. The amount of water vapour in the air.

2. The amount at saturation point for that temperature.

As these values are difficult to measure, the technique for measuring RH relies on using a standard chart called a psychrometric chart and also obtaining RH from the chart using 2 temperature measurements relating to the above values. The 2 temperature measurements made are:

- The dry bulb measurement of the air.
- The wet bulb measurement of the air.

The **dry bulb temperature** is a measurement using a standard thermometer *(see 'surrounding temperature' section above)*.

The **wet bulb temperature** is measured using a specialised thermometer in which the bulb is covered with a wick which has been wetted with distilled water. When the water evaporates from the wick, heat is removed from the bulb by the evaporating cooling effect and the thermometer will show a reading that is lower than that of the dry bulb reading. The rate of water evaporation is directly related to the amount of water in the surrounding atmosphere. When there is a saturated atmosphere no evaporation will take place and the two readings will be the same - thus the RH value will be 100%.

Both the wet and dry bulb temperature readings can be plotted onto a psychometric chart which results in the relative humidity reading.

Hygrometers are used for measuring relative humidity:

Whirling Hygrometer (or Sling Psychrometer) - This resembles an old fashioned football rattle and is a very basic design. It consists of a wet and dry bulb thermometer mounted side by side in a frame which is rotated by hand. When it is rotated air is forced to flow over the bulbs. A small reservoir supplies the wick surrounding the bulb of the wet bulb thermometer with distilled water. Although very effective it is quite limited in its uses as it only gives a reading for a particular spot where the sample was taken and it needs to be checked very frequently to ensure that the distilled water reservoir is not empty.

Static Hygrometer - This is the static hygrometer or masons hygrometer. This is not very accurate and must be positioned in an area free from draughts as it relies on natural ventilation to induce evaporation of the wet bulb's wick.

Forced Draught Hygrometer - This is also known as an Assmann Hygrometer and is extremely accurate. It is of a similar design to the static hygrometer in that it contains **wet** and **dry** bulb thermometers mounted in a frame but it has a fan that forces an air flow across the bulbs rather than relying upon natural ventilation.

Air velocity/wind speed

This is measured using an anemometer. The most common kind is one that consists of three or four cups attached to short rods that are connected at right angles to a vertical shaft. As the wind blows, it pushes the cups, which in turn rotate the shaft. The number of turns per minute is translated into wind speed by a system of gears similar to the speedometer on a car. It is important, however, to appreciate that air movement seldom comes from only one direction. It is therefore important to ensure that air movement from all directions is measured. There are several types of instruments that will achieve this, the main ones for field use being:

- **Thermo-anemometers** - relies on the rate of cooling of heated resistance wire or thermocouple. The rate of cooling is dependent on air movement that causes circuit balance changes which are translated into velocity rate via a meter. They are portable battery powered instruments which give instantaneous readings.
- **Kata Thermometer** - looks like an alcohol thermometer with a large bulb. The bulb is placed in warm water until the alcohol rises to an upper reservoir. The thermometer is wiped dry and suspended in the air. The time that the column falls between two marks is measured. This rate of fall is a function of air movement which can be calculated via nomograms. This instrument is less convenient than the thermoanemometer and relies on there being a source of hot water. It comes in several sizes but is accurate at low wind speeds (>10 m per min).

Mean radiant temperature

The most common way of measuring mean radiant temperature is by using a thermometer which has the bulb encased in the centre of a 15 cm diameter copper sphere which has been painted matt black. Radiant heat is absorbed into the globe without being influenced by air currents. This is known as a **Vernon Globe thermometer** or **a black globe thermometer** and is suspended at the point of measurement for normally at least 20 minutes. This is known as the globe temperature.

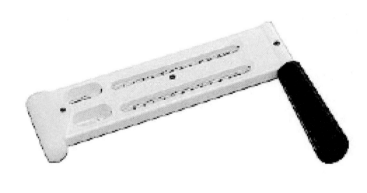

Figure B8-16: Globe thermometer.   *Source: : www.novalynx.com*   Figure B8-17: Whirling hygrometer.   *Source: www.paint-test-equipment.co.uk.*

Metabolic rate

Work rates can be calculated by considering the metabolic rate for various activities. As with the clothing index given later, these are widely available in tables, e.g.:

N.B. A typical male adult has a body area of 1.8m^2.

ACTIVITY	RATE (W/m² body surface)	Watts/Person 1.8m²
Sleeping	43	60
Resting	47	80
Sitting	60	100
Standing	70	120
Strolling (1.5 mph)	107	190
Walking (3 mph)	154	300
Running (10 mph)	600	1080
Sprinting (15 mph)	2370	4270
Shivering	330	600

Figure B8-18: Metabolic rates.

Source: ACT.

Clothing

Clothing indices are designed to indicate the insulating properties of clothing. An example of this is the Clo value:

1 Clo = 0.155m² °C/W - Measurement of resistance	1 tog = 0.1m² & °C/W	
	Naked	0
	Shorts	0.1
	Light summer clothing	0.5
	Indoor clothing	1.0
	Heavy suit	1.5
	Polar clothing	3.4
	Practical maximum	5

Figure B8-19: Typical Clo values (from Fanger).

Source: ACT.

Duration of exposure

Prolonged exposure can lead to fatigue, lowered concentration, slowed reflexes and loss of physical co-ordination. Any one of these things increases the possibility of an injury occurring. For example, if an employee should faint as a result of heat stress, there is a possibility of an injury from falling or striking objects.

Vibration from tools and equipment also presents increased risk to the operator in cold conditions. As air temperature drops, risk from falling tools that cause significant hand-transmitted or whole body vibration may be increased.

Workers must be able to function efficiently both physically and mentally to sustain work practices that will not place them at risk. If exposure to heat or cold leads to fatigue or discomfort, this could impair decision-making and affect the ability to follow safe working procedures.

OUTLINE OF HEAT INDICES

Effective temperature (ET) and corrected effective temperature (CET)

The effective temperature and corrected effective temperature were early attempts to quantify thermal stress dating back to the 1920s.

The effective temperature (ET) uses both wet and dry bulb temperatures. The corrected effective temperature (CET) uses the same criteria corrected for radiant heat. It is calculated using nomograms which are available for different clothed states (e.g. semi-nude and light summer clothed). The following measurements are required in order to calculate the CET. These are:

■ Wet bulb temperature.
■ Wind velocity.
■ Globe temperature or air temperature if they are the same.

The World Health Organisation recommended that the following limits should apply:

■ 30°C CET - sedentary work.   ■ 28°C CET - light work.   ■ 26.5°C CET - heavy work.

Wet bulb globe temperature (WBGT)

The wet bulb globe temperature (WBGT) was originally developed for military use for personnel on active service in the desert. It takes into account humidity, the air temperature and radiant heat. WBGT was brought in during the 1950s as an easier and more practical method to quantify thermal stress. The WBGT is calculated using the following equations:

Activity	Formula
Outdoor work with a solar load:	$WBGT = 0.7WB + 0.2GT + 0.1DB$
Indoor work / Outdoor work without a solar load:	$WBGT = 0.7WB + 0.3GT$

Figure B8-20: WBGT calculations.

Source: ACT.

WB natural wet bulb temperature.   DB dry-bulb temperature (this is the air temperature).   GT globe thermometer temperature (this is the radiant temperature).

The natural wet bulb temperature means that the wet bulb temperature reading on the whirling hygrometer is taken without rotating the instrument thus it is naturally, rather than forcibly, ventilated.

The readings are then compared against a psychrometric chart. *Example* guideline limits for work-rest regimes are given in the following table:

Example only - not for field use

Work : Rest Regime		Work load	
	Light	Moderate	Heavy
Continuous work	30.0	26.7	25
75% Work : 25% Rest each hour	30.6	28.0	25.9
50% Work : 50% Rest each hour	31.4	29.4	27.9
25% Work : 75% Rest each hour	32.2	31.1	30.0

Source: ACT.

Figure B8-21: Maximum permissible WBGT readings °C.

Thus a worker in an environment of 30 °C WBGT could:

1. Perform continuous light work.

2. Carry out light to moderate work for 30 minutes and rest for 30 minutes of each hour (i.e. do slightly less than moderate work).

3. Perform heavy work for 15 minutes and rest for 45 minutes of each hour.

Heat stress index (HSI)

The heat stress index (HSI) is calculated by using a formula or by charts. The upper limit for safety is an HSI which exceeds 100%. HSI is obtained by estimating two values:

The required evaporative heat loss (by sweating) to achieve heat balance (E_{req}).

The maximum evaporative heat loss possible in that environment (E_{max}).

If E_{req} is less than or equal to E_{max} then work can continue without any problem. When E_{req} is greater than E_{max} then there will be heat build up and working time should be limited.

The following measurements are required:

- Metabolic work rate.
- Air velocity.
- Air temperature.
- Wet-bulb temperature.
- Globe temperature.

Predicted 4-hour sweat rate (P4SR)

The predicted 4 hour sweat rate is obtained from charts (nomogram). This takes into account work rates and the clothing worn. The preferred standard is a sweat rate of below 2.7 litres in 4 hours. In any event the maximum sweat rate should not exceed 4.5 litres in 4 hours.

Wind chill index (WCI)

The wind chill index is relevant to work in low temperatures and takes both air velocity and temperature into account. This can be obtained from charts. WCI represents heat lost from the body in k cal h^{-1} m^2.

ASSESSMENT OF EXPOSURES TO THERMAL ENVIRONMENT EXTREMES

Risk assessment

(Source: WorkCover NSW September 2001).

Risk assessment involves considering the:

- Risks that any identified hazard can cause to an employee or other person in the workplace.
- Likelihood of an injury or illness occurring.
- Likely severity of any injury or illness that may occur.

Employers should also read any available health and safety information related to the hazard; identify the factors that may contribute to the risk; and identify the action necessary to control the risk.

Employers should think about:

- The potential sources of heat/cold.
- The number of people involved.
- The type of work to be performed.
- The work practices in use.
- The type of plant, machinery and equipment to be used.
- The premises and working environment including their layout/condition.
- The capability, skill, experience and age of the people doing the work.

Risk assessment must be done in consultation with employees. The risk assessment should be documented. Employers should list the potential injuries and diseases that can occur, from the most to the least serious, e.g. 'death by freezing' to 'fatigue'. The most serious risks are the ones that should be dealt with first.

Eliminate or control the risk

Once the risks are identified, the employer must work to eliminate any risk to the health and safety of all employees or other persons at the workplace. If it is not reasonably practicable to eliminate the risk, the employer must control the risk. The employer is responsible for ensuring risks are controlled, and that the method of control is working.

Eliminate the risk - discontinue the activity; think about using a different, less dangerous piece of equipment; fix faulty ventilation; use safer materials or chemicals.

Control the risk - if the employer can't eliminate the risk, they should think about redesigning the equipment/processes so that less hazardous equipment or materials may be used. Otherwise, the employer should control the risk by:

1. Substituting the hazard (with a hazard that gives rise to a lesser risk; changing the plant/work method).

2. Isolating the hazard (restricted work area).

3. Engineering controls (ventilation; exhaust ducting; thermostats).

4. Administrative controls and safe work practices (specific training/work instructions).

5. PPE (insulated gloves, warm clothing or face shields).

Summary

■ Eliminating the risk gives the best result and should be adopted where practicable.
■ Controlling the risk (measures 1-3) are less effective, require more frequent reviews of the hazards and systems of work.
■ Controlling the risk (measure 5) is the least preferred way of dealing with hazards, but should be used when all other methods are simply not practicable or feasible.

Any new control measures should be evaluated to ensure they are effective and safe and that they create no new hazards. Clear work procedures must be developed and documented and made available to employees, with specific training where applicable.

Controls

CONTROL MEASURES TO IMPROVE UNSATISFACTORY THERMAL ENVIRONMENT PARAMETERS

(See also 'risk assessment' and 'eliminate or control the risk' in the section above).

In order improve the thermal environment it is first necessary to consider what constitutes a pleasant environment. The recommended conditions for comfort are:

1. The temperature should be compatible with comfort:
■ The mean radiant temperature should preferably be equal to or slightly higher than the air temperature.
■ Temperature gradients should not exceed approximately $3^{\circ}c$ over the height of a person.
■ Excessive radiant heat should not fall on the heads of occupants.
■ There should not be large asymmetrics in the radiant fields (e.g. cold window, hot surfaces).
2. Air movement should be approximately 0.1 - 0.2 m/s. Higher values may be desirable in summer. Lower values are likely to cause 'stuffiness'.
3. Air movement should be variable rather than uniform.
4. The relative humidity should be in the range of 40 - 70%

(after Bedford).

Alternatively the conditions which cause discomfort are:
■ Thermal differences, e.g.:
  • Underheating in winter.
  • Overheating in summer.
Or else:
■ Conditions not matched to activity and clothing:
  • Cold draughts which affect feet in particular as cold air drops (e.g. from windows).
  • Cold surfaces (e.g. windows give localised radiation loss, for example, to the neck).
  • Localised high radiant conditions - particularly uncomfortable if to the head (the extreme being 'sunstroke').
  • Low air movement - stuffiness, oppressiveness.
  • Dry air (<30% RH) - sore throats, inflamed sinuses etc.
  • Moist air (>70%) - stuffiness. Particularly uncomfortable when activity rate increased.
  • Asymmetric conditions e.g. air or radiant temperature gradients.

There are a limited number of ways in which control measures can be applied. The variables which must be taken into consideration are the:

1.   Time and frequency of work.

2.   The rate of work.

3.   Heat exchange with the environment by:
     - Convection.
     - Radiation.
     - Sweat loss.

4.   Clothing index.

Thus an area with high temperature and humidity is problematic because sweat is not able to evaporate easily. This can be treated in a combination of ways including:

■   Increasing air flow (e.g. fans).
■   Reducing humidity (e.g. dehumidifiers).
■   Reducing clothing.
■   Reducing work rates, frequency and exposure.

Psycho-social agents

Learning outcomes

On completion of this element, candidates should be able to:

B9.1   Outline the effects of work-related stress on individuals, its identification, control and the applicable legal and other standards.

B9.2   Outline the effects on health & safety at work of alcohol, prescribed and unprescribed drugs, appropriate testing methods and the effective implementation of management systems and support.

B9.3   Outline the issues, risk factors and appropriate controls for work-related violence.

Content

This page is intentionally blank

ELEMENT B9 - PSYCHO-SOCIAL AGENTS

This page is intentionally blank

B9.1 - Stress

Definition of stress

There are a number of definitions of stress in existence but for the purposes of this Element, the Health and Safety Executive's definition from the publication "Tackling Work-Related Stress" (HSE, ISBN 0-7176-2050-6) will be used:

"The adverse reaction people have to excessive pressure or other types of demand placed on them".

However, other terms which broaden understanding of the nature of stress include:

- Any force which interferes with a person's ability to control their emotional and physical state within a comfortable range and which prevents them from producing a control strategy for that force.
- A broad range of problems which unduly test a person's psychological, physiological or social system and the response of that system to the problems.
- A physiological state in which the mental and physical energy expended to cope with pressure exceeds the body's ability to replace that energy.

Individuals have different reactions to pressure and varying methods of controlling those reactions. For example, a mundane and routine job which may be the preferred choice of an employee comfortable with a familiar and undemanding role may cause stress in another employee who would prefer an unpredictable, challenging, fast-paced role. The reverse of this situation would be true for other individuals.

Problems may arise when the pressure faced by the individual appears overwhelming and uncontrollable. The individual may consider that they are not in possession of the skills necessary to control the stress and therefore feel unable to cope. Stress, whatever the cause, is brought about and made worse by an individual's inability to cope and it is stress which results in physical and mental harm.

The subject of stress is complex, varied and complicated by the fact that many people suffer from stress caused at work, outside of work or a combination of both. Many people come to work against a background of problems at home which may involve family/relationship, financial, health and legal issues to name but a few. These problems, which are outside the employer's responsibility, may cause an employee to be more vulnerable to work related stress.

In addition, the problems associated with stress are often made worse by sceptical employers and colleagues. However, in terms of statistics, the problem appears to be increasing rapidly as illustrated by the following figures:

- Trades Union Congress (TUC) estimates that 3 in 5 employees complain of stress.
- 6.5m working days were lost in 1995 through stress related issues.
- The number was estimated to be 13m in 2004.
- The cost to the UK economy is £7 billion.
- Working days lost through stress are 50 times greater than those lost through industrial accidents.

In a more recent report by the HSE, 'Stress–related and psychological disorders', the following statistics were provided:

The 2006/07 survey of Self-reported Work-related Illness (SWI06/07) prevalence estimate indicated that around 530 000 individuals in Britain believed in 2006/07 that they were experiencing work-related stress at a level that was making them ill.

Source: www/HSE.gov.uk/statistics

Identification of stress

Identifying the main sources of stress is the most effective first step in stress management. This provides the basis for targeting intervention strategies at an individual and organisational level.

USING RISK ASSESSMENT, QUALITATIVE AND QUANTITATIVE DATA TO IDENTIFY STRESS

The main technique used to help identify an actual or potential stress related problem is risk assessment during which a combination of qualitative and quantitative data is used. Risk assessments can be effectively used to determine the extent and sources of workplace stress. However, although some sources of stress may be easy to identify such as increased working hours and traumatic working conditions during prolonged emergency incidents, others may be more difficult to identify such as bullying.

Most risk assessments utilise questionnaires which cover work activities, health/well-being and perceived sources of stress. The process must have guaranteed confidentiality or inaccurate/dishonest responses may result. The length of questionnaires varies greatly but importantly must not be too long that there is an unwillingness to complete it, nor too short that it fails to generate useful data. Online questionnaires have the advantage of ease of data collection and analysis but must be secure to prevent unauthorised access.

Other qualitative and quantitative data which is frequently used includes that listed below.

Quantitative methods include the use of:

- Sickness/absence data such as increased absenteeism-especially short-term.
- Accident data including increasing frequency or significant patterns in accidents.
- Productivity data such as reduced performance, quality and efficiency.
- Staff turnover records analysed for reasons for departure.
- Staff questionnaires to ascertain attitudes, concerns, etc.

Qualitative methods include the use of:

- Informal talks with staff sometimes using independent third-parties to "interview".
- Staff performance appraisals giving staff opportunities to raise issues.
- Focus groups to discuss and raise concerns in a group environment.
- Return to work interviews to ascertain possible links between stress and absence from work.

USING PHYSICAL, EMOTIONAL AND BEHAVIOURAL SIGNS TO IDENTIFY STRESS

Stress can cause numerous minor disorders which create discomfort but which may also lead to serious ill-health. There are a number of physical, emotional and behavioural signs of stress which may become apparent to colleagues, supervisors and managers. Recognising these signs or symptoms is an important part of any strategy to manage work related stress illnesses. Stress will manifest itself in a variety of ways with different people but the following are common symptoms:

Physical signs of stress

- Heart and circulatory problems-palpitations, pain/tightness in the chest, heart attack, stroke.
- Repeated colds, flu or other infections.
- Menstrual pattern changes.
- Rapid weight gain/loss.
- Tiredness, fainting.
- Skin complaints-eczema, psoriasis, sweating, baldness.
- Digestive system problems-indigestion, nausea/vomiting, stomach cramps, irritable bowel syndrome (IBS).

Emotional signs of stress

- Mood swings/irritability.
- Cynicism.
- Anxiety, nervousness, apprehension.
- Loss of confidence.
- Lack of self-esteem.
- Lack of concentration/ lack of enthusiasm.
- Panic attacks.

Behavioural signs of stress

- Poor quality work.
- Increased smoking, alcohol/drug use.
- Insomnia.
- Loss of appetite or overeating.
- Poor time management.
- Accident proneness.
- Impaired speech.
- Too busy to relax.

Certain symptoms are important warning signs that action should be taken to identify and tackle the cause of the stress. Medical advice should be sought if symptoms such as some of these listed below are experienced.

- Frequent heartburn, diarrhoea, inability to swallow.
- Memory/concentration impairment.
- Inability to make decisions.
- Difficulty in problem solving.
- Recurring headaches/migraines.
- Feeling of faintness.
- Prone to illness.
- Palpitations/chest pain.
- Frequent use of self-prescribed drugs.
- Anger, irritation, tearfulness and frustration are common emotions.

It should be noted that many of the symptoms listed are experienced by individuals who are not suffering from stress. However, if the symptoms are uncharacteristic of that individual, begin to occur in combination or occur at a time when the individual is known to be experiencing pressures at home or at work, they could be indicative of stress related illness.

CAUSES OF STRESS

Causes of stress, or stressors, are many and varied and occur in both private and work lives. The "Life Events" checklist handout identifies a number of events associated with varying levels of stress. A completed checklist will provide an estimate of the increased risk of ill-health, in its broadest terms, associated with a combination of events experienced by an individual. At the very least, the checklist is a useful tool for supervisors and managers to use to identify the sort of events in private lives which may trigger problems amongst the staff for which they are responsible. For example, it is foreseeable that a member of staff going through a divorce, problems with children, a major illness in the family, bereavement, house move or similar will experience increased pressure for a period of time.

There are many causes of stress in the working environment. The causes can be classified as organisational factors, personal factors and physical factors.

Some causes are very specific and predictable such as during times of change such as mergers or when redundancies are being planned. Others are more general and may exist over a longer period of time such as poor working relationships, long working hours, boredom, poor workstation design, harassment and bullying.

Organisational factors

A workplace which is characterised by poor organisational factors is likely to generate unacceptable levels of stress in employees. Important issues include:

- How the organisation is managed.
- Individual roles in the organisation.
- Level of support provided for staff.
- Degree of consultation and control over work.
- Consistency.
- Sufficient staffing levels.

Stress can be created by insufficient staff, vacant posts, excess staff resulting in spare time and boredom, lack of variety of tasks, poor communication between functions, lack of training, inconsistency in approach by employer/manager, shift work/piece work/bonus systems, emphasis on competitiveness, lack of responsibility and lack of support from subordinates/peers/employer.

Personal relationships including bullying and harassment

Stress is frequently associated with personal and social relationships. At work, the following stressors may cause problems:

- Poor relationships with colleagues/subordinates/manager.
- Isolation from or rejection by colleagues.
- Lack of ability to delegate tasks.
- Lack of feedback from managers.
- Personality conflicts.
- Racial / sexual harassment.
- Bullying.
- Lack of opportunity.
- Lack of social contact at work.

Improving personal relationships at work and attempting to modify people's attitudes and behaviour is a difficult and time-consuming process. Effective strategies include regular communication with staff, provision of accurate and honest information on the effect of organisational changes on them, adopting partnership approaches to problems, provision of support.

Physical factors in the workplace

Poor physical working conditions and inadequate work equipment are common causes of stress. In the case of working conditions, the following, which are self-explanatory, are common stressors:

- Lack of space/privacy.
- Inadequate lighting/ventilation.
- Unreasonable temperature.
- Poor welfare facilities.
- Excessive noise/vibration.
- Hazardous working conditions.
- Dirty and untidy workplaces.

In the case of work equipment, the following are common stressors:

- Work equipment unsuitable for location/task/operator.
- Poor working order.
- Prone to breakdowns.
- Associated with production of noise/fumes/vibration.
- Design of equipment hinders the work.
- Uncomfortable or difficult to use.

Working hours

Working excessive hours, typically 60 or more hours per week, can be a significant stressor. The results of a joint study conducted by the International Stress Management Association UK & Royal and Sun Alliance concluded that there are four main causes of stress at work:

- Long working hours-typical for many people at work at present.
- Poor work/life balance-family/private life suffers due to long working hours, work tasks taken home.
- Excessive workload/deadline pressures-which may be caused by down-sizing or unrealistic targets being set.
- Unsatisfactory working conditions-poor physical conditions which cause ill-health and low morale are the norm in many workplaces.

Non-work related stressors

The main reasons for employee absence from work with non-work related stressors are bereavement, relationship/marital problems, family pressures and medical conditions. These factors make take on increasing significance if an employee is experiencing excessive pressure at work.

LEGAL OBLIGATIONS AND CASE LAW RELATING TO STRESS

Employer's legal obligations are outlined in the following:

- Health and Safety at Work etc. Act (HASAWA) 1974.
- The Management of Health and Safety at Work Regulations (MHSWR) 1999.
- The Working Time Regulations (WTR) 1998.
- Employers liability under Common Law.
- Disability Discrimination Act 1995

Under HASAWA 1974 Section 2, the statement: "It is the duty of every employer to ensure, so far as is reasonably practicable, the health, safety and welfare of all employees" , applies to an employee's mental as well as physical health. The employer has a duty to prevent or control the risk of physical or mental harm caused by exposure to excessive pressure at work.

Under HASAWA 1974 Section 7, the statement: "All employees shall take reasonable care of themselves and others who might be affected by their acts or omissions" suggests that employees should perhaps take steps to inform the employer of stress affecting their health (taking reasonable care of themselves). This Section also implies that employees should not act in ways which may cause stress for others, for example, through bullying (that is, *not* taking reasonable care of others).

MHSWR 1999 Regulations 3 and 4 require employers to make suitable and sufficient assessments of risks to the health and safety of employees who may be affected by their work activities. Control measures can then be based upon such assessments. Therefore, stress should be managed using the methods employed for other hazards at work:

- Identify the hazards.
- Assess who may be harmed and how.
- Evaluate the level of risk and decide if current precautions are adequate or whether more should be done.
- Record the findings.
- Review and revise the assessment as necessary.

MHSWR 1999 Regulation 13 requires every employer to take employees' capabilities into account when allocating tasks. Therefore, an assessment of the abilities of an employee should be made prior to allocating tasks to the individual. The physical and mental capabilities of the individual should be considered along with their experience, training and knowledge.

MHSWR 1999 Regulation 14 requires employees to inform their employer of shortcomings in the employer's health and safety arrangements. This requirement implies that employees should inform their employer of the stress that they are suffering or otherwise make it obvious that there is impending harm to their health due to work-related stress.

Under English law, a claimant would bring a case for work-related stress under the common law tort of negligence and would be required to prove:

- The employer owed a duty of care.
- That duty of care was breached.
- As a direct result of the breach of duty, harm was caused.

In addition, there is the question of 'foreseeability'. Foreseeability will depend upon what an employer knows or ought reasonably to know about the individual employee. An employer can assume that an employee can cope with the normal pressures of a job unless the employer knows of some particular problem or vulnerability.

In the landmark case, *Lancaster v Birmingham City Council (1999)*, liability was admitted when an employee had taken three periods of sick leave and had then been medically retired. The City Council conceded that it failed to act upon complaints from Mrs Lancaster and had failed to give her adequate training and guidance to do her job, which had changed from a technical role in a backroom to a pressurised job on a front desk dealing directly with housing issues.

Previous periods of ill-health leave meant that it was foreseeable that failure to act would result in injury.

Sutherland v Hatton and others [2002] EWCA Civ 76 [reasonableness in relation to harm from stress at work]

Statute ref. These claims were brought in common law negligence

Facts The Court of Appeal heard four appeals by employers against compensation awards to employees who had suffered stress-induced psychiatric illness.

Decision Three of the appeals succeeded. The Court ruled that the general principle was that employers should not have to pay compensation for stress-induced illness unless such illness was reasonably foreseeable. Employers are normally entitled to assume that employees can withstand the normal pressures of a job. The Court set out a number of practical propositions for future claims concerning workplace stress. These are as follows:

- Employers do not have a duty to make searching inquiries about employees' mental health. They are entitled to take what they are told by employees at face value unless they have good reason to disbelieve the employees' statements.
- Where an employee wishes to remain in a stressful job and the only alternative is demotion or dismissal, the employer is not in breach of duty in allowing the employee to continue.
- Indications of impending harm to health at work must be clear enough to show an employer that action should be taken, in order for a duty on an employer to take action to arise.
- An employer is in breach of duty where he fails to take reasonable steps bearing in mind the following: the size of the risk; the gravity of the harm; the cost of preventing the harm; any justification for taking the risk.
- No type of work may be regarded as intrinsically dangerous to mental health.
- Employers who offer confidential counselling advice services, with access to treatment, are unlikely to be found in breach of their duty of care in relation to workplace stress.
- Employees must show that their illness has been caused by a breach of duty and not merely by occupational stress.
- The amount of compensation will be reduced to take account of pre-existing conditions or the chance that the employee would have become ill in any event.

The Court of Appeal dealt with the following cases:

1. Penelope Hatton, a schoolteacher who had been awarded £90,000 compensation for depression and debility. Her employer's appeal was allowed on the grounds that her workload was no greater than her colleagues' and her absences could be put down to reasons other than workplace stress.

2. Olwen Jones, a local authority employee who had suffered from depression and anxiety as a result of overwork. It was foreseeable that her workplace conditions would cause harm, therefore the employer's appeal against an award of £150,000 damages was dismissed.

3. Leon Barber, a teacher, developed symptoms of depression. He was awarded £100,000 compensation. The employer's appeal was allowed on the grounds that the claimant had not told the employers about his illness until he suffered a breakdown.

4. Melvyn Bishop, a factory worker awarded £7,000 compensation following a nervous breakdown and attempted suicide. The employer's appeal was allowed because the Court ruled that the demands of his work had not been excessive.

Source: Croner's Health and Safety Case Law 2003.

The Court of Appeal stated that an employer who offers a confidential advice service, with referral to:

- Appropriate counselling and treatment services, is unlikely to be found in breach of duty. This may be acceptable under the tort of negligence in that a court would consider the employer to have taken reasonable steps to discharge the duty of care.

However, in order to discharge statutory duties, an employer would be expected to proactively identify causes of work-related stress, undertake risk assessments and implement measures, so far as reasonably practicable, to prevent or control the risk of physical or mental harm. In other words, the duty of care under civil law can be discharged more easily than the criminal law duty of care contained in Section 2 HSAWA 1974 and Regulation 3 MHSWR 1999.

Walker v Northumberland County Council [1995] IRLR 35 [employers' duty of care in relation to mental ill-health arising from excessive workload].

Facts Mr Walker was employed as a social worker dealing with cases of child abuse. His workload increased steadily over the years and in 1986 he had a nervous breakdown. When he recovered and returned to work, he was promised additional resources to help him with his workload, but they failed to materialise. He had a second breakdown six months later and had to retire. Mr Walker sued the council claiming they were in breach of their duty of care to provide a safe working environment.

Decision The council were not held liable for the first breakdown as they could not reasonably have foreseen Mr Walker was exposed to a significant risk of mental illness through his job. They were, however, liable for the second breakdown, given that the same circumstances were there that caused the first. (After the first breakdown, the council had notice of the particular risk facing the plaintiff and could have taken steps to reduce the stress, by reducing his workload and providing greater assistance). The second breakdown was a reasonably foreseeable risk. The court accepted that this could have caused some disruption to other services provided by the council, but this did not outweigh the obligation to protect the plaintiff against a serious risk to his health. The council were found to have failed in their duty of care by not providing effective support to alleviate Mr Walker's suffering. The decision is indistinguishable, but what matters is the view that an employer can be under a duty of care to provide an employee with assistance, of uncertain scope and duration, to enable him to perform his contractual duties.

House of Lords decision in Barber v Somerset County Council [2004] UKHL 13 [employers' liability in damages for the mental breakdown; duty owed when problem known or should have been known].

Facts One of the co-joined cases heard by the Court of Appeal in February 2002 was taken to the House of Lords in April 2004. Maths teacher Leon Barber was the only one to appeal the decision to the House of Lords. The council employed Mr Barber, a 52 year old schoolteacher, as head of mathematics in a comprehensive school; he worked long hours about which he complained of 'work overload'. Following a period of sickness because he was 'overstressed and suffered from depression', he suffered a mental breakdown at school.

Decision On a majority of four to one, the appeal was allowed and he was awarded damages of almost £37,000. The decision was based upon the following important facts:

- The employer should have taken action after Barber separately informed each member of the management team of the pressure he was experiencing at work.
- Barber was treated unsympathetically after a three week absence.
- No attempt was made to reduce his workload upon return to work and he subsequently suffered a nervous breakdown.
- Lack of action by the employer breached the duty of care requirement.
- Barber's ill-health was foreseeable.

The school owed Mr Barber a duty of care, and their breach of that caused the claimant's nervous breakdown. The employer's duty to take some action arose when Mr Barber informed separately each member of the school's senior management team of his problems. However, nothing was done to help him. The senior management team should have made inquiries about Mr Barber's problems and seen what they could have done to ease them, instead of brushing him off unsympathetically or sympathising but simply telling him to prioritise his work. (Stokes v Guest, Keen and Nettlefold (Bolts and Nuts) Ltd [1968] applied).

DISABILITY DISCRIMINATION ACT (DDA) 1995

An employee suffering from a stress related illness may be protected by the DDA 1995. The Act defines a disability as "a physical or mental impairment which has a substantial and long-term adverse effect on a person's ability to carry out normal day-to-day activities". Most stress cases are associated with mental impairments of one form or another but the DDA 1995 limits these to those which result from or consist of "a clinically well-recognised mental illness". The impairments also have to be "long-term", that is lasting or likely to last 12 months or more. Temporary or short-term stress-related conditions do not attract the protection of the DDA 1995.

However, for cases which do come under the DDA 1995, the employer must make "reasonable adjustments" to enable the employee to continue with their existing job. Reasonable adjustments may include

- Altering the content of the job.
- Shorter or different working hours.
- Rehabilitation following absence from work.
- Additional holidays/unpaid leave.
- Provision of extra support.
- Permitting absence for medical treatment.
- Higher than usual tolerance of absence.

If continuation in the existing job is impossible, redeployment of the employee may need consideration. If an employer is considering dismissing the employee, the dismissal must be approached in the correct way to avoid claims of both unfair dismissal and disability discrimination. Factors which may be taken into account in deciding whether dismissal was justified include the length of absences, any health and safety risks associated with the job, whether the employee is an important worker or not and the scale of any reasonable adjustments already made by the employer.

Controls

Reducing the level of occupational stress is by any standards a major undertaking if attempted in isolation. An organisation that is forward thinking and progressive will have in place systems to apply and monitor health and safety along with policies and procedures to cover all aspects of staff development and the correct implementation of appropriate regulations.

- In order to reduce stress, there are a number of interventions that may be adopted by organisations. These include
- Introducing a Stress Policy to demonstrate to employees, trades unions and the HSE that the organisation recognises stress as a serious issue worthy of a commitment to manage the problem
- Promoting general health awareness initiatives within the organisation such as diet, exercise and fitness programmes
- Addressing the issue of work-life balance which may include the consideration of job-share, part-time work, voluntary reduced hours, home-working, flexitime etc
- Providing training and support for employees, supervisors and all levels of management in the form of stress awareness and stress management training, as appropriate
- Providing access to occupational health practitioners, counselling support or employee assistance programmes

To assist employers further, the HSE has developed guidance for organisations on how to tackle work related stress, together with yardsticks against which they can measure their performance. The guidance is in the form of Management Standards. The standards can be found at www.hse.gov.uk/stress/standards.

THE MANAGEMENT STANDARDS FOR WORK RELATED STRESS

The Management Standards define the characteristics or culture of an organisation where stress is being managed effectively.

The Standards were launched in November 2004. As far as complying with the Standards is concerned, the HSE is trying the voluntary approach first but will enforce against failures to assess the risks of stress if necessary.

The Standards are based upon the 6 main stress factors of demands, control, change, relationships, role and support. Each standard defines a desired state (best practice) to be achieved in several areas.

- **Demands** - includes issues like workload, work patterns and the work environment.
  The standard is that employees indicate they can cope with the demands of the job and there are systems in place locally to respond to any individual concerns.
- **Control** - how much say the person has in the way they do their work.
  The standard is that employees indicate that they are able to have a say about the way they do their work and there are systems in place locally to respond to any individual concerns.
- **Support** - includes the encouragement, sponsorship and resources provided by the organisation, line management and colleagues.
  The standard is that employees indicate that they receive adequate information and support from their colleagues and superiors and there are systems in place locally to respond to any individual concerns.
- **Relationships** - Includes promoting positive working to avoid conflict and dealing with unacceptable behaviour.
  The standard is that employees indicate that they are not subjected to unacceptable behaviours, e.g. bullying at work and there are systems in place locally to respond to any individual concerns.
- **Role** - whether people understand their role within the organisation and whether the organisation ensures that the person does not have conflicting roles.
  The standard is that employees indicate that they understand their role and responsibilities and there are systems in place locally to respond to any individual concerns.
- **Change** - how organisational change (large and small) is managed and communicated in the organisation. The standard is that employees indicate that the organisation engages them frequently when undergoing organisational change and there are systems in place locally to respond to any individual concerns.

B9.2 - Substance misuse

The legal position

Employers have a general duty under the **Health and Safety at Work etc Act 1974** (HSAWA) to ensure, as far as is reasonably practicable, the health, safety and welfare at work of their employees. They also have a duty under the **Management of Health and Safety at Work Regulations 1999** (MHSWR), to assess the risks to the health and safety of their employees. If employers knowingly allow an employee under the influence of drug misuse to continue working and his or her behaviour places the employee or others at risk, the employer could be prosecuted. Employees are also required to take reasonable care of themselves and others who could be affected by what they do at work.

The **Transport and Works Act 1992** makes it a criminal offence for certain workers to be unfit through drugs and/or drink while working on railways, tramways and other guided transport systems. This extends to work such as train driving or signal operation (sometimes called 'safety critical work'). The operators of the transport system would also be guilty of an offence unless they had shown all due diligence in trying to prevent such an offence being committed.

The **Road Traffic Act 1988** (RTA) states that any person who, when driving or attempting to drive a motor vehicle on a road or other public place, is unfit to drive through drink or drugs shall be guilty of an offence. An offence is also committed if a person unfit through drink or drugs is in charge of a motor vehicle in the same circumstances.

Alcohol

THE EFFECTS OF ALCOHOL

Many people participate in the drinking of alcohol without it causing problems in their personal life or work. However, what is seen as the misuse of alcohol can affect the workplace by causing absence from work and risk of accidents.

"17% of personnel directors described alcohol consumption as a 'major problem' for their organisation."

Figure B9-1: Study of Personnel Directors in 1994 referred to in "Don't mix it!". *Source: HSE "Don't mix it!" IND(G)240L 11/96.*

The presence of alcohol-related problems at work may be identified from some of its effects:

- Lateness.
- Absenteeism.
- Extended work breaks.
- Loss of productivity and poor performance.
- Health and safety hazards or accidents.

- Unsafe behaviour.
- Poor morale.
- Poor employee relations.
- Poor discipline.
- Poor customer relations.

Various estimates have been made of the affect of alcohol on workplace absenteeism; figures vary but indicate that it may be 3-5% of all work absences. There are no accurate national figures that identify alcohol as a factor in workplace accidents, although some organisations do take steps to monitor this as an accident causation factor, particularly in organisations that have identified 'safety critical work' conducted by employees.

In order to understand the problem of alcohol and the workplace it is important to understand the effects of alcohol.

Alcohol is absorbed into your bloodstream within a few minutes of being drunk and carried to all parts of your body including the brain.

The concentration of alcohol in the body, known as the 'blood alcohol concentration', depends on many factors, but principally, how much you have drunk, how long you have been drinking, whether you have eaten, and your size and weight. It is difficult to know exactly how much alcohol is in your bloodstream or what effect it may have.

It takes a healthy liver about 1 hour to break down and remove 1 unit of alcohol. A unit is equivalent to 8 gm or 10 ml (1 cl) of pure alcohol. The following all contain one unit of alcohol:

A half pint of average strength beer, lager or cider (3.5%ABV), a single 250ml measure of spirits (40%ABV), a small glass of wine (9%ABV).

If someone drinks 2 pints of ordinary strength beer at lunchtime or half a bottle of wine (i.e. 4 units), they will still have alcohol in their bloodstream 3 hours later. Similarly, if someone drinks heavily in the evening they may still be over the legal drink drive limit the following morning.

Black coffee, cold showers and fresh air won't sober someone up. Only time can remove alcohol from the bloodstream.

Figure B9-2: The effects of alcohol. *Source: HSE "Don't mix it!" IND(G)240L 11/96.*

Many organisations reflect the national limit for driving when deciding if an individual has too much alcohol in their system. The legal limit of alcohol in the body is:

- 35 micrograms (μg) per 100 millilitres of breath.
- 80 milligrams (mg) per 100 millilitres of blood.
- 107 milligrams per 100 millilitres of urine.

This limit is often equated to two pints (4 units) of ordinary strength beer. For an average weight male this is said to be a rough approximation, but should not be used as a general rule. There are significant differences between male and female absorption rates and many physiological factors combine to affect the amount of alcohol showing in the system.

Past statistics show that of 90,000 drivers who are convicted, over 15,000 say they are on their way to work, or on business.

Figure B9-3: Driving convictions for alcohol. *Source: Fleetplan website dated 10/06/2004.*

Even at low levels of consumption the body is affected by alcohol reducing reaction time and impeding co-ordination. It also affects thinking, judgement and mood and can have a significant effect on behaviour when conducting routine work. Whilst large amounts of alcohol in one session can put a strain on the body's functions, in particular the liver, it can also affect muscle function and stamina. Drinking alcohol raises the drinker's blood pressure and this can increase the risk of coronary heart disease and some kinds of stroke. Regularly drinking more than the 'daily benchmarks' also increases the risk of cirrhosis of the liver. The effect of alcohol is not limited to physical effects - people who drink very heavily may develop psychological and emotional problems, including depression.

	Men	**Women**
No significant risk to health	3 - 4 units	2 - 3 units
Increased risk to health if consistently drink	4 units	3 units

Figure B9-4: Daily benchmarks for alcohol. *Source: HSE "Don't mix it!" IND(G)240L 11/96.*

The daily benchmarks are a useful guide for good health and do not represent a 'safe limit' in the way that the levels set for driving do. These limits do have value in the workplace in that they can be used to promote a healthy person strategy that may encourage more people to drink at lower levels, thus reducing the number of people at risk of the adverse effects of alcohol while at work. It should be noted that these benchmarks relate to average adults in average health and do not relate to young people who have not reached physical maturity. Individuals that consume alcohol look to the positive effects of alcohol to support their consumption. It is claimed that some studies have identified that people that regularly drink small quantities of alcohol live longer; the main reason is stated to be the protection from coronary heart disease that this gives. However the HSE "Guide for employers on alcohol at work" advises:

"This protective effect is only significant when people reach a stage of life when they are at risk of coronary heart disease. For men, this is over the age of 40. For women, it is after the menopause. The benefits come from drinking small amounts of alcohol fairly regularly - i.e. between 1 and 2 units a day. No overall additional benefit comes from drinking more than 2 units a day, or from drinking a particular type of drink (e.g. red wine)."

Figure B9-5: Protective effect of alcohol. *Source: HSE "Don't mix it!" IND(G)240L 11/96.*

In the absence of more specific limits organisations are likely to use those limits set for driving vehicles subject to the Road Traffic Act. This is a practical limit with which workers are familiar and it would be difficult for a fork lift truck driver to expect a lower standard for operating a vehicle in a workplace. It should be remembered that whilst this is a useful limit organisations may opt for a lower limit.

The adverse effects of alcohol on health and safety are higher in some work activities than others. Activities that are classed as 'safety critical' in a general workplace might include those where reaction, co-ordination, dexterity, judgement and balance are essential. This might include operation of machinery, work at a height or in a confined space, work near traffic, using hazardous equipment such as a knife in butchery trades or being in control of animals. Though this is not a complete list it serves to illustrate the principle that being adversely affected by alcohol is not appropriate when involved in high risk work.

TESTING FOR ALCOHOL

There are different methods of testing for alcohol in the body. Testing for alcohol generally relies on breath testing since this is non-invasive, accurate and has been accepted as best practice.

To dispel any doubts over the validity of the testing methods you should only use devices that are approved by the Home Office as used by the British Police.

Disposable and re-usable electronic breath test equipment is available. The disposable tests comprise a mouthpiece and colourmetric tube which is calibrated to change colour at a given level of alcohol in the breath of the person providing the sample. They can be obtained calibrated to determine different levels of alcohol in the breath.

The electronic version of this device provides a direct and accurate reading. Because the device may be used for other people it is essential that routines be used which ensure the device is properly purged/re-set between tests. The Disposable type may be kept in a sealed bag to assist as evidence, printers may be added to the electronic versions that can document the test and enable the person tested to sign it accepting its accuracy.

Figure B9-6: Disposable breath test equipment. *Source: Grendonstar.*

Figure B9-7: Electronic breath test equipment. *Source: Grendonstar.*

Testing for alcohol can be used in various ways, for example:

- As part of a selection process for job applicants.
- Routine tests, for example, at the start of a shift.
- Random tests.
- After an accident.
- Where there is evidence of drinking that contravenes rules.

Alcohol testing can be a sensitive issue and securing the acceptance of the workforce to the principle of testing is essential if the practical and legal issues involved are to be overcome. Agreement to the principle of testing must be incorporated in each member of staff's contract of employment to be effective. In addition written consent of the individual should be obtained for each test. It should be clear what the consent is for i.e. specifically for alcohol and therefore not for clandestine testing for other substances or medical problems. Medical confidentiality should be assured and the results of the tests should only be communicated such that managers know whether an employee is considered fit or unfit for work. Testing requires a 'confidence procedure' to ensure the test sample is related to the correct person and is safeguarded from being tampered with. Where test methods other than using direct reading instruments are used this is particularly important in order to reduce the risk of error. Samples should be carefully controlled and an accredited laboratory used for the analysis. The National Measurement Accreditation Service provides such accreditation.

PLANNING TO COPE WITH THE EFFECTS OF ALCOHOL ON HEALTH AND SAFETY

- Find out it you have a problem with alcohol or the risk of alcohol affecting work.
- Evaluate the ways in which alcohol may affect your work.
- Consider methods and routes of consultation with employees.
- Decide how and to what extent your organisation expects employees to limit their drinking.
- Consider the options for the identification of employees with alcohol problems and decide a strategy.
- Establish and publicise how employees can confidentially alert the employer to their problem and obtain help.
- Decide at what point and in what circumstances an employee's drinking will be treated as a matter for discipline rather than a health problem.
- Establish a formal written alcohol policy which encompasses the above.
- Provide managers and employees with information and where necessary training.

GUIDANCE AND SUPPORT TO STAFF

An organisation's strategy for managing alcohol issues will be underpinned by providing guidance and support to staff. In the first instance this will be in the form of a policy on alcohol which will set out the organisation's perspective on the issue and how it plans to respond to it. In the first instance, the guidance needs to clarify if the policy is driven by the underlying health issue related to alcohol, other organisational decisions such as company image or religion, identified health and safety risks and/or a strict legal duty to take action. The first stage of support would usually involve dialogue with those affected. This may represent a radical change to their way of life and involve amendments to what they see as their employment contract. It is essential that all such issues are considered and a lead-in period may be decided on to deal with all these factors - if this is acceptable when balanced against legal duties. As the policy would usually apply to all workers it will affect senior management. The guidance to be provided needs to include:

■ The identified need, including the effects of alcohol.
■ Policy.
■ Any limits set within the policy translated to practical situations for different types of worker.
■ How someone may identify if they have an alcohol problem.
■ Confidential methods of reporting alcohol problems.
■ The effects of reporting a problem, including the support that would be provided - adjustment to work, a period agreed to conform with policy, counselling options.
■ The circumstances in which an employee's drinking will be treated as a matter of discipline.
■ Discipline steps and consequences.

Managers of employees can be expected to play an important role in the strategy to manage alcohol as it affects work. They will be expected to communicate, support and enforce the policy - it is important that they accept the policy and the strategy may take particular care to ensure that managers get support in conforming to the policy themselves. Part of the training of managers could include techniques on how to respond to a person with an identified problem. Though this is likely to include listening strategies and discussion of options it is unlikely that it will extend to the provision of counselling. It is important that employees with established alcohol problems receive professional assistance, including support from a recognised competent counsellor.

How access to such a counsellor can be obtained should be considered at an early stage in establishing a policy on alcohol, there are specialist organisations and individuals that can assist with counselling support. If uncertain, access can usually be obtained through a general practitioner health practice.

Prescribed and controlled drugs

THE EFFECTS OF DRUGS

As with alcohol the adverse effects of the misuse of drugs on work takes the form of absenteeism or impaired performance (including the associated risks to health and safety).

> 'Drug misuse' refers to the *use* of illegal *(controlled)* drugs and the *misuse*, whether deliberate or unintentional, of prescribed drugs and substances such as solvents.

Figure B9-8: Drug misuse term used by HSE.   *Source: HSE Drug Misuse at Work a guide to employers INDG91.*

Drug misuse can harm the employee both physically and mentally and, through their actions, other people may be harmed because their health and safety is endangered in general or more specifically because they are involved with the use of mobile equipment or they may act violently in unexpected situations. Though the topic of drug misuse is being treated separately it should be remembered that simultaneous use of alcohol and drugs is particularly dangerous.

Drugs can affect the brain and the body in a number of ways. They can alter the way a person thinks, perceives and feels, and this can lead to mistaken priorities, impaired judgement or concentration. Drug misuse can also bring about the neglect of general health and well-being. This may adversely influence performance or health and safety at work as clothing or other aspects of appearance may become inappropriate, for example for the operation of machinery, even when the misuse takes place outside the workplace.

The variety of drugs that may be misused may have a variety of effects, including:

■ Drowsiness.
■ An unaccountable sense of well-being, even when conducting safety critical tasks - e.g. work at a height, railway maintenance activities, working in a sewer.
■ Sudden mood changes.
■ Unexpected alertness and confidence.
■ Unusual assertion of well-being towards others.
■ Talkative.
■ Unusual irritability or aggression.
■ Poor levels of motivation.
■ Inability to focus on critical detail.
■ A tendency to become confused.
■ Abnormal fluctuations in concentration.
■ Heightened sense of awareness - for example of smells or their surroundings.
■ Abnormal fluctuations in energy.
■ Deterioration in relationships with other employees, customers or management.
■ Impaired job performance.
■ Poor time-keeping.
■ Increased short-term sickness absence.
■ Dishonesty and theft (arising from the desire or need to purchase expensive drugs).

Though these are offered as possible signs of drug misuse some of them could also be signs of other problems such as anxiety, stress or association with strong beliefs such as religion.

The effects of drug misuse has led to legislation designed to control it, namely, the Misuse of Drugs Act (MDA)1971, though this is not specifically health and safety legislation, it is still valid to workplaces. Nearly all drugs with misuse and/or dependence liability are covered by it. The Act makes the production, supply and possession of these controlled drugs unlawful except in certain specified circumstances (for example, when they have been prescribed by a doctor). If you knowingly permit the production or supply of any controlled drugs, the smoking of cannabis or certain other activities to take place on your premises you could be committing an offence. The Act lists the drugs that are subject to control and classifies them in three categories according to their relative harmfulness when misused. It should be noted that on 29 January 2004 cannabis was re-defined as a class C drug. As a controlled drug, production, supply and possession remains illegal, it is only the penalties that have changed.

CLASS A includes ecstasy, cocaine, heroin, LSD, mescaline, methadone, morphine, opium and injectable forms of Class B drugs.

CLASS B includes oral preparations of amphetamines, barbiturates, codeine and methaqualone (Mandrax).

CLASS C includes most benzodiazepines (e.g. Temazepam, Valium), other less harmful drugs of the amphetamine group, cannabis, cannabis resin, and anabolic steroids.

Figure B9-9: Classified drugs.   *Source: HSE Drug Misuse at Work a guide to employers INDG91 (amended to reflect re-classification of cannabis).*

METHODS OF TESTING FOR DRUGS

Strategies for drug testing have similar features and considerations as testing for alcohol. Testing is only likely to be acceptable to employees if it can be seen to be part of an organisation's occupational health policy and is clearly designed to prevent risks to the misuser and others. As with alcohol the railway industry is bound by the Transport and Work Act 1992 to take active steps to prevent employees conducting 'safety critical work' whilst under the influence of drugs. This has involved the use of testing at the time of selection or promotion, after accidents/incidents, and on a random basis. Various methods of testing for drugs are available, many products provide an immediate feedback at point of use, without recourse to specialist laboratories.

There are different methods of testing for drugs in the body. Urine, blood, hair and oral testing can all be sampled and each testing method has merits depending on the testing criteria.

Urine testing is inexpensive, accurate and gives a good detection window on drug use (approximately 3 - 30 days). Screening can be carried out on-site providing results within minutes (approximately 10 - 16 minutes). They use detection strips added to the urine sample or small kits where a quantity of urine is added and detection is shown by indicator marks, providing a direct reading. They are usually limited to detection of a single drug or group of drugs, though multi-drug kits and devices are available to test for such drugs as heroin, cannabis, amphetamines, cocaine and methadone. Positive samples can be sent to a laboratory for legally defensible confirmation.

Figure B9-10: Urine strip drug test. *Source: Access Diagnostic Tests UK.*   Figure B9-11: Urine strip drug test. *Source: Access Diagnostic Tests UK.*

Oral testing generally provides shorter detection windows than other tests. In some cases samples have to be sent to a laboratory for analysis, which is one of the main reasons why urine instant testing is often preferred in the workplace as it provides a result at point of sample. Oral testing is becoming more common for pre-employment testing since time waiting for results is not as an important factor. Electronic analysis instruments are available to provide an on site result within minutes.

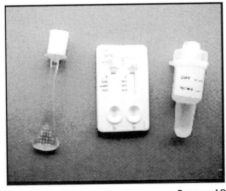

Figure B9-12: Saliva test kit.   *Source: ADrugtests4u.*   Figure B9-13: Saliva sampling instrument.   *Source: Drager.*

Hair testing is comparatively more expensive but provides much longer detection windows (up to 90 days), hence it is generally used to confirm abstinence for individuals undergoing counselling and treatment or to provide lifestyle information on high value job applicants.

Whichever method of test is used it is important to establish confidence in the test process and if the test may lead to disagreement, litigation or discipline it is important to establish what are often called 'chain of custody' protocols.

PLANNING TO COPE WITH THE EFFECTS OF DRUGS ON HEALTH AND SAFETY

The strategy for dealing with misuse of drugs is very similar to that for alcohol, one of the essential ingredients being a formal policy established through employee consultation. Other important features are clear lines for communication of a problem from the individual or others, confidentiality, support and, as appropriate, referral to counselling. It is a useful proactive approach to establish a policy on drugs even if there is no current evidence of misuse.

GUIDANCE AND SUPPORT TO STAFF

It is essential that the misuse of drugs policy be supported by a programme of awareness for all staff, whatever the level or role. In addition, it is important to identify those that will need additional information and training, for example, those involved with recruitment and induction or those that staff with a problem may refer to.

The need for confidentiality if an employee admits to a drugs problem is important. People who misuse drugs with a drugs problem may be persuaded to come forward if they are assured that their problems will be dealt with sensitively and confidentially. However, the organisation's legal position must also be considered. It may be necessary to remove a person from 'safety critical work' while the misuse is being brought under control. Employees with a drug problem should have the same rights to confidentiality and support as they would if they had any other medical or psychological condition.

It is therefore usual practice to inform managers of the unsuitability of the person to work, but not the reason. It should be remembered that it may be very difficult for people to admit to themselves or others that they have a drug problem. They may feel there is a stigma attached to drug misuse and they may well fear reprisals if they admit to taking illegal drugs. Policy and practice should seek, as far as possible, to treat drug misuse as a health issue rather than an immediate cause for dismissal or disciplinary action. It may be necessary to assist the employee by providing time off work in order to get help, advice or counselling. This might be from your organisation's occupational physician or nurse (if you have one), their general practitioner, health unit or a specialist organisation providing support for drug misuse.

As with alcohol, part of the training of managers could include techniques on how to respond to a person with an identified problem. Though this is likely to include listening strategies and discussion of options it is unlikely that it will extend to the provision of counselling. It is important that employees with established drug misuse problems receive professional assistance, including support from a recognised competent counsellor.

B9.3 - Violence

Identification

WORK-RELATED VIOLENCE

Definition of 'violence'

> The exertion of physical force so as to inflict injury on or damage to persons or property; action or conduct characterised by this.

Figure B9-14: Definition of violence.   *Source: The Shorter Oxford English Dictionary.*

The HSE defines violence as:

> *'Any incident in which a person is abused, threatened or assaulted in circumstances relating to their work'.*

The definition includes violence to employees at work by members of the public, whether inside a workplace or elsewhere, when the violence arises out of the employees' work activity. For example, this might include violence to teachers from pupils, to doctors/nurses from patients, to peripatetic employees whose work involves visiting the sick, or collecting payments, to security staff or to officials enforcing legislation. It would not include violence to persons when not at work, e.g. when travelling between home and work or violence outside their normal working hours, even though where such risks were significant, employers might wish to take action to safeguard their employees.

Figure B9-15: Definition of work-related violence (WRV).   *Source: HSE in their publication "Violence at work: a guide for employers" (INDG 69).*

Physical violence can involve incidents which:

- Require first aid treatment.
- Require medical assistance.
- Cause injury.

The HSE definition extends this to include incidents which:

- Involve a threat, even if no physical injury results.
- Involve verbal abuse.
- Involve non-verbal abuse (e.g. stalking).
- Involve other threatening behaviour.

> "Any incident where persons are abused, threatened or assaulted in circumstances related to their work, involving an explicit or implicit challenge to their safety, well being or health"   *(Wynne et.al.(1996)*

Figure B9-16: Extended definition of work-related violence (WRV).   *Source: HSE review of workplace-related violence (CRR143).*

This extends the dictionary definition to include verbal abuse and threats as well as physical attack. Physical attacks are comparatively rare with abuse and threats being most common. In addition, definitions are widening their scope from "workplace" to "work-related", to include incidents connected with work but which may not take place in the workplace. This gradual widening of definitions can lead to an increase in subjectivity in deciding what is to be included. Employees may have a different perspective of what constitutes abuse or threat. The inclusion of incidents involving verbal abuse and behaviour perceived as threatening moves the scope and numbers of potential incidents from the relatively small number of objective incidents involving physical injury to a larger number of subjective incidents involving perceived threat.

There are many views on definitions for work-related violence, but these too are a matter of perspective. The HSE review of workplace related violence reports their view that "any working definition should be produced locally".

This perspective being influenced by Lamplugh and Pagan (1996) who noted:

"A definition of a problem is not an end in itself but an initial collective effort to raise the awareness of the problem in order to promote effective strategies. A working definition should hence take into account the context and culture of the organisation, and should be developed as a flexible tool for understanding, building commitment, and developing polices, procedures and working practices."

Lamplugh and Pagan (1996)

Figure B9-17: Note on a working definition of work-related violence (WRV).　　　　*Source: HSE review of workplace-related violence (CRR143).*

Organisations and employees working for them will have a wide variety of opinions of what is an acceptable definition and as expressed by Lamplugh and Pagan the creation of an acceptable working definition for any organisation is an excellent opportunity for employee consultation. Through the involvement of employees the policies, procedures and practices, including appropriate reporting, are more likely to be effective.

Extent of problem

The latest statistics on violence at work were published in 2004 in the report of the British Crime Survey conducted by the Home Office and the Health and Safety Executive (HSE). The number of incidents of physical assaults and threats were shown by the report to have reduced has fallen since 1995. The report 'Violence at work: Findings from the 2002/2003 BCS' established that the:

Number of incidents of violence experienced by workers in England and Wales was 849,000 in 2002/03. Since a peak of 1,310,000 in 1995, the extent of violence at work reported in the British Crime Survey has been on a downward trend. The level is now similar to that reported in 1991.

Figure B9-18: Incident of work-related violence (WRV).　　　　*Source: http://www.hse.gov.uk/violence/index.htm.*

The survey report is based on self-report data and uses a narrower definition than many of the above definitions, restricting data to actual assaults. The definition of violence at work used in this report is:

"All assaults or threats, which occurred while the victim was working, that were perpetrated by members of the public."

Physical **assaults** include common assault, wounding, robbery and snatch theft. Threats include both verbal threats, made to or against the respondent, and non-verbal intimidation. These are mainly threats to assault the victim, though some threats relate to damaging property or harming others. The term violence is used in this report to refer to both assaults and threats. However, threats are not usually included in other BCS measures of violence.

Members of the **public** are clients or customers who the victim did not know before the incident or people previously known to the victim, including friends, neighbours and local children.

Excluded are incidents in which there was a domestic relationship between the offender and victim (partners, ex-partners, relatives or household members) and incidents in which the offender was a **work colleague**. Cases of domestic violence and violence between colleagues have been excluded as these incidents are likely to be very different in nature from those involving members of the public.

Figure B9-19: Definition of work-related violence (WRV) used in BCS survey.　　　*Source: report 'Violence at work: Findings from the 2002/2003 BCS'.*

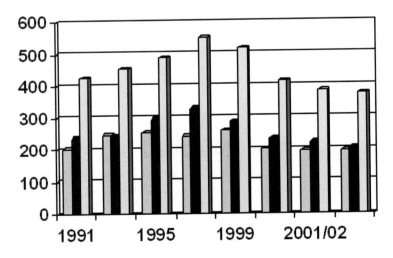
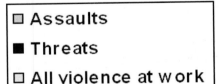

Figure B9-20: Number of victims of violence at work.　　　　*Source: report 'Violence at work: Findings from the 2002/2003 BCS'.*

From data within the BCS 2002/03 report it is concluded that the estimated risk of a worker being a victim of actual or threatened violence at work is low. 1.7 per cent of working adults were the victim of one or more violent incidents at work in the year before their interview. Based on the number of adults in working employment this represents an estimated 376,000 workers who had experienced violence at work, 196,000 had been assaulted by a member of the public while they were working and 203,000 had been threatened.

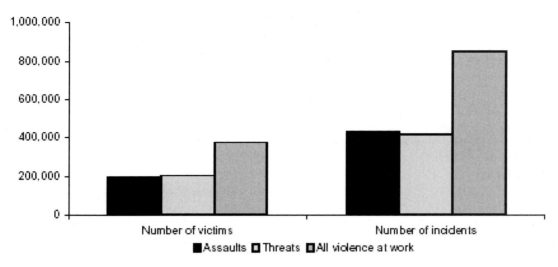

Figure B9-21: Number of victims and incidents of violence at work.   *Source: report 'Violence at work: Findings from the 2002/2003 BCS'.*

The statistics used in *Figure B9-20* (*'Number of victims of violence at work'*) shows the number of victims over time and shows a decline from the peak in 1995; *Figure B9-22 - below* shows the number of incidents that have occurred over the same period of time.

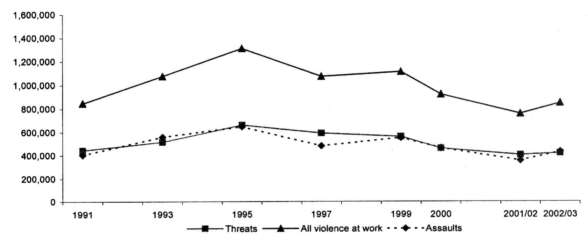

1. Source 1992, 1994, 1996, 1998, 2000, 2001, 2001/02 and 2002/03 BCS.

2. Based on adults of working age, in employment.

Figure B9-22: Number of incidents of violence at work over time.   *Source: report 'Violence at work: Findings from the 2002/2003 BCS'.*

It should be noted that the BCS generally defines violence more narrowly than the HSE and other agencies, restricting it to actual assaults. The definition used for the 1996 survey was:

Incidents of violence (wounding, common assault, robbery and snatch theft) occurring while the victim was working.

Figure B9-23: Definition of violence.   *Source: 1996 British Crime Survey (BCS).*

Workers in the protective services, for example, police officers, were most at risk of violence at work. 14% of workers in protective services experienced violence in 2002/3. Health and social welfare associate professionals, including nurses, medical and dental practitioners were also at relatively high risk. The survey revealed that 5% experienced violence.

Physical attacks are obviously dangerous, but serious or persistent verbal abuse can be a significant problem too, as it can cause damage to employees' health through anxiety and stress.

Consequences for organisations and individuals

Organisations have become increasingly concerned about violence at work. This can lead to both poor morale and a poor image for the organisation, with the consequent difficulties in recruiting or retaining staff and the effect on confidence in the business and its profitability. It can also be expensive with extra costs relating to:

■   Absenteeism.

■   Higher insurance premiums.

■   Civil compensation payments.

For the individual employee, physical violence can cause pain, distress and even disability or death. Verbal abuse or threats, particularly if they are serious or persistent, can affect the individuals' health through the mental anguish caused by stress or anxiety.

Concern about violence at work varied considerably with occupation. Thirty-six per cent of health and social welfare associate professionals, such as youth workers, were very or fairly worried about assaults at work, compared with three per cent of science and technology professionals, for example, mechanical engineers.

Overall, 0.5 per cent of workers said that worrying about workplace violence had a 'great deal' of impact on their health, and two per cent said that it affected their health 'quite a bit'.

Twenty-two per cent of workers who had contact with members of the public thought it very or fairly likely that they would be threatened at work in the next year. Ten per cent of workers with face-to-face contact with the public thought it very or fairly likely that they would be assaulted.

Sixty-seven per cent of workers who had face-to-face contact with the public said they had not received any form of training in how to deal with violent or threatening behaviour.

Figure B9-24: Level of concern about violence at work amongst workers.   Source: report 'Violence at work: Findings from the 2002/2003 BCS'.

RISK FACTORS

General issues

Reports on work-related violence consider age, gender and occupation, the most significant of these being occupation. Though there is no statistically significant difference in incidence of violence to men or women there is a significant increase with increased age, for example, 2.6% women over 45 compared with 0.8% for women 16-24. Though other factors than age may influence the incidence it tends to illustrate a higher risk for those over the age of 45. Violence at work can be inflicted by:

- Clients or customers.
- Members of the general public.
- Co-workers and fellow employees (including bullying).

While bullying at work is increasingly recognised as a significant problem, the main emphasis of this unit is on other forms of violence. The great majority of violent incidents occur in situations where the victim is providing (or not as the case may be) a service and the aggressor is the client or customer for that service. The 1996 British Crime Survey (BCS) indicated that the following worker groups were at increased risk of violence:

- The protective services, especially police, security guards and the fire service (17 times average).
- Health and welfare (4 times average).
- Teachers (above average).
- Others groups identified as being at high risk are staff in takeaway food outlets, bar and retail staff, Department of Social Security staff, transport workers, milkmen and taxi drivers.

Additional risk factors to consider include:

- When incidents occur.
- Where incidents occur.
- Influence of factors such as alcohol, drugs and mental health.
- The relationship with the person likely to be violent.

Percentage very / fairly worried	Assaults
Health and social welfare associate professionals	36
Protective service occupations	33
Health professionals	26
Sales occupations	23
Transport and mobile machine drivers and operatives	21
Managers and proprietors in agriculture and services	21
Caring personal service occupations	18
Leisure and other personal service occupations	16
Teaching and research professionals	15
Elementary administration and service occupations	15
All	13
1. Source 2001/02 and 2002/03 BCS	
2. Based on adults of working age, in employment	
3. Full details of the SOC occupations within each of the groups are given in Appendix B.	

Figure B9-25: Occupations with a high level of worry about assaults at work.   Source: Report 'violence at work: findings from the 2002/2003 BCS'.

People working with public in caring/teaching professions

Health care

Acts of violence at work have long been of real concern in the health services due to the necessarily close interaction with the public, some of whom may be mentally disturbed or suffering from alcohol and other drug abuse problems. The 1996 British Crime Survey reported the following incidents in relation to heath workers:

Occupation	Incidents per 10 000 workers
Medical practitioners	762
Nurses and midwives	580
Other health-related occupations	830
All survey subjects	251

Figure B9-26: Risk of work-related violence to health workers.   Source: Home Office Research and Statistics Directorate, British Crime Survey 1996.

As previously stated the definition of violence includes: wounding, common assault, robbery and snatch theft, excluding incidents committed by partners, ex-partners, relatives or other household members occurring while the victim said that they were working. Key risk factors for healthcare staff include:

- Working alone.
- Working after normal working hours.
- Working and travelling in the community.
- Handling valuables or medication.
- Providing or withholding a service.
- Exercising authority.
- Working with people who are emotionally or mentally unstable.
- Working with people who are under the influence of drink or drugs.
- Working with people under stress.

Education sector / teaching professions

Teachers, support staff and volunteers in the education sector may be at risk of violence from pupils and their parents, and from other visitors. Many of those working in the education sector consider violence at work to be one of the most serious problems that they face. This has been exacerbated by incidents such as the shootings at Dunblane Primary School, the machete attack in Wolverhampton and an attack with a home-made flame thrower on pupils taking examinations in Northern Ireland. These incidents have involved mainly intruders and Lord Cullen's Public Inquiry into the Dunblane shootings emphasised that employers need to consider the protection of the school population as a whole from intruders.

The HSE publication "Violence in the Education Sector" deals with many of these problems. While it retains an emphasis on schools, the general principles outlined can be applied throughout the education sector. The issue of pupil on pupil violence, other than where this creates a risk to staff, is not addressed nor does it consider the particular problems experienced by high-security research departments within universities, although some of the general advice given may be relevant.

This publication identifies the following activities, and those who undertake them, as situations where the risk of violence may be increased:

Activities	People
Looking after premises (caretaking).	Site supervisors (e.g. caretakers), porters, security staff.
Lone Working.	Cleaning staff, library staff, head-teachers, principals, teachers, lecturers, site supervisors, maintenance and administrative staff.
Home visiting, off-site working.	Education welfare officers, education social workers, teachers, researchers, psychologists etc.
Evening working.	Teaching staff, library staff, cleaning staff, education welfare officers, youth and community workers, site supervisors, bursars, students.
Running licensed premises in education establishments.	Bar staff.
Looking after animals/research with animals.	Animal house technicians, teaching staff, research workers.
Working with pupils with behavioural difficulties.	Teachers, educational psychologists, day-care helpers, nursery nurses.
Looking after money.	Bursars, clerical and finance staff, headteachers, teachers, school secretaries.
Disciplining/supervising/students.	Headteachers, teachers, lunchtime supervisors, lecturers.
Dealing with angry parents or relatives of pupils.	Headteachers, teachers, principals, lecturers, school secretaries, bursars, receptionists.

Figure B9-27: Risk of violence.   Source: Violence in the Education Sector, HSE.

Working with psychiatric clients or alcohol/drug impaired people

Workers who come into contact with psychiatric clients or alcohol/drug impaired people are at increased risk of experiencing violence when working. Both of these characteristics can have an effect on a person's perception, sense of values or restraint, and their co-ordination. These factors, coupled with a potential for restricted ability to communicate, can cause the person to feel frustrated, threatened or to misunderstand a situation, particularly if this is an offer of help that brings the worker in close proximity with the person. In other situations the person might be one whose psychiatric tendencies make them prone to commit violence. In the case of alcohol/drug impaired people the simple fact that their control over their own body is diminished may mean that they could cause injury to workers without intention.

Working alone

Lone workers are those who work by themselves without close or direct supervision. Examples of lone workers include:

Persons who work in a static location:

- Only one person works on the premises (e.g. small workshops, petrol stations, kiosks, shops and those who work at home).
- People work separately from others (e.g. in factories, warehouses, some research and training establishments, leisure centres or fairgrounds).
- People work outside normal hours (e.g. cleaners, security, special production, maintenance or repair staff).

Persons who work away from their base (mobile workers):

- On construction, plant installation, maintenance and cleaning work, electrical repairs, lift repairs, painting and decorating, vehicle recovery.
- Agricultural and forestry workers.
- Service workers, e.g. rent collectors, postal staff, social workers, home helps, district nurses, pest control workers, drivers, engineers, architects, estate agents, sales representatives and similar professionals visiting domestic and commercial premises.

Home visiting

As identified above home visiting is frequently an activity that is done alone and carries particular risks of violence based on the fact that it is at a person's home and that it is done alone. The fact that it is a person's home means that there is usually little control over it as a workplace. It is a possibility that the home visit may be attended by a number of people at a time, for example, relatives of a sick person. Though many home visits are routine there are times that there may be an increased tension related to the visit, due to the anxiety or frustration of the people being visited. A home contains many ordinary, everyday items which may be used against a worker in a violent act. This increases the degree of harm that may be caused and in some cases may make violence more likely to move from the verbal to the physical. The layout of homes being visited, such as a single entrance/exit flat, makes it more difficult for the worker to leave the home and avoid a potentially violent situation before it escalates.

Handling money/valuables

Workers involved in handling money/valuables are at risk of being involved in planned or opportunist theft. Theft accompanied by actual violence or a threat of violence is commonplace. Organisations involved in industries that know they are targets have generally evaluated the risks and taken steps to minimise them, for example, in petrol stations, banks or security transfer activities. Those organisations where money or valuables are seen as a secondary or incidental activity of their operation are at particular risk as they will not have well developed strategies to deal with the risks. Examples might be charities handling fund-raised money, a person emptying coin operated launderette machines, shop keepers banking takings or organisations that pay wages in cash.

In addition to money employers have to consider workers that handle valuables, though the term 'valuable' has a wide definition and what is not valuable to an organisation or worker may be valuable to a person who wants it. Obvious valuables that may place someone at risk include drugs for medical treatment, a mobile phone, laptop or even the company car they drive. All of these may represent an increased risk of violence to obtain them from a worker.

Inspection and enforcement duties

Workers involved in inspection and enforcement duties are at increased risk because despite any good intentions they will be seen by some people in an adversarial perspective. Distrust, anxiety and frustrations may accompany the execution of these duties leading to a heightened tension and an increased risk of violence. These duties may be carried out on a forced rather than planned basis which in itself could lead a person to have offensive behaviour and possibly become violent. If the duties are carried out by an individual alone similar issues as those referred to with regard to lone working apply. Increased risks exist when carrying out these duties with regard to work that makes use of equipment that may be used as a weapon of violence. For example, a shot gun for farmers, dogs for scrap yards, knives for catering or butchery trades.

THE LEGAL DUTIES TO PROTECT EMPLOYEES FROM VIOLENCE

Health and Safety at Work etc. Act (HASAWA) 1974

An employer's responsibilities under HASAWA 1974 s2 extend to protecting staff from violence. In the decided case West Bromwich Building Society v Townsend [1983] IRLR 147, a principal environmental health officer served an improvement notice on the building society requiring the installation of screens to protect staff against attack. Although in the particular circumstances of that case, the High Court found for the Society, in his summing up Mr Justice McNeill stated that protecting staff from violent attack was **not out with** an employer's responsibilities under HASAWA 1974 s.2.

HASAWA 1974 is a wide ranging Act and could be applied to almost any incident of violence at work. However, it is HSE policy not to enforce the Act where there is other more specific legislation. In practice it is intended that attention should focus on protecting employees where there is a significant risk of violence from members of the public. An exception to this general rule would be where skylarking or other incidents between employees warranted action under HASAWA 1974 s.7.

The Management of Health and Safety at Work Regulations (MHSWR) 1999

The Regulations require employers to assess risks to employees and make arrangements for their health and safety by effective planning, organisation, control, monitoring and review. Where appropriate, employers must assess the risks of violence to employees and, if necessary, put in place control measures to protect them

Although there is no general legal prohibition on higher risk factors such as working alone, the broad duties of the Health and Safety at Work Act and the Management of Health and Safety at Work Regulations still apply. Therefore employers need to ensure, so far as is reasonably practicable the health, safety and welfare at work of employees. Risk assessments and the resultant appropriate planning, organisation, control and monitoring and review arrangements are also required.

The Reporting of Injuries, Diseases and Dangerous Occurrences Regulations (RIDDOR) 1995

Employers must notify their enforcing authority in the event of an accident at work to any employee resulting in death, major injury or incapacity for normal work for three or more days. This includes any act of non-consensual physical violence done to a person at work.

The Safety Representatives and Safety Committees Regulations (SRSCR) 1977 and The Health and Safety (Consultation with Employees) Regulations (HSCER) 1996

Employers must inform, and consult with, employees in good time on matters relating to their health and safety. Employee representatives, either appointed by recognised trade unions under SRSCR 1977 or elected under HSCER 1996 may make representations to their employer on matters affecting the health and safety of those they represent.

Sex Discrimination Act 1975 and Race Relations Act 1976

Both these Acts deal in part with verbal abuse in specific contexts and are enforced by the Equal Opportunities Commission (EOC) and the Commission for Racial Equality (CRE) respectively. CRE and EOC only pursue cases of abuse between employees. There are no formal agreements between the CRE, EOC or HSE/HELA on the subject of demarcation but enforcement officers should normally refer cases of sexual or racial abuse to these bodies.

Employers' common law duties

An employer's duties under common law and employment law have been interpreted as including a duty to protect staff from violent attack from the public. If an employee considers the employer has failed in his/her duty of care, redress is available on 2 fronts. If injury has occurred the employer can be sued for negligence. If, however, no injury has occurred but the employee has left the job because he/she considered the risk of injury unacceptable, then it might be possible in some cases for the employer to be sued.

Violence between employees should normally be dealt with as a personnel matter by the employer, but reasonably practicable measures need to be taken by employers to satisfy their legal duty under HASAWA 1974, particularly so where the employer is aware of the likelihood of violence occurring.

Public Order Act (POA) 1986

The Public Order Act 1986 (POA) is enforced by the police and covers threats and abuse as well as physical assault. There could be some interplay between the POA and HASAWA 1974 where cases of violence occur. However, police action under the POA will be directed against the perpetrator of the violence, whereas HSE's & Local Authorities' activities will be directed towards assessing whether the employer complied with his/her general duties under HASAWA 1974. The POA also only applies after an offence has been committed and cannot be used to require preventive measures beforehand.

RISK IDENTIFICATION METHODOLOGY

Management of violence at work

A four stage strategy for managing violence can be adopted by employers:

Stage 1:   Finding out if there is a problem.

Stage 2:   Deciding what action to take.

Stage 3:   Taking action.

Stage 4:   Checking what has been done.

This is an ongoing process which should be repeated, if stage 4 shows there is still a problem. Essentially, stages 1 and 2 are completed by carrying out a risk assessment. From this policy and procedures for violence at work can be developed.

Use of staff surveys

In order to complete Stage 1 (finding out if there is a problem) then hazards should be identified. This is the first step of the risk assessment process. The management perception may be that violence is not a problem at your workplace or that incidents are rare. A staff survey carried out by a major oil company of forecourt employees showed that they believed that increased customer violence was the most serious threat to their personal health and safety.

A staff survey can be carried out by informal discussion between workers and managers, supervisors or safety representatives. A more formal approach would be the use of a questionnaire to find out whether employees feel threatened in their work activities. The results of the survey should be publicised in order to reassure staff that the problem is recognised.

Incident reporting

Incident reporting should be encouraged and detailed records kept of all events - including verbal abuse and threats. You may find it useful to record the following information:

- An account of what happened.
- Details of the victim(s), assailant(s) and any witnesses.
- The outcome, including working time lost to both the individual(s) affected and to the organisation as a whole.
- Details of the location of the incident.

There are many reasons why employees may be reluctant to report incidents of aggressive behaviour which make them feel threatened or worried. For example, they may for instance feel that accepting abuse is part of the job. Records should be kept in order to allow the full extent of the problem to be built up. Employees should be both encouraged and expected to report incidents promptly and fully.

Incidents should be classified in order to aid analysis. Classifications could include:

- Place.
- Potential severity.
- Time.
- Who was involved.
- Type of incident.
- Possible causes.

It is important that each incident is examined in order to establish whether there could have been a more serious outcome. Again, a simple classification system could be used to decide on the severity of incidents:

- Fatal injury.
- First aid injury (including for emotional shock).
- Counselling.
- Emotional trauma (feeling of being at risk or distressed).
- Major injury.
- Out-patient treatment.
- Absence from work (record number of days).

While it may be easy to classify major injuries, it may be more difficult to define serious or persistent verbal abuse. The classification guidelines should be detailed enough to ensure consistency in classifying all incidents that worry staff.

Once data has been gathered then analysis can be carried out in order to identify patterns. Common causes such as areas or times can be established. Appropriate control measures can then be targeted where they are needed most. For example, a Trade Union survey found that, after 12 separate shop robberies, each incident occurred between 5 and 7 p.m. This could be used to improve the security measures for late night opening shops.

Useful information can also be gathered from outside the organisation. Trade and professional organisations and trade unions can provide information about patterns of violence linked to certain work situations, Articles in the local, national and technical press might contain details of relevant incidents and potential problem areas.

Risk assessment

Having defined the extent of the problem, then the next step in the risk assessment process is to decide what action to take. (Stage 2). This involves deciding who might be harmed, and how and then risk evaluation.

The first task is to identify those employees at risk. For example, people whose job entails personal contact with the public are normally vulnerable. If necessary, potentially violent people should be identified in advance so that the risks from them can be minimised.

Risk evaluation entails the consideration of existing control measures. If the existing arrangements and precautions already in place are not adequate then more controls will be required. Factors which can be influential include:

- The level of training and information provided.
- The environment.
- The design of the job.

Controls

STRATEGY FOR PLANNING TO COPE WITH VIOLENCE

Guidance to staff on dealing with an incident

Aside from possible physical injuries, someone involved in a violent incident, can suffer severe distress. In some cases, the psychological effects can be long term and debilitating. This can include post traumatic stress disorder (PTSD). Planning is needed to ensure a quick response in order to avoid long-term distress to victims. The following factors should be considered:

Debriefing: Victims will need to talk through their experience as soon as possible after the event. It should be remembered that verbal abuse can be just as upsetting as a physical attack.

Time off work: Individuals will react differently and may need differing amounts of time to recover. In some circumstances they might need specialist counselling.

Legal help: In serious cases legal help may be appropriate.

Other employees: May need guidance and/or training to help them to react appropriately.

Legal constraints regarding 'reasonable force'

A person who is subjected to violence is entitled to protect himself if he is put in fear of his life or the safety of his person. He must not, however, use more force than is necessary or reasonable in the circumstances. This is the basis for the defence of Self-Defence (also known as Private Defence) against a charge related to assault and battery. Legally, **assault** is a threat to apply force immediately to the person of the victim and battery is the actual application of force. If accepted this is a complete defence because it negates the unlawful nature of the assault carried out in self defence.

Support for staff post-incident including training for managers in counselling

The need for counselling varies between individuals. Reaction to a violent incident ranges from anxiety attack, phobias, guilt and self-blame through to post traumatic stress disorder (PTSD). The severity of the violence is not necessarily related to the victim's response. Personality has much to do with the psychological impact. Some people, who are said to have "an external locus of control", are classified as 'type A' personalities. Type As are thought to suffer a more exaggerated psychological impact than that which non-type As would suffer. Victims are thought to suffer three distinct phases:

1. The impact phase: The victim experiences emotions ranging from shock, fear, vulnerability; sleep loss, fatigue and anger are experienced.

2. The recoil phase: The victim tries to make sense of the incident (why me?).

3. The reorganisation phase: The victim eventually regains control of their emotions.

Support on return to work should be considered, especially if the aggressor is still within the working environment. If an employee suffers an injury, loss or damage from a crime then useful information can be obtained from the Home Office leaflet "Victims of Crime" which gives then useful advice - including how to apply for compensation. It should be available from libraries, police stations, Citizens Advice Bureaux and victim support schemes.

COMMUNICATION SYSTEMS

Passing on information on risks from individual clients

Risk assessments should include the identification of increased risk from individual client, situations and areas. In some situations it may not be acceptable for an individual to visit high risk clients by themselves. Alternatively it may not be appropriate for certain employees (e.g. a woman or a young person) to carry out certain visits. A progressive client classification scheme could be used in order to decrease the risk of violence. It should be noted however that while some people are predisposed to be violent due to physiological and environmental factors, some incidents of physical violence consist of a single act of violence without any preceding interaction or escalation.

Recording of staff whereabouts and recognition when staff are overdue

Where people work away from a fixed point in higher risk activities, such as community nurses that visit in the home to administer drugs to patients, it is usual to establish simple systems where their visits are recorded and balanced against a proposed time sheet for the day. This helps to establish where they should be at any point in time. Systems for calling in to confirm progress and the worker's well-being enable progress sheets to be updated and to observe when a worker is overdue for an appointment at a given location. An agreed protocol needs to be in place to act promptly to deal with an observation that a worker is overdue. Usually this will include a call to the person, if they are equipped to receive one, and the escalation to involve the police if necessary.

Use of mobile communication equipment

Clearly, individuals who work alone visiting clients should not be at more risk than other employees. This may require extra control measures which should include precautions to take account of both normal work and foreseeable emergencies. Employers should consider the use of mobile communication equipment for workers that may need to gain assistance rapidly or for those that need to confirm their safe condition intermittently. Equipment could include:

- Regular telephone or radio contact between the lone worker and supervision.
- The use of automatic warning devices which operate if specific signals are not received periodically from the lone worker.
- Other alarm devices for use in the event of an emergency and which are operated manually or automatically by the absence of activity.

STAFF TRAINING

Recognition of situations where violence could result

Training should be provided to all employees at risk from violence. It may also be appropriate to train managers so that they can recognise the problems associated with violent and aggressive incidents, and how to manage them.

The objective of training is to bring about a reduction in both the number and seriousness of incidents. Further benefits include:

- A reduction in the psychological effects of incidents.
- An improved response to incidents.
- An improvement in staff morale.

A training programme might include:

Theory: understanding aggression and violence in the workplace.

Prevention: assessing danger and taking precautions including causes of violence.

Interaction: with aggressive people. This includes the recognition of warning signs, relevant interpersonal skills and details of working practices and control measures.

Post-incident action: incident reporting procedures, investigation, counselling and other follow-up.

There are various levels of training ranging from basic through to the more advanced skills required to defuse, de-escalate and avoid incidents. Some workers, for example those working in mental health, may need training in breakaway, control and restraint techniques.

Detailed training records should be kept.

Interpersonal skills to defuse aggression

Workers that may be exposed to the risk of violence should be trained in the use of interpersonal skills to defuse an aggressive situation. The training does not need to be overly complicated but will often develop a heightened awareness of how the workers' behaviour can add to or reduce the risk of violence, frequently providing a better perspective of how the other person sees things. If this consideration is taken into account at recruitment or selection it may help to prevent workers that do not have these skills being placed in work with a risk of violence.

Use of language and body language

Two of the critical factors to consider when analysing and preventing violence are the language and body language of the worker and violent person. In the first instance it is possible for the worker to precipitate violence not because of what they say but because of how they say it. In addition, many situations that are moving towards a violent situation can be identified by the person's language and body language. This provides an opportunity to re-assess if the worker is contributing to the move towards violence and use the interpersonal skills to defuse the situation.

OTHER CONTROL MEASURES

Cash free systems

The handling of money is a high risk factor associated with violence. Where possible, effort should be made to use cash free systems. Technology has enabled this for many quite ordinary activities. For example, drink and food machine vending organisations can work in association with companies to provide swipe card systems that automatically debit a person's card when purchases are made. Even the company does not need to handle money as they can make adjustment to the person's salary to account for the cost of credit on the swipe card. Many organisations do not pay staff using cash which avoids the drawing and distribution of cash to employees, a high risk for the employer and for the employee that needs to make their way from their workplace carrying a significant sum of money.

Layout of public areas and design of fixtures and fittings

The provision of better seating, decor, lighting in public waiting rooms and more regular information about stress factors such as delays can be beneficial in reducing and managing violent situations. Potential weapons / missiles should be identified and then modified or removed. It must not be forgotten that weapons can include ones which pose a biological threat (e.g. used syringe needles).

Care should be taken when deciding on controls. In one housing department it was found that protective screens made it difficult for staff and the public to speak to each other. This caused tension on both sides. Management and safety representatives agreed a package of measures including taking screens down, providing more comfortable waiting areas and better information on waiting lists and delays. This package of measures reduced tension and violent incidents.

Employees are likely to be more committed to the measures if they help to design them and put them into practice. A mix of measures often works best. Concentrating on just one aspect of the problem may make things worse in another. An overall view must be taken and the risks to employees balanced against any possible reaction of the public. An atmosphere that suggests employees are worried about violence can sometimes increase its likelihood.

Use of cameras, protective screens and security-coded doors

The following physical measures can be taken to reduce the risk of violence such as:

- Video cameras or alarm systems.
- Coded security locks on doors to keep the public out of staff areas.
- Wider counters and raised floors on the staff side of the counter to give staff more protection.
- Protective screens.
- Escape routes.
- Barriers.
- Security patrols.
- Emergency call systems such as panic buttons and personal alarms.

These measures act both as visual deterrents to people that might commit violent acts and to provide comfort and assurance to workers.

Use of panic buttons and personal alarms

Where workers are in close proximity to people that may be violent, such as in interviews for benefit claims, it is important to anticipate this likelihood. Workers should have a clear perspective of what constitutes potentially violent behaviour and have ready access to assistance. This may be best provided by equipping them with an alarm, on their person or at the workstation, for them to call for help when they feel threatened.

Other

The threat of violence does not stop when the work period has ended. It is good practice to make sure that employees can get home safely. For example, where employees are required to work late, employers might help by arranging transport home or by ensuring a safe parking area is available.

Ergonomic factors

Learning outcomes

On completion of this element, candidates should be able to:

B10.1 Outline the conditions and effects resulting from poor ergonomics in the workplace and the risk reduction methods that can be applied.

B10.2 Explain the ill-health effects associated with the use of display screen equipment together with appropriate risk assessment and control strategies.

B10.3 Explain the assessment and control of risk from manual handling activities and the main injuries that can occur.

Content

Relevant statutory provisions

Health and Safety (Display Screen Equipment) Regulations (DSE) 1992 (and as amended 2002)

Manual Handling Operations Regulations (MHOR) 1992 (and as amended 2002)

This page is intentionally blank

B10.1 - Ergonomics

Conditions likely to result from lack of attention to ergonomic principles

WRULDS

Work related upper limb disorders [WRULD]

Were first defined in medical literature as long ago as the 19th century as a condition caused by *forceful, frequent, twisting and repetitive movements.*

WRULD covers well known conditions such as tennis elbow, flexor tenosynovitis and carpal tunnel syndrome. It is usually caused by the conditions detailed above and aggravated by excessive workloads, inadequate rest periods and sustained or constrained postures, the result of which is pain or soreness to the inflammatory conditions of muscles and the synovial lining of the tendon sheath. Present approaches to treatment are largely effective, provided the condition is treated in its early stages.

Clinical signs and symptoms: local aching pain, tenderness, swelling, crepitus (a grating sensation in the joint).

GENERAL MUSCULOSKELETAL EFFECTS OF POOR POSTURE

(Source: HSG121, 'A Pain in Your Workplace? and www.betterhealthchannel.com').

General musculoskeletal effects can include backache, sore shoulders or elbows and numb or tingling wrists and hands. Such health problems manifest themselves in different ways, such as:

- Cases of injury to backs and limbs.
- Sickness absence.
- Aches and pains.
- Poor product quality.
- High material waste.
- Low output.
- Frequent employee complaints and rest stops.
- 'Do-it-yourself' improvements to workstations and tools, e.g. seat padding.
- Employees wearing bandages, splints, rub-ons, copper bracelets.

General musculoskeletal disorders can cause muscle fatigue and tension that ultimately lead to poor posture. The complications of poor posture include back pain, spinal dysfunction, joint degeneration, rounded shoulders and a potbelly. When such musculoskeletal disorders are related to work, they are often caused by poor workplace or job design. The risk factors for musculoskeletal disorders may act alone or in combination (when the risk is generally increased), and include:

- Awkward and uncomfortable working postures (e.g. bending, stretching and static postures).
- Manual handling.
- Repeating an action too frequently.
- Exerting too much effort.
- Working too long without adequate breaks.
- Adverse working conditions (e.g. hot, cold).
- Psycho-social factors (e.g. high job demands, time pressures and lack of control).
- Employers not receiving and acting on reports of symptoms quickly enough.

Symptoms of poor posture can include:

- Rounded shoulders.
- Potbelly.
- Bent knees when standing or walking.
- Head that either leans forward or backward.
- Back pain.
- Body aches and pains.
- Muscle fatigue.
- Headache.

Postural mechanisms

Poor posture interferes with a number of the body's postural mechanisms, including:

- Slow-twitch and fast-twitch muscle fibres.
- Muscle strength and length.
- Nervous system feedback on the body's position in space.

Slow-twitch and fast-twitch muscle fibres

Skeletal muscle is made up of two types of muscle fibre - slow-twitch and fast-twitch. Generally, slow-twitch muscle fibres are found in the deeper muscle layers. They help us to maintain posture without too much effort, and contribute to balance by 'sensing' our position and relaying this information to the brain. Fast-twitch muscle fibres are used for movement and activity.

Slow-twitch fibres burn energy slowly and can keep working for a long time without tiring. However, fast-twitch fibres quickly run out of steam. Poor posture causes muscle fatigue because it calls on the fast-twitch fibres instead of slow-twitch fibres to maintain the body's position.

Muscle strength and length

Over time, poor posture that demands support from fast-twitch fibres causes the deeper supporting muscles to waste away from lack of use. Weak, unused muscles tend to tighten, and this shortening of muscle length can compact the bones of the spine (vertebrae) and worsen posture.

Nervous system feedback on the body's position in space

The deeper layers of muscle are concerned with 'sensing' our position in space and relaying this information to the brain. If this function is taken over by muscles that mainly contain fast-twitch fibres, the brain gets an incomplete picture. The brain assumes that the body needs to be propped up to counteract the effects of gravity, so it triggers further muscle contraction. This adds to the general fatigue and pain felt by the person with poor posture.

Listen to your body

Good posture feels effortless, which is why traditional 'good posture' suggestions like throwing your shoulders back and sticking out your chest may feel uncomfortable too. Instead, listen to your body. Make minor adjustments while standing and sitting. Which position feels the easiest and most graceful? In most cases, concentrating on other tasks (such as work) can direct attention away from any feelings of physical discomfort. Get into the habit of regularly tuning in to your body. If you feel muscle tension or fatigue, move into another position.

Improve your general posture

Suggestions include:

- Remember the rule of 'curve reversal' - for example, if you've been leaning over your desk, stretch back the other way.

- Perform stretching exercises two or three times per week to boost muscle flexibility.

- Exercise regularly to improve muscle strength and tone.

- Stretch your neck muscles regularly by turning your head from one side to another.

- Your abdominal muscles support your lower back, so make sure they are in good condition. Do 'abdominal crunches' (lie on your back and curl your ribcage and pelvis as close together as possible) rather than straight-backed sit-ups (which exercise the muscles of the hips and thighs).

- Avoid standing on one foot for long periods of time.

- Cross your legs at the ankle, rather than the knee.

TYPICAL WORKPLACE EXAMPLE

The following example is sourced from HSG121, 'A Pain in Your Workplace?':

VDU operation

Body area affected: shoulder, arm.

Risk factors: awkward posture.

Type of solution: workspace organisation.

Task

A news agency employee used a VDU for about 70% of the day to download, input and verify numerical information. He was right-handed and used a mouse much of the time.

Problem

The individual got pain in the top of his right arm and shoulder.

Assessing the task and finding the solutions

Because of the way the equipment was laid out at the workstation, the employee's posture was uncomfortable and restricted. The monitor was in the right-hand corner of the workstation, but the mouse and pad were on the left of the keyboard. Being right-handed, the employee reached across his body every time he used the mouse. It was difficult to sit like this for ling periods, and frequently reaching across his body posed a risk of injury.

Looking at the whole workstation, it was also clear that when the employee was sitting at a comfortable typing height with his arms flat and level with the work surface, his feet didn't reach the floor. This put pressure on the back of his legs and made sitting uncomfortable.

The equipment was rearranged. The VDU monitor was put on the left-hand side of the workstation, and the mouse on the right of the keyboard, so the employee no longer had to reach across his body. A foot rest was found to support his legs.

The employee felt more comfortable overall, and the painful symptoms in his right shoulder have gone.

Note

The arrangement of equipment in a workstation is one of the main things that decide the worker's posture. It is also a part of the work environment - especially in offices - that the worker can change to get more comfortable. It costs nothing. This example shows how simple rearrangements by the worker can have a big impact on comfort. This often leads to higher productivity and quality.

Other typical workplace examples of general musculoskeletal disorders can be found in HSG121, 'A Pain in Your Workplace?'.

Risk reduction measures

ERGONOMIC DESIGN OF TOOLS, EQUIPMENT AND WORKPLACES

Some ergonomic factors relating to the design of work activities

Tools, equipment and materials

- There should be a definite and fixed place for all tools and materials.
- Tools, materials and controls should be positioned close in and directly in front of the operator.
- Materials and tools should be located to permit the best sequence of operations.
- Tools and materials should be pre-positioned wherever possible.
- Handles such as those used on cranks and screwdrivers should be designed to permit as much of the surface of the hand to come into contact with the handle as possible.
- Levers, crossbars and hand wheels should be located in such positions that the operator can manipulate them with the least change in body position and with the greatest mechanical advantage.

Visibility

- Provisions should be made to minimise eyestrain. Good illumination is the first requirement for clear vision.
- Activities requiring eye attention should take place within the normal area of vision.

Comfort

- The height of the work surface and the chair should preferably be such that alternate sitting and standing to work are easily possible.
- A chair of the type and height to permit good posture should be provided for each worker.

Movement

- Momentum should be employed to assist the worker wherever possible, and it should be reduced to a minimum if it must be overcome by muscular effort.
- Rhythm is essential to the smooth and automatic performance of an operation, and the work should be arranged to permit easy and natural rhythm wherever possible.

Hands and arms

- The hands should be relieved of all work that can be done more advantageously by a jig, fixture or a foot-operated device.
- Smooth, continuous motions of the hands are preferable to zigzag motions or straight-line motions involving sudden and sharp changes in direction.
- The two hands should begin as well as complete their motions at the same time.
- Hand motions should be at the minimum with which it is possible to perform the work satisfactorily.
- Motions of the arms should be made in opposite and symmetrical directions and should be made simultaneously.

Risk reduction by design

Equipment must be suitable, by design, construction or adaptation, for the actual work it is provided to do. This should mean in practice that when employers provide equipment they should ensure that it has been produced for the work to be undertaken and that it is used in accordance with the manufacturer's specifications and instructions. If employers choose to adapt equipment then they must ensure that it is still suitable for its intended purpose.

Designers should establish health and safety features that reduce risk at the design stage. Consideration should be given to all aspects of use. In addition, design should minimise risks at all phases of the life of the equipment including:

- Construction.
- Transport.
- Installation.
- Commissioning.

- De-commissioning.
- Dismantling.
- Disposal/recycling.

Wherever practicable, dangerous parts should be eliminated or effectively enclosed at the initial design. If they cannot be eliminated, then suitable safeguards should be incorporated as part of the design. Provision should be made to facilitate the fitting of alternative types of safeguards on machinery where it is known that this will be necessary because the work to be done on it will vary.

At the design stage arrangements should be made where practicable to eliminate the need to expose any dangerous parts during operation, examination, lubrication, adjustment or maintenance.

There are then two principles to bear in mind:-

- As a first principle, as many hazards as possible should be avoided by suitable choice of design features.
- Secondly, where it is not possible to avoid these hazards, the factors which influence the magnitude of the risk should be examined, i.e. reducing speed or distance of movement, force, torque, inertia, and by use of surfaces that are as smooth as possible.

JOB ROTATION / WORK ROUTINE

The job

- Tasks should be designed in accordance with ergonomic principles so that the limitations to human performance can be taken into account. Matching the job to the man will ensure that he is not overloaded, physically or mentally.
- Physical matching includes the whole workplace environment as well as considerations of such things as strength, reach, freedom of movement etc.
- Mental match involves the individual's ability to absorb information and make decisions as well as his perception of the task.
- Any mis-match between the requirements of the job and the worker's abilities provides potential for human error!

The major considerations in the design of the job include:

- Identification and detailed examination of the critical tasks that the individual is expected to do and an appraisal of any likely errors.
- An evaluation of the decisions that the operator will be called upon to make and an appraisal of the contributions of the human and automatic actions to safety factors.
- The application of ergonomic principles to the design of machinery and equipment including the display of information, panel layouts and the design and accessibility of control devices.
- The design and presentation of procedure manuals and operating instruments.
- Organisation and control of the working environment, including the workspace, access for maintenance, lighting, noise, heating (for cooling), where necessary and ventilation.
- Provision of the correct tools and equipment, including the correct instructions for their safe use. Also the provision of a system for the maintenance, repair and safe storage of such tools and equipment.
- The scheduling of work patterns, including systems of shift working, control of fatigue and stress and the arrangements for emergency operations in a crisis situation.
- Arrangements for efficient communication for both routine and emergency situations.

This is reinforced by Regulation 4 (Daily Work Routine of Users) of the Health and Safety (Display Screen Equipment) Regulations (DSE) 1992 which states:

"Employers shall plan activities and provide such breaks or changes in work activity to reduce employees' workload on that equipment".

B10.2 - Display screen equipment

Ill-health effects

MUSCULOSKELETAL INJURY AND DISCOMFORT

Many cases of repetitive strain injuries (RSI) and work related upper limb disorders (WRULD) can be related to excessive periods of continuous intensive work at a keyboard combined with a badly designed workstation. This could result in musculoskeletal problems, visual fatigue and mental stress. Mostly, these are only temporary. However, a small minority of those who suffer upper limb disorders as a result of display screen work experience serious pain or disability.

In recognition of industry's immediate need for guidance on Visual Display Units (VDU) use, Regulations were introduced on 1 January 1993, and subsequently were amended in 2002.

The Regulations are directed not only to the protection of employees, but others who may be working at the employers premises who habitually use display screen equipment as a significant part of their normal work. Such employees of the employer are defined by the regulations as 'users'. Others are defined as 'operators' under the regulations and this would include for example, agency staff and contractors working in the host employers premises. The regulations place a duty on the employers of both categories of employee, i.e. 'users' and 'operators'. The host employer who uses 'others' to do work at their premises is required to carry out an assessment of risk for both 'users' and 'operators', but the employer only has a duty to train, inform and pay for eye tests for their own employees who they have classified as 'users'.

The Regulations apply to workstations first put into service by the employer after 31 December 1992 and to workstations already in service after 31 December 1996. The Regulations were designed with current typical office VDU work in mind and the following main factors must form part of any assessment:

- *Screen:* readable and stable image, adjustable, glare free.
- *Keyboard:* usable, adjustable, key tops legible.
- *Work Surface:* allow flexible arrangement, spacious, glare free, document holder as appropriate.
- *Work Chair:* appropriate, adjustable plus suitable foot rest.
- *Leg Room and Clearances:* to facilitate postural change.
- *Lighting:* provision of adequate contrast, no direct or indirect glare or reflections.
- *Noise:* distracting noise minimised.
- *Environment:* no excessive heat, adequate humidity.
- *Software:* appropriate to the task and adapted to user capabilities, provide feedback on system status, no clandestine monitoring.

The employer must also assess rest breaks. Rest breaks must reflect the mix of demands made by the job, and must be of appropriate length and frequency to prevent fatigue.

The Regulations impose an entitlement to give display screen users ophthalmological examinations to include eye and eyesight tests. Any corrective appliances needed specifically for display screen work must be provided, with any related costs being borne by the employer.

The *Management of Health and Safety at Work Regulations (MHSWR) 1999* require all employees to be consulted on and be allowed to participate with any proposals or changes. All relevant training and information must also be provided to the employee.

The Regulations should reduce the incidence of RSI, WRULD, eye-strain and headaches amongst VDU workers.

It is estimated that the additional costs of equipping a new workstation will be considerably offset by the reduction in sick leave and thus the resulting gain in output. Indeed, this should also help to reduce the increasing number of court cases being heard against employers for negligence in preventing employees suffering in this area.

EYE AND EYESIGHT EFFECTS

Do not result from DSE, nor does DSE use make them worse. Temporary fatigue, sore eyes and headaches can be produced by poor positioning of DSE, pool legibility and flicker. Prolonged work can have some effect.

FATIGUE AND STRESS

Results from poor job design, work organisation, social isolation and high speed work - can be identified in assessment and by consulting workforce.

Assessment of risk from display screen equipment use

EQUIPMENT

Display screen

- The characters on the screen shall be well-defined and clearly formed, of adequate size and with adequate spacing between the characters and lines.
- The image on the screen should be stable, with no flickering or other forms of instability.
- The brightness and the contrast between the characters and the background shall be easily adjustable by the operator or user, and also be easily adjustable to ambient conditions.
- The screen must swivel and tile easily and freely to suit the needs of the operator or user.
- It shall be possible to use a separate base for the screen or an adjustable table.
- The screen shall be free of reflective glare and reflections liable to cause discomfort to the operator or user.

Keyboard

- The keyboard shall be tiltable and separate from the screen so as to allow the operator or user to find a comfortable working position avoiding fatigue in the arms or hands.
- The space in front of the keyboard shall be sufficient to provide support for the hands and arms of the operator or user.
- The keyboard shall have a matt surface to avoid reflective glare.
- The arrangements of the keyboard and the characteristics of the keys shall be such as to facilitate the use of the keyboard.
- The symbols on the keys shall be adequately contrasted and legible from the design working position.

Work desk or work surface

- The work desk or work surface shall have a sufficiently large, low-reflectance surface and allow a flexible arrangement of the screen, keyboard, documents and related equipment.
- The document holder shall be stable and adjustable and shall be positioned so as to minimise the need for uncomfortable head and eye movements.
- There shall be adequate space for operators or users to find a more comfortable position.

Work chair

- The work chair shall be stable and allow the operator or user easy freedom of movement and a comfortable position.
- The seat shall be adjustable in height.
- The seat back shall be adjustable in both height and tilt.
- A footrest shall be made available to any operator or user who wishes one.

ENVIRONMENT

- Levels of noise should not be distractive.
- Low humidity, less 40% Relative Humidity (RH) as may cause sore eyes and facial acne.
- Lighting levels should be appropriate.
- Adequate space for working.

INTERFACE BETWEEN COMPUTER AND OPERATOR / USER

FIGURE 1

SUBJECTS DEALT WITH IN THE SCHEDULE

① ADEQUATE LIGHTING

② ADEQUATE CONTRAST, NO GLARE OR DISTRACTING REFLECTIONS

③ DISTRACTING NOISE MINIMISED

④ LEG ROOM AND CLEARANCES TO ALLOW POSTURAL CHANGES

⑤ WINDOW COVERING

⑥ SOFTWARE: APPROPRIATE TO TASK, ADAPTED TO USER, PROVIDES FEEDBACK ON
SYSTEM STATUS, NO UNDISCLOSED MONITORING

⑦ SCREEN: STABLE IMAGE, ADJUSTABLE, READABLE, GLARE/REFLECTION FREE

⑧ KEYBOARD: USABLE, ADJUSTABLE, DETACHABLE, LEGIBLE

⑨ WORK SURFACE: ALLOW FLEXIBLE ARRANGEMENTS, SPACIOUS, GLARE FREE

⑩ WORK CHAIR: ADJUSTABLE

⑪ FOOTREST

Figure B10-1: Interface between computer and user.   *Source: Guidance on Regs, Health and Safety (Display Screen Equipment) Regulations 1992.*

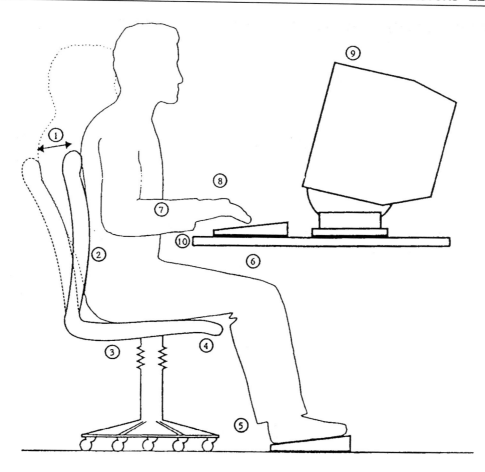

FIGURE 2

SEATING AND POSTURE FOR TYPICAL OFFICE TASKS

① SEAT BACK ADJUSTABILITY

② GOOD LUMBAR SUPPORT

③ SEAT HEIGHT ADJUSTABILITY

④ NO EXCESS PRESSURE ON UNDERSIDE OF THIGHS AND BACKS OF KNEES

⑤ FOOT SUPPORT IF NEEDED

⑥ SPACE FOR POSTURAL CHANGE, NO OBSTACLES UNDER DESK

⑦ FOREARMS APPROXIMATELY HORIZONTAL

⑧ MINIMAL EXTENSION, FLEXION OR DEVIATION OF WRISTS

⑨ SCREEN HEIGHT AND ANGLE SHOULD ALLOW COMFORTABLE HEAD POSITION

⑩ SPACE IN FRONT OF KEYBOARD TO SUPPORT HANDS/WRISTS DURING PAUSES IN KEYING

Figure B10-2: Interface between computer and user.   *Source: Guidance on Regs, Health and Safety (Display Screen Equipment) Regulations 1992.*

Analysis of DSE workstations

Regulation 2 (Analysis of Workstations - Employers' Duties) of the DSE Regulations 1992 states that:

"In line with good health and safety practice and all recent legislation, employers have a duty to analyse workstations for the purpose of assessing the health and safety risks of persons working with display screens".

- Risks must be reduced to the lowest possible extent.
- Assessments must be reviewed when they are suspected to be no longer valid.

To this end, display screen assessments should be conducted.

DSE ASSESSMENT

Purpose

To identify display screens mainly used to display line drawings, graphs, charts or computer generated graphics. (Not screens whose main use is to show television or film pictures). Having identified a specific requirement, the first thing to consider is the possibility of (foreseeable) risks or injuries, immediately or cumulatively due to the work.

Where risk or injury is foreseeable, perhaps as the result of past experience, then steps must be taken to eliminate or reduce (as appropriate) this element of the job, so far as is reasonably practicable. Often it is not practicable to totally eliminate all risks, but steps must be taken to minimise the chance of injury through ongoing evaluation and monitoring.

Short-term

Training of a practical nature, particularly on the job, can bring swift improvements, but, without constant reinforcement, will equally swiftly degenerate to old routines.

Constant reinforcement

- Regular on-job training.
- Good job instruction.
- Regular supervision.
- Propaganda such as posters, competitions, company magazine articles.
- Briefing groups.

Actions to eliminate

Any work where the operator is subject to:

- Excessive work periods without breaks.
- Poor postural problems i.e. twisting movements.
- Visual problems.
- Fatigue and stress.
- Poor lighting/glare.
- Excessive noise/temperature.

Additional considerations/potential problems

- Incorrect humidity can create additional hazards, such as static electricity, perspiration and sore eyes and one must make allowances for the effects of these in the assessment.
- Perceived conflicts over production "at all costs" - problems which can only be resolved by management through commitment and effective communication. Perhaps with helpful propaganda.
- Worker attitudes, particularly to change - some may need more training and supervision than others.

Health and safety management tool

- Establish a policy.
- Gain commitment from both Manager and user.
- Develop an action plan (which may be as follows):
    1. Carry out a survey of each area.
    2. Identify tasks.
    3. Identify equipment.
    4. Identify users.
    5. Group similar tasks.
    6. Identify priorities (from Company history, media and medical comment) for conducting assessments.
    7. Assess risks, analyse tasks and break-down into short-term, long-term actions.
    8. Establish a time-scale related to practicability, cost, dates for renewal of equipment and tools.

Whilst there will never be a completion date due to changing circumstances, a reasonable time-scale to get most things as good as possible may be a minimum of three to five years for large users of equipment.

Suitability of equipment

Display screen, keyboard, work desk or work surface, work chair - all of these should be assessed - see the earlier section in this Element sub-titled: 'Assessment of risk from display screen equipment use'.

Distance between workstation areas

Assess access and egress and consider shared equipment with respect to position of user.

Assessing the working environment

A thorough DSE assessment includes a detailed examination of the working environment.

What do we assess? Some of the main areas for consideration are:

Floors

The floor should be assessed to ensure it is level for both the workstation and the users chair, to ensure the display screen and the chair are in correct alignment and additional postural problems are not avoided.

Housekeeping

Housekeeping is an important factor when it comes to slips and trips. Items of equipment, rubbish bins and trolleys all find themselves on the route of persons working with VDU equipment.

Extremes of temperature, high humidity

Injury risk is increased:

- By high temperature/humidity where fatigue will occur quicker - look for signs of perspiration.
- Low temperatures can cause fingers to get cold and feet to become numb. Extra clothing may restrict movement.

Lighting

- Poor lighting prevents documents from being read easily.
- Excessive lighting results in eye strain.
- Reflective surfaces may cause glare.
- Control daylight with curtains or roller blinds.

How do we quantify these factors? Quantification comes through measurements, the simplest instrument required being a tape measure. Other more sophisticated equipment is also required if the results are to be meaningful to enable comparison with standards and to measure progress and improvement.

Equipment required

Thermometer - to measure air and surface temperatures. BS 7179 recommends an ideal temperature range of 190 - 230 for Display Screen Equipment operation.

Hygrometer - to measure relative humidity. BS 7179 recommends an ideal humidity range of 40 - 60% for Display Screen Equipment operation. BS 5958 gives advice on the control of static electricity.

Lightmeter - to measure luminance.

Sound Meter - to measure noise in the work area. BS 7179 recommends a maximum limit of 60 dB for on screen work, but where work demands a particularly high degree of concentration 55 dB should not be exceeded.

Control measures

ERGONOMIC CONSIDERATIONS OF EQUIPMENT AND WORKSTATION DESIGN

Should take account of:

Equipment:	Screen:	positioning, character definition, character stability.
	Keyboard:	tiltable, character legibility.
	Desk:	size, matt surface.
	Chair:	adjustable back and height, footrest available.
Environment:	Noise:	levels of noise not distractive.
	Lighting:	levels appropriate, contrast between surroundings balanced.
	Space:	adequate for work conducted.
Person/software interface:	Software:	easy to use.
	Work rate:	not governed by software.
	Monitoring:	operator/user informed.

DAILY WORK ROUTINE OF USERS

- Improved design or working areas.
- Better training and supervision.
- Adjustment of workloads and rest periods.
- Provision of special tools.
- Health surveillance aimed at early detection.

OTHER CONTROLS

Eye and eyesight testing

Regulation 5 (Eyes and Eyesight) of the DSE Regulations 1992 states that:

"For DSE users, the employer shall provide, on request, an eyesight test carried out by a competent person".

Training and information

In addition, Regulation 6 (Provision of Training) of the DSE Regulations 1992 states:

"The employer shall ensure that the employee is provided with adequate health and safety training in the use of any workstation upon which he may be required to work".

Further, Regulation 7 (Provision of Information) of the DSE Regulations 1992 states:

"Every employer shall ensure that operators and users at work are provided with adequate information about all aspects of health and safety relating to their workstations, to them, and to their work".

See also - Relevant Statutory Provisions - Element B11 - Health and Safety (Display Screen Equipment) Regulations (DSE) 1992 - as amended by the Health and Safety (Miscellaneous Amendments) Regulations 2002.

B10.3 - Manual handling

Introduction

Manual handling operations can cause many types of injury. The most common injuries are to the back: rupture of intervertebral discs ('prolapsed disc'), muscle strain and sprain. Tendons and ligaments can also be over-stretched and torn, and rupture of a section of the abdominal wall can cause a hernia. Loads with sharp edges can cause cuts, and dropped loads can result in bruises, fractures and crushing injuries.

Around 25% of all reported injuries to the appropriate enforcing authority have been attributed to the manual lifting and handling of loads. Legislation contained in the Factories Act 1961 and a few other regulations were concerned only with the weight of the load, i.e. Factories Act 1961 - Section 72:

"A person shall not be employed to lift, carry or move any load as to be likely to cause injury to him"

This gave the impression that only the load weight was the problem - or was it? There are a number of other factors that need to be considered if industry is ever to reduce the problem of back injuries.

With the regulations below the whole ergonomics of carrying out the task must be considered, i.e. the **assessment approach.**

It is hoped that these guidance notes will enable users to carry out an assessment on tasks within their companies, thus reducing the risk of injuries.

MANUAL HANDLING OPERATIONS REGULATIONS (MHOR) 1992

The regulations establish a clear hierarchy of measures.

- Avoid hazardous manual handling operations so far as is reasonably practicable.
- Make a suitable and sufficient assessment of any hazardous manual handling operations that cannot be avoided.
- Reduce the risk of injury so far as is reasonably practicable.

Legal requirements

All employers have a common law duty of care to ensure their employees' health and safety at work.

This is reinforced by the Health and Safety at Work etc. Act (HASAWA) 1974.

The above mentioned have a wide interpretation and the new regulations have the effect of being much more specific on concerning the duties of the employer.

Each employer shall:

1. So far as is reasonably practicable, **avoid** the need for his employees to undertake any manual handling operations which involve a risk of their being injured.

2. Where it is not reasonably practicable to avoid the need for his employees to undertake any manual handling operations which involve a risk of their being injured, they shall:

- Make a suitable and sufficient **assessment** of all such manual handling operations.

- Take appropriate steps to **reduce the risk** of injury to employees undertaking any such manual handling operations to the lowest level reasonably practicable.

- Take appropriate steps to provide employees with general indications and where it is reasonably practicable, precise **information** on:

  - The weight of each load.

  - The heaviest side of any load whose centre of gravity is not positioned centrally.

The new regulations are also very specific on the duties expected from employees.

Each employee shall:

1. Make full and proper use of any equipment or system of work provided by his employer.
2. Inform his employer about any physical condition suffered by him which might reasonably be considered to affect his ability to undertake manual handling operations safely.

This is in addition to the general responsibilities imposed on him by the HASAWA 1974, sections 7 & 8.

See also - Relevant Statutory Provisions - Element B11 - Manual Handling Operations Regulations (MHOR) 1992.

Main injuries from manual handling

SPRAINS/STRAINS, FRACTURES, LACERATIONS

Muscular sprains and strains - normally occur in the back or in the arm and wrists. Caused by the stretching of muscular tissue beyond its normal capacity leading to weakening or bruising and painful inflammation of the area.

Fractures - normally affect the feet through dropping of the load. Fractures of the hand can also occur but are not so common.

Lacerations - caused by the handling of loads with unprotected sharp corners or edges.

Built-in hazards of the package or load

The following, in combination with poor manual handling technique, can result in workplace accidents leading to injury to employees:

- Poor packaging, wet or broken packs.
- Large packages - hard to hold properly.
- Large packages - obstructing the carrier's view.
- Fragile packaging likely to split.
- Sharp edges or corners.
- Smooth with no grip.
- Containing powders which frequently escape.
- Centre of gravity of load not in centre.

Assessment of risk from manual handling operations

The factors to which the employer must have regard, and questions he must consider when making an assessment of manual handling operations, are:

- The task.
- The load.
- The working environment.
- Individual capability.

Each factor in turn should be looked at to determine whether there is a risk of injury. When this has been completed the information can then be processed giving a *total risk assessment.*

The following are constituents of the individual factors that should be approached to help you achieve Total Risk Assessment.

FACTORS	QUESTIONS	Yes	Level of Risk		
			H	M	L
The Task	Does it involve: Holding load at distance from trunk? Unsatisfactory bodily movement or posture? especially: Twisting the trunk Stooping Excessive movement of load?, especially: Excessive lifting or lowering distances Excessive pushing or pulling distances Risk of sudden movement of load Frequent or prolonged physical effort Insufficient rest or recovery periods				
The Load	Is it: Heavy? Bulky or Unwieldy? Difficult to grasp? Unstable, or with contents likely to shift? Sharp, hot or otherwise potentially damaging?				
The Working Environment	Are there: Space constraints preventing good posture? Uneven, slippery or unstable floors? Variations in level of floors or work surfaces? Extremes of temperature, humidity or air movement? Poor lighting conditions?				
Individual Capability	Does the job: Require unusual strength, height, etc.? Create a hazard to those who have a health problem? Require special knowledge or training for its safe performance?				

Figure B10-3: Manual handling risk assessment. *Source: HSE Manual handling (Manual Handling Operations Regulations 1992) Guidance L23.*

NUMERICAL GUIDELINES FOR ASSESSMENT-HANDLING OPERATIONS

Lifting

The Regulations set no specific requirements such as weight limits. An assessment then based on a range of relevant factors should be used to determine whether there is a risk and whether there is a need for any remedial action. A full assessment of every manual handling operation could be a major undertaking and might involve wasted effort and resources.

The following guidelines set out an *approximate* boundary within which manual handling operations are unlikely to create a risk of injury sufficient to warrant more detailed assessment. This should enable assessment work to be concentrated where it is most needed. Even operations lying within the boundary should be avoided or made less demanding wherever it is reasonably practical to do so.

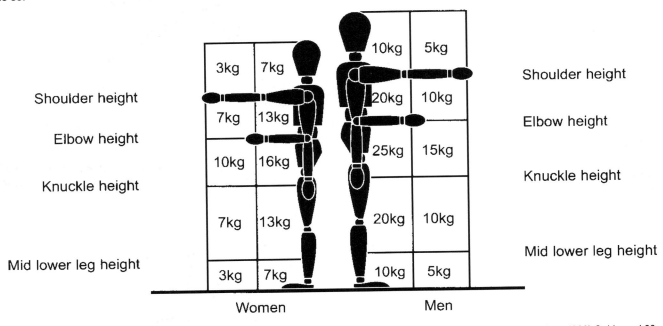

Figure B10-4: Guideline figures.   *Source: HSE: Manual Handling (Manual Handling Operations Regulations 1992) Guidance L23.*

The guideline figures are not weight or force limits. They may be exceeded where a more detailed assessment shows it is safe to do so. However, even for a minority of fit, well-trained individuals working under favourable conditions the guideline figures should not normally be exceeded by more than a factor of about 2. The guideline figures for weight and force will give reasonable protection to nearly all men and between one half and two thirds of women. To provide the same degree of protection to nearly all working women the guideline figures should be reduced by about one third.

Carrying

The guideline figures for manual handling operations involving carrying are similar to those given for lifting and lowering. It is assumed that the load is held against the body and is carried no further than about 10 metres without resting. If the load is carried over a longer distance without resting the guideline figures may need to be reduced. Where the load can be carried securely on the shoulder without attendant lifting (i.e. unloading sacks from a lorry) a more detailed assessment may show that it is safe to exceed the guideline figure.

Pushing and pulling

Guideline figures for manual handling operations involving pushing and pulling, whether the load is slid, rolled or supported on wheels are as follows. The guideline figure for starting or stopping the load is a force of about 250 newtons (i.e. a force of about 25 Kg as measured on a spring balance). The guideline figure for keeping the load in motion is a force of about 100 newtons. It is assumed that the force is applied with the hands between knuckle and shoulder height. If this is not possible the guideline figures may need to be reduced. No specific limit is intended as to the distances over which the load is pushed or pulled provided there are adequate opportunities for rest or recovery.

Handling while seated

The guideline figures for handling operations carried out while seated are given below and apply only when the hands are within the box zone indicated. If handling beyond the box zone is unavoidable a more detailed assessment should be made.

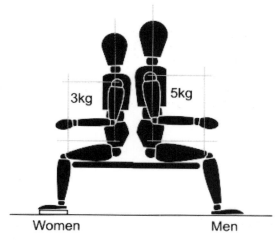

Figure B10-5: Handling while seated.

Source: HSE: Manual Handling (Manual Handling Operations Regulations 1992) Guidance L23.

Twisting

The basic guideline figures for lifting and lowering should be reduced if the handler twists to the side during the operation. As a rough guide the figures should be reduced by about 10% where the handler twists through 45° and by about 20% where the handler twists through 90°.

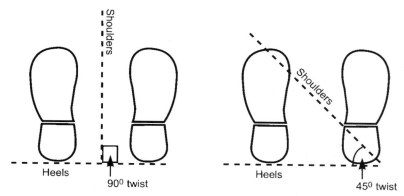

Figure B10-6: Twisting.

Source: HSE: Manual Handling (Manual Handling Operations Regulations 1992) Guidance L23.

Remember - these guideline figures should not be regarded as precise recommendations and should be applied with caution, noting particularly the assumptions on which they are based.

Assumptions

- The handler is standing or crouching in a stable body position with the back substantially upright.
- The trunk is not twisted during the operation.
- Both hands are used to grasp the load.
- The hands are not more than shoulder width apart.
- The load is positioned centrally in front of the body and is itself reasonably symmetrical.
- The load is stable and readily grasped.
- The work area does not restrict the handler's posture.
- The working environment (heat, cold, wet, condition of floor) and any personal protective equipment used do not interfere with performance of the task.

ASSESSING THE TASK

Headroom

Stooping to move an item is a bad movement but stooping to lift a load is even more likely to cause injury. The worst move is to stoop, lift and twist. A little time spent watching people at work will soon show that this is a common combination, such as in removing items from under racking, particularly from pallets, or boxes of paper from low shelves and in maintenance of vehicles, conveyors, machinery etc.

Where stooping and twisting cannot be designed out of the task, then it may require help with the lifting element.

Working on different levels

Carrying loads up steps, stairs, and ladders can be problematic:

- Climbing ladders requires one hand at least to grip the ladder.
- Stairs, even in good condition, can cause trips, often dependent on other factors such as type of shoes, height or weight of package, wearing bifocal spectacles or passing others going in the opposite direction.
- Doors at the top and bottom of stairs may well open in the opposite direction to travel and may be spring-loaded.

Height of storage

The height of storage of loads is important in that the object will be to eliminate lifting. Best height for storage or benches is around waist-height, particularly for heavy items.

Where pallets of heavy items, say up to 50 kg each, are used it may be sensible to put the pallet on top of two other empty pallets with the object of ensuring that the operator does not have to stoop too low.

Holding loads away from the body

Holding loads away from the body causes additional and mostly unnecessary stress on the back. At arms length the load that can be handled may be reduced by as much as 80%.

Loads should be held close to the body where possible as this allows the body and its clothing to give frictional help in stabilising the load. Also it allows the arms to be brought into the sides and thus reduce stress on the neck, shoulders and arms. The issue of protective clothing may encourage people to hold loads close to their bodies. This can be a problem in an office environment where people handle heavy, often dusty, materials somewhat infrequently and are therefore 'not entitled' to protective clothing.

Posture

When assessing the task, there should be enough room to enable the person lifting to get into a good posture. A good base is essential and this consists of getting the feet well apart, as much as 75 cm, and bending the knees until the thigh is at 90^0 to the lower leg. Arms should be between the knees. Feet should be flat on the floor.

Where the person lifting cannot get this distance between the feet, heels tend to rise from the floor, toes take the stress and balance is lost.

Remember that these rules also apply to women. It is therefore essential that due consideration is given to their mode of dress before asking them to carry out lifting operations. Failure to do so will almost certainly result in compromise solutions which may result in injuries.

Static loads

Holding static loads can rapidly cause fatigue in muscles particularly when the arms are extended above the head. In fact, all work above the head has a similar effect. The pains and often immobility (temporary) are called upper limb disorders.

Tools

Tools which require a very firm grip can also create upper limb problems if the handles are narrow and dig into the soft tissues of the hands. The problem is compounded where the pressure has to be held for several seconds at a time, or where the application of pressure is very frequent.

Lifting loads whilst seated

There is usually an element of twisting involved when lifting whilst seated. This problem may be compounded by reaching and bending with the added possibility of the seat moving or tipping.

Personal Protective Equipment (PPE)

The wearing of PPE can add additional stress to persons carrying out a manual handling task and care should be taken to ensure that the PPE does not become a hazard. Comfort and mobility are the two areas which need assessing. Often the combination of work rate and PPE results in excessive temperature, stress, early fatigue, and could, with an unfit person, endanger their health.

ASSESSING THE LOAD

Assessing the load means not only considering its weight but:

1. Physical size - can it be lifted between the knees from the ground by one person?   If not, then assistance may be required.
2. The centre of gravity of a load, i.e. will it twist when lifted?
3. Flexible loads such as bags of cement may shift and strain the back of the carrier.
4. Hot loads, be they tar for a paint or food in a container, require protective equipment and great care.
5. Loads which can cut or pierce the hands or body require protective equipment and a good system of work.
6. Extremely cold loads offer hazards which range from the lack of grip to "frost burn" of the skin if protective clothing is not used.
7. Loads may contain toxic or corrosive substances and may require assessment under other regulations such as; The Control of Substances Hazardous to Health Regulations (COSHH) 2002.
8. Loads with fragile or damaged packaging have potential to damage feet and legs or even the back if a package breaks suddenly.

ASSESSING THE WORKING ENVIRONMENT

Assessing the working environment in the main is looking at an area and really seeing what is there. The difficulty is that this takes considerable experience in dealing with problems over a long period of time in order to become sensitised to seeing the hazards. Fortunately, training and a belief in what one is doing can speed up the process.

Floors

It may be sensible to assess the floor first, because the results of trips, slips and falls can be compounded when someone is lifting or carrying a load. Uneven or slippery floors create unpredictability and make the person carrying the load tense, which in itself causes fatigue. A partial slip or trip under these circumstances will cause a person's balance to be lost and a sudden reaction of the muscles may cause soft tissue injuries.

Housekeeping is an important factor when it comes to slips and trips. Pallets, items of plant or equipment, rubbish bins, trucks and trolleys all find themselves on the route of persons handling loads. Studs often protrude from floors long after items of plant have been removed, duck-boards get moved into passages and packaging material is left to be moved later.

Distance between storage areas

The carrying of loads should be restricted to a minimum and due consideration should be given to using mechanical means where distances are more than a few metres.

Carrying loads around blind corners is another area with accident potential.

Extremes of temperature, high humidity or windy conditions

Injury risk is increased:

1. By high temperatures/humidity where fatigue will occur quicker, perspiration may cause hands to become wet and reduce grip.
2. Low temperatures can cause fingers to get cold and loose grip, feet to become numb and balance more difficult to achieve. Extra clothing may restrict movement and in extreme conditions floors may become slippery, packages will be harder to grip and may even be stuck together or to the ground by ice.
3. Working in high winds carries the penalty of difficulty of control of loads of large area, often compounded by dust.

Poor lighting

Poor lighting prevents a person from seeing the condition of floors and noting any trip or slip potential. Damaged packaging may go unnoticed until the load drops apart during lifting or carrying.

Where handling takes place in an area used by mechanical/electrical transport, the lighting is poor and persons appear from behind racking or stacks, then drivers may not have time to take avoiding action. The sudden appearance of the vehicle would throw the load-carrying person off-balance and result in muscle injury.

Similarly, where loads have to be carried from a bright area into a dark area, e.g. from bright sunlight into a warehouse, accidents will happen.

ASSESSING INDIVIDUAL CAPABILITY

People have varying degrees of capabilities which may not be obvious from observation when they are not working.

When assessing the individual it should be done in conjunction with the assessment of the task and the load in mind.

1. Levels of medical fitness can be checked.
2. Training records of manual handling instruction should be available.
3. Recent past history of work will also indicate a person's abilities.
4. Care must be taken when assessing persons who are:
- Overweight.
- Frail.
- Old.
- Young.
- Relatively inactive types.
- Women (who may not be capable of lifting/handling the loads).
- Pregnant women.
- Depending on the task, exclusion or inclusion might depend upon:
  - Physical size.
  - Height.
  - Willingness (often a useful measure).
5. When protective clothing is required - will the person be able to cope wearing it?

Control measures

REDUCING THE RISK

Having completed the assessment each manual handling operation should now be examined to take in appropriate steps to reduce the risk of injury to the lowest level reasonably practicable.

The same structured approach used during the assessment of risk can be used, considering in turn, the task, the load, the working environment and individual capability. The emphasis given to each of these factors will depend on the results of your initial assessment, i.e. where routine handling operations are being carried out in circumstances which are fairly unchanging, for example, in manufacturing processes, the task and the workplace are the probable areas for improvement. However areas where circumstances are constantly changing, construction sites for example, it may be more beneficial to look at the load and in addition the individual, training etc.

AUTOMATION/MECHANICAL ASSISTANCE

The MHOR 1992 and accompanying guidance provide guidelines to prevent the risk of injury to employees whilst carrying out manual handling operations. The first step identified is to avoid hazardous manual handling; as part of this, a consideration is:

- Could the process be automated or mechanised e.g. provide sets of wheels; use sack trolleys; use hand pallet trucks; use hoists, slings; use fork lift trucks.

Mechanical assistance involves the use of handling aids; although this may retain some elements of manual handling, bodily forces are applied more efficiently. Examples are:

Levers	Reduces bodily force to move a load. Can avoid trapping fingers.
Hoists	Can support weights, allowing handler to position load.
Trolley, Sack Truck Roller Conveyer	Reduces effort to move loads horizontally.

Chutes	A way of using gravity to move loads from one place to another.
Handling Devices	Hand-held hooks or suction pads can help when handling a load that is difficult to grasp.

ERGONOMICS

In the past, emphasis was nearly always placed on load weight and in some cases lifting techniques. Emphasis now must be given to all the factors involved in manual handling operations, task, load working environment and individual capability. This should be carried out with a view to fitting the operation to the individual rather than the other way round.

TASK LAYOUT AND WORK ROUTINE

Again, another step in the MHOR 1992 is to reduce the risk of injury. This can be reduced in several ways, including:

The task
- Use mechanical aids to eliminate or reduce handling.
- Store loads are at optimum heights.
- Design a logical work layout.
- Employ a team for heavy or awkward loads.
- Adopt a better work routine to improve posture, frequency of load handling, and rest pauses.
- Use of protective clothing such as gloves, overalls and boots.

Experience has shown that handling accidents are the results of poor workplace design, poor package design and often poor housekeeping, rather than due to the physical size or capabilities of the operator. Considerations are:

Basic design of a work area in which:
- *Manual handling is at a minimum* - regarding lifting, pushing, pulling and particularly carrying of loads over a distance.
- *Handling aids are available* - such as conveyors, vehicles, tracks, trolleys, cranes, chain blocks etc., all in good repair, tested and part of a safe system of work backed up by adequate training.

Workplace environment
- *Heat* - operators require water to replace body fluids lost as sweat. Sweat can cause bad grip, operators tire and tempers can flare.
- *Humidity* - all the symptoms for heat, but aggravated! Floors can become moist and slippery whilst packages containing relatively cool products can sweat and become difficult to handle, particularly where the packaging is metal.
- *Cold* - fingers and toes can become numb making grip and stability hazardous. Bulky clothing can restrict the operator's lifting position. Reactions become slow.
- *Lighting* - sufficient to see and be seen, sufficient to see damage to load or packaging, and sufficient to note obstacles.
- *Noise* - noise, like vibration, can affect the operator mentally and mistakes can happen. Sudden noise can result in the dropping of a load and of the operator going off balance. Vibration can cause problems with grip.
- *Space* - sufficient to allow the operator room to practice good handling methods.
- *Free from 'built-in hazards'* - Such as conduit routed across floors, split level working areas or transport without defined routes.
- *Good Housekeeping* - clean and tidy working areas, orderly stacks of products or materials.
- *Good Safety Arrangements* - planning of the safest routes for transport or cranes, pedestrian routes marked, prohibition of unauthorised persons.
- *Availability of Drinking Water* - how available should depend on sweat loss, due to environment and exertion.

Physical properties of the task
- Package size.
- Weight.
- Shape.
- Flexibility - i.e. plastic bags of chemicals where the contents move or shift centre of gravity.
- Rigidity.
- Handholds - are they appropriate and in the right place for a good lift?

MODIFYING THE LOAD

Another way to reduce the risk of injury is to consider:

The load
- Reduce the weight or bulk of the load.
- Make it easier to grasp or provide handholds.
- Make the load more stable so the weight does not shift.

When considering the physical properties of the task, operators should be able to hold a package into the body with elbows into the sides. It is imperative that the operator can see over the load. Any package that has an off-centre centre of gravity should be clearly marked and carrying points indicated. If the physical properties of the load indicate potential problems for manual handling, then the operator should consider modifying the load in line with the MHOR 1992 to enable safe, successful, manual handling.

REORGANISING THE WORK ENVIRONMENT

Further, the MHOR 1992 states that to reduce the risk of injury, you should also consider:

The working environment
- Allow room for manoeuvre.
- Ensure floors are suitable, in good condition, and free from obstruction or spillage.

- Avoid work near slopes or changes in level.
- Avoid temperature and ventilation extremes and provide adequate lighting.

There should always be adequate gangway space and working area to allow room to handle and manoeuvre during manual handling operations. Lack of head room could cause stooping, while constrictions caused by poor work station, adjacent machinery etc. should also be avoided. In many cases problems are simply caused by lack of attention to good housekeeping. Where ever possible all manual handling tasks should be carried out on a single level. If tasks are to be carried out on more than one level, access should preferably be by a gentle slope or failing that properly positioned and well maintained stairs/steps. Steep slopes should be avoided. Work benches should be of a uniform height, thus reducing the need for raising or lowering loads.

Finally, look at the general working environment. A comfortable working environment i.e. heating, ventilating and lighting will all help to reduce the risk of injury.

PERSONAL CONSIDERATIONS

The final area of consideration in the MHOR 1992, when considering ways to reduce the risk of injury is:

Individual capacity

- Pay particular attention to those more vulnerable to injury as a result of manual handling activities, e.g. pregnant women, those who have back trouble, or suffer other health problems.
- Provide comprehensive instruction and training on all aspects of manual handling, include details of the weight distribution of the load where possible.

Individual capability

The individual's state of health, fitness and strength can significantly affect the ability to perform a task safely. An individual physical capacity can also be age related, typically climbing until the early 20's and declining gradually from the mid 40's. It is clear then that an individual's condition and age could significantly affect the ability to perform a task safely.

Studies though have shown no close correlation between any of the above and injury incidence.

There is therefore insufficient evidence for reliable selection of individuals for safe manual handling on the basis of such criteria. It is however, recognised, that there is often a degree of self-selection for work that is physically demanding.

Training

Employers should ensure that all employees who carry out manual handling operations receive the necessary training to enable them to carry out the task in a safe manner.

A training programme should include:-

- How potentially hazardous loads may be recognised.
- How to deal with unfamiliar loads.
- The proper use of handling aids.
- The proper use of personal protective equipment.
- Features of the working environment that contribute to safety.
- The importance of good housekeeping.
- Factors affecting individual capability.
- Good handling techniques.

It should always be remembered that training is not a "One Off Situation", it should be on-going and monitored, for it is only by doing this that companies can ensure that they will cope with the requirements of good health and safety practices.

Main points of kinetic handling techniques

The foundations of good lifting techniques have been around for some considerable time. The basic lift consists of the six following principles:

Figure B10-7: Basic lifting techniques.

Source: HSE Guidance L23.

Putting it all into practice; i.e.

1. Assess the load before attempting a lift
2. Begin with load between the feet; the leading foot should be in line with the side of the load, pointing in the direction of movement.
3. Bend knee, tuck chin in and keep back straight. Generally grip the load at the upper outer corner on the side of the leading foot, tilt it slightly and grip the opposite corner with the other hand. (Ensure the palm, not fingers take weight).
4. Keep your arms close to body, move rear hand forward along the lower edge of the load. Stand up in one movement, keeping the load in contact with the body at all times.
5. Keep load close to the body when carrying it.
6. To lower the load, reverse the procedure, bending knees, whilst tilting the load to avoid trapping fingers.

Always Remember:

Lift the load smoothly - Do not jerk.

Relevant Statutory Provisions

Content

Chemicals (Hazard Information and Packaging for Supply) Regulations (CHIP 3) 2002

Law considered in context / more depth in Element B2.

Arrangement of Regulations

1) Citation and commencement.
2) Interpretation.
3) Application of these Regulations.
4) Meaning of the approved supply list.
5) Classification of substances and preparations dangerous for supply.
6) Safety data sheets for substances and preparations dangerous for supply.
7) Advertisements for substances dangerous for supply.
8) Packaging of substances and preparations dangerous for supply.
9) Labelling of substances and preparations dangerous for supply.
10) Particular labelling requirements for certain preparations.
11) Methods of marking or labelling packages.
12) Child resistant fastenings and tactile warning devices.
13) Retention of classification data for substances and preparations dangerous for supply.
14) Notification of the constituents of certain preparations dangerous for supply to the poisons advisory centre.
15) Exemption certificates.
16) Enforcement, civil liability and defence.
17) Transitional provisions.
18) Extension outside Great Britain.
19) Revocations and modifications.

Schedule 1   Classification of substances and preparations dangerous for supply.
Schedule 2   Indications of danger and symbols for substances and preparations dangerous for supply.
Schedule 3   Classification provisions for preparations dangerous for supply.
Schedule 4   Classification provisions for preparations intended to be used as pesticides.
Schedule 5   Headings under which particulars are to be provided in safety data sheets.
Schedule 6   Particulars to be shown on labels for substances and preparations dangerous for supply and certain other preparations.
Schedule 7   British and International Standards relating to child resistant fastenings and tactile warning devices.
Schedule 8   Modifications to certain enactments relating to the flashpoint of flammable liquids.

The Chemicals (Hazard Information and Packaging for Supply) Regulations (CHIP 3) 2002 apply to those who supply dangerous chemicals. They are based on European Directives, which apply to all EU and European Economic Area (EEA) Countries. The Directives are constantly reviewed and changed when necessary. When changes do occur to the Directives, CHIP is changed as well (about once a year). CHIP may be changed by amending Regulations or if there are major changes, the principal Regulations are revised.

The Regulations are designed to protect people's health and the environment by:
■   Identification of the hazardous properties of materials (classification).
■   Provision of health and safety information to users (safety data sheet and label).
■   Packaging of materials safely.
CHIP introduces a new scheme to classify products based upon a calculation method.

Outline of main points

REGULATION 6 (1)

*'The supplier of a substance or preparation dangerous for supply **shall** provide the recipient of that substance or preparation with a safety data sheet containing information under the headings specified in Schedule 5 to enable the recipient of that substance or preparation to take the necessary measures relating to the protection of health and safety at work and relating to the protection of the environment and the safety data sheet shall clearly show its date of first publication or latest revision as the case may be.'*

The test of adequacy of the information provided in a safety data sheet is whether the information enables the recipient to take the necessary measures relating to the protection of health and safety at work and relating to the protection of the environment.

This does not mean that the safety data sheet will take the place of a risk assessment which would require specific detail of the circumstances in which the chemical is to be used.

GUIDANCE ON THE CONTENTS OF SAFETY DATA SHEETS

The headings shown here are those specified in Schedule 5 of C(HIP) 2. However, information given here is indicative of the issues to be addressed by the person compiling the safety data sheet and do not impose an absolute requirement for action or controls.

Identification of the substance/preparation and the company
- Name of the substance.
- Name, address and telephone number (including emergency number) of supplier.

Composition/information on ingredients
- Sufficient information to allow the recipient to identify readily the associated risks.

Hazards identification
- Important hazards to man and the environment.
- Adverse health effects and symptoms.

First-aid measures
- Whether immediate attention is required.
- Symptoms and effects including delayed effects.
- Specific information according to routes of entry.
- Whether professional advice is advisable.

Fire fighting measures
- Suitable extinguishing media.
- Extinguishing media that must not be used.
- Hazards that may arise from combustion e.g., gases, fumes etc.
- Special protective equipment for fire fighters.

Accidental release measures
- Personal precautions such as removal of ignition sources, provision of ventilation, avoid eye/skin contact etc.
- Environmental precautions such as keep away from drains, need to alert neighbours etc.
- Methods for cleaning up e.g. absorbent materials. Also, "Never use…."

Handling and storage
- Advice on technical measures such as local and general ventilation.
- Measures to prevent aerosol, dust, fire etc.
- Design requirements for specialised storage rooms.
- Incompatible materials.
- Special requirements for packaging/containers.

Exposure controls/personal protection
- Engineering measures taken in preference to personal protective equipment (PPE) 1992.
- Where PPE is required, type of equipment necessary e.g. type of gloves, goggles, barrier cream etc.

Physical and chemical properties
- Appearance, e.g. solid, liquid, powder, etc.
- Odour (if perceptible).
- Boiling point, flash point, explosive properties, solubility etc.

Stability and reactivity
- Conditions to avoid such as temperature, pressure, light, etc.
- Materials to avoid such as water, acids, alkalis, etc.
- Hazardous by-products given off on decomposition.

Toxicological information
- Toxicological effects if the substance comes into contact with a person.
- Carcinogenic, mutagenic, toxic for reproduction etc.
- Acute and chronic effects.

Ecological information
- Effects, behaviour and environmental fate that can reasonably be foreseen.
- Short and long term effects on the environment.

Disposal considerations
- Appropriate methods of disposal e.g. land-fill, incineration etc.

Transport information
- Special precautions in connection with transport or carriage.
- Additional information as detailed in the Carriage of Dangerous Goods by Road Regs (CPL) 1994 may also be given.

Regulatory information
- Health and safety information on the label as required by C(HIP) 2.
- Reference might also be made to Health and Safety at Work etc Act (HASAWA) 1974 and Control of Substances Hazardous to Health Regulations (COSHH) 2002.

Other Information

- Training advice.
- Recommended uses and restrictions.
- Sources of key data used to compile the data sheet.

RISK PHRASES AND SAFETY PHRASES

More useful information to help ensure the safe use of dangerous substances comes in the form of risk phrases and safety phrases. These are often displayed either on the container label or in the safety data sheet. There are currently 48 risk phrases and 53 safety phrases. Some examples are given below and detailed information can be found in the ACOP to C(HIP) 2.

Risk Phrase		Safety Phrase	
R3	Risk of explosion by shock, friction, fire or other sources of ignition.	S2	Keep out of reach of children.
R20	Harmful by inhalation.	S20	When using do not eat or drink.
R30	Can become highly flammable in use.	S25	Avoid contact with eyes.
R45	May cause cancer.	S36	Wear suitable protective clothing.
R47	May cause birth defects.	S41	In case of fire and/or explosion do not breathe fumes.

Absence of hazard symbols or risk and safety advice does not mean the item is harmless.

Chemicals (Hazard Information and Packaging for Supply) (Amendment) Regulations 2005

Law considered in context / more depth in Element B2.

These Regulations came into force 31st October 2005.

The principal Regulations shall be amended as follows.

(2) In regulation 2(1) -

(a) for the definition of "the approved supply list" substitute -

"the approved supply list" means the document entitled "Information Approved for the Classification and Labelling of Dangerous Substances and Dangerous Preparations (Eighth Edition)" approved by the Health and Safety Commission on 26 July 2005;"; - (updated from April 2002)

(b) omit the definition of "the CDGCPL Regulations".

(3) In regulation 5(12)(a), for "and" substitute "or" - *this changes the meaning of the term "supply".*

(4) In regulation 7(3)(a), for the words "the CDGCPL Regulations" substitute "the Carriage of Dangerous Goods and Use of Transportable Pressure Equipment Regulations 2004".

(5) In regulation 8(1), for the words "Subject to regulations 9 and 10 of the CDGCPL Regulations (which allow combined carriage and supply labelling in certain circumstances) and paragraphs (8) to (12)" substitute "Subject to regulation 8A and paragraphs (8) to (12)".

(6) In regulation 9(2), for the words "regulations 9 and 10 of the CDGCPL Regulations (which allow combined carriage and supply labelling in certain circumstances)" substitute "regulation 8A".

(7) Omit regulations 13 and 18(2).

(8) In Part II of Schedule 3, in Table VIA, in line 1 for "0.%" substitute "0.1%" - *reclassification of gaseous substances or preparations to be assigned R45 or R49.*

(9) In Part I of Schedule 5—

(a) in paragraph 2(4), for "22(1)" substitute "6";

(b) in paragraph 3(5), for "(2)" substitute "(3)".

Control of Asbestos Regulations (CAR) 2006

Law considered in context / more depth in Elements B3, B4 and B5.

Arrangement of Regulations

Part 1 Preliminary

1) Citation and commencement.

2) Interpretation.

3) Application of these Regulations.

Part 2 General requirements

4) Duty to manage asbestos in non-domestic premises.

5) Identification of the presence of asbestos.

6) Assessment of work which exposes employees to asbestos.

7) Plans of work.

8) Licensing of work with asbestos.

9) Notification of work with asbestos.

10) Information, instruction and training.

11) Prevention or reduction of exposure to asbestos.

12) Use of control measures etc.

13) Maintenance of control measures etc.

14) Provision and cleaning of protective clothing.

15) Arrangements to deal with accidents, incidents and emergencies.

16) Duty to prevent or reduce the spread of asbestos.

17) Cleanliness of premises and plant.

18) Designated areas.

19) Air monitoring.

20) Standards for air testing.

21) Standards for analysis.

22) Health records and medical surveillance.

23) Washing and changing facilities.

24) Storage, distribution and labelling of raw asbestos and asbestos waste.

Part 3 Prohibitions and related provisions

25) Interpretation of prohibitions

26) Prohibitions of exposure to asbestos

27) Prohibition of the importation of asbestos

28) Prohibition of the supply of asbestos

29) Prohibition of the use of asbestos

30) Labelling of products containing asbestos

31) Additional provisions in the case of exceptions and exemptions

Part 4 Miscellaneous

32) Exemption certificates.

33) Exemptions relating to the Ministry of Defence

34) Extension outside Great Britain.

35) Existing licences and exemption certificates

36) Revocations, amendments and savings.

37) Defence.

Schedule 1   Particulars to be included in a notification.

Schedule 2   The labelling of raw asbestos, asbestos waste and products containing asbestos.

Outline of main points

The Control of Asbestos Regulations (CAR) 2006 emphasis is placed on assessment to exposure; licensing and notification; exposure prevention, reduction and control; adequate information, instruction and training for employees: monitoring and health surveillance. The Regulations also clearly apply to incidental exposure.

Identification and assessment

Before any work with asbestos is started the employer must ensure a thorough assessment of the likely exposure is carried out. Such an assessment must identify the type of asbestos involved in the work, or to which the employees are likely to be exposed. The assessment must also determine the nature and degree of any exposure and the steps required to prevent or reduce the exposure to the lowest level reasonably practicable.

Assessments must be reviewed regularly and when there is reason to suspect that the original assessment is invalid or there is a significant change in the work to which the original assessment related. Assessments should be revised accordingly to take account of any such changes, etc.

Plan of work

Employers must also prepare a suitable 'plan of work' before any work involving asbestos removal from buildings, structures, plant or installations (including ships) is undertaken. Such 'plans of work' must be retained for the duration of the work. The 'plan of work' should address the location, nature, expected duration and asbestos handling methods involved with the work, and the characteristics of the protection and decontamination equipment for the asbestos workers and the protection equipment for any others who may be affected by such work. The asbestos risk assessment and plan of work must be kept on site.

Licensing and Notification

Where the work with asbestos requires a licence the enforcing authority must be notified at least 28 days prior to commencement of the work (a lesser time may be agreed by mutual consent). Significant changes must also be notified.

Under these regulations, anyone carrying out work on asbestos insulation, asbestos coating or asbestos insulating board (AIB) needs a licence issued by HSE unless they meet one of the exemptions:

- If employee exposure is sporadic and low intensity, i.e. the concentration will not exceed 0.6 fibres per cm^3 measured over 10 minutes; and exposure will not exceed the Control Limit; and the work involves short non-continuous maintenance activities. This latter stipulation will be where one person works with the materials for less than one hour in a seven-day period. The total time spent by all workers on the work should not exceed a total of two hours.
- The materials being removed have asbestos fibres firmly linked in a matrix, e.g. asbestos cement.
- Encapsulation or sealing of asbestos-containing materials which are in good condition.
- Air monitoring and control, and the collection and analysis of samples to find out if a specific material contains asbestos.

Even if a licence is not required the rest of the requirements of the Asbestos Regulations must still be complied with. If the work is licensable, there are a number of duties:

- Notify the enforcing authority responsible for the site where the work is: HSE or the local authority, at least 28 days before work begins. A shorter time may be agreed by the enforcing authority, e.g. in emergencies. The notification should be in writing and the particulars are specified in Schedule 1.
- Designate the work area (see regulation 18 for details).
- Prepare specific asbestos emergency procedures.
- Pay for employees to undergo medical surveillance.

Information, instruction and training

Employees exposed to asbestos must be provided with adequate information, instruction and training to understand the risks associated with asbestos and the necessary precautions. Employees who carry out work in connection with the employer's duties under these Regulations should also be given adequate information, instruction and training to do their work effectively. Under Regulation 10, refresher training must also be provided.

Prevention or reduction of exposure

Wherever possible the employer must prevent exposure of asbestos to the employees. Where this is not reasonably practicable the employer must reduce the exposure to the lowest level reasonably practicable other than by using respiratory protective equipment (RPE). If the asbestos exposure is in connection with a manufacturing process or the installation of a product, then the prevention of such exposure should be achieved by the substitution of asbestos for a less harmful substance, where practicable. RPE, where used, must reduce exposure to as low as is reasonably practicable below Control Limits.

Any personal protective equipment (respiratory protective equipment and protective clothing must comply with the health and safety requirements of any relevant design or manufacturing EU Directives applicable to such personal protective equipment and which are implemented in the UK.

Control limits

These Regulations have a single Control Limit for all types of asbestos - 0.1 fibres per cubic centimetre of air averaged over a continuous period of 4 hours. The Control Limit is the maximum concentration of fibres in the air averaged over the time period that must not be exceeded.

Short term exposures must also be strictly controlled and worker exposure should not exceed 0.6 fibres per cubic centimetre of air averaged over any continuous 10 minute period, using RPE if exposure cannot be reduced sufficiently using other means.

In the event of a unexpected escape of asbestos in the workplace at a concentration that is liable to exceed the control limit, the employer must ensure that only persons necessary to deal with the situation are permitted into the affected area and that such persons are provided with the appropriate personal protective equipment (respiratory protective equipment and protective clothing). Employees and other persons who may have been affected by the escape should be informed immediately.

Control measures

Employers must ensure that any measures provided to control the risks of exposure from asbestos are properly used or applied so far as is reasonably practicable. Likewise employees have a duty to use any control measures provided in the proper manner and to report any defects immediately. All control measures, including respiratory protective equipment (RPE), must be maintained in a clean and efficient condition and a suitable record of the work carried out in accordance with this provision must be kept for five years. RPE must be tested and examined and should be face-fit tested to the user (ACOP requirement).

Local exhaust ventilation equipment must be regularly examined and tested at suitable intervals by a competent person.

Where protective clothing is required to be provided to reduce the risks of exposure it must be either safely disposed of as asbestos waste, or adequately cleaned at certain intervals, after use in the specified manner. The spread of asbestos from one place to another must be prevented or reduced to the lowest level that is reasonably practicable.

Cleanliness

Any areas where asbestos work is carried out, or any plant/machinery used in connection with that work, must be kept in a clean state and be capable of being thoroughly cleaned. When considering work which creates asbestos dust, regard should be made as to the design and construction of the building to facilitate cleaning. Provision should be made for a suitable and adequate fixed vacuum system.

Provision and Cleaning of Protective Clothing

Adequate and suitable protective clothing shall be provided where necessary. Disposable overalls should be treated as asbestos waste and non-disposable protective clothing should be washed after every shift and the wastewater filtered.

Arrangements to deal with accidents, incidents and emergencies

Employers should have emergency procedures in place for any accident, incident or emergency relating to asbestos. Information should be provided to the emergency services so that when they attend an incident, they can protect themselves against the risks from asbestos.

Duty to prevent or reduce the spread of asbestos

Contaminated plant or equipment should be thoroughly decontaminated before it is moved for use elsewhere or for disposal. Persons should also be decontaminated every time they leave the work area.

Cleanliness of premises and plant

Asbestos dust and debris must be cleaned up as work progresses and not allowed to accumulate. Dustless methods, e.g. vacuuming with a type H vacuum should be used. When work comes to an end, all traces must be removed before handing the workplace over.

Designated areas

Work areas where employees would be liable to be exposed to asbestos, other than due to exempt activities, must be designated as 'asbestos areas' and where the 'control limit' is likely to be exceeded designated 'respirator zones'. Designated areas/zones must be clearly and separately demarcated and identified by notices and only permitted persons allowed to enter. Employees must not eat, drink or smoke in these areas.

Monitoring

A monitoring programme must be set up to record the efficiency of the control measures in reducing or preventing exposure to asbestos. Suitable records of the monitoring results must be kept. Health records are required to be kept for 40 years, while other records must be retained for at least five years. Laboratories carrying out clearance tests and personal sampling must be accredited to EN 45001.

Health records

Where employees are exposed to asbestos above the 'action level', the employer is obliged to keep health records for the affected persons. Such records must be kept for at least 40 years. Employees who are exposed to asbestos above the 'action level' are also required to undergo medical surveillance. Medical examinations prior to employment and then at intervals not exceeding two years must be provided by the employer who will keep a certificate issued by the Employment Medical Adviser or appointed doctor of all such examinations in the individual's file. The employer is also obliged to provide the appropriate facilities which enable medical examinations to be carried out. Original medical certificates (not copies) must be given to workers.

Washing and changing facilities

Where employees are exposed to asbestos at work, the employer must provide suitable and adequate washing and changing facilities. Such facilities would include the provision of somewhere to store protective clothing and personal clothing not used at work. There must also be somewhere to store respiratory protective equipment.

Storage and labelling

Raw asbestos and asbestos waste must always be stored and transported in sealed, properly labelled containers.

Supply of products containing asbestos

No one may supply a product which contains asbestos unless it is for disposal.

Approved Code of Practice

The regulations are accompanied by an Approved Code of Practice and Guidance - "Work with materials containing asbestos" L143. There is a separate ACoP / guidance for regulation 4 of CAR 2006 "The management of asbestos in non-domestic premises" L127.

Control of Lead at Work Regulations (CLAW) 2002

Law considered in context / more depth in Elements B3, B4 and B5.

Arrangement of Regulations

1) Citation and commencement.
2) Interpretation.
3) Duties under these Regulations.
4) Prohibitions.
5) Assessment of the risk to health created by work involving lead.
6) Prevention or control of exposure to lead.
7) Eating, drinking and smoking.
8) Maintenance, examination and testing of control measures.
9) Air monitoring.
10) Medical surveillance.
11) Information, instruction and training.
12) Arrangements to deal with accidents, incidents and emergencies.
13) Exemption certificates.
14) Extension outside Great Britain.
15) Revocation and savings.

Schedule 1   Activities in which the employment of young persons and women of reproductive capacity is prohibited.

Schedule 2   Legislation concerned with the labelling of containers and pipes.

Outline of main points

The **Control of Lead at Work Regulations (CLAW) 2002** aims to protect people at work exposed to lead by controlling that exposure. The Regulations, which are summarised below, apply to any work which exposes people to lead.

Exposure to lead must be assessed by employers so that they may take adequate measures to protect both employees and anyone else who may be exposed to lead at work. Once the level of exposure has been assessed, then adequate measures can be taken ranging from simple maintenance of good washing facilities through to the provision of control measures such as respiratory equipment and constant medical surveillance. The Regulations prohibit the employment of young persons and women of reproductive capacity from some manufacturing, smelting and refining processes (specified in Schedule 1).

WORK WITH LEAD

The Regulations apply to any work which exposes employees or others to lead. In practical terms, this means any work from which lead arises:

a.   in the form of lead dust, fume or vapour in such a way as it could be inhaled.

b.   in any form which is liable to be ingested such as powder, dust, paint or paste.

c.   in the form of lead compounds such as lead alkyls and compounds of lead, which could be absorbed through the skin.

Employers' duties under the 2002 Regulations extend to any other people at work on the premises where work with lead is being carried on.

Lead assessment

Before employers (or a self employed person) can take adequate measures to protect people from lead at work, they need to know exactly what the degree of risk of lead exposure is. The level of risk dictates the measures to be taken. The employer's first duty, therefore, is to assess whether the exposure of any employee is liable to be significant. The next step is to determine the nature and degree of exposure. The assessment must be made before the work is commenced and revised where there is a reason to suspect that it is incorrect.

The purpose of the assessment is to determine whether or not exposure to lead is significant. Where exposure is significant then the employer must, so far as is reasonably practicable, ensure the prevention or adequate control of exposure by means other than the provision of personal protective equipment (PPE). Where control measures are not sufficient on their own and PPE is issued then it must comply with the PPE Regulations or be of a type approved by the Health and Safety Executive (HSE). When deciding controls the employer must take reasonable steps to ensure that they are being used and employees are under a duty to make full and proper use of control measures, PPE or any other measures dictated by the Regulations.

Control measures

Employers must, so far as is reasonably practicable, provide such control measures for materials, plant and processes as will adequately control the exposure of their employees to lead otherwise than by the use of respiratory protective equipment or protective clothing by those employees. Again, personal protective equipment and clothing should be used as a last resort. Employers are under a duty to restrict access to areas to ensure that only people undertaking necessary work are exposed.

If other control measures are inadequate, respiratory protective equipment must be provided for employees exposed to airborne lead. Employees must also be provided with protective clothing where they are significantly exposed to lead. Respiratory protective equipment (RPE) or protective clothing should comply with any UK legislation which implements relevant EU 'design and manufacture' Directives.

Employers must also carry out an assessment before selecting RPE or protective clothing to ensure it will satisfy the necessary requirements and provide adequate protection. The assessment should define the characteristics required by the RPE or protective clothing in order to be suitable, and compare these characteristics against those of the protective equipment actually available. RPE must be examined and tested at appropriate intervals and records kept for a minimum period of 5 years.

Control measures, respiratory equipment and protective clothing must be maintained in an efficient state, in efficient working order and good repair. Employers should ensure that employees use the measures provided properly and employees must make full and proper use of all respiratory protective equipment or protective clothing provided, report defects immediately to the employer and take all reasonable steps to ensure RPE or protective clothing is returned to its storage accommodation after use.

Eating, drinking and smoking are prohibited in any place that is, or is liable to be, contaminated with lead.

Occupational exposure limits

Control limits for exposure to lead in atmosphere are:

■   For lead other then lead alkyls, a concentration of lead in air which any employee is exposed of 0.15 mg per m^3 (8 hour TWA).

■   For lead alkyls a concentration of lead of 0.10 mg per m^3 (8 hour TWA).

Air monitoring in relevant areas must be carried out at least every 3 months. This interval can be increased to 12 months providing that there are no material changes to the workplace and lead in air concentrations have not exceeded 0.10 mg per m^3 on two previous consecutive occasions.

Medical surveillance

Employees subject to, or liable to be, significantly exposed (or for whom a relevant doctor has certified that they should be) must be placed under medical surveillance by an employment medical adviser or appointed doctor. The Regulations set down action levels for blood-lead concentrations, which are:

■   20 g/dl for women of reproductive capacity, or   ■   35 g/dl for any other employee.

Levels for urinary lead concentration are also specified. The adviser or doctor can certify that employees should not be employed on work which exposes them to lead or can only be employed under certain conditions. An investigation must be made when blood-lead action levels are exceeded.

Employees exposed to lead at work are under a duty to present themselves, in normal working hours, for medical examination or such biological tests as may be required. Employers and employees have a right to appeal against decisions made by relevant doctors.

Information, instruction and training

Every employer must ensure that adequate information, instruction and training is given to employees who are liable to be exposed to lead so that they are aware of the risks from lead and the precautions which should be observed. Information must also be given about the results relating to air monitoring and health surveillance and their significance. Adequate information, instruction and training must also be given to anyone who is employed by the employer to carry out lead assessments, air monitoring, etc.

Records

Adequate records must be kept of assessments, examination and testing of controls, air monitoring, medical surveillance and biological tests. Those records should be made available for inspection by employees (although not health records of identifiable individuals). Specific recording requirements are made in respect of female employees who are, or who are likely to be, exposed to significant levels of lead. Air monitoring records must be kept for at least 5 years and individual medical records for 40 years.

Control of Noise at Work Regulations 2005

Law considered in context / more depth in Element B7.

The implementation of the European Physical Agents (Noise) Directive as the Control of Noise at Work Regulations 2005 came into force on 06 April 2006. These regulations replaced the Noise at Work Regulations 1989. The main changes are the reduction by 5dB of the exposure levels at which action has to be taken, and the introduction of a new exposure limit value and a specific requirement on health surveillance.

ARRANGEMENT OF REGULATIONS

1) Citation and commencement.
2) Interpretation.
3) Application.
4) Exposure limit values and action values.
5) Assessment of the risk to health and safety created by noise at the workplace.
6) Elimination or control of exposure to noise at the workplace.
7) Hearing protection.
8) Maintenance and use of equipment.
9) Health surveillance.
10) Information, instruction and training.
11) Exemption certificates from hearing protection.
12) Exemption certificates for emergency services.
13) Exemptions relating to the Ministry of Defence.
14) Extension outside Great Britain.
15) Revocations and amendments.

OUTLINE OF MAIN POINTS

Changes to the action levels

The values of the actions levels associated with noise at work have been lowered and their names have been changed. The first action level is reduced from *85 dB(A) down to 80 dB(A)* and will be known as the *lower exposure action value.* Meanwhile, the section level is reduced from *90 dB(A) down to 85 dB(A)* and will be known as the *upper exposure action value*. The Regulations also allow the employer to average out the exposure to noise over a one week period instead of the previous normal eight hour period, in situations where the noise exposure varies on a day-to-day basis. When determining noise levels for the purposes of determining exposure action levels, the noise exposure reducing effects of hearing protection may not be taken in to account.

Where exposure is at, or above, the *lower exposure action value* (80 dB(A)) the employer has a duty to provide hearing protection to those employees that request it. The employer also has a duty to information, instruction and training on the risks posed by exposure to noise and the control measures to be used.

Where the exposure it at, or above, the *upper exposure action value* (85 dB(A)) the employer is also required to introduce a formal programme of control measures. The measures to be taken as part of this programme of control measures will depend on the findings of the noise risk assessment (see below).

The Control of Noise at Work Regulations 2005 also introduces a new value known as the *exposure limit value*. When evaluating the risks to employees from noise, the employer needs to take account of the exposure limit values. These are limits set both in terms of daily (or weekly) personal noise exposure (LEP,d of 87 dB) and in terms of peak noise ($LCpeak$ of 140 dB). The exposure action values, take account of the protection provided by personal hearing protection (unlike the two exposure action values). *If an employee is exposed to noise at or above the exposure limit value, then the employer must take immediate action to bring the exposure down below this level.*

Summary of exposure limit values and action values

The lower exposure action values are: A daily or weekly personal noise exposure of 80 dB (A-weighted)

A peak sound pressure of 135 dB (C-weighted)

The upper exposure action values are: A daily or weekly personal noise exposure of 85 dB (A-weighted)

A peak sound pressure of 137 dB (C-weighted)

The exposure limit values are: A daily or weekly personal exposure of 87 dB (A-weighted)

A peak sound pressure of 140 db (C-weighted)

Noise risk assessment and control measures

The requirement for a noise risk assessment carries through from the Noise at Work Regulations 1989 into the Control of Noise at Work Regulations 2005. Employers are required (in accordance with the general risk assessment and control measure hierarchy contained in Schedule 1 to the Management of Health and Safety at Work Regulation 1999) to ensure that the risks associated with employees' exposure to noise are eliminated where this is reasonably practicable. Where elimination is not reasonably practicable, then the employer must reduce the risks down to as low a level as is reasonably practicable.

Regulation 6(2) of the proposed Control of Noise at Work Regulations 2005 introduces the requirement for a formal programme of control measures and states:

If any employee is likely to be exposed to noise at or above an upper exposure action value, the employer shall reduce exposure to a minimum by establishing and implementing a programme of organisational and technical measures, excluding the provision of personal hearing protectors, which is appropriate to the activity and consistent with the risk assessment, and shall include consideration of:

(a)   Other working methods which eliminate or reduce exposure to noise.

(b)   Choice of appropriate work equipment emitting the least possible noise, taking account of the work to be done.

(c)   The design and layout of workplaces, work stations and rest facilities.

(d)   Suitable and sufficient information and training for employees, such that work equipment may be used correctly, in order to minimise their exposure to noise.

(e)   Reduction of noise by technical means including:

(i)   in the case of airborne noise the use of shields, enclosures, and sound-absorbent coverings.

(ii)   in the case of structure-borne noise by damping and isolation.

(f)   Appropriate maintenance programmes for work equipment, the workplace and workplace systems.

(g)   Limitation of the duration and intensity of exposure to noise.

(h)   Appropriate work schedules with adequate rest periods.

If the risk assessment indicates an employee is likely to be exposed to noise at or above an upper exposure action value, the employer shall ensure that

- the area is designated a Hearing Protection Zone;
- the area is demarcated and identified by means of the sign specified for the purpose of indicating "ear protection must be worn" (to be consistent with the Health and Safety (Safety Signs and Signals) Regulations 1996)
- the sign shall be accompanied by text that indicates that the area is a Hearing Protection Zone and that employees must wear personal hearing protectors while in that area;
- access to the area is restricted where this is technically feasible and the risk of exposure justifies it and shall make every effort to ensure that no employee enters that area unless they are wearing personal hearing protectors.

Maintenance

There is a duty on the employer to maintain the control introduced to protect employees. This will include maintenance of acoustic enclosures, etc as well as the maintenance of machinery (as required under the Provision and Use of Work Equipment Regulations 1998) to control noise at source.

Health Surveillance

Under the Control of Noise at Work Regulations 2005, employees who are regularly exposed to noise levels of 85 dB(A) or higher must be subject to health surveillance, including audiometric testing. This constitutes a big change from the previous Regulations that only required an employer to carry out health surveillance where the employee was subject to noise levels of 95 dB(A) or higher. Where exposure is between 80 dB and 85 dB, or where employees are only occasionally exposed above the upper exposure action values, health surveillance will only be required if information comes to light that an individual may be particularly sensitive to noise induced hearing loss.

Summary

The Control of Noise at Work Regulations 2005 became part of UK health and safety law in April 2006. They introduce levels for employees to control exposure down to, including a new exposure limit value, above which employers are obliged to take immediate action to reduce exposure. These new lower limits mean that about a further million workers will be afforded protection by these new Regulations. The requirements for risk assessments, control measures and health surveillance have been updated, but are broadly similar to previous requirements.

(Source: www.lrbconsulting com & www.hse.gov.uk)

Control of Vibration at Work Regulations 2005

Law considered in context / more depth in Element B7.

Hand-arm vibration (HAV) and whole body vibration (WBV) are caused by the use of work equipment and work processes that transmit vibration into the hands, arms and bodies of employees in many industries and occupations. Long-term, regular exposure to vibration is known to lead to permanent and debilitating health effects such as vibration white finger, loss of sensation, pain, and numbness in the hands, arms, spine and joints. These effects are collectively known as hand-arm or whole body vibration syndrome.

These Regulations introduce controls, which aim substantially to reduce ill-health caused by exposure to vibration. These Regulations came into force on 06 July 2005.

ARRANGEMENT OF REGULATIONS

1) Citation and commencement.

2) Interpretation.

3) Application.

4) Exposure limit values and action values.

5) Assessment of the risk to health created by vibration at the workplace.

6) Elimination or control of exposure to vibration at the workplace.

7) Health surveillance.

8) Information, instruction and training for persons who may be exposed to risk from vibration.

9) Exemption certificates for emergency services.

10) Exemption certificates for air transport.

11) Exemption relating to the Ministry of Defence etc.

12) Extension outside Great Britain.

13) Amendment of the Offshore Installations and Wells (Design and Construction, etc.) Regulations 1996.

OUTLINE OF MAIN POINTS

Regulation 4 states the personal daily exposure limits and daily exposure action values, normalised over an 8-hour reference period.

	Daily exposure limits	Daily exposure action values
Hand arm vibration	5 m/s^2	2.5 m/s^2
Whole body vibration	1.15 m/s^2	0.5 m/s^2

Regulation 5 requires the employer to make a suitable and sufficient assessment of the risk created by work that is liable to expose employees to risk from vibration. The assessment must observe work practices, make reference to information regarding the magnitude of vibration from equipment and if necessary measurement of the magnitude of the vibration.

Consideration must also be given to the type, duration, effects of exposure, exposures limit / action values, effects on employees at particular risk, the effects of vibration on equipment and the ability to use it, manufacturers' information, availability of replacement equipment, and extension of exposure at the workplace (e.g. rest facilities), temperature and information on health surveillance. The risk assessment should be recorded as soon as is practicable after the risk assessment is made and reviewed regularly.

Regulation 6 states that the employer must seek to eliminate the risk of vibration at source or, if not reasonably practicable, reduce it to a minimum. Where the personal daily exposure limit is exceeded the employer must reduce exposure by implementing a programme of organisational and technical measures. Measures include the use of other methods of work, ergonomics, maintenance of equipment, design and layout, information, instruction and training, limitation by schedules and breaks and the provision of personal protective equipment.

Regulation 7 states that health surveillance must be carried out if there is a risk to the health of employees liable to be exposed to vibration. This is in order to diagnose any health effect linked with exposure to vibration. A record of health shall be kept of any employee who undergoes health surveillance. If health surveillance identifies a disease or adverse health effect, considered by a doctor to be a result of exposure to vibration, the employer shall ensure that a qualified person informs the employee and provides information and advice. In addition the employer must also review risk assessments and the health of any other employee who has been similarly exposed and consider alternative work.

Regulation 8 states that employers must provide information, instruction and training to all employees who are exposed to risk from vibration. This includes any organisational and technical measures taken, exposure limits and values, risk assessment findings, why and how to detect injury, health surveillance entitlement and safe working practices. The requirement for information, instruction and training extends to persons whether or not an employee, but who carries out work in connection with the employers duties.

Control of Substances Hazardous to Health Regulations (COSHH) 2002

Law considered in context / more depth in Elements B2, B3, B4, B5 and B6. See also – Control of Substances Hazardous to Health (Amendment) Regulations 2004.

Arrangement of Regulations

1) Citation and commencement.

2) Interpretation.

3) Duties under these Regulations.

4) Prohibitions on substances.

5) Application of regulations 6 to 13.

6) Assessment of health risks created by work involving substances hazardous to health.

7) Control of exposure.

8) Use of control measures etc.

9) Maintenance of control measures.

10) Monitoring exposure.

11) Health surveillance.

12) Information etc.

13) Arrangements to deal with accidents, incidents and emergencies.

14) Exemption certificates.

15) Extension outside Great Britain.

16) Defence in proceedings for contravention of these Regulations.

17) Exemptions relating to the Ministry of Defence etc.

18) Revocations, amendments and savings.

19) Extension of meaning of "work".

20) Modification of section 3(2) of the Health and Safety at Work etc Act 1974.

Schedule 1   Other substances and processes to which the definition of "carcinogen" relates.

Schedule 2   Prohibition of certain substances hazardous to health for certain purposes.

Schedule 3   Special provisions relating to biological agents.

Schedule 4   Frequency of thorough examination and test of local exhaust ventilation plant used in certain processes.

Schedule 5   Specific substances and processes for which monitoring is required.

Schedule 6   Medical surveillance.

Schedule 7   Legislation concerned with the labelling of containers and pipes.

Schedule 8   Fumigations excepted from regulation 14.

Schedule 9   Notification of certain fumigations.

Appendix 1   Control of carcinogenic substances.

Annex 1   Background note on occupational cancer.

Annex 2   Special considerations that apply to the control of exposure to vinyl chloride.

Appendix 2   Additional provisions relating to work with biological agents.

Appendix 3   Control of substances that cause occupational asthma.

NOTE the main impact to the latest version of the COSHH Regulations concern the control of substances that cause occupational asthma.

Outline of main points

REGULATIONS

Reg. 2   ### Interpretation

"Substance hazardous to health" includes:

1) Substances which under The Chemicals (Hazard Information and Packaging) Regulations (CHIP 3) 2002 are in categories of very toxic, toxic, harmful, corrosive or irritant.

2) A substance listed in Schedule 1 to the Regs or for which the HSC have approved a maximum exposure limit or an occupational exposure standard.

3) A biological agent.

4) Dust in a concentration in air equal to or greater than:

■ 10 mg/m^3 inhalable dust as an 8hr TWA, or

■ 4mg/m^3 respirable dust as an 8hr TWA.

5) Any other substance which creates a health hazard comparable with the hazards of the substances in the other categories above.

Reg. 3   ### Duties

Are on employer to protect:

Employees

Any other person who may be affected, except:

■ Duties for health surveillance do not extend to non-employees.

■ Duties to give information may extend to non-employees if they work on the premises.

Reg. 4   ### Prohibitions on Substances

Certain substances are prohibited from being used in some applications. These are detailed in Schedule 2 to Regs.

Reg. 5   ### Application of Regs. 6 - 13

Regs. 6 - 13 are made to protect a person's health from risks arising from exposure. They do not apply if:

The following Regs already apply:

- The Control of Lead at Work Regulations (CLAW) 2002.
- The Control of Asbestos at Work Regulations (CAWR) 2002.

The hazard arises from one of the following properties of the substance:

- Radioactivity, explosive, flammable, high or low temperature, high pressure.
- Exposure is for medical treatment.
- Exposure is in a mine.

Reg. 6

Assessment

Employer must not carry out work which will expose employees to substances hazardous to health unless he has made an assessment of the risks to health and the steps that need to be taken to meet the requirements of the Regs.

The assessment must be reviewed if there are changes in the work and at least once every 5 years.

A suitable and sufficient assessment should include:

- An assessment of the risks to health.
- The practicability of preventing exposure.
- Steps needed to achieve adequate control.

An assessment of the risks should involve:

- Types of substance including biological agents.
- Where the substances are present and in what form.
- Effects on the body.
- Who might be affected.
- Existing control measures.

Reg. 7

Control of Exposure

1) Employer shall ensure that the exposure of employees to substances hazardous to health is either prevented or, where this is not reasonably practicable, adequately controlled.

2) So far as is reasonably practicable (1) above except to a carcinogen or biological agent shall be by measures other than personal protective equipment (PPE).

3) Where not reasonably practicable to prevent exposure to a carcinogen by using an alternative substance or process, the following measure shall apply:

- Total enclosure of process.
- Use of plant, process and systems which minimise generation of, or suppress and contain, spills, leaks, dust, fumes and vapours of carcinogens.
- Limitation of quantities of a carcinogen at work.
- Keeping of numbers exposed to a minimum.
- Prohibition of eating, drinking and smoking in areas liable to contamination.
- Provision of hygiene measures including adequate washing facilities and regular cleaning of walls and surfaces.
- Designation of areas/installations liable to contamination and use of suitable and sufficient warning signs.
- Safe storage, handling and disposal of carcinogens and use of closed and clearly-labelled containers.

4) If adequate control is not achieved, then employer shall provide suitable PPE to employees in addition to taking control measures.

5) PPE provided shall comply with The Personal Protective Equipment at Work Regulations, 2002 (dealing with the supply of PPE).

6&7) For substances which have a maximum exposure limit (MEL), control of that substance shall, so far as inhalation is concerned, only be treated if the level of exposure is reduced as far as is reasonably practicable and in any case below the MEL.

Where a substance has an occupational exposure standard (OES), control of that substance shall, so far as inhalation is concerned, only be treated as adequate if the OES is not exceeded or if it is, steps are taken to remedy the situation as soon as reasonably practicable.

8) Respiratory protection must be suitable and of a type or conforming to a standard approved by the HSE.

9) In the event of failure of a control measure which may result in the escape of carcinogens, the employer shall ensure:

Only those who are responsible for repair and maintenance work are permitted in the affected area and are provided with PPE.

- Employees and other persons who may be affected are informed of the failure forthwith.

Reg. 8

Employer shall take all reasonable steps to ensure control measures, PPE, etc. are properly used/applied.

Employee shall make full and proper use of control measures, PPE etc. and shall report defects to employer.

Reg. 9

Maintenance of Control Measures

Employer providing control measures to comply with Reg.7 shall ensure that it is maintained in an efficient state, in efficient working order and in good repair and in the case of PPE in a clean condition, properly stored in a well-defined place checked at suitable intervals and when discovered to be defective repaired or replaced before further use.

- Contaminated PPE should be kept apart and cleaned, decontaminated or, if necessary destroyed.
- Engineering controls - employer shall ensure thorough examination and tests.
- Local exhaust ventilation (LEV) - Once every 14 months unless process specified in Schedule 4.
- Others - At suitable intervals.
- Respiratory protective equipment - employer shall ensure thorough examination and tests at suitable intervals.
- Records of all examinations, tests and repairs kept for 5 years.
-

Reg. 10

Monitoring Exposure

Employer shall ensure exposure is monitored if

- Needed to ensure maintenance of adequate control.
- Otherwise needed to protect health of employees.
- Substance/process specified in Schedule 5.

Records kept if:

- There is an identified exposure of identifiable employee - 40 years.
- Otherwise - 5 years.

Reg. 11

Health Surveillance

1) Where appropriate for protection of health of employees exposed or liable to be exposed, employer shall ensure suitable health surveillance.
2) Health surveillance is appropriate if:
- • Employee exposed to substance/process specified in Schedule 6.
- • Exposure to substance is such that an identifiable disease or adverse health effect can result, there is a reasonable likelihood of it occurring and a valid technique exists for detecting the indications of the disease or effect.
3) Health records kept for at least 40 years.
4) If employer ceases business, HSE notified and health records offered to HSE.
5) If employee exposed to substance specified in Schedule 6, then health surveillance shall include medical. surveillance, under Employment Medical Adviser (EMA) at 12 monthly intervals - or more frequently if specified by EMA.
6) EMA can forbid employee to work in process, or specify certain conditions for him to be employed in a process.
7) EMA can specify that health surveillance is to continue after exposure has ceased. Employer must ensure.
8) Employees to have access to their own health record.
9) Employee must attend for health/medical surveillance and give information to EMA.
10) EMA entitled to inspect workplace.
11) Where EMA suspends employee from work exposing him to substances hazardous to health, employer of employee can apply to HSE in writing within 28 days for that decision to be reviewed.

Reg. 12

Information etc.

Employer shall provide suitable and sufficient information, instruction and training for him to know:

- Risks to health.
- Precautions to be taken.

This should include information on:

- Results of monitoring of exposure at workplace.
- Results of collective health surveillance.

If the substances have been assigned a maximum exposure limit, then the employee/Safety Representative must be notified forthwith if the MEL has been exceeded.

Reg. 13

Arrangements to deal with accidents, incidents and emergencies.

To protect the health of employees from accidents, incidents and emergencies, the employer shall ensure that:

- Procedures are in place for first aid and safety drills (tested regularly).
- Information on emergency arrangements is available.
- Warning, communication systems, remedial action and rescue actions are available.
- Information made available to emergency services: external and internal.
- Steps taken to mitigate effects, restore situation to normal and inform employees.
- Only essential persons allowed in area.

These duties do not apply where the risks to health is slight or measures in place Reg 7(1) are sufficient to control the risk.

The employee must report any accident or incident which has or may have resulted in the release of a biological agent which could cause severe human disease.

NOTE the main impact to the latest version of the COSHH Regulations concern the control of substances that cause occupational asthma.

APPENDIX 3 CONTROL OF SUBSTANCES THAT CAUSE OCCUPATIONAL ASTHMA

This relates certain regulations specifically to substances with the potential to cause asthma.

- Regulation 6 - assessment of risk to health created by work involving substances hazardous to health, (i.e. substances that

- may cause asthma).
- Regulation 7 – prevention or control of exposure to substances hazardous to health, (i.e. substances that may cause occupational asthma).
- Regulation 11 – health surveillance, (for employees who are or may be exposed to substances that may cause occupational asthma).
- Regulation 12 – information, instruction and training for persons who may be exposed to substances hazardous to health, to include: typical symptoms of asthma, substances that may cause it, the permanency of asthma and what happens with subsequent exposures, the need to report symptoms immediately and the reporting procedures.

Training should be given, including induction training before they start the job.

SCHEDULE 3 ADDITIONAL PROVISIONS RELATING TO WORK WITH BIOLOGICAL AGENTS

Regulation 7(10)

Part I Provision of general application to biological agents

1   Interpretation.

2   Classification of biological agents.

The HSC shall approve and publish a "Categorisation of Biological Agents according to hazard and categories of containment" which may be revised or re-issued.

Where no approved classification exists, the employer shall assign the agent to one of four groups according to the level of risk of infection.

Group 1 - unlikely to cause human disease.

Group 2 - can cause human disease.

Group 3 - can cause severe disease and spread to community.

Group 4 - can cause severe disease, spread to community and there is no effective treatment.

3   **Special control measures for laboratories, animal rooms and industrial processes**

Every employer engaged in research, development, teaching or diagnostic work involving Group 2, 3 or 4 biological agents; keeping or handling laboratory animals deliberately or naturally infected with those agents, or industrial processes involving those agents, shall control them with the most suitable containment.

4   **List of employees exposed to certain biological agents**

The employer shall keep a list of employees exposed to Group 3 or 4 biological agents for at least 10 years. If there is a long latency period then the list should be kept for 40 years.

5   **Notification of the use of biological agents**

Employers shall inform the HSE at least 20 days in advance of first time use or storage of Group 2, 3 or 4 biological hazards. Consequent substantial changes in procedure or process shall also be reported.

6   **Notification of the consignment of biological agents**

The HSE must be informed 30 days before certain biological agents are consigned.

Part II Containment measures for health and veterinary care facilities, laboratories and animal rooms.

Part III Containment measures for industrial processes.

Part IV Biohazard sign.

The biohazard sign required by regulation 7(6)(a) shall be in the form shown below -

Figure B11-1: Biohazard sign.   *Source: Stocksigns.*

Part V Biological agents whose use is to be notified in accordance with paragraph 5(2) of Part I of this Schedule

- Any Group 3 or 4 agent, or
- Certain named Group 2 agents.

Control of Substances Hazardous to Health (Amendment) Regulations 2004

These Regulations make minor amendments to The Control of Substances Hazardous to Health Regulations 2002 and came into force on 17th January 2005 and 6th April 2005.

Arrangement of Regulations

1)   Citation and commencement.

2)   Amendments of the Control of Substances Hazardous to Health (Amendment) Regulations 2004.

3)   Amendment of the Chemicals (Hazard Information and Packaging for Supply) Regulations 2002.

4)   Amendments of the Control of Lead at Work Regulations 2002

Outline of main points

The main change is that maximum exposure limits (MELs) and occupational exposure standards (OESs) have been replaced by the new workplace exposure limits (WELs).

Health and Safety (Display Screen Equipment) Regulations (DSE) 1992

Law considered in context / more depth in Element B10. See also – Health and Safety (Miscellaneous Amendments) Regulations (MAR) 2002 – below.

Arrangement of Regulations

2)   Every employer shall carry out suitable and sufficient analysis of workstations.

3)   Employers shall ensure that equipment provided meets the requirements of the schedule laid down in these Regulations.

4)   Employers shall plan activities and provide such breaks or changes in work activity to reduce employees' workload on that equipment.

5)   For display screen equipment (DSE) users, the employer shall provide, on request, an eyesight test carried out by a competent person.

6 & 7) Provision of information and training.

Outline of main points

WORKSTATION ASSESSMENTS (REGULATION 2)

Should take account of:

- Screen   -   positioning, character definition, character stability etc.
- Keyboard   -   tilt able, character legibility etc.
- Desk   -   size, matt surface etc.
- Chair   -   adjustable back and height, footrest available etc.
- Environment -   noise, lighting, space etc.
- Software   -   easy to use, work rate not governed by software.

INFORMATION AND TRAINING (REGULATIONS 6 & 7)

Should include:

- Risks to health.
- Precautions in place (e.g. the need for regular breaks).
- How to recognise problems.
- How to report problems.

Health and Safety (Miscellaneous Amendments) Regulations (MAR) 2002

See also – DSE 1992, MHOR 1992, PPER 1992 and WHSWR 1992.

These Regulations make minor amendments to UK law to come into line with the requirements of the original Directives and came into force on 17th September 2002. In relation to this publication, the Regulations that are effected by the amendments are:

- Health and Safety (Display Screen Equipment) Regulations (DSE) 1992.
- Manual Handling Operations Regulations 1992.
- Personal Protective Equipment at Work Regulations 1992.
- Workplace (Health, Safety and Welfare) Regulations 1992.

Arrangement of Regulations

1)   Citation and commencement.

2)   Amendment of the Health and Safety (First-Aid) Regulations 1981.

3)   Amendment of the Health and Safety (Display Screen Equipment) Regulations 1992.

4)   Amendment of the Manual Handling Operations Regulations 1992.

5)   Amendment of the Personal Protective Equipment at Work Regulations 1992.

6)   Amendment of the Workplace (Health, Safety and Welfare) Regulations 1992.

7)   Amendment of the Provision and Use of Work Equipment Regulations 1998.

8)   Amendment of the Lifting Operations and Lifting Equipment Regulations 1998.

9)   Amendment of the Quarries Regulations 1999.

Outline of main points (relevant to this publication only)

REGULATION 3 - AMENDMENT OF THE HEALTH AND SAFETY (DISPLAY SCREEN EQUIPMENT) REGULATIONS 1992

The Health and Safety (Display Screen Equipment) Regulations 1992 shall be amended -

(a)   by substituting for regulation 3 the following regulation -

"Every employer shall ensure that any workstation which may be used for the purposes of his undertaking meets the requirements laid down in the Schedule to these Regulations, to the extent specified in paragraph 1 thereof.";

(b)   by substituting for paragraphs (1) and (2) of regulation 5 the following paragraphs -

(1) Where a person -

(a) is a user in the undertaking in which he is employed; or
(b) is to become a user in the undertaking in which he is, or is to become, employed,

the employer who carries on the undertaking shall, if requested by that person, ensure that an appropriate eye and eyesight test is carried out on him by a competent person within the time specified in paragraph (2).
(2) The time referred to in paragraph (1) is -

(a) in the case of a person mentioned in paragraph (1)(a), as soon as practicable after the request; and
(b) in the case of a person mentioned in paragraph (1)(b), before he becomes a user.";

(c)   in paragraph (3) of regulation 5 by inserting, after the words "has been provided", the words "(whether before or after becoming an employee)";

(d)   by substituting for paragraph (1) of regulation 6 the following paragraphs -

(1) Where a person -

(a) is a user in the undertaking in which he is employed; or
(b) is to become a user in the undertaking in which he is, or is to become, employed,

the employer who carries on the undertaking shall ensure that he is provided with adequate health and safety training in the use of any workstation upon which he may be required to work.

(1A) In the case of a person mentioned in sub-paragraph (b) of paragraph (1) the training shall be provided before he becomes a user.".

REGULATION 4 - AMENDMENT OF THE MANUAL HANDLING OPERATIONS REGULATIONS 1992

Regulation 4 of the Manual Handling Operations Regulations 1992 shall be amended by adding the following paragraph -

"(3) In determining for the purposes of this regulation whether manual handling operations at work involve a risk of injury and in determining the appropriate steps to reduce that risk regard shall be had in particular to -

(a)   the physical suitability of the employee to carry out the operations;
(b)   the clothing, footwear or other personal effects he is wearing;
(c)   his knowledge and training;
(d)   the results of any relevant risk assessment carried out pursuant to regulation 3 of the Management of Health and Safety at Work Regulations 1999;
(e)   whether the employee is within a group of employees identified by that assessment as being especially at risk; and
(f)   the results of any health surveillance provided pursuant to regulation 6 of the Management of Health and Safety Regulations 1999.".

REGULATION 5 - AMENDMENT OF THE PERSONAL PROTECTIVE EQUIPMENT AT WORK REGULATIONS 1992

The Personal Protective Equipment at Work Regulations 1992 shall be amended -

(a)   by substituting for sub-paragraphs (a) and (b) of paragraph (3) of regulation 4 the following sub-paragraphs -

"(a) it is appropriate for the risk or risks involved, the conditions at the place where exposure to the risk may occur, and the period for which it is worn;
(b) it takes account of ergonomic requirements and the state of health of the person or persons who may wear it, and of the characteristics of the workstation of each such person;";

(b)   by adding to regulation 4 the following paragraph -

"(4) Where it is necessary to ensure that personal protective equipment is hygienic and otherwise free of risk to health, every employer and every self-employed person shall ensure that personal protective equipment provided under this regulation is provided to a person for use only by him.";

(c)   in paragraph (2) of regulation 6, by adding the following sub-paragraph -

"(d) an assessment as to whether the personal protective equipment is compatible with other personal protective equipment which is in use and which an employee would be required to wear simultaneously.";

(d)   in paragraph (1) of regulation 9 by adding after sub-paragraph (c) the words "and shall ensure that such information is kept available to employees"; and

(e)   in paragraph (3) of regulation 9 by adding the following paragraph -

"(3) Without prejudice to the generality of paragraph (1) the employer shall, where appropriate, and at suitable intervals, organise demonstrations in the wearing of personal protective equipment.".

REGULATION 6 - AMENDMENT OF THE WORKPLACE (HEALTH, SAFETY AND WELFARE) REGULATIONS 1992

The Workplace (Health, Safety and Welfare) Regulations 1992 shall be amended -

(a)   in regulation 2(1), by inserting, before the definition of "new workplace", the following definition -

"disabled person" has the meaning given by section 1 of the Disability Discrimination Act 1995;

(b)   in the definition of "workplace" in regulation 2(1), by deleting the words "but shall not" to the end of the definition;

(c)   by inserting after regulation 4 the following regulation -

     " **Stability and solidity**
     4A. Where a workplace is in a building, the building shall have a stability and solidity appropriate to the nature of the use of the workplace.";

(d)   in regulation 5(3) -

(i) by deleting the word "and" after sub-paragraph (a);
(ii) by adding the word "and" after sub-paragraph (b); and
(iii) by adding the following sub-paragraph -

" (c) equipment and devices intended to prevent or reduce hazards";

(e)   by deleting regulation 6(3);
(f)   in regulation 7, by inserting the following paragraph -

" (1A) Without prejudice to the generality of paragraph (1) -

(a) a workplace shall be adequately thermally insulated where it is necessary, having regard to the type of work carried out and the physical activity of the persons carrying out the work; and
(b) excessive effects of sunlight on temperature shall be avoided.";

(g)   in paragraph (2) of regulation 24, by adding the words "and the facilities are easily accessible, of sufficient capacity and provided with seating";

(h)   in regulation 25, by substituting for paragraph (3) the following paragraph -

" (3) Rest rooms and rest areas shall -

(a) include suitable arrangements to protect non-smokers from discomfort caused by tobacco smoke; and
(b) be equipped with -

       (i) an adequate number of tables and adequate seating with backs for the number of persons at work likely to use them at any one time; and
       (ii) seating which is adequate for the number of disabled persons at work and suitable for them.";

(i)   by inserting after regulation 25 the following regulation -

" **Disabled persons**
25A. Where necessary, those parts of the workplace (including in particular doors, passageways, stairs, showers, washbasins, lavatories and workstations) used or occupied directly by disabled persons at work shall be organised to take account of such persons.".

SUMMARY OF AMENDMENTS:

- That all DSE workstations should conform to the recognised standard as stated in the DSE Regulation. Also DSE eyesight tests to be provided for users as soon as practicable after the request or, for prospective employees or users, before becoming a user.
- Risk assessments for Manual Handling Operations must take into account the physical suitability of the employee, the PPE being worn, the persons knowledge and training, whether the individual is "especially at risk" and the results of any health surveillance.
- PPE must be appropriate for the risk or risks, the conditions in the workplace where exposure to the risk may occur and the period it is to be worn. It must also take into account ergonomic requirement, the state of health of the person wearing it and the workstation characteristics.
- Minor changes to the definitions in the Workplace (Health, Safety and Welfare) Regulations and to the wording about thermal insulation of buildings and avoidance of excessive effects of sunlight. Also requires rest rooms to include suitable arrangements to protect non-smokers from smoke discomfort, to have adequate tables and seating with backs and an adequate amount of suitable seating for the disabled.

Ionising Radiations Regulations (IRR) 1999

Law considered in context / more depth in Element B8.

Arrangement of regulations

PART I   **Interpretation and General**

1)   Citation and commencement.

Schedule 9.   Modifications.

Outline of main points

These Regulations supersede and consolidate the Ionising Radiations Regulations 1985 and the Ionising Radiation (Outside Workers) Regulations 1993.

The Regulations impose duties on employers to protect employees and other persons against ionising radiation arising from work with radioactive substances and other sources of ionising radiation and also impose certain duties on employees.

The Regulations are divided into 7 Parts.

Manual Handling Operations Regulations (MHOR) 1992

Law considered in context / more depth in Element B10. See also – Health and Safety (Miscellaneous Amendments) Regulations (MAR) 2002.

Arrangement of Regulations

1)   Citation and commencement.

2)   Interpretation.

3)   Disapplication of Regulations.

4)   Duties of employers.

5)   Duty of employees.

6)   Exemption certificates.

7)   Extension outside Great Britain.

8)   Repeals and revocations.

Outline of main points

1)   **Citation and commencement**

2)   **Interpretation.**

"Injury" does not include injury caused by toxic or corrosive substances which:

- Have leaked/spilled from load.
- Are present on the surface but not leaked/spilled from it.
- Are a constituent part of the load.

"Load" includes any person or animal.

"Manual Handling Operations" means transporting or supporting a load including:

- Lifting and putting down.
- Pushing, pulling or moving by hand or bodily force.
- Shall as far as is reasonably practicable.

3)   **Disapplication of regulations**

4)   **Duties of employers**

4) (1)(a)   **Avoidance of manual handling**

The employer's duty is to avoid the need for manual handling operations which involve a risk of their employees being injured - as far as is reasonably practicable.

4) (1)(b)(i)   **Assessment of risk**

Where not reasonably practicable make a suitable and sufficient assessment of all such manual handling operations.

4) (1)(b)(ii)   **Reducing the risk of injury**

Take appropriate steps to reduce the risk of injury to the lowest level reasonably practicable.

4) (1)(b)(iii)   **The load - additional information**

Employers shall provide information on general indications or where reasonably practicable precise information on:

- The weight of each load.
- The heaviest side of any load whose centre of gravity is not central.

4) (2)   **Reviewing the assessment**

Assessment review:

- Where there is reason to believe the assessment is no longer valid.
- There is sufficient change in manual handling operations.

5)   **Duty of employees**

Employees shall make full and proper use of any system of work provided for his use by his employer.

6)   **Exemption certificates**

7)   **Extension outside Great Britain**

8)   **Repeals and revocations**

Schedule 1   Factors to which the employer must have regard and questions he must consider when making an assessment of manual handling operations.

Schedule 2   Repeals and revocations.

Appendix 1   Numerical guidelines for assessment.

Appendix 2   Example of an assessment checklist.

Thus the Regulations establish a clear hierarchy of measures:

1.   Avoid hazardous manual handling operations so far as is reasonably practicable.
2.   Make a suitable and sufficient assessment of any hazardous manual handling operations that cannot be avoided.
3.   Reduce the risk of injury so far as is reasonably practicable.

Notification of New Substances Regulations (NONS) 1993

Law considered in context / more depth in Element B2.

Arrangement of Regulations

1)   Citation and commencement.
2)   Interpretation.
3)   Application of these Regulations.
4)   Full notifications.
5)   Requirements for further testing for substances notified under regulation 4.
6)   Reduced notification requirements for substances placed on the market in quantities of less than one tonne per year by a single manufacturer.
7)   Notifications relating to polymers.
8)   Placing of notified substances on the market.
9)   Requirements for further information.
10)   Follow-up information.
11)   Notification of substances previously notified.
12)   Substances manufactured outside the Communities.
13)   Further notifications of the same substances and avoidance of duplication of testing on vertebrate animals.
14)   Tests under these Regulations to conform to the principles of good laboratory practice.
15)   Notifications and reports to be in English.
16)   Risk assessments.
17)   Information to be sent by the competent authority to the European Commission.
18)   Disclosure of information provided under Part II of these Regulations.
19)   Treatment of confidential information.
20)   Substances appearing in the list of notified substances.
21)   Enforcement and civil liability.
22)   Prohibition of importation and placing on the market of unnotified substances.
23)   Exemption certificates.
24)   Fees for notifications etc.
25)   Revocations, amendments and transitional provisions.

Schedule 1   Characteristic properties of dangerous substances.
Schedule 2   Information required to be in the technical dossiers.
Schedule 3   Additional information and tests required under regulation 5.
Schedule 4   Fees for notifications etc.

Outline of main points

Introduction to NONS 93

Chemicals play a major part in all our lives: making clothing and consumer goods, controlling pests, increasing yields in agriculture, combating disease, making machinery run efficiently. Most chemicals have beneficial effects on our lives and can be made and used without harm. However, they can also have unintended harmful effects on people (workers, consumers or others just going about their everyday lives) and on the environment. A variety of legislation seeks to ensure that these possible harmful effects are avoided.

The UK chemical industry is the nation's fourth largest manufacturing industry and the UK manufacturing sector's number one export earner. The UK chemicals industry is also one of the largest in Europe.

NONS 93 and the seventh amendment directive (92/32/EEC)

NONS 93 implements part of a European Community (EC) Directive, commonly known as the Seventh Amendment Directive. The Directive is called this as it is the seventh time the EC's Dangerous Substances Directive (67/548/EEC), originally adopted in 1967, has been amended. NONS 93 replaces the Notification of New Substances Regulations 1982, as amended in 1986 and 1991.

The directive aims to protect people and the environment from the possible harmful effects of new substances and to create a 'single market' in new substances across the EC.

Substance

A substance in this case means a chemical such as sodium chloride (common salt). A preparation (i.e. a deliberate mixture of such substances) is not subject to these regulations, but one or more of its constituent parts may be.

New substance

A new substance is one which is not on a list called the European Inventory of Existing Commercial Chemical Substances (EINECS).

The single market

The Seventh Amendment is a single market directive. This means it has been adopted by the EC to lay down common trading requirements between EC Member States.

The Directive helps create this single market by ensuring that notification requirements are the same in all EC Member States and that a notification accepted in one Member State is valid for all of them; i.e. notification requirements are harmonised across the EC. This should save notifiers time and money and make trade between Member States easier. NONS 93 brings this into effect in the UK. Appendix 2 discusses the enlargement of the single market to include some members of the European Free Trade Association (EFTA).

Objective of NONS 93

NONS 93 aims to identify the possible risks posed to people and the environment from the placing on the market of new substances. It does this by obtaining information about them in a systematic way so that, if necessary, recommendations for control can be made.

Nons 93 requires those placing a new substance on the market to:

a.   Notify to a competent authority their intention to place a new substance on the market; and

b.   Provide the competent authority with certain information on the substance.

c.   (a) and (b) together comprise a notification.

Functions of the competent authority

The competent authority (CA) has a number of functions under the Regulations. These are concerned with the general running of the system. Most of the functions of the CA are stated as duties in the Regulations, as the notification system will only work efficiently and effectively if CAs carry out their functions within certain timescales.

Placing on the market

Placing on the market means making a substance available to another person. This includes selling it, lending it to someone else, passing it on, giving it away and importing it into the EC (i.e. control of the substance passes from one person to another).

The competent authority

The competent authority is the Health and Safety Executive (HSE) and the Department of the Environment (DoE) acting jointly.

The key functions of the competent authority are:

- Evaluating notification dossiers.
- Providing a risk assessment.
- Requiring additional information from notifiers where necessary.
- Advising on interpretation of the seventh amendment directive and NONS 93.
- Co-operating with other member state (CAS).
- Co-operating with the European Commission (CEC).

The functions of the CA and the role of the European Commission and other member state competent authorities are discussed in more detail in appendix 3.

Confidentiality

In the interests of openness and the public's right of access to environmental information, certain information submitted by notifiers is available to anyone who asks for it. The information available is limited, however, as some information submitted by notifiers could give their competitors a commercial advantage if it were made available.

Risk and proportionality

The precise notification and risk assessment requirements in NONS 93 depend on the quantity of the new substance to be, or already, placed on the EC market and relate to the risks it is likely to pose. More information is generally required if the amount placed on the market is large than would be the case for small quantities.

In most cases the Regulations make it clear what a notification should contain. However, the competent authority will ensure, wherever possible, within the constraints of the Seventh Amendment, that the information required is proportional to the likely risk posed by the new substance. This means that for substances that can be demonstrated by the notifier to pose little risk, some elements of a notification may be considered by the CA to be unnecessary or unjustifiable (for example, in terms of animal welfare) or it may be possible to 'read across' data from an analogous substance.

Because of the constraints imposed by the Regulations and the Seventh Amendment, it will not normally be possible to alter the notification requirements at Level 1 and Level 2.

Substances that are placed on the market solely for 'simple transfers' (i.e. from one site to another only), in small quantities and which seem unlikely to have any hazardous properties may be seen by the competent authority as posing little risk. Notifiers of substances which may fall within this group are therefore advised to discuss the notification requirements with the competent authority before starting any testing. Notifiers of substances which were not notifiable prior to NONS 93 and have already been placed on the market, are also advised to discuss notification requirements with the CA prior to testing.

Where the competent authority has clear discretion under the Regulations (for example, where substances subject to research and development can be treated as having been notified) the information required will also be proportional to the risk.

The 'proportionality' approach outlined above should help reduce the resources spent on unnecessary tests, by industry in generating them and by the competent authority in evaluating them, and be beneficial in terms of animal welfare.

The competent authority's commitment to notifiers and the public

The CA appreciates the importance, both as part of the EC-wide system and to the chemicals industry, of carrying out its duties efficiently. The CA has therefore set itself standards in discharging these duties in a 'NONS Charter'. The Charter is set out in Appendix 4.

Main points from the NONS charter:

The CA will;

- Respond promptly and courteously to enquiries.
- Issue receipts within three days of receiving a notification dossier.
- Say whether a notification dossier is in compliance with regulations, normally within seven to ten working days.
- Clearly set out the reasons if a notification dossier is rejected.
- Maintain the confidentiality of certain information.
- Make non-confidential information available to the public on request.

Personal Protective Equipment at Work Regs (PPER) 1992

Law considered in context / more depth in Elements B4 and B5. See also – Health and Safety (Miscellaneous Amendments) Regulations (MAR) 2002.

Arrangement of Regulations

1) Citation and commencement.
2) Interpretation.
3) Disapplication of these Regulations.
4) Provision of personal protective equipment.
5) Compatibility of personal protective equipment.
6) Assessment of personal protective equipment.
7) Maintenance and replacement of personal protective equipment.
8) Accommodation for personal protective equipment.
9) Information, instruction and training.
10) Use of personal protective equipment.
11) Reporting loss or defect.
12) Exemption certificates.
13) Extension outside Great Britain.
14) Modifications, repeal and revocations directive.

Schedule 1	Relevant Community.
Schedule 2	Modifications.
Part I	Factories Act 1961.
Part II	The Coal and Other Mines (Fire and Rescue) Order 1956.
Part III	The Shipbuilding and Ship-Repairing Regulations 1960.
Part IV	The Coal Mines (Respirable Dust) Regulations 1975.
Part V	The Control of Lead at Work Regulations 1980.
Part VI	The Ionising Radiations Regulations 1985.
Part VII	The Control of Asbestos at Work Regulations 1987.
Part VIII	The Control of Substances Hazardous to Health Regulations 1988.
Part IX	The Noise at Work Regulations 1989.
Part X	The Construction (Head Protection) Regulations 1989.
Schedule 3	Revocations.

Part I

Outline of main points

2) Personal protective equipment (PPE) means all equipment (including clothing provided for protection against adverse weather) which is intended to be worn or held by a person at work and which protects him against risks to his health or safety.

3) These Regulations do not apply to:
- Ordinary working clothes/uniforms.
- Offensive weapons.
- Portable detectors which signal risk.
- Equipment used whilst playing competitive sports.
- Equipment provided for travelling on a road.

The Regulations do not apply to situations already controlled by other Regulations i.e.
- Control of Lead at Work Regulations 1998.
- Ionising Radiation Regulations 1999.
- Control of Asbestos at Work Regulations 1987 (and as amended 1999).
- CoSHH Regulations 1999.
- Noise at Work Regulations 1989.
- Construction (Head Protection) Regulations 1989.

4) Suitable PPE must be provided when risks cannot be adequately controlled by other means. Regulation 4 shall ensure suitable PPE:
- Appropriate for the risk and conditions.
- Ergonomic requirements.
- State of health of users.
- Correctly fitting and adjustable.
- Complies with EEC directives.

5) Equipment must be compatible with any other PPE which has to be worn.

6) Before issuing PPE, the employer must carry out a risk assessment to ensure that the equipment is suitable.
- Assess risks not avoided by other means.
- Define characteristics of PPE and of the risk of the equipment itself.
- Compare characteristics of PPE to defined requirement.
- Repeat assessment when no longer valid, or significant change has taken place.

7) PPE must be maintained.
- In an efficient state.
- In efficient working order.
- In good repair.

8) Accommodation must be provided for equipment when it is not being used.

9) Information, instruction and training must be given on:
- The risks PPE will eliminate or limit.
- Why the PPE is to be used.
- How the PPE is to be used.
- How to maintain the PPE.

Information and instruction must be comprehensible to the wearer/user.

10) Employers shall take reasonable steps to ensure PPE is worn.
- Every employee shall use PPE that has been provided.
- Every employee shall take reasonable steps to return PPE to storage.

11) Employees must report any loss or defect.

The Guidance on the Regulations points out:

"Whatever PPE is chosen, it should be remembered that, although some types of equipment do provide very high levels of protection, none provides 100%".

PPE includes the following when worn for health and safety reasons at work:

- Aprons.
- Adverse weather gear.
- High visibility clothing.
- Gloves.
- Safety footwear.
- Safety helmets.

- Eye protection.
- Life-jackets.
- Respirators.
- Safety harness.
- Underwater breathing gear.

PPE comes almost last of the measures to be taken to control hazards:

Eliminate

Reduce by substitution

Isolate

Control

Personal Protection

Discipline

There are some good reasons why PPE is used as a last resort:

- PPE only protects the wearer and not others who may be in the area and also at risk.
- The introduction of PPE may bring another hazard such as impaired vision, impaired movement or fatigue.

Protection will depend upon fit in many cases, i.e. respirators, breathing apparatus, noise protection devices. Not only does this presuppose that adequate training and instruction have been given, it also presupposes that other individual conditions have been assessed, such as:

- Long hair.
- Wearing of spectacles.
- Stubble growing on men's faces which may have an adverse effect on protection.

PPE will not be suitable unless:

- It is appropriate to the risk involved and the prevailing conditions of the workplace.
- It is ergonomic (user-friendly) in design and takes account of the state of health of the user.
- It fits the wearer correctly, perhaps after adjustment.
- It is effective in preventing or controlling the risk(s) [without increasing the overall risk], so far as is practicable.
- It must comply with EEC directives or other specific standards.

It must be compatible with other equipment where there is more than one risk to guard against.

Training and instruction will include both:

- ***Theoretical training*** - where the reasons for wearing the PPE, factors which may affect the performance, the cleaning, maintenance and identification of defects are discussed.
- ***Practical training*** - wearing, adjusting, removing, cleaning, maintenance and testing are practised.

Workplace (Health, Safety and Welfare) Regulations (WHSWR) 1992

Law considered in context / more depth in Element B8. See also – Health and Safety (Miscellaneous Amendments) Regulations (MAR) 2002.

Arrangement of Regulations

1) Citation and commencement.
2) Interpretation.
3) Application of these Regulations.
4) Requirements under these Regulations.
5) Maintenance of workplace, and of equipment, devices and systems.
6) Ventilation.
7) Temperature in indoor workplaces.
8) Lighting.
9) Cleanliness and waste materials.
10) Room dimensions and space.
11) Workstations and seating.
12) Condition of floors and traffic routes.
13) Falls or falling objects.
14) Windows, and transparent or translucent doors, gates and walls.
15) Windows, skylights and ventilators.
16) Ability to clean windows etc. safely.
17) Organisation etc. of traffic routes.
18) Doors and gates.
19) Escalators and moving walkways.
20) Sanitary conveniences.
21) Washing facilities.
22) Drinking water.
23) Accommodation for clothing.
24) Facilities for changing clothing.
25) Facilities for rest and to eat meals.
26) Exemption certificates.
27) Repeals, saving and revocations.

Schedule 1   Provisions applicable to factories which are not new workplaces, extensions or conversions.
Schedule 2   Repeals and revocations.

Outline of main points

SUMMARY

The main requirements of the Workplace (Health, Safety and Welfare) Regs 1992 are:

1)   *Maintenance* of the workplace and equipment.

2)   *Safety* of those carrying out maintenance work and others who might be at risk (e.g. segregation of pedestrians and vehicles, prevention of falls and falling objects etc.).

3)   Provision of *welfare* facilities (e.g. rest rooms, changing rooms etc.).

4)   Provision of a safe *environment* (e.g. lighting, ventilation etc.).

ENVIRONMENT

Regulation 1	New workplaces, extensions and modifications must comply now. Older workplaces have until 1 January 1996 to get up to standard.
Regulation 4	Requires employers, persons in control of premises and occupiers of factories to comply with the regulations.
Regulation 6	Ventilation - enclosed workplaces should be ventilated with a sufficient quantity of fresh or purified air (5 to 8 litres per second per occupant).
Regulation 7	Temperature indoors - This needs to be reasonable and the heating device must not cause injurious fumes. Thermometers must be provided. Temperature should be a minimum of 16°C or 13°C if there is physical effort.
Regulation 8	Lighting - must be suitable and sufficient. Natural light if possible. Emergency lighting should be provided if danger exists.
Regulation 10	Room dimensions and space - every room where persons work shall have sufficient floor area, height and unoccupied space (min 11 cu.m per person).
Regulation 11	Workstations and seating have to be suitable for the person and the work being done.

SAFETY

Regulation 12	Floors and traffic routes must be of suitable construction. This includes absence of holes, slope, uneven or slippery surface. Drainage where necessary. Handrails and guards to be provided on slopes and staircases.
Regulation 13	Tanks and pits must be covered or fenced.
Regulation 14	Windows and transparent doors, where necessary for health and safety, must be of safety material and be marked to make it apparent.
Regulation 15	Windows, skylights and ventilators must be capable of opening without putting anyone at risk.
Regulation 17	Traffic routes for pedestrians and vehicles must be organised in such a way that they can move safely.
Regulation 18	Doors and gates must be suitably constructed and fitted with any necessary safety devices.
Regulation 19	Escalators and moving walkways shall function safely, be equipped with any necessary safety devices and be fitted with emergency stop.

HOUSEKEEPING

Regulation 5	Workplace and equipment, devices and systems must be maintained in efficient working order and good repair.
Regulation 9	Cleanliness and waste materials - workplaces must be kept sufficiently clean. Floors, walls and ceilings must be capable of being kept sufficiently clean. Waste materials shall not be allowed to accumulate, except in suitable receptacles.
Regulation 16	Windows etc. must be designed so that they can be cleaned safety.

FACILITIES

Regulation 20	Sanitary conveniences must be suitable and sufficient and in readily accessible places. They must be adequately ventilated, kept clean and there must be separate provision for men and women.
Regulation 21	Washing facilities must be suitable and sufficient. Showers if required (a table gives minimum numbers of toilets and washing facilities).
Regulation 22	Drinking water – an adequate supply of wholesome drinking water must be provided.
Regulation 23	Accommodation for clothing must be suitable and sufficient.
Regulation 24	Facilities for changing clothes must be suitable and sufficient, where a person has to use special clothing for work.
Regulation 25	Facilities for rest and eating meals must be suitable and sufficient.

Index

NOTES